THE NEW REVISED CAMBRIDGE GED PROGRAM:

Social Studies

By
Karen Wunderman, M.A., M.Ed.

CAMBRIDGE Adult Education
Prentice Hall Career & Technology
Englewood Cliffs, New Jersey 07632

Production Editor: **Shari Toron**
Cover Design: **Ben Santora**
Cover Art: **Kunio Owaki/The Stock Market**
Prepress Buyer: **Ray Keating**
Manufacturing Buyer: **Lori Bulwin**
Scheduler: **Leslie Coward**
Illustrator: **Alice B. Thiede, CARTO-GRAPHICS**

 © 1992 by Prentice-Hall, Inc.
A Simon & Schuster Company
Englewood Cliffs, New Jersey 07632

Printed in the United States of America
10 9 8 7 6 5 4 3

ISBN 0-13-116435-X

Prentice-Hall International (UK Limited, *London*
Prentice-Hall of Australia Pty. Limited, *Sydney*
Prentice-Hall Canada Inc., *Toronto*
Prentice-Hall Hispanoamericana, S. A., *Mexico*
Prentice-Hall of India Private Limited, *New Delhi*
Prentice-Hall of Japan, Inc., *Tokyo*
Simon & Schuster Asia Pte. Ltd., *Singapore*
Editora Prentice-Hall do Brasil, Ltda., *Rio de Janeiro*

The New Revised Cambridge GED Program

Executive Editor

James W. Brown

Senior Editor

Robert McIlwaine

Development Editor

Julie Scardiglia

Writers

Karen Wunderman
Gloria Levine
Stella Sands
Jerry Howett
Beverly Ann Chin
Michael Ross
Alan Hines
Donald Gerstein

Consultants/Reviewers

Marjorie Jacobs
Cecily Bodner
Diane Hardison
Dr. Margaret Tinzman
Nora Chomitz
Bert C. Honigman
Sylvester Pues

Photo Researchers

Page Poore
Julie Scardiglia

Permissions Editor

Wesley Hall

Contents

To the Student

What is the Social Studies Test?

The Social Studies Test of the GED Tests examines your ability to understand, use, analyze, and evaluate social studies material. Questions are based on reading passages and graphic materials in the five branches of social studies: history, geography, economics, political science, and behavioral science.

What Are the Reading Passages Like?

The reading passages on the GED Social Studies Test will vary in length. Some will be only one short paragraph, while others will be several paragraphs long. The shorter passages may have only one question to answer; longer ones usually have two or three. In addition to written text, you will also be given graphic materials. These consist of maps, charts, graphs, and political cartoons. You will learn how to read graphic materials and answer questions about them in this book.

How Many Questions Are on the Test?

The Social Studies Test has 64 multiple-choice questions. The percentages of questions in each content area are as follows:

- History (including global issues)   25%
- Geography   15%
- Economics   20%
- Political Science   20%
- Behavioral Science (Anthropology, Psychology, Sociology)   20%

Roughly two-thirds of the questions will be based on reading passages (each no longer than 250 words). One-third of the questions will be based on graphic materials (maps, charts, graphs, and political cartoons). You will have 85 minutes to complete the Social Studies Test.

What Kinds of Questions Are on the Test?

The GED consists of four levels of questions: comprehension, application, analysis, and evaluation.

Comprehension questions. These questions require you to show that you understand the material you have read. To demonstrate your comprehension, you will be asked to restate and summarize basic information and concepts. You will also be asked to figure out the unstated meaning of some of the information given.

Application questions. These questions require you to understand the information you are given and to apply that understanding to new situations. To answer application questions, you have to be able to see similarities between the idea or situation you have read about and another idea or situation.

Analysis questions. These require you to understand ideas and think about relationships among them. An example of analysis-level thinking is understanding cause and effect. You use what you have read and knowledge you already have to understand how one thing makes another happen. Distinguishing facts from opinions, recognizing unstated assumptions, and distinguishing conclusions from supporting statements are also examples of analysis-level thinking.

Evaluation questions.   These questions require you to decide how valid an argument is or how well the data presented support a conclusion. You also have to be able to recognize the role that values play in beliefs and indicate logical faults in arguments. The percentages of questions designed to test each thinking skill break down as follows:

- Comprehending Ideas   20%
- Applying Ideas   30%
- Analyzing Ideas   30%
- Evaluating Ideas   20%

The Five GED Tests

There are five content areas tested by the GED: writing skills, social studies, science, literature and the arts, and mathematics. The specifics of each test are listed below.

- *Writing Skills, Part I:*   You will have 75 minutes to answer 55 questions (Sentence Structure 35%; Usage 35%; Mechanics 30%). Most questions involve detecting and correcting errors.
- *Writing Skills, Part II:*   You will have 45 minutes to write a 200-word composition. The topic will be familiar to most people.
- *Social Studies:*   You will have 85 minutes to answer 64 questions (History 25%; Geography 15%; Economics 20%; Political Science 20%; Behavioral Science 20%—Note: in Canada, Geography is 20% and Behavioral Science is 15%). Most questions are based on reading passages. About 1/3 are based on graphic material.
- *Science:*   You will have 95 minutes to answer 66 questions (Biology 50%; Physical Sciences 50%). Most questions are based on reading passages. Others are based on graphic material.
- *Literature and the Arts:*   You will have 65 minutes to answer 45 questions (Popular Literature 50%; Classical Literature 25%; Commentary 25%). Questions are based on reading passages.
- *Mathematics:*   You will have 90 minutes to answer 56 questions (Arithmetic 50%; Algebra 30%; Geometry 20%). Most of the questions are word problems.

Actual passing scores differ from area to area, but regardless of where you are, there are two scores you will need to pay attention to. One is the *minimum score* you must get on each test. If your area sets a minimum score of 35, that means you have to score at least 35 points on *each* of the five tests. The second score is a *minimum average score* on all five tests. If your area requires a minimum average of 45, that means you have to get a total of 225 points to pass (45 × 5 = 225). To pass the GED, you must meet *both* requirements: 1) the minimum score on each of the five tests, and 2) the minimum average score for all five tests. Failure to meet one or the other score will result in failure to pass the GED.

All is not lost if you don't pass the test the first time around. You can take one or all five tests again if you don't pass. You will receive a different form of the test each time you take it, but the experience of having taken the test before should improve your score the next time around. Of course, you will want to study again to be fully prepared for the test.

Good places to contact are: the office of the superintendent of schools in your area; a vocational education center; local community colleges; and adult education courses. Or, write to: General Education Development
GED Testing Service of the American
Council on Education
One Dupont Circle
Washington, D.C. 20036

How To Be A Better Test-Taker

Often you will hear people say that they are not good test takers. These people may be quite intelligent and get good grades in school, but they simply do not do well on standardized tests. You may think of yourself as one of these people, but there are things people can do to improve their chances of doing well on a test. Listed below are some helpful hints to make you a better test taker.

- *Study the Content Areas of the GED*
- *Practice Taking Tests*
- *Be Well-Rested for the Actual Test*
- *Allow Yourself Enough Time*
  to Get to the Test Center
- *Follow Directions Carefully*

- *Pay Attention to the Time*
- *Use Your Test-Taking Skills*
- *Answer All Questions on the Test*
- *Mark Your Answers Carefully*
- *Above All, Relax*

How This Book's Content Can Help You on the GED

The content of this book can help you prepare for the Social Studies test on the GED in three important ways:

Reading Skills: Clear step-by-step instruction teaches you many new ways to find the information you want in whatever you read, which will help you answer questions on the GED and make your reading more active and stimulating.

Social Studies Knowledge: All the major areas covered by the GED are presented in easy-to-read lessons, which connect the material to the world you live in.

GED Practice: This book will give you a maximum of practice in answering GED-type multiple choice questions. It includes GED-type questions in every single lesson and has three times as many full-scale GED practice tests as any other Social Studies GED text.

How This Book's Design Can Help You on the GED

This book has been designed to help you develop the thinking skills you will need for the GED. If you really make use of its features, you will do better on the exam.

Prereading Prompts, Key Words, Headings: Use these features to bring to mind whatever you already know about the topic of each lesson, to look over the main parts of it and focus on its content, *before* you start reading. These *prereading* features can help you understand—and remember—what you read: a big help for the GED.

Model and Practice Questions: Every reading skill is taught to you by using an example of a GED question—a model or practice question. You are taught step-by-step how to get the right answer and why the other answers are incorrect. Study these sample questions well, and you will do much better on the lesson exercise questions that come right after them.

Lesson Exercises and Answer Keys: The more than 140 multiple-choice questions in these exercises are the best possible preparation for the GED. Just as important are their answer keys, which show you where you went wrong, or why you chose the correct answer. If you understand the steps in thinking in these answer keys, you can apply the thinking skills you learn on the GED.

PREDICTION

Introduction

Imagine that you were going to take the GED test today. How do you think you would do? In which areas would you perform best, and in which areas would you have the most trouble? The Predictor Test that follows can help you answer these questions. It is called a Predictor Test because your test results can be used to predict where your strengths and your weaknesses lie in relation to the actual Social Studies Test of the GED.

The Predictor Test is like the actual GED test in many ways. It will check your skills as you apply them to the kind of social studies passages you will find on the real test. The questions are like those on the actual test.

How to Take the Predictor Test

The Predictor Test will be most useful to you if you take it in a manner close to the way the actual test is given. If possible, you should complete it in one sitting, with as little distraction as possible. So that you have an accurate record of your performance, write your answers neatly on a sheet of paper, or use an answer sheet provided by your teacher.

As you take the test, don't be discouraged if you find your are having difficulty with some (or even many) of the questions. The purpose of this test is to predict your overall performance on the GED and to locate your particular strengths and weaknesses. So relax. There will be plenty of opportunities to correct any weaknesses and retest them.

You may want to time yourself to see how long you take to complete the test. When you take the actual Social Studies Test, you will be given 85 minutes. The Predictor Test is about half as long as the actual test. If you finish within 42½ minutes, you are right on target. At this stage, however, you shouldn't worry too much if it takes you longer.

When you are done, check your answers by using the answer key that begins on page 14. Put a check by each item you answered correctly.

How to Use Your Score

At the end of the test, you will find a Performance Analysis Chart. Fill in the chart; it will help you find out which areas you are more comfortable with, and which give you the most trouble.

As you begin each chapter in the book, you may want to refer back to the Performance Analysis Chart to see how well you did in that area of the Predictor Test.

PREDICTOR TEST

TIME: 42 ½ minutes

Directions: Choose the one best answer to each question.

1. A balance of trade is the difference in value between what a country sells to other countries (exports) and what it buys from them (imports). If a country's total exports are worth more than its total imports, it has a balance of trade surplus. If the opposite is true, it has a balance of trade deficit. Countries try to have surpluses.

   The best strategy for a country that wants to achieve a balance of trade surplus would be to

   (1) decrease the value of both imports and exports
   (2) increase the value of imports and decrease the value of exports
   (3) decrease the value of imports and increase the value of exports
   (4) keep the value of imports at the same level but increase the value of exports
   (5) increase the value of both imports and exports

2. Members of both the Senate and the House of Representatives participate in lawmaking. But the two bodies have some separate responsibilities. All bills concerning spending and money matters must begin in the House. However, only the Senate can ratify treaties and confirm the president's appointments. Which of the following would have to begin in the House?

   (1) consideration of the president's proposed budget for the year
   (2) confirmation of the appointment of a federal judge
   (3) ratification of a treaty on arms control
   (4) confirming a U.S. representative sent to the United Nations
   (5) establishing a commission to study manned space flights

Items 3 and 4 are based on the following graphs.

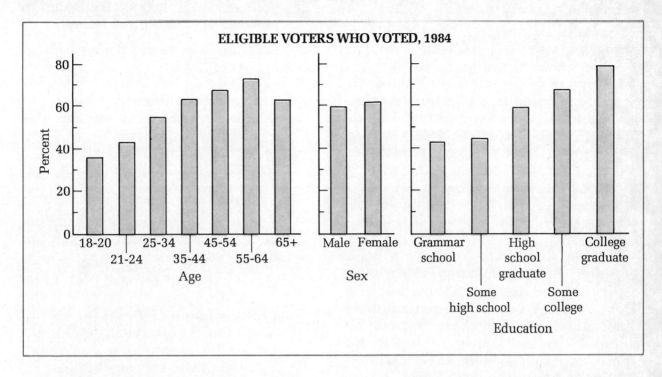

ELIGIBLE VOTERS WHO VOTED, 1984

3. Judging from information on the graphs, which of the following people is LEAST likely to have voted in 1984?

(1) a 20-year-old male with a grammar-school education
(2) a 25-year-old female high-school graduate
(3) a 34-year-old male high-school graduate
(4) a 55-year-old male college graduate
(5) a 65-year-old female with some high-school education

4. Judging from information on the graphs, a civic group that is trying to get nonvoters to register and vote should direct its efforts especially toward

(1) women
(2) high-school graduates
(3) college graduates
(4) young adults
(5) senior citizens

Items 5 to 8 are based on the following passage.

Love is important in raising children, psychologists say, but it is not enough. Discipline is also necessary.

Discipline is not a simple matter of "dos" and "don'ts." It means setting well-defined limits for the child and allowing the child to move freely within those limits. Different parents may set different limits. That is, some will be stricter than others. This is all right. What matters is that parents don't constantly change the limits. Consistency is important.

Parents should try to strike a good balance. Authoritarian parents give their children responsibilities but few rights. Overly permissive parents give their children lots of rights but few responsibilities. Parents should avoid these extremes, giving their children both rights and responsibilities.

Parents' methods of disciplining are also important. Most parents use some physical punishment. It is also natural and appropriate for them to express anger, of a controlled kind, at children who misbehave. In addition, parents may discipline their children by "withdrawal of love," for example, by temporarily refusing to speak to a child. These methods of disciplining, used occasionally, are acceptable. But it is if far better to emphasize praise and approval, when the child behaves well, and discussion, when there is a problem.

5. A father has a policy that no sweets are allowed. While standing at the grocery store checkout counter, his child spots some candy. She begins to beg, and the father, wanting to avoid a scene, buys it for her. A few days later the child asks for some bubble gum.

The father becomes angry and yells at her. Which advice from the passage is he failing to follow?

(1) Children need love as well as discipline.
(2) Children need rights as well as responsibilities.
(3) Use of physical punishment should be limited.
(4) Rules should be consistent.
(5) Praise and approval can be important.

6. Which of the following statements best summarizes the main point of the passage?

(1) What children need most of all is discipline.
(2) Discipline of the right sort is important in raising children.
(3) Children should be given both rights and responsibilities.
(4) Discipline should include praise and discussion, not just punishment.
(5) Communication between parents and children is important.

7. A child who usually does well in school comes home one day with a bad report card. Based on the passage, which of the following is the best approach for a parent to take?

(1) Wait to see if the next report card shows improvement.
(2) Yell at the child and send him to his room.
(3) Discuss the report card with the child and try to find out what happened.
(4) Take the child to a movie and try to help the child feel better.
(5) Ignore the child, as a way of expressing disapproval.

8. Which of the following statements in NOT a recommendation of the passage?

(1) Love is important in raising a child.
(2) Discipline should be mainly a matter of "dos" and "don'ts."
(3) Discussion is important.
(4) Children need well-defined limits.
(5) Children need a certain amount of freedom.

Item 9 is based on the following graph.

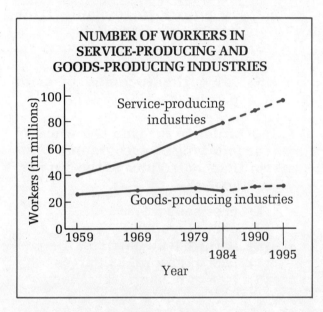

NUMBER OF WORKERS IN
SERVICE-PRODUCING AND
GOODS-PRODUCING INDUSTRIES

9. During the period shown in the graph, many women entered the labor force. The statement concerning these new members of the labor force that is best supported by the graph is that many women

(1) went into the service-producing industries
(2) went into the goods-producing industries
(3) went into low-paying careers
(4) suffered periods of unemployment
(5) had to retrain because of changes in the economy

Items 10 to 12 are based on the following information.

In the course of its history, the United States has pursued a number of different goals in dealing with other countries. Listed below are several of these foreign policy goals, with brief descriptions of each.

(1) **Isolationism:** avoiding close military, political, and economic relationships with other countries
(2) **Imperialism:** adding territory by means of force; acquiring an empire
(3) **Intervention:** using diplomatic and/or military means to support national political and/or business interests abroad
(4) **Alliances:** pursuing military and economic partnerships with other countries or groups of countries
(5) **Détente:** trying to relax tensions with potentially hostile countries in order to preserve peace

10. In his last speech as president, George Washington advised his country to steer clear of all political entanglements with other nations. This advice was followed. The main foreign policy goal in the earliest years of this country was

(1) isolationism
(2) imperialism
(3) intervention
(4) alliances
(5) détente

11. President Taft encouraged American businessmen to invest in the countries of Central America and the Caribbean. When disturbances broke out in the Central American country of Nicaragua in 1912, Taft sent in the U.S. Marines to protect American lives and property. The foreign policy goal Taft was emphasizing was

(1) isolationism
(2) imperialism
(3) intervention
(4) alliances
(5) détente

12. In 1949 the United States, Canada, and ten Western European nations signed the North Atlantic Pact. The pact said that if any of the nations signing were to be attacked, the other nations would come to its defense. In signing the North Atlantic Pact, the United States was pursuing a foreign policy goal of

(1) isolation
(2) imperialism
(3) intervention
(4) alliances
(5) détente

Items 13 to 14 are based on the following passage.

Around the world there are millions of people who go hungry. The problem of hunger is especially serious in many of the developing countries of Africa, Asia, and Latin America.

The reason for hunger often isn't insufficient food production. Many countries that in the past weren't producing enough have now greatly increased their crop yields, thanks to new agricultural technologies. Yet people continue to go hungry. Often the reason for hunger is poverty. People are simply too poor to buy the food they need. Sometimes the reason is distribution. That is, people who are hungry may live in regions where it is very difficult to transport large supplies of food, because the country lacks modern transportation systems. Certain types of terrain—mountains, deserts, rainforests—make building such systems extremely difficult and sometimes impossible.

13. Judging from information in the passage, a long-range solution for the problem of hunger would require the governments of the developing countries to

(1) improve the agricultural technologies used
(2) obtain more food aid from abroad
(3) increase their food exports
(4) increase their food imports
(5) raise the incomes of poor people

14. According to the passage, which of the following is a geographical factor that contributes to the problem of hunger?

(1) poor soils
(2) poor climates
(3) natural land barriers
(4) lack of natural resources
(5) lack of modern technology

Item 15 is based on the following cartoon.

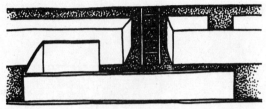

Löffler/Borba/Belgrade

15. This cartoon was created when the countries of Eastern Europe first became free of control by the Soviet Union in the late 1980s and rejected the Communist systems which they had lived under since the late 1940s. The artist suggests that they will suffer all of the following EXCEPT

(1) they will fall back into tyranny very soon
(2) they will be surrounded by barriers from the old social order
(3) they will celebrate freedom before they really have it
(4) they will have difficulty finding their way to a new life
(5) they will have difficulty seeing their whole situation

Items 16 to 18 are based on the following passage.

Blue-collar workers have always made up a large part of the membership of labor unions. For many years the number of jobs for blue-collar workers grew steadily. Today, however, there is a declining need for blue-collar workers. Many unions are suffering as a result.

Union leaders and members often blame the problem on tough foreign competition. Because Americans are buying more foreign goods, they say, U.S. factories are being forced to shut down. This is only part of the explanation, however. More important has been the shift toward high technology in factories and offices. Because of this shift, the makeup of the labor force is changing. Certain kinds of jobs are being created, others are being lost. Unions will have to adjust to these changes if they are to survive.

16. The most important cause of the situation unions face that is discussed in the passage is

(1) decreased membership
(2) the loss of blue-collar jobs
(3) anti-union legislation
(4) American manufacturers' inability to compete with foreign companies
(5) the change toward new technology in the workplace

17. Judging from information in the passage, the most effective strategy for unions today probably would be to

(1) push for restrictions on imports
(2) take a tougher stance when negotiating contracts with employers
(3) try to unionize new sorts of workers
(4) oppose the use of new technology
(5) raise union dues

18. Based on the passage, the LEAST likely to be experiencing problems would be a union for

 (1) textile and garment workers
 (2) teachers
 (3) machinists
 (4) auto workers
 (5) steel workers

Items 19 to 22 refer to the following chart.

CHECKS AND BALANCES		
EXECUTIVE POWER (given mainly to the president)	**LEGISLATIVE POWER** (given mainly to congress)	**JUDICIAL POWER** (given mainly to the courts)
The President makes treaties. The President is the Commander in chief of the Armed Forces.	The Senate must approve all treaties. Only Congress may declare war. Congress may impeach and convict a President.	The Supreme Court may declare a presidential act unconsititutional.
The President carries out the laws.	Only Congress may pass laws.	The courts interpret laws. The Supreme Court may declare a law unconstitutional.
The President may veto laws.	Congress can override a veto with a two-thirds vote.	Congress can propose an ammendment to the constitution if the Supreme Court declares a law unconstitutional. The ammendment must be approved by three fourths of the states' legislatures.
The President appoints judges, ambassadors, and other officials. The President appoints judges. The President may grant pardons and reprieves.	The Senate must approve all appointments. The Senate approves the appointment of the judges. Congress may impeach and convict any federal judge.	

19. According to the information in the chart, the President would NOT be able to

    (1) appoint a relative as ambassador to a foreign country

    (2) declare war on another country

    (3) give commands to the navy during wartime

    (4) make a treaty with another country

    (5) carry out a law preventing terrorism

20. The main purpose of the checks and balance system is to

    (1) prevent any branch of the government from becoming too powerful

    (2) establish a way for the President, Congress, and the Supreme Court to work together

    (3) make the Constitution adaptable to changing times

    (4) make sure that all citizens are fairly represented

    (5) encourage the government to be more efficient

21. Which of the following statements is NOT an example of the checks and balances system?

    (1) Congress passes laws, and the courts interpret laws.

    (2) The President can veto laws, and Congress can override the president's veto.

    (3) The President can pardon people convicted of crimes.

    (4) The Supreme Court may declare a law unconstitutional, and Congress may then propose to amend the Constitution.

    (5) The President appoints judges and the Senate approves the appointments.

22. In 1987 Congress passed a multi-billion-dollar highway bill. This bill provided funds for new highways and bridges in many states and raised the speed limit on some rural highways to 65 mph. President Reagan vetoed the bill because he considered it too costly. In a close vote Congress overrode his veto, so that the bill became law. This bill became law because of which of the following aspects of the checks and balance system?

    (1) executive power checked by legislative power

    (2) executive power checked by judicial power

    (3) legislative power checked by executive power

    (4) legislative power checked by judicial power

    (5) judicial power checked by legislative power

23. The problem of "groupthink" occurs in all kinds of groups—from groups advising the president of the United States to decision-making groups in corporations and small groups as well. Groupthink is the tendency of people in groups to become so concerned with agreeing with their leader, or with one another, that they are unable to think on their own or express criticism. Not surprisingly, bad decisions often result.

To avoid groupthink a leader might do all of the following EXCEPT

    (1) encourage the group to sometimes meet without him or her

    (2) get the opinion of outside experts

    (3) have the group meet more often

    (4) encourage those in the group to openly express their views

    (5) rotate group membership, so there is always someone new

24. The federal government has a budget deficit. That is, it spends more money than it earns. The government earns money largely through taxes. Individuals and corporations are required to give the government a certain percentage of the money they earn. The government spends money largely on national defense and on benefit payments to individuals. Benefit payments include unemployment compensation, for workers who have lost their jobs, and social security, for workers who have reached retirement age.

Which of the following would be most likely to lessen, rather than add to, the budget deficit?

(1) More people become unemployed.
(2) More people reach retirement age.
(3) Corporations earn larger profits.
(4) A law is passed to develop an expensive new defense program.
(5) A law is passed lowering taxes.

Item 25 is based on the following chart.

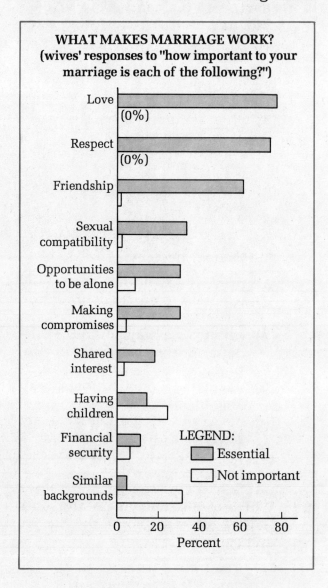

25. According to the values expressed by the wives' responses on the chart, which of the following would be the *least relevant* for a successful marriage?

(1) a stubborn husband
(2) a husband with the same race and religion
(3) a wealthy husband
(4) a sexually responsive husband
(5) a husband who puts the family first

Items 26 to 30 are based on the following passage.

The initial policy of the U.S. government was to treat Native American tribes as nations, or independent governments. In keeping with this policy, Congress negotiated treaties with the tribes of the Great Plains. These treaties established large areas as permanent Native American territory. However, miners and farmers traveling west wanted land. All the treaties were broken.

The Plains tribes fought fiercely against white settlers and the U.S. Army. The whites, however, had better weapons and, with the coming of the railroad and the telegraph, better transportation and communication. Also, the whites exterminated the buffalo, on which the Indians depended for food and other necessities. By the 1880s, most of the Plains tribes had been forced onto two large reservations. Once this happened, their power to wage war was severely limited.

The Dawes Act of 1887 divided reservations into farms and promised U.S. citizenship to Native Americans if they became farmers and gave up their tribal practices. The act was an attempt to help that Native Americans. It was, however, also an effort to make them change their way of life. By and large the act was a failure. In the 1920s and 1930s the U.S. Congress, recognizing that Native Americans wanted to preserve their own way of life, passed some new laws. From now on, U.S. citizenship would be automatic. No conditions would be attached. The tribes were to be encouraged to govern themselves.

26. Which of the following was NOT a factor leading to the defeat of the Plains tribes?

   (1) The U.S. Army had superior weapons.
   (2) The U.S. Army was better able to transport its men.
   (3) The U.S. Army divisions had better means of communicating vital information to one another than did the Native Americans.
   (4) Many Native Americans became farmers and gave up their tribal practices.
   (5) The buffalo herds were killed.

27. According to the passage, fighting between the Plains tribes and the soldiers virtually came to an end once

   (1) the U.S. government began negotiating treaties
   (2) the Native Americans were forced onto reservations
   (3) miners and farmers settled the Great Plains
   (4) railroads were built across the plains
   (5) the Native Americans agreed to change their way of life

28. According to the passage, why did the Dawes Act fail?

   (1) The tribes had been forced onto reservations.
   (2) Previous treaties had been broken.
   (3) The Native Americans wanted to keep their own culture and way of life.
   (4) The Native Americans didn't want to become U.S. citizens.
   (5) The Native Americans weren't interested in farming.

29. The U.S. government has had a number of policies toward the Native Americans. Judging from information in the passage, one similarity between its earliest and most recent policies is that both

(1) encourage the Native Americans to farm the land
(2) encourage the Native Americans to live on reservations
(3) treat the tribe as a unit of government for the Native Americans
(4) attempt to destroy the Native Americans' way of life
(5) emphasize the integration of Native Americans into the larger society

30. Which of the following statements best describes what has happened over time to the Native american way of life?

(1) When the plains were settled and the buffalo exterminated, the Native American way of life was ended.
(2) When the Native Americans were forced onto reservations, their way of life was destroyed.
(3) Over time, the Native Americans became farmers and abandoned their way of life.
(4) The settlement of the Great Plains had no effect on the Native American way of life.
(5) Despite some changes, the Native Americans have preserved their way of life.

Items 31 to 32 are based on the graph on page 13.

31. Which statement best summarizes the age distributions of Mexico and Sweden?

(1) Mexico and Sweden have similar patterns of age distribution.
(2) Mexico's population is more evenly distributed in terms of age than Sweden's.
(3) Overall, Mexico has a younger population than Sweden.
(4) Overall, Sweden has a younger population than Mexico.
(5) Mexico has a larger proportion of both very old people and very young people than Sweden does.

32. Which one of the following conclusions is best supported by the graphs?

(1) Mexico is a larger country than Sweden.
(2) Mexico has more people living in larger cities than Sweden does.
(3) Mexico has better medical care than Sweden.
(4) Mexico's standard of living will improve more rapidly than Sweden's.
(5) Mexico's population will grow at a faster rate than Sweden's.

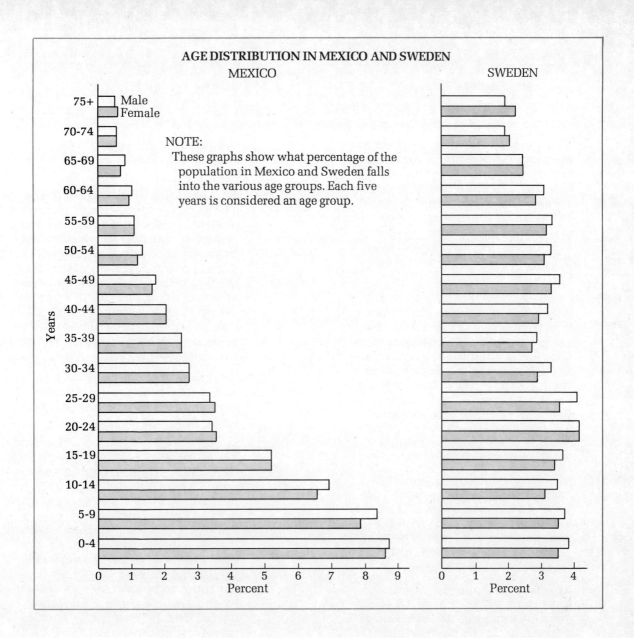

AGE DISTRIBUTION IN MEXICO AND SWEDEN

MEXICO

SWEDEN

NOTE:
These graphs show what percentage of the population in Mexico and Sweden falls into the various age groups. Each five years is considered an age group.

Male
Female

Years:
75+
70-74
65-69
60-64
55-59
50-54
45-49
40-44
35-39
30-34
25-29
20-24
15-19
10-14
5-9
0-4

Percent

ANSWERS AND EXPLANATIONS FOR THE PREDICTOR TEST

1. **(3)** *Analysis/Economics.* Since a surplus is possible only if exports are worth more than imports, the country will have to decrease the value of its imports and increase the value of its exports. Choice (4) is also a possible strategy, but it will not be the best one because the value of imports doesn't go down.

2. **(1)** *Comprehension/Political Science.* As a money matter, the national budget the president proposes must first be considered in the House. (2) and (3) are the two Senate responsibilities listed in the passage. (4) is also an example of a presidential appointment which the Senate would approve. (5) would be an act by the president; neither Senate or House would approve it.

3. **(1)** *Analysis/Political Science.* In each of the three graphs, the 20-year-old male who has a grammar-school education falls into the group that voted least. Therefore, of the people described, he is the least likely to have voted.

4. **(4)** *Application/Political Science.* Less than 40 percent of 18-to 20-year-olds voted (and less than 45 percent of 21- to 24-year-olds). The civic group would therefore be most interested in changing the voting habits of young adults.

5. **(4)** *Application/Behavioral Science.* By sometimes breaking his policy on sweets and other times insisting on it, the father is failing to apply rules consistently.

6. **(2)** *Comprehension/Behavioral Science.* The passage is basically talking about children's need for discipline and about the kind of discipline children need. Choice (1) in fact contradicts the passage, which opens by saying that both love and dicipline are important. The other incorrect choices, al-though in keeping with the passage, are each discussed in only part of it.

7. **(3)** *Application/Behavioral Science.* The passage states that discussion in situations where problems have arisen is "far better" than direct expression of anger (2) or "withdrawal of love" (5). (4) illustrates the behavior of an overly permissive parent, and (1) shows parental action that does not set well-defined limits for the child, neither praising, blaming nor discussing the child's behavior.

8. **(2)** *Comprehension/Behavioral Science.* The passage specifically says that discipline is more than just "dos" and don'ts.

9. **(1)** *Evaluation/Economics.* The number of workers in goods-producing industries remained about the same. Therefore (2) is false. The number of workers in service-producing industries increased greatly. Therefore, women entering the labor force were far more likely to have gone into service-producing industries. This will continue to be the case, as shown by the graph's projections (the dotted lines). The graph provides no information about (3), (4) and (5).

10. **(1)** *Application/History.* The emphasis on steering clear of entanglements with other countries is characteristic of a policy of isolationism.

11. **(3)** *Application/History.* Taft's policy of using military means to support U.S. business interests in Central America was an example of intervention.

12. **(4)** *Application/History.* In signing the North Atlantic Pact, the United States was pursuing a foreign policy goal of alliances, in this case of alliance for defense purposes.

13. (5) *Evaluation/Geography.* Poverty is a major reason for hunger. Therefore, to really deal with hunger, the incomes of the very poor must somehow be raised. Another major reason for hunger, we are told, is lack of transportation to distribute the food, but this reason is not among the choice's offered. The passage says new agricultural technologies already produce enough food, so (1) is wrong. (2), (3) and (4) are not discussed.

14. (3) *Analysis/Geography.* People in developing countries sometimes go hungry because they live in areas that are difficult to transport food to because of the terrain. (1), (2) and (4) are geographical factors but they do not contribute to hunger according to the passage. In fact, the passages say that with new agricultural technologies, these hungry regions produce enough food despite the drawbacks of their soils, climates and supply of natural resources. (5) is not a geographical factor; because of the mention of "new agricultural technologies" it is not a contributing factor to hunger.

15. (1) *Analysis/Political Science.* All the other choices describe one possible meaning of the cartoon. The man in the cartoon, who is shouting "Freedom!," is surrounded by a confusing network of walls and hallways that looks endless, with no clear exit to another place. This means that he is being compared to someone entering a maze. He is climbing out of a lower area of walled-off spaces and darkness into an area even more filled with walls. The cartoon therefore clearly suggests (2), (3), (4) and (5). There is, however, nothing to suggest that the man is going to "fall back" down the ladder into the condition where he was before he got this far toward freedom. So (1) is the one difficulty the artist does not foresee for these people.

16. (5) *Comprehension/Economics.* We are told that the most important cause of the union's problems is the "shift toward high technology in factories and offices." (4) is a cause, but less important. (1) and (2) are effects of (5). They describe the union's problems not the causes of these problems.

17. (3) *Evaluation/Economics.* Jobs that have typically been "union jobs" are being lost. New kinds of jobs are becoming important. Therefore, to remain healthy, unions must try to unionize workers in jobs that are new jobs or that have existed but haven't typically been union jobs. Having less power, unions would face defeat if they pursued the actions listed in the other choices.

18. (2) *Analysis/Economics.* Union membership has declined mainly in fields where blue-collar jobs predominated and high technology has changed the kinds of jobs available. These characteristics are not true of the teaching field.

19. (2) *Application/Political Science.* The chart shows that although the president is commander in chief of the armed forces, only Congress may declare a war. All the other choices are executive powers of the President.

20. (1) *Evaluation/Political Science.* The chart shows that each of the three branches of government "checks," or limits, the powers of the other branches. This arrangement therefore serves to prevent any branch from becoming too powerful.

21. (3) *Comprehension/Political Science.* As the chart makes clear, checks and balances are between branches of government. All the examples with the exception of choice (3) involve two branches. The chart shows no check from the judicial or legislative branch on this particular example of executive power, the granting of Presidential pardons.

22. (1) *Analysis/Political Science.* This example actually involves two checks. The veto of the bill was an executive check on legislative power. The bill became law, however, because the veto was overridden by Congress. Therefore it became law because of a legislative check on executive power.

23. **(3)** *Evaluation/Behavioral Science.* More frequent meetings, by increasing group contact, would, if anything, enourage groupthink. All the other choices would discourage groupthink, either by bringing in outside views or by helping those in the group form and express their own opinions.

24. **(3)** *Analysis/Economics.* Corporations pay the government a certain percentage of the money they earn. So if they make larger profits, the government earns more money. This would lessen the budget deficit. All the other choices would add to the deficit.

25. **(2)** *Analysis/Behavioral Science.* The women whose opinions are shown on the chart consider "Similar backgrounds" the least important or relevant to a good marriage. All the other choices refer to characteristics of husbands that they consider more important. (1) refers to "Making Compromises," (3) to "Financial Security," (4) to "Sexual Compatibility," and (5) to "Having Children."

26. **(4)** *Comprehension/History.* The passage does not state that many Native Americans became farmers and gave up their way of life. In fact, the opposite is implied. Therefore, this could not be a reason for the Native American's defeat. All the other choices are mentioned in the passage.

27. **(2)** *Comprehension/History.* The passage explains that once the Native Americans had been forced onto reservations, they could no longer put up an effective resistance. (3) is a reason the Native Americans were driven from their land, not a reason they stopped fighting. (4) is a reason they were at a disadvantage against white settlers, though they fought on for many years. Treaties were signed with the Native Americans and all were broken from the start of western settlement, so (1) is wrong. The entire last paragraph implies the opposite of (5).

28. **(3)** *Comprehension/History.* The passage states that the Dawes Act was in part an attempt to make the Native Americans change their way of life. It also states that the act failed and that the laws replacing it were based on the recognition that the Native Americans wanted to keep their way of life. From this it can be inferred that the Dawes Act failed because it went against the Native Americans' desire to preserve their culture.

29. **(3)** *Analysis/History.* The U.S. government's earliest policy was to treat the tribes as governments and therefore make treaties with them. Its most recent policy, shaped by the acts of the 1920s and 1930s, is to recognize the importance of the tribes and to encourage tribal self-government. In both cases, the tribe is being treated as a unit of government. (1), (2) and (4) do not refer to the earliest and latest periods but to the 1880s and early 20th century, when Native Americans were on reservations and were being encouraged to farm. Nothing suggests that (5) was ever a U.S. government policy toward Native Americans.

30. **(5)** *Evaluation/History.* The passage describes a situation in which the Native American way of life has changed but endured. The other choices, which indicate either no change or complete change, are incorrect.

31. **(3)** *Comprehension/Geography.* Mexico has a large percentage of its population concentrated in the younger age groups (0-4, 5-9, 10-14, etc.). Sweden does not. Therefore, Mexico's population is, overall, younger than Sweden's. All the other choices are false, inaccurate summaries of information on the graphs.

32. **(5)** *Evaluation/History.* The graphs show that Mexico has a younger population than Sweden. This means that a greater percentage of Mexico's population is at the age of having children or will be reaching that age soon. As a greater percentage of its population will be having children, Mexico will experience faster population growth than Sweden. None of the other choices are supported by the graphs.

Predictor Test

Performance Analysis Chart

Directions: Circle the number of each item that you got correct on the Predictor Test. Count how many items you got correct. Write the grand total correct over the denominator, **32**, at the lower right corner of the chart. (For example, if you got 28 items correct, write 28 so that the fraction reads 28/**32**.) Divide the numerator by the denominator to find what percentage of the items you got correct.

	History (page 40)	Geography (page 214)	Economics (page 174)	Political Science (page 122)	Behavioral Science (page 242)	TOTAL CORRECT
Comprehension	26, 27, 28		16	2, 15, 21	6, 8	—— 10
Application	10, 11, 12			4, 19	5, 7	—— 7
Analysis	29	14	1, 18 24	3, 22	25	—— 8
Evaluation	30	13, 32	9, 17	20	23	—— 7
TOTAL CORRECT	—— 8	—— 4	—— 6	—— 8	—— 6	—— 32

The page numbers in parenthesis indicate where in this book you can find the beginning of specific instruction about the various fields of social studies.

READING STRATEGIES FOR THE SOCIAL STUDIES TEST

(Credit: American Airlines)

PREREADING: PREVIEWING, BRAINSTORMING, AND PREDICTING

You may think that the only thing that will matter when you take the GED is how much you know about the subject matter. Certainly, your chances of doing well are greatly improved by knowing your subject. But your performance on the test will also be determined by how quickly and how well you can understand the material. By using *reading strategies*, you can gather information more effectively and cut right to the heart of the questions you will be asked to answer.

Prereading is an important reading strategy. You probably already use it a lot without even realizing it. With our busy lives, many of us don't have the time to read all the articles in the newspapers or magazines we get. We have to limit ourselves to those articles that are of particular interest to us. We do this by *previewing* them. We glance at the name of the article, some of the first sentences of the paragraphs, the illustrations and the captions. From this information, we can *predict* fairly well what the article is about. Then we decide if we want to take the time to read it.

On the GED test, you won't be deciding whether or not to read a passage; you'll have to read it to be able to answer the questions. But previewing and predicting can help you get an idea of what a passage and its questions are about *before* you actually read them. This helps you better understand and absorb the material when you do read it.

Another prereading strategy is *brainstorming*. To brainstorm means to think of everything you know about a subject. Brainstorming helps you apply old information to new situations and come up with solutions to problems that might not otherwise have occurred to you. In your day-to-day living, you might brainstorm when you get stuck following complicated instructions, such as hooking up the components of a stereo system. If you're halfway through and realize there aren't enough places to plug everything in, you could brainstorm. Think of everything you know about the path the electronic signals take in going from one component to another. Similarly, brainstorming can help you on the GED by summoning up all you know about a topic—both what you have learned from books and what you have learned from your experience. You can then use the information to help you answer questions.

PREVIEWING

Previewing a reading passage and the corresponding test items on the GED helps you get the most out of the passage when you actually read it. To preview social studies material, follow these steps:

(1) Find where the directions begin and end.

(2) Get a sense of how long the passage is and how many questions follow it.

(3) Get a sense of the form of the material. Is it all written text? Is there a graph? a table? a cartoon? Is there both graphic material and written text?

(4) Pay close attention to headings, captions, and labels. What clues do they give you?

(5) Look for words that are emphasized in the text. Emphasized words may be boldfaced (in dark print), underlined, capitalized, repeated, or italicized (in slanted print). These are key words that tell you what the passage is about.

Try out your previewing skills with this passage and the question that follows it. First quickly review the steps in previewing. Then look at the passage and the question below.

> The destructiveness of World War II inspired 46 nations to meet in San Francisco and form a world body that would unite to "save the succeeding generations from the scourge of war." As a result of this meeting, the **United Nations** was founded in June 1945. Today the United Nations has its headquarters in New York. There, the General Assembly, with its 180 members, discusses world issues and recommends courses of action. The Security Council, with 27 seats, gives the major countries a permanent place and the right to veto any proposal.

1. Which of the following sentences best restates the definition of the United Nations? "The United Nations is a world body that

(1) was founded after World War II"

(2) consists of a General Assembly and Security Council"

(3) consists of 27 member nations"

(4) consists of 180 member nations"

(5) was designed to prevent future war"

(Credit: United Nations/M. Grant)

First, you should have located the directions and given the passage and question a quick going-over. You should have noticed that there was only one question. Perhaps you even read the question quickly. Next you should have noticed that the material is all in the form of written text. There are no graphics, no labels, no headings. But there are emphasized words. The bold-faced words in this passage give you an idea what the passage is all about. They also help you locate the answer to the question.

Once you have previewed the material, go back and read it carefully. Look at *every* answer choice. Since United Nations is boldfaced in the passage, you should look in that general area to find the answer to the question. The correct answer to the question is choice (5).

Previewing may seem like a lot of work now, and you may think that it takes more time than it's worth. But as you improve your previewing skills, you will find that it becomes almost second nature, and it will save you time in the end.

QUESTIONING AS YOU READ

Asking questions as you read is another good reading strategy. Think about what happens when you read an exciting story. You might find yourself asking questions about what's going to happen next, or who a new character is, or—when it's a murder mystery—who did it? As you read, without realizing it, you are asking these questions, looking for clues and asking more questions as the story unfolds. If the story is well written, all your questions will be answered by the end of the book.

You will want to make guesses and predictions about the reading material on the GED, too. This will help you read with a plan in mind: to find the answers to your questions. To question social studies material, follow these steps:

(1) After you preview the material, ask a question that you might find the answer to as you read.

(2) Predict the answer to your question.

(3) Read to see if your prediction is correct.

Use what you have just learned to question the following passage:

> Four of the United States' pioneering women travelers were Annie Smith Peck, Delia J. Akeley, Marguerite Harrison, and Louise Arner Boyd. Peck (1850–1935) was a mountain climber. Akeley (1875–1970) was an *anthropologist*. Harrison (1879–1967) was a documentary filmmaker, and Boyd (1887–1972) was an Arctic explorer.

1. The four women have in common that they were all
   (1) pioneer women in colonial America
   (2) among the first famous American women travelers
   (3) the first women world travelers
   (4) photographers who filmed the wonders of the Arctic
   (5) mountain climbers who climbed the world's highest peaks

Sally Ride (Credit: NASA)

After previewing the material, you should have formulated a question. In this case, you can rephrase item 1 as a question: "What did these four women have in common?" Before reading the passage to answer the question, you should make your own prediction. You may have noticed the capitalized word Arctic, or the italicized *anthropologist*. From this you might predict that the four women were anthropologists who explored the Arctic. Your next step would be to see if your prediction holds up. Read the passage. You will find that your prediction is not confirmed. Only Boyd is mentioned in regard to the Arctic, and only Akeley was an anthropologist. Reading the entire passage tells you that the four women had different backgrounds and different pursuits. What they had in common was that they were all American, all women, and all travelers. So choice (2) is the correct answer.

Continue to ask yourself questions as you read. It will help you stay actively involved in gathering information. Whether your predictions are right or wrong isn't important. Your purpose is to streamline the reading process by gathering information quickly and effectively. Asking questions and making predictions can help you achieve this goal.

CHAPTER 1

What is **social studies**? If you look at the word **social**, you will see that it has the same root as the word **society**. Societies are large, organized groups of people who have many thing in common: what they believe, how they live, where they live, and how they interact. So social studies is the study of people and how they live together.

(Credit: Marc Anderson)

Prereading Prompt

Think about how it would feel to know nothing about your place in the world, about what is going on around you. You would probably feel lost—perhaps even frightened. Throughout history, people have recognized the need to let each generation know what has come before it. Whether told around a campfire or written in a textbook, passing on the story of humankind has been important to every civilization.

Introduction to Social Studies

What Is Social Studies?

Like most people, you are probably curious about the world you live in and the people who inhabit it. What determines where and how people live? Why are some countries wealthy and some poor? Why do countries have different customs, different systems of government? What causes people to behave the way they do?

These questions and the topics they address are all part of *social studies*. Finding the answers can help you learn why the world is the way it is, and how it got to be that way.

Of course, the answers to these questions are complex. People are complicated beings, and groups of people, such as communities and societies, are even more complicated. You can simplify the study of groups of people by finding common threads that tie them together. Take the United States as an example. There are over 245 million people in this country who come from different backgrounds, speak different languages, and have different ideas. But they are associated with each other for some common purpose. In this case, it is because we believe in a free and democratic way of life. This isn't to say that everyone agrees on all political issues; listening to one political discussion would prove that notion incorrect. But we do share a political system, a history, a common language and an economic system.

Looking at all societies in this way can help us understand ourselves as people who share the same planet. The field of social studies can help us understand the past and plan for the future. Together we can make the world a better place to live.

Key Words

communities—groups of people living in the same area under a common government

societies—larger groups of people that share political and economic systems, language, and history

culture—a group's beliefs and way of life

The Social Sciences That Make Up Social Studies

Prereading Prompt

When something is seen out of context—out of its surroundings—it can be difficult to understand. For example, a machine part from a TV or a car may not mean much until you see how it fits into the rest of the machine. In the same way, words you do not understand at first can be understood by seeing how they fit in with the words around them. This lesson will introduce many new words. When you see an unfamiliar word, look for clues in the words that you *do* understand in its context.

Key Words

History—the study of people and events in the past
Geography—the study of the relation ship between the regions of the Earth and the creatures that live in them
Economics—the study of how wealth is made and distributed
Political Science—the study of various types of government
Behavioral Sciences—sciences that study human behavior

You already know that social studies is the study of people in society. What does this really mean? Let's break it down and examine the five main branches of social studies.

History is probably the first branch of study that comes to mind when people think about social studies. History is the record of human events, the actual story of humankind. There are many kinds of history, as every person, every country, and every idea has a history.

Another branch of social studies is **geography**. Geography is the study of the relationship between people and the Earth. There are two types of geography. *Physical geography* is the study of the Earth itself—its surface, its climate, and its structure. *Cultural geography* is concerned with the distribution of the world's population—the areas where people live and how the physical geography of these particular regions affects how they live.

Economics is the branch of social studies that deals with the financial condition of a country: how it produces goods and services; how the wealth from these goods and services is distributed among the people; and how the country's goods and services are traded throughout the world.

A fourth branch of social studies is **political science**. This is the study of the various types of governments that exist in the world and how they operate. Representative democracy and dictatorship are two types of government. Though very different from each other, both have roots that can be traced back to ancient and even prehistoric times.

The last branch of social studies is **behavioral science**. This includes the fields of psychology, sociology, and anthropology. These sciences all have to do with people and their behavior. *Psychology* is the study of the mind—how it works and how it affects what people do. *Sociology* is concerned with the various relationships among people in a society—what roles people play and what groups they associate with. *Anthropology* is the study of groups of people, including large groups, such as an entire country, or smaller groups within a society. It studies their beliefs and their way of life (including food, language, art, sports, and religion)—their *culture*.

Often you will find that the branches of social studies overlap. If you are studying a particular event in history, such as the American Revolution, you will also likely study geography and economics as they relate to this period. Since people and their lives are so connected with each other, few events can ever be looked at in isolation.

Understanding Words by Context Clues

When something is seen out of **context**—out of its surroundings—it can be difficult to understand. Look at the following sentence: "The President hated to look at the flag." It doesn't make much sense. But add a second sentence: "The President hated to look at the flag. It was torn and covered with mud." Now the first sentence makes sense. The context of the second sentence gives you the full, clear meaning.

Unfamiliar words can also be understood by their context. By picking up everything you *do* know from the sentence, you will often be able to figure out what a word means. When you come across a word you don't know, brainstorm. Think of everything that comes to mind about the word. For example, you may not know exactly what "inauguration" means, but you probably have heard the word associated with the President of the United States. You probably know that it has something to do with a *new* president, one who is just taking office. Taking what you know about the word, you guess that inauguration means "a formal ceremony that begins a term in public office."

In addition to brainstorming about an unfamiliar word, you can look for clues in words around it that will help you figure out its meaning. Sometimes the answer will be given right in the sentence. In this lesson, for instance, you are given the exact dictionary meaning—the **definition**—of several new words: for example, psychology, sociology, and anthropology. Definitions are the easiest clues to the meaning of new words.

Often, however, a new word is not defined exactly. You have to look for other clues in the words around it that you already know—other context clues. For instance, the lesson says that sociology "is concerned with the various relationships among people in society." You can understand the exact meaning of the word "relationships" here by looking at the words right after it: "what roles people play and what groups they associate with." This kind of clue is called a **paraphrase**. It gives the meaning of a word or a phrase that comes right before it by restating it in other words. Often it begins with "in other words" or with the word "or," or—as here—with a dash.

Another kind of context clue is an **example**. You can see this used in the way the meaning of the word "culture" is given in the lesson: "their beliefs, and their way of life (including food, language, art, and sports)—their culture." Putting all these examples together defines "culture."

Sometimes a word is defined indirectly, by stating what the word does *not* mean, or by stating what its opposite is. This kind of context clue is called **contrast**. An example of contrast is in the passage below. You are told "we do not have *chaos* in the U.S. On the contrary, the U.S. is a strong and orderly political union." Here, the meaning of chaos is therefore the opposite of a strong and orderly political union. So chaos must be a situation in which there is no strong or orderly political union in a society. It must mean disorder and lack of unity.

Read the following passage and see if you can use context clues to figure out the meaning of "conglomerate" and "ethnic." Brainstorm quickly, because you probably already know something about these words.

> The United States is a *conglomerate* of people. The 50 states are populated by people from every *ethnic* group and every religion in the world. They include whites from Europe, Asians, and Africans, as well as people from Latin America and the Middle East. They also include Catholics, Protestants, Jews, Moslems, Buddhists, and other kinds of believers. It is amazing that we do not have *chaos* in the U.S. On the contrary, the U.S. is a strong and orderly political union. All these people share the American Dream of working to provide a better future for their children and to maintain a democratic way of life.

You have heard the word "ethnic" before, but you can figure out its exact meaning by looking at its context. You can see that the sentence about Catholics and others gives examples of religions. So you can figure out that the sentence before it gives examples of ethnic groups. The examples are of people of different races who come from different parts of the world. Therefore, ethnic must mean the characteristics people have from their race and the parts of the world they come from.

You can figure out *conglomerate* by putting several clues together. The first sentence says that the U.S. is a conglomerate of people. The second sentence says that the U.S. includes people from every ethnic and religious group in the world. The last two sentences tell us that all these people are parts of a union. So if the United States is a conglomerate of people, a conglomerate must be a union of many different parts—here, of people. You may have to figure out other words to get the meaning of a main word like "conglomerate," which is the key word of the topic sentence of the paragraph. But you can do it, step by step, using what you already know and using context clues.

One final context clue is **parallelism.** When two statements talk about the same things in slightly different ways, they are said to be parallel, just as two railroad or subway tracks go in the same direction side by side. The lesson says that cultural geography studies "the areas where people live and how the physical geography of these particular *regions* affects how they live." It is clear that "these particular regions" refers to the same thing as "the areas where people live," so "region" must mean geographical area.

Practice

The Practice item is based on the following paragraph.

A topic often discussed in social studies courses is political elections. In most elections, candidates run on different platforms. In the presidential election of 1988, however, voters complained that the candidates did not talk about the issues. Instead, they made speeches about patriotism, loyalty to the flag, and human values. These are not ideas that deal with real social problems. Americans want specific solutions to such issues as the national debt, unemployment, crime, the homeless, and the environment. American voters want candidates to have definite platforms.

1. In the passage, the meaning of
   platform is
   (1) a speech about human values
   (2) a stage to stand on
   (3) a set of solutions
   (4) a particular statement
   (5) a national problem

Choice (3) is correct. You can find this answer by using two context clues: contrast and parallelism. You can use parallelism to connect "platforms" with "solutions to such issues." The statement that "Americans want specific solutions to such issues" is parallel to the statement "American voters want candidates to have definite platforms." Both sentences tell us what Americans want from candidates, and "specific" and "definite" mean the same thing. So you could guess that "platforms" mean "solutions to such issues." The examples of issues are also clues to what "platform" might mean: it would offer solutions to such things as the national debt and the homeless.

You can use context clues to eliminate wrong answers, too. We are told that candidates in 1988 gave speeches "about patriotism . . . and human values" "instead of" talking about the issues. This contrast between their speeches and what platforms talk about means that (1) and (4) are wrong. By using parallelism, you can see that "real social problems" and "such issues" mean the same thing. We are told that Americans want solutions to these problems, or issues, not that they want the problems themselves, so (5) is wrong. You can eliminate (2) by combining prior knowledge with what you read. You know that a platform can be a stage to stand on, but you read that voters want to know what the candidates stand *for*, not what they stand *on*.

Items 1 and 2 are based on the following passage.

Sociologists have been following a disturbing trend in the nation's urban areas: the trend toward *gentrification*. It has always been difficult for the urban poor and lower middle class to find decent, affordable housing. The general movement toward gentrification is making the problem worse. In recent years many poor and lower-income neighborhoods have been redeveloped into upper-middle-class areas filled with expensive restaurants and fashionable shops. Since no public housing is being built, the trend toward gentrification is leaving the urban poor with two choices: to live in crowded, run-down ghettos, or else be homeless on the streets.

1. What is the most likely definition of *gentrification*?
    (1) a prejudice against certain ethnic groups
    (2) a growth in the number of upper-middle-class areas
    (3) an eviction of lower-middle-class people
    (4) a change of poor neighborhoods into wealthy neighborhoods
    (5) an increase in the number of homeless people

2. The word *trend* in the passage means a
    (1) redevelopment of areas
    (2) general movement
    (3) gentrification process
    (4) new neighborhood
    (5) upper-middle-class fashion

Item 3 is based on the following passage.

The United States is a paradise for people studying physical geography. The land is full of landforms of opposite extremes: high mountains and deep canyons; dry deserts and fertile plains; high buttes and low valleys.

3. The meaning of *butte* is
    (1) a sunken plain
    (2) a dry river bed
    (3) a wide swamp
    (4) a steep hill
    (5) a deep canyon

Answers are on page 369.

How Social Scientists Report Information

Prereading Prompt

When you drive to a strange town you read a map to find the names of the places and streets you need to know. To remember these details you may sum them up in your own words. Finding details and restating information are useful skills you will learn more about in this lesson. They can help you deal with the information social scientists report.

Key Words

charts—designs of columns or rows that organize information
statistics—information given in numbers

The people who write television guides know that bits and pieces of information are difficult to understand if they are not organized. That's why TV listings are organized into charts showing channels, air times, and names of shows. **Charts** organize information and make it easier to remember and use.

For the same reason, social scientists use graphs and charts to present **statistics**, or numerical information. Suppose an economist wanted to show how a change in the price of automobiles affected the number of cars sold. She could use a *line graph*, as in Figure 1-1. A sociologist who wanted to look at the number of people working in manufacturing and industry over a century could use a *bar graph*, as in Figure 1-2.

Another kind of graph is the *circle graph*, or pie chart. The full circle represents 100 percent. The circle is then divided like a pie to show parts of the whole. Circle graphs are useful to show what percentage of the whole a given group represents.

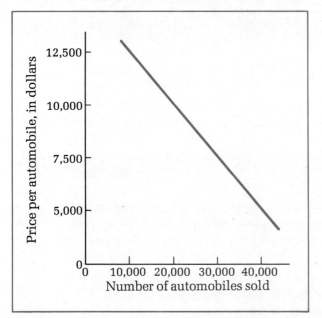

Fig. 1–1

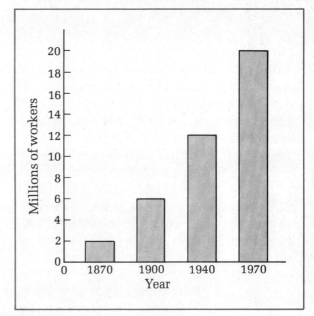

Fig. 1–2

A useful tool for historians is the *timeline*. Historians use one continuous line to represent the course of history, placing events on the line according to when they occurred. Usually the line runs from left to right, with the earliest events on the left and the more recent on the right.

Maps are often used by historians, and are also very useful to geographers. Maps can show climate, the physical features of the Earth's surface, the location of natural resources, centers of population, and many other kinds of information.

Often it doesn't make sense to use a chart, graph, or map to report information. Details can be given in written paragraphs, or *text*. For example, statistics show that 73.9 percent of Americans live in cities and 26.1 percent in rural areas. The numbers are easy to compare, so there is no need for a chart. Written text also allows the social scientist to discuss the meaning of details. Text is most useful when it does not include many statistics, but rather explanations, ideas, and details.

Finding Details

Social scientists work with a lot of *details*—bits of information about topics. Details answer the questions, When? Where? Who? What? How? and Why? A good newspaper reporter knows this and attempts to answer these questions when writing. When you read something, such as a newspaper or this book, you are looking for specific details. On the GED test, you will be asked to find details to show that you understand written passages.

To look for details, start by brainstorming about the topic. Then ask yourself what you want to learn from the passage. While you read, look for the answers to your questions. When you've finished reading, review what you've learned. What details did you find to answer your questions? Try this method with the following passage, which is about a government study of acid rain.

> The federal government has spent ten years and $500 million to study the effects of acid rain. Acid rain is rain, snow, or sleet that has become acidic by picking up airborne particles of pollution. By disturbing the natural balance of chemicals in the soil, acid rain can kill trees and plants. One telltale sign is evergreen trees that begin to turn orange and eventually die. Lakes, fed by run-off from rain and snow, also become acidic. When this happens, the water can no longer support fish and plant life.

Your first step in brainstorming before reading is to think about what you know about acid rain. You've probably heard about it on the news and know that it has something to do with pollution. Next is to ask yourself what you would learn by reading the passage, questions such as, "Exactly what is acid rain? What effects does it have? How much did the study cost?" While reading the passage, you looked for answers to these and other questions you may have had. When you finished reading, you should have reviewed the details that answered your questions. You learned that acid rain comes from pollution, that it can kill plants and animals, and that the government spent $500 million to study the problem. If you had trouble remembering the details, you could go back to the passage and quickly find them.

Use what you've learned to answer the following question: How many years did the government spend studying acid rain? You may remember that the study took ten years. If not, you could quickly find the answer in the passage.

Restating Information

When you're driving somewhere strange and get lost, the best thing to do is stop and ask for directions. Usually, after a person has given you directions, you will repeat them aloud, in your own words. There's a good reason for doing this—it's much easier to remember details if you review them and put them into language that is meaningful to you.

Restating information helps you review, organize, and comprehend it. In Lesson 2 a lot of information was given on how social scientists report information. Can you remember what you read? Take a minute to go back and review the passage. Look at the words in italics or boldface. Review the key points of the passage. Put them in your own words. Repeat the words and the ideas, either aloud or in your head. Try doing this with the definition of a circle graph. How would you restate the information given? You might say, "A circle graph is round like a pie and is divided into sections, like slices of a pie. Each 'slice' is a percentage of the whole." Once you've visualized this and put it in your own words, you'll find it much easier to remember.

Now let's see how well you can restate what you've read by doing a Practice question.

Practice

The Practice item is based on the information in Lesson 2 on how social scientists report information.

Where do most Americans live?
(1) Americans are divided about equally between the city and the country.
(2) 26.1 percent of Americans live in rural areas.
(3) More than a quarter of all Americans live in cities.
(4) Many Americans live in suburbs.
(5) Roughly three-quarters of all Americans live in cities.

To answer this question, you would first need to recognize which choice is a *restatement* of information from the passage. Choices (2), (3), and (5) all contain information from the passage. Choices (1) and (4) do not, and so can be eliminated. Choice (2) uses the same wording as the passage, but doesn't answer the question. Choice (3) is a restatement of information from the passage, but doesn't answer the question either. How many more than a quarter live in cities? Is it a majority (more than 50 percent)? There's no way to know from this statement. Choice (5), however, restates the information that 73.9 percent of Americans live in cities. This is a clear majority, and answers the question.

Lesson 2 Exercises

Items 1 to 3 are based on the following paragraph.

Columbus is generally credited with discovering America. Evidence suggests however, that the North American continent was visited much earlier by a Norse Viking named Leif Eriksson. The details are sketchy, but Eriksson reportedly explored what is now southern Canada or the northern U.S. in the year 1000. Some scholars think there may have been an even earlier expedition to the area, around 986, by the Icelander Bjarni Herjulfsson. It is certain, however, that in 1492 Columbus reached the Caribbean. Columbus was Italian, although his expedition was financed by Spain. Columbus made three more voyages to the Americas before his death in 1506. John Cabot, an Italian who sailed under the English flag, explored much of the North American coast in 1498. Ponce de Leon, a Spaniard sailing for Spain, explored the Caribbean and Florida in 1513. The "Age of Discovery" had begun.

1. An historian might plot the information in the passage on a time line. What event would he or she plot at the far left of the time line?
   (1) Cabot explores North American coast.
   (2) Eriksson reaches North America.
   (3) Columbus lands in the Caribbean.
   (4) Ponce de Leon explores Florida.
   (5) Herjulfsson reaches North America.

2. According to the passage, Columbus
   (1) was Spanish, but sailed under the Italian flag
   (2) was the third explorer to reach the New World
   (3) reached the North American continent in 1492
   (4) was from the same country as Ponce de Leon
   (5) landed in the Caribbean in 1498

3. How many voyages did Columbus make to the Americas?
   (1) one
   (2) two
   (3) three
   (4) four
   (5) five

Answers are on page 369.

CHAPTER 2

American history is not just the study of dry dates in old books. It is all the unique ideas, all the fascinating people and events, all the things that have made the United States different from any other country in the world. From the Revolution to Woodstock, from the Civil War to the civil rights movement, from the discovery of the New World to the first moon landing, this is American history.

(Credit: U.S. Immigration Museum, Ellis Island, New York)

Prereading Prompt

President John F. Kennedy said that America was a nation of immigrants. The different groups of people who have come here have different ideas of American history. American history has been written mostly by European immigrants. Can you think of other ways that American history might be written?

American History

What Is American History?

American history begins with the discovery of the New World. Why was it called the New World? After all, the North and South American continents existed long before Europeans stumbled on them in their search for a short-cut to Asia. The Native Americans were here for centuries before the Europeans settled here. What was "new" about this world?

The answer lies in whose view of history you take. Typically, American history has been written by people who were descended from Europeans. They took a **Eurocentric** point of view. The word Eurocentric is similar to *egocentric*, which means self-centered, and **ethnocentric**, or from the point of view of one race or culture (ethos-centered). Eurocentric means European-centered. From a Eurocentric point of view, the New World was new; no European had been there before. The Eurocentric version of history is what we all have been taught in school.

There have been movements to teach American history from other points of view. Think about it: American history from the perspective of African Americans would be very different from the European version. For black Americans, American history does not begin "in fourteen-hundred-ninety-two, when Columbus sailed the ocean blue." Rather, it begins when the first slave ships landed on the African shores and captured people to bring back to America. From their perspective, American history would be told in a very different way from what we usually read in history books.

Native Americans also have a different view of American history. For one thing, they were already here when the Europeans arrived. Imagine how it must have been for them, to have Europeans take their land and destroy their way of life. American history from the Native American perspective would be very different, indeed.

This doesn't mean that Eurocentric American history is incorrect. It is merely slanted in a different direction, with emphasis on different events and ideas. There are different sides to every story, and American history is no exception.

Key Words

ethnocentric—from the point of view of one race or culture
eurocentric—from a European point of view

The New World

Prereading Prompt

You already know that Christopher Columbus discovered America. You probably also know that other explorers came to the New World after him. Do you know what they were looking for? Do you know what changes in Europe inspired them to explore foreign lands?

Key Words

Crusades—"holy" wars against the Moslems to regain the Holy Land
Renaissance—meaning rebirth, the period from the 14th to the 16th centuries characterized by the revival of art, literature, and learning
New World—the Western Hemisphere, consisting of North America, Central America, and South America

In Europe of the 12th through 15th centuries, the stage was being set for the discovery of the New World. First, in the 1100s, came the **Crusades**, or the European Christian armies sent to Jerusalem (modern Israel) to take back the Holy Land from the Moslems. Men returned from the Crusades with exotic perfumes, spices, and other luxury items that were foreign to Europeans. This awakened an interest in establishing trade with foreign lands. Second, starting around 1300, a new interest in the great philosophy, science, and art of ancient Greece produced a rebirth of learning called the **Renaissance**. The Renaissance inspired new ideas and new curiosity about the world. Inventions such as the compass facilitated exploration. Third, European nations were ruled by powerful kings and queens who sought wealth and power. They financed attempts to find riches and establish colonies in foreign lands.

Europeans of the 15th century knew what lay to the east; the vast Asian continent was a huge obstacle to trade with the Far East. So explorers from all over Europe set out to find what lay to the west. As far as they knew, there was only ocean, and then Asia. One by one, beginning with Columbus, they found land—but not the Far East. The Age of Discovery led to the discovery of the Americas—the **New World**.

If the 1500s was the age of discovery, the 1600s was the age of settlement in the New World. In search of gold, Spain established settlements in Mexico, South America, the Caribbean, and Florida. France had colonies in Canada, where abundant wildlife supported a lively fur trading business. In 1607, England established its first permanent colony at Jamestown, Virginia, to grow tobacco. Other colonies were settled by the Pilgrims, Puritans, Catholics, and Quakers, who sought religious freedom in the New World.

Fig. 2–1 Virginia Indians, as seen by Raleigh's expedition, 1585. (Credit: Theodore deBry, engraving after the watercolor by John White, 1590, New York Public Library).

Finding the Main Idea of a Paragraph

Paragraphs are made up of sentences containing details about a particular topic. The topic is what the paragraph is about. While all of the sentences in a paragraph should relate to the topic, one sentence usually contains the most important statement made about the topic. This sentence contains the *main idea* of the paragraph. All of the other sentences should contain details that support the main idea.

Look at the first paragraph in the preceding lesson on the New World. What is the topic? Generally, the paragraph is about Europe in the 12th through 15th centuries. Now look for the main idea. The main idea is the most important thing the writer says about the topic. The sentence that states the main idea is called **the topic sentence**. Is there one sentence that is most important, giving the main idea of this paragraph? The first sentence does: "In Europe of the 12th through 15th centuries, the stage was being set for the discovery of the New World." All the other sentences contain details that support this main idea. They tell what events led up to and made possible the discovery of the New World. In this paragraph, as is often the case, the main idea is contained in the first sentence.

Sometimes the main idea is stated at the end of a paragraph. Look at the second paragraph in the preceding section. In this case, the first sentence is *not* the most important, and is not a summary of the information in the paragraph. It is a detail. But the last sentence is a summary. It is the main idea of the paragraph. The paragraph is about how explorers came to discover the New World: "The Age of Discovery led to the discovery of the Americas—the New World." The other sentences give the details of what led to that discovery.

Remember, when looking for the main idea of a paragraph, first find the topic, then look for the most important statement made about the topic—the topic sentence. When you've found this sentence, test it against the other sentences of the paragraph. They must support the sentence you've identified as the main idea. Remember, too, that on the GED the main idea in a question may be in different words from what was in the paragraph. The exercises that follow may contain restated main ideas, as on the GED.

Practice

The Practice item is based on the following paragraph.

The story of Columbus' life is one of disappointed hopes and unrealized greatness. He didn't sail his historic voyage to prove the world was round; in the 15th century most people already knew that. His mission was to find a route to the Far East by going west. To get financial backing for his trip, he had to promise huge returns on investors' capital. Columbus made four voyages across the Atlantic to find the Orient, the last one specifically against royal orders. He returned in disgrace and soon died. Tragically, he never understood his great achievement: that he had discovered the New World.

1. The tragedy of Columbus' life was that he failed to
   (1) prove the world was round and become famous
   (2) find a route to the Far East and become rich
   (3) pay back his investors and avoid disgrace
   (4) realize his discovery was great and overcome his disappointments
   (5) realize his hopes were false and sail directly east

To find the main idea, you first need to find the topic. What is it? Columbus' voyages across the Atlantic. What is the most important thing the paragraph says about the topic? The first sentence says that his life was a story of "disappointed hopes and unrealized greatness." The last sentence says "Tragically, he never understood his great achievement: that he had discovered the New World." This achievement was greater than his hopes of finding a route to the Far East or getting rich. Columbus' tragedy is that he did not realize this. So (4) is the correct answer, and (2) and (3) are incorrect. Choice (1) is wrong because the second sentence says he did not sail to prove the world was round. Choice (5) is wrong because it is not stated anywhere that he should have sailed east.

Lesson 1 Exercises

Items 1 through 3 are based on the following paragraph.

After Columbus landed in the New World in 1492, other explorers learned more about it and the world beyond it. Henry Cabot, sailing under the English flag, explored much of the North American coast in 1497–1498. At the same time, an Italian named Amerigo Vespucci was exploring the South American coast. It was becoming clear that there was in fact a new world, made up of at least one continent that was separate from Asia. By 1522, Ferdinand Magellan and Juan Sebastian del Cano became the first Europeans to sail the Pacific. Magellan died before finishing the trip, but the expedition sailed across the Atlantic, around the southern tip of South America, across the Pacific, and finally back to Europe. The world was indeed round, and there was more than one way to get to the Far East.

1. The main significance of the Magellan/del Cano voyage was that they
   (1) sailed around the tip of South America
   (2) circumnavigated (sailed around) the entire globe
   (3) achieved for Spain what Columbus had failed to do
   (4) were the first Europeans to sail the Pacific
   (5) kept Italy from colonizing the New World

2. All the explorers who sailed after Columbus
   (1) explored South America rather than North America
   (2) gained knowledge about the New World and the globe
   (3) found out the New World was only one continent
   (4) sailed the Pacific as well as the Atlantic Oceans
   (5) found out there was only one way to the Far East

3. We celebrate Columbus Day rather than Vespucci Day, or Magellan Day, or Cabot Day because
   (1) Columbus was the first European to land in the New World
   (2) Columbus made four voyages to the New World
   (3) Magellan died before finishing the voyage
   (4) Cabot didn't realize he had reached the New World
   (5) Vespucci explored with a partner, del Cano

Answers are on page 369.

From English Colonies to an American Nation

Prereading Prompt

You know that the United States were originally English colonies and that they became a nation by revolting against England. Do you know why the colonies rebelled? Do you know why England changed its policy toward the colonies and drove them to rebellion? You will learn these things in this lesson.

Key Words

Revolutionary War—the American Revolution; war in which the colonists won independence from English rule
Declaration of Independence—the official announcement in 1776 in which American colonists declared themselves free from the rule of Great Britain

The United States changed from thirteen English colonies into an independent nation by going through two wars and breaking with their mother country. By the 1700s, more than a million people lived in the 13 British colonies in North America. These colonies fell into three groups: The *New England Colonies* of Massachusetts, New Hampshire, Rhode Island, and Connecticut; the *Middle Colonies* of New York, New Jersey, Pennsylvania, and Delaware; and the *Southern Colonies* of Maryland, Virginia, North Carolina, South Carolina, and Georgia.

The colonists were in a strange position: they were expected to be loyal to England, but they weren't given all the rights of English citizens. When it was convenient for the monarchy, England intervened in the colonists' affairs. Otherwise they left them to fight among and govern themselves. This policy changed, however, after the French and Indian War.

This war, begun in 1753, was a race between France and England for control of the Ohio Valley. At the end of the war in 1763, the signing of the Treaty of Paris left France with just two tiny fishing villages in Canada. England, now with colonies all over the globe, was stretching its financial limits to defend these territories. The monarchy looked to the colonies, with their prosperous trading, to help pay off its huge war debt.

King George III enacted the Stamp Act in 1765, imposing heavy taxes on legal documents and newspapers. The colonists rose up in opposition, and the tax was repealed. In 1767, King George tried taxing the colonists again, levying taxes on tea, glass, paint, and paper. The colonists responded by dumping tea from British cargo ships into Boston Harbor, a rebellion that came to be known as the Boston Tea Party. It was becoming clear that the colonists were not going to accept this form of government, which taxed them but in which they had no say.

Boston Massacre 1770
(Credit: Library of Congress)

England responded to the uprisings by sending troops, and the colonists organized against them. With the outbreak of fighting in Massachusetts in 1775, the **Revolutionary War** began. In 1776, the colonists issued their **Declaration of Independence**, in which they objected to "taxation without representation" and declared themselves free from British rule. It would be seven long years before the colonists would achieve their goal.

Finding the Main Idea of a Passage

You already know how to find the main idea of a paragraph: identify the topic, then look for the sentence stating the most important thing the writer says about the topic. This important idea is general enough to include all the other ideas in the paragraph. The sentence that states this main idea is the topic sentence of the paragraph.

As with finding the main idea of a paragraph, begin by figuring out what the topic of the passage is. What is the topic of the passage in Lesson 2? It is *the change of the United States from English colonies into a nation*. The next step is to look for the sentence that states the most important idea about the topic, or the topic sentence of the passage. The first sentence contains the main idea of the passage: "The United States changed from 13 English colonies into an independent nation by going through two wars and breaking with their mother country." This sentence states the most important and general thing that is said about the topic.

The last step is to test this topic sentence, to make sure the main idea of each paragraph supports it. To do this, you look at the topic sentence of each paragraph.

Go back and read the first paragraph of the passage. Which sentence contains the main idea? The first sentence does: "By the 1700s, more than a million people lived in the 13 British colonies in North America." This is the most important sentence in the paragraph. The remaining sentences support it.

Now find the main idea of the second paragraph. Again it is the first sentence: "The colonists were in a strange position: they were expected to be loyal to England, but they weren't given all the rights of English citizens." What is the main idea of the third paragraph? "The monarchy looked to the colonies, with their prosperous trading, to help pay off its huge war debt." The fourth paragraph? "It was becoming clear that the colonists were not going to accept this form of government, which taxed them but in which they had no say." And the last paragraph? "With the outbreak of fighting in Massachusetts in 1775, the **Revolutionary War** began."

Do all these topic sentences support the main idea? Yes. The main idea statement covers all the ideas in these sentences.

What if you don't find the main idea of the passage right away? Then do the last step first, and look for the main idea of each paragraph. This will give you a more complete picture of what the writer is saying about the topic. Then look for a sentence that covers all these main ideas. That will be the main idea of the passage.

Practice

The Practice item is based on the following passage.

Benjamin Franklin was an important and popular figure in colonial America because he contributed so much to its intellectual and public life. He began his long career as a printer. He was born in 1706 in Boston, but spent many years in London learning printing. Later he set up his own shop in Philadelphia. From this shop came words of wisdom to the colonists, many of them printed in *Poor Richard's Almanack*.

Franklin held many official posts in his life, among them postmaster of Philadelphia and printer of the province of Pennsylvania. He helped make Philadelphia the home of the first lending library, the first public hospital, and the first fire insurance company. He also founded the academy that later became the University of Pennsylvania.

Franklin was well known as a researcher and inventor. His most daring research demonstrated that lightning was a form of electricity, which led to the invention of the lightning rod. Other inventions that are still used in some form today include the Franklin stove and bifocals.

In his later years, Franklin spent many years abroad and served as ambassador to France. He even took a small part in writing the U.S. Constitution. He died in 1790. His funeral was attended by over 20,000 people, the largest gathering ever assembled in Philadelphia up to that time.

Franklin was a major figure in early America mainly because he
(1) was responsible for many inventions still in use today
(2) made many different contributions to life in the colonies
(3) was a colonist at heart even though he spent many years abroad
(4) made Philadelphia an important center in the colonies
(5) was an ambassador and worked on the Constitution

Follow the three-step process to find the main idea of the passage. First, identify the topic (Benjamin Franklin). Next, look for the most important thing said about the topic. The first sentence in the passage states its main idea: "Benjamin Franklin was an important and popular figure in colonial America because he contributed so much to its intellectual and public life." This is the most important, general idea in the passage. Choice (2) is a restatement of this idea, so it is the correct answer. Choices (1), (4), and (5) are details that are all covered by this main idea. Choice (3) is not stated anywhere in the passage.

Remember: if you do not find the main idea of a passage right after a first reading, look for ideas of all the paragraphs. Then look for a statement that summarizes them. Check your main idea to see if it is supported by the topic sentences of all the paragraphs.

Lesson 2 Exercises

1. The colonists wanted their independence from Great Britain in order to
   (1) avoid taxes on items such as tea and paper
   (2) avoid paying off England's war debt
   (3) elect a ruler other than King George III
   (4) get all the rights of English citizens
   (5) be able to govern themselves

Items 2 and 3 are based on the following passage.

The Declaration of Independence, now a sacred American document, was a hotly contested issue in its time, and it took years to get it officially signed. On June 7, 1776, Richard Henry Lee of Virginia first proposed to the Continental Congress that the colonies declare their independence from England. The issue was finally put to a vote on July 1st. South Carolina and Pennsylvania were against independence. Delaware was divided over the issue, and New York's delegation awaited further instructions from their state. After much debate and persuasion, on July 2nd the Congress voted unanimously to declare independence.

On July 4th, the text that proclaimed independence was adopted by the congress. Official signing of the document, however, did not begin until August 2nd. For almost a year, the document traveled in different delegates' baggage, picking up signatures. After stops in Maryland, Pennsylvania, New Jersey, and New York, it finally found its way back to Washington in 1800. Despite these delays, the Declaration became an object of extreme national pride and a model for other new nations.

2. In the debate over the Declaration of Independence, the most important fact was that it was
   (1) put to a vote in less than a month
   (2) opposed by southern as well as northern states
   (3) intensely debated
   (4) first proposed by a leading southerner
   (5) approved unanimously

3. The main point of the passage is that the Declaration
   (1) is an object of great national pride
   (2) was the result of long and intense discussion
   (3) serves as a model for nations seeking freedom and democracy
   (4) was adopted by both northern and southern colonies
   (5) was almost rejected by the Continental Congress

Answers are on page 370.

Forming an American Government

Prereading Prompt

Independence Day doesn't mark the anniversary of America's independence from Great Britain; it marks the anniversary of the day the Second Continental Congress adopted the Declaration of Independence, July 4, 1776. The U.S. government has lasted for over two centuries. Why has the system worked so well? Find out in the next lesson.

Key Words

Articles of Confederation—the first framework for a national government in the United States
Federalists—people who believed in a strong central government
Anti-Federalists—people who believed the states should have the main power in government

The Declaration of Independence was written primarily by Thomas Jefferson. Our system of government is founded on the ideas in this document: that all people are created equal; that all people have certain rights that cannot be taken away; that government should be designed by and for the people being governed; that the people have the right to change or dissolve any government that is contrary to these ideas.

The Declaration of Independence was sent to the British monarchy, which refused to give the colonies their independence. A seven-year war—the American Revolution—followed, ending with the signing of the Treaty of Paris in 1783. With this, the independence of the 13 American states was officially recognized.

Independence, however, brought its own problems. How would the states be governed? Who would decide? What laws would be in effect in the meantime?

Even before the Revolution was over, the colonists had recognized the need for government. In 1781, they had adopted the Articles of Confederation, which provided for a "league of friendship" among the independent states. A strong central government was not formed because there were so many separate interests among the different states. Most powers remained with the states. This caused problems when the states needed to act as a group or with each other. For instance, the central government could declare war, but the states weren't required to supply men to form an army. Also, it was difficult to do business across state lines because each state had its own currency.

For the new nation to survive, a stronger central government would have to be formed. This government would have to be strong enough to hold the states together but also recognize the rights of the states to rule themselves. In 1787, a Constitutional Convention was held in Philadelphia to meet this challenge.

Major arguments developed between the **Federalists** and the **Anti-Federalists**. The new government would have to be a federal government; that is, a union of states who would give up some, but not all, powers to the central government. The Federalists wanted a strong central government that could control the individual states. The Anti-Federalists feared that, if there were a strong central government, the people and states would have to give up too many rights and freedoms.

Enormous political differences also developed between states with large populations and those with smaller populations. There didn't seem to be a fair way to give equal representation, to keep the large states from asserting their power over the smaller ones. A solution to these problems had to be found.

Months of debates and arguments followed. Proposals were made and rejected, but in democratic fashion compromises were reached. The chart on page 52 shows how the major disputes were settled. The result was a written plan for a system of basic laws that would govern the nation; this is called the United States Constitution. By August 1788, each state had ratified the Constitution, which became the law of the land.

Finding a Detail in a Graphic

Charts are most useful when they separate a lot of information into categories. Look at the chart in the lesson. Although the information is given in words, separating it down into boxes and categories makes it easier to find and understand. There are three headings: "Issue," "Problems," and "Solution." These headings make it easy to find the specific details about the compromises made at the Constitutional Convention. For example, look at the chart and find out how the issue of representing all the people and all the states was resolved. First, look in the column labeled "Issue." You will see that this is issue #1. How was this issue resolved? Look in the column labeled "Solution." It tells you about the Connecticut Compromise and how it solved the problem.

The Constitution: Problems and Solutions		
Issue	Problems	Solution
1. To represent fairly all people and all states in national government	• Large states wanted representation based on population (the Virginia Plan) • Small states wanted each state to have equal representation regardless of size (the New Jersey Plan)	*The Connecticut Compromise.* The legislature will have two houses: (a) the House of Representatives, in which representation is based on population; (b) the Senate, in which each state has equal representation
2. How to count slaves in the population for purposes of representation	• States in the South wanted slaves included in the population count for purposes of representation but not taxation • Northern states, where there were few slaves, didn't want slaves included for representation	*The Three-fifths Compromise.* Five slaves would be counted as three whites for both representation and taxation
3. How to elect the national executive (president)	• One plan called for direct election by all the people • Another claimed the people weren't educated enough to elect the national executive directly	*Electoral Compromise.* The people would choose electors, who in turn would do the actual voting, representing groups of people rather than individuals

Fig. 2–2

The beauty of a well-designed chart is that you can jump in at any point and find the details you need. For example, suppose you needed to know what the Three-fifths Compromise was. If you knew nothing about it, you wouldn't get many hints from its name (three-fifths of what?). But if you use the chart, you will see the Three-fifths Compromise listed under the category "Solution." Then work backwards to find out what the issue was and what problems were involved.

Practice

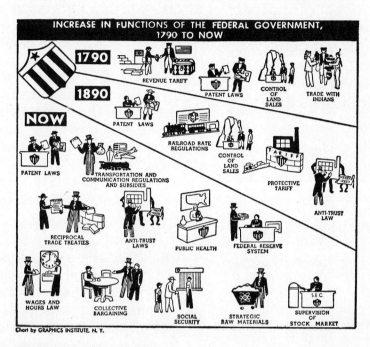

INCREASE IN FUNCTIONS OF THE FEDERAL GOVERNMENT, 1790 TO NOW

Fig. 2–3

Look at the following diagram and then answer the question.

According to the diagram, which of the following functions was the federal government *not* responsible for in 1790?

(1) control of land sales
(2) revenue tariff
(3) antitrust law
(4) trade with Native Americans
(5) patent laws

The chart is divided into three sections that show what the government was responsible for in 1790, 1890, and now. To find out what the government was *not* responsible for in 1790, you would look first at the section for 1790. Your next step would be to compare each choice to the ones in that section. Choice (1), control of land sales, is in the 1790 section and so is not correct. It is also in the 1890 section, but this is not relevant to the question. Choice (2), revenue tariff, is also in the 1790 section, so it is incorrect. Choices (4) and (5) are both in the 1790 section and are therefore incorrect.

Choice (3), antitrust law, is in the 1890 section as well as the "Now" section. But it is *not* in the 1790 section. Antitrust laws didn't exist in 1790 and were therefore not a responsibility of the federal government. So (3) is the correct answer.

Lesson 3 Exercises

1. The election of a national executive (president) was first established by
   (1) the Declaration of Independence
   (2) the Treaty of Paris (1793)
   (3) the Articles of Confederation
   (4) the Constitution
   (5) the Federalists

   Items 2 and 3 are based on the chart in Lesson 3.

2. The Connecticut Compromise was fair to
   (1) large states
   (2) small states
   (3) the state of Connecticut and other Northern states
   (4) slave states
   (5) all states

3. The Northern states didn't want slaves counted as part of the population because this would give the South an unfair edge in representation; there were many more slaves in the South than in the North. By accepting the Three-fifths Compromise, which counted more than half of the slaves for representation, what did the North get in return?
   (1) More than half the slaves were also counted for taxation.
   (2) Slaves were not permitted to vote.
   (3) The large states were given the same number of representatives in the Senate as the small states.
   (4) Less than half the slaves were counted for representation.
   (5) More slaves were permitted to go north to even out the population.

Answers are on page 370.

Lesson 4

The Growth of the United States

Prereading Prompt

You may have heard someone speak about his or her "manifest destiny" when discussing plans for the future. Do you know the original meaning of this phrase? As our young nation grew, it tried to keep out of foreign alliances and wars and to keep foreign powers out of the Western Hemisphere. Why do you suppose that was true?

Key Words

Monroe Doctrine—a U.S. policy forbidding foreign nations from having colonies or influence in the Western Hemisphere
Manifest Destiny—the belief that the U.S. was destined to expand west to the Pacific Ocean
Louisiana Purchase—The huge central region of North America bought by the U.S. from France in 1803

When George Washington became the first president in 1789, there was a strong feeling of *nationalism* among the newly united states. People were proud to be American, and the country kept to itself, preferring to concentrate on its own problems and stay out of European affairs. When Thomas Jefferson became president in 1801, he maintained this policy of neutrality. Americans went about the business of making a new nation.

Property and who owned it became major issues. The land to the west of the 13 states remained unsettled. People without land or running from the law or without money fled to the western frontier.

The West prospered as more settlers arrived, but growth caused problems, too. Most notable was the fact that the region's main waterway, the Mississippi River, was controlled by a foreign power. The Louisiana Territory, making up the central region of the continent, had been owned by France and then by Spain. In 1800, the land was given back to France. In 1803, President Jefferson bought the territory for $15 million.

With the **Louisiana Purchase**, the size of America doubled. An official government expedition, headed by Lewis and Clark, was sent to explore the new territory. The idea of **Manifest Destiny**—that America was meant to expand west to the Pacific—became very popular.

But as the United States expanded, new problems arose. The slave-holding South and non-slave-holding North struggled to gain control of the new territories. Their differences in economy and way of life became key political issues. Furthermore, people in the East viewed the western frontiersmen as uncivilized outlaws. Strong divisions threatened the new Union.

In 1812, some parts of the country wanted to end the policy of neutrality by involving the United States in the ongoing war between England and France. Jefferson resisted, but when England began seizing U.S. ships on the high seas, the United States entered the *War of 1812* against Great Britain.

After the war, there was a new surge of nationalism. Americans refocused their energy on domestic affairs, particularly western settlement. In 1823, the **Monroe Doctrine** was issued, reinforcing American neutrality and nationalism. It stated that the United States would not interfere in European affairs. More important, however, it declared that the United States would not allow foreign nations to establish any influence or colonies in the Western Hemisphere, from Canada to the bottom of South America.

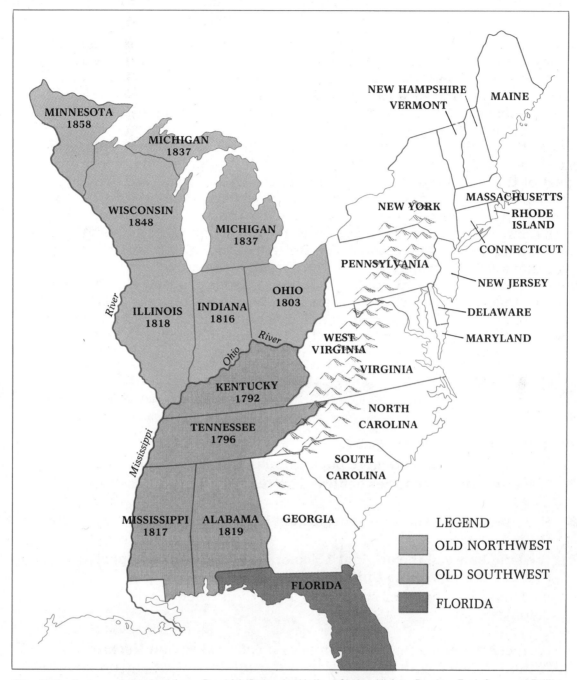

Fig. 2–4 Source: Adapted from Paul M. Roberts, *United States History Review Text*, Second Edition (New York: AMSCO School Publications, 1989), p. 139. Used with permission.

Finding the Main Idea in a Graphic

You already know how to find the main idea of a paragraph or passage. You look for a topic sentence that tells you the most important thing about the topic. With graphic material, since there are no sentences, you have to look for the most important idea the graphic shows you. Look at the details and see what main idea they support. Don't get hung up on the details—see how they fit together to give you the "big picture."

Look at the map on page 57. What details does it show? On the right, the part that is not shaded, are the original 15 states, plus Florida, which was not part of the United States at the time. To the left, or west, are two areas: the gray area is the old southwestern territory; the blue area is the old northwestern territory. These are bordered by the Mississippi River. The dates given for each state are the years that each attained statehood. Keeping in mind the title of the lesson ("The Growth of the United States"), what can you say about this map? What is the overall idea here?

The first thing that might strike you about this map is that the blue and gray areas together are roughly the same size as the white area. This means that the acquisition of this land doubled the size of the original United States. Keep this in mind when you do the Practice question.

Practice

According to the map on page 57,

(1) the old Northwest had more population than the old Southwest

(2) twice as many territories achieved statehood after 1803 as before 1796

(3) the land to the west of the Mississippi River was twice the size of the United States

(4) the land between the original 13 colonies and the Mississippi River doubled the size of the United States

(5) by 1858 the number of states was more than twice the original 13 colonies

The correct answer is (4). The map makes it easy to see that the size of the United States doubled with the addition of the old Northwest and old Southwest. This is the main idea of the map. Choice (1) is incorrect because the map shows nothing about population. Choices (2) and (5) can be proved incorrect by the map, and are details anyway. Choice (3) cannot be proved correct or incorrect by this map because the map doesn't show all the land west of the Mississippi.

1. The Monroe Doctrine and the idea of Manifest Destiny showed that Americans in the early 19th century were most interested in
   (1) gaining new territories
   (2) neutrality
   (3) statehood for new territories
   (4) states' rights
   (5) a strong union

Item 2 is based on the following cartoon.

2. The cartoon represents
   (1) the Louisiana Purchase
   (2) the War of 1812
   (3) Manifest Destiny
   (4) America's push to the West
   (5) the Monroe Doctrine

Uncle Sam Says, "Keep Out."

(Source: Graphics Institute, N.Y.C.)

Item 3 is based on Figure 2-4.

3. The map shows that
    (1) all the states of the old North-
        west were larger than the first
        15 states
    (2) all the states of the old South-
        west were larger than the first
        15 states
    (3) the states of the old Southwest
        and Florida had a warmer cli-
        mate than the states of the old
        Northwest
    (4) the Mississippi touches more
        states of the old Southwest
        than of the old Northwest
    (5) the first 15 states were more
        mountainous than the states of
        the new territories

Answers are on page 370.

Sectionalism, Slavery, and Secession

Prereading Prompt

Think about how different the various regions of the United States are today. When you listen to someone from Texas and then to someone from Boston, it's hard to believe they're from the same country.

In the 1850s, regional differences of all kinds threatened to tear the U.S. apart. As you read, keep in mind your knowledge of today's conflicts.

Key Words

sectionalism—identification with one's region rather than one's country
Industrial Revolution—a period of growth in factory production and mechanization that began in England in the mid-18th century and spread to America in the 19th century

By the middle of the 19th century, the United States was in danger of breaking up. Americans were proud to be Americans, but increasingly they identified more with the section of the country where they lived than with the country as a whole. This attitude, known as **sectionalism**, showed itself in a dislike for people of other regions.

To a large extent, sectionalism was based on economic differences. In the North, where farming was difficult because of the hilly, rocky soil, the economy was based on industry. The North got cotton for textile manufacturing from the South and agricultural products from the West. The **Industrial Revolution** contributed to the growth of the North as a manufacturing region. The North was also the banking center of the nation.

In the South, the way of life was based on plantation farming. The availability of slave labor, the warm climate, and the rich soil made agriculture most profitable. Tobacco, rice, and sugar were raised, but cotton was king. With the invention of the cotton gin by Eli Whitney in 1793, the cotton industry soared. Because the South was almost entirely agricultural, it had to rely on the North for manufactured goods and loans.

The economy of the West was based on the small family farm. Western settlers raised enormous amounts of wheat, rye, corn, and meat. Because the West was primarily agricultural, it was dependent on the North in the same way the South was. Like the South, the West resented its economic dependence on the North. Both regions particularly resented the North's efforts to place taxes, called *tariffs*, on foreign manufactured goods they might want to buy instead of Northern products.

In addition to economic differences, slavery was a major issue that contributed to sectionalism. Slavery was not profitable on the small farms of the North and West, and many people in these regions were also morally opposed to it. A small but influential group of Northerners, the *abolitionists*, wanted to abolish, or eliminate, slavery. In the South, however, the economy depended on slave labor. Southerners argued that the slaves were better off on plantations than they had been in Africa; that freeing them would endanger the lives of white Southerners; and that the South treated its slaves better than the North treated its factory workers.

Before 1854, there were two major political parties, the Whigs and the Democrats. In 1854, the Republican Party was founded on an antislavery platform. In 1860, a Republican named Abraham Lincoln became the nation's 16th president. The South was outraged. South Carolina immediately seceded from the Union. Six other Southern states withdrew soon after. The leaders of the secession met in February 1861 and formed the *Confederate States of America*, with Jefferson Davis as their president.

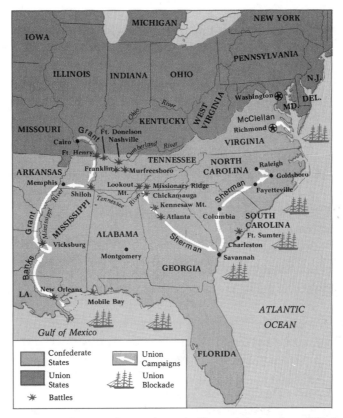

Fig. 2–5 Source: Reproduced with permission from "Civil War, American" in *Children's Brittannica*, © 1989 by Encyclopaedia Brittannica, Inc.

Making Inferences

Imagine that you are watching TV. The space shuttle is lifting off from Cape Canaveral. The camera pans the audience on the ground, their eyes trained on the rising rocket. Suddenly, there are screams. Some people are crying. Others clasp their hands to their mouths.

What has happened? Something good? Not likely. How do you know? You know because you have the ability to put clues together to figure out what is not directly told. You can *infer* that something bad has happened. When people cry, when people scream, we know from experience that something terrible has happened. In this case, the space shuttle *Challenger* exploded shortly after lift-off in January 1986.

How do you infer meaning from written social studies material? Again, you have to find information that is not directly stated in the passage. You have to use what *is* stated as clues to help you figure out—infer—the unstated information.

For example, you read in the preceding lesson that the Republican Party was founded in 1854 on an antislavery platform. You can infer from this that there was antislavery sentiment in the country at the time. The Republicans must have believed that they had enough support to make it worth forming a political party. You can infer this unstated information from other information in the passage and from your own logical reasoning. Use these skills to answer the Practice item.

Practice

According to the lesson, the West was dependent on the North for which of the following?

(1) manufactured goods and textiles
(2) cotton and bank loans
(3) textiles and agricultural products
(4) bank loans and manufactured goods
(5) manufactured goods and agricultural products

Choice (4) is the correct answer. To find the answer, you would first review what you *do* know. The text states that the South depended on the North for manufactured goods and loans. It also says that the West was dependent on the North in the same way that the South was. You can infer that it depended on the North for loans and manufactured goods. Choice (5) is wrong because it puts one true clue together with one false clue to make a false inference: it is true that the West depended on the North for manufactured goods, but not for agricultural products (which the West produced); for the same reason, (3) is incorrect. In (2), it is true the West depended on the North for bank loans, but not for cotton, which the South produced. Choice (1) is incorrect because it fails to mention loans, and both the South and West depended on the North for loans as well as manufactured goods.

1. It is probably true of the Whig and Democratic parties that before 1854 they
   (1) were not strongly antislavery
   (2) were strongly antislavery
   (3) didn't think slavery was an important issue
   (4) underestimated Lincoln's popularity
   (5) were allied with the South

Items 2 and 3 are based on the following passage.

Because the economy of the North was primarily industrial, most Northerners were Federalists. They favored a strong central government that would impose taxes on foreign goods that competed with U.S. manufactured goods. They also wanted a strong federal government that could settle the issue of slavery.

Most Southerners, on the other hand, tended to be Anti-Federalists. They believed in states' rights and resented the interference of the federal government, particularly over the issue of slavery.

2. Southerners were afraid of a strong central government because they
   (1) were Anti-Federalists
   (2) were against anything the North favored
   (3) feared the government might outlaw slavery
   (4) didn't want taxes imposed on foreign goods
   (5) thought it would impose taxes on their agricultural products

3. According to the passage, the tariff policy of the North seemed designed to
   (1) keep the price of Southern products high
   (2) tax the South for owning slaves
   (3) keep the price of foreign goods high
   (4) interfere with agricultural activity
   (5) keep the North more industrial than the South

Answers are on page 370–371.

Lesson 6

The Civil War

Prereading Prompt

The Union had existed for little more than half a century when the Civil War broke out. Would the great experiment in democratic government end so soon? You know that the Union survived, but do you know why the North won the war? How were the states reunited? Find out in this lesson.

Key Words

Confederacy—the 11 Southern states that seceded from the United States
Union—the remaining 23 Northern and border states that didn't secede
Emancipation Proclamation—the order issued by Lincoln that freed slaves in the Confederacy only

The issues that split the nation in the 1860s wouldn't go away. Slavery, states' rights, secession—people were so divided over these issues that many families fought the war on both sides. A phrase often associated with the Civil War is "brother against brother." The war divided the country, and the battle wounds were deep. But the issues couldn't be ignored.

Ultimately, 11 Southern states seceded to join the **Confederacy**. This left 19 free states and four slave-holding states in the **Union**. Between 1861 and 1865 the nation was torn by bloody battles, fought mostly in the South.

The Union had some advantages over the South: more factories to produce weapons; twice as many railroads; more than twice the population; a steady supply of food from the West; and 75 percent of the nation's financial resources. The Confederacy also had advantages, however. Many outstanding military leaders, such as General Robert E. Lee, were loyal to the South.

Also, Southern soldiers were thought to be slightly superior to their Northern counterparts because they were used to an outdoor life. Another advantage was that most battles took place on familiar turf in the South. Finally, the South believed it could count on the support of England and France, both heavy importers of cotton.

Richmond, VA ruins
(Credit: Library of Congress)

Even with a brilliant military leader in General Lee, the South simply couldn't overcome the North's advantages. The South was dealt another blow when President Lincoln issued the **Emancipation Proclamation**, which ordered that all slaves be freed from the Confederacy on January 1, 1863. It did not, however, free slaves from the border states that were allied with the Union or in Southern states already conquered. The Confederacy lost 180,000 slaves—many of whom were added to the ranks of the Union army.

On April 9, 1865, General Robert E. Lee surrendered to General Ulysses S. Grant at Appomattox, Virginia. The war was over. The North had won and the Union had been preserved—the hard way. The Southern economy was devastated. The nation started on the long road to recovery.

Inferring the Main Idea of a Paragraph

You already know how to locate the main idea of a paragraph. Often it is given in the first or the last sentence—the topic sentence. But sometimes you have to figure out, or infer, the main idea. You have to come up with a summary statement about the paragraph on your own. In Lesson 5, you learned how to infer information that is not stated directly. In this lesson, you will learn how to infer an unstated main idea.

Look back at the first paragraph of the preceding passage. You can see what the topic is: the issues of the war and the fact that these issues divided the country in a painful way. So what is the main idea—the most important thing said about the topic? Abe Lincoln said it eloquently in this quote borrowed from the Bible: "A house divided against itself cannot stand." Put simply, the topic sentence for this paragraph might read: *The Civil War was fought to keep the United States from being split in two.*

Use the details of a paragraph to check that your statement is really the main idea. Look at each detail in the paragraph. Does it support your main idea? If so, you have probably come up with a good statement. Try this with the first paragraph from this lesson. The summary statement, or main idea, was *The Civil War was fought to keep the United States from being split in two.* Now look at each detail: (1) the issues wouldn't go away and couldn't be ignored; (2) people were so divided over the issues that even family members fought each other; (3) the war divided the country. Each of these details supports the inferred main idea. Always test the sentence you have chosen as the main idea by making sure the details support it.

Practice

Which statement is true according to paragraph 3 of the lesson?
- **(1)** The North had more advantages than the South and so would win the war.
- **(2)** The South had more advantages than the North and so would win the war.
- **(3)** Neither side had more advantages than the other.
- **(4)** Both sides had advantages, and either side could win.
- **(5)** The advantages of both sides canceled each other out.

The correct choice is (4). The paragraph lists important advantages of both sides. The only thing you can safely infer is that either side could win. Choice (1) is incorrect. It is true the paragraph lists five advantages for the North and four for the South, but it does not suggest that the North would therefore win the war. Choices (2) and (3) are both incorrect because they are details and contradict statements in the paragraph. Choice (5) is incorrect because you know that the North's advantages helped it win the war.

1. Based on the content of the Emancipation Proclamation, Lincoln's probable reason for freeing the slaves was that he thought
   (1) all slavery was evil
   (2) slaves would be happier in the North
   (3) slaves in the border states were treated better than slaves in the deep South
   (4) slaves should be allowed to fight for their freedom
   (5) freeing the slaves would help the North win the war

Items 2 and 3 are based on the following passage.

The Confederate States of America developed a governmental structure that was almost identical to that of the old Union. There was a president, a two-house congress, and a judicial branch. Laws were passed and enacted by the same process as provided in the U.S. Constitution. The primary difference was that fewer powers were given to the central government. This was a major issue among the Southern states—a large part of their disagreement with Lincoln and their reason for seceding. Southerners thought their constitution was closer to the original principles of the constitution written in Philadelphia in 1787. When the Confederacy decided that it needed its own flag, some members proposed a slightly modified version of the Union flag, the Stars and Stripes.

2. The main difference between the way the Confederate and Union governments were structured suggests that
   (1) The South disagreed with Lincoln on how to structure the government
   (2) a key issue for the South was giving the states more power to govern themselves
   (3) the South wanted to keep African Americans out of government office
   (4) slavery was not the root of disagreements between the North and South
   (5) many Southerners were Federalists

3. By the form of its government, and by its choice of a flag, the Confederacy showed that it
   (1) saw itself as the legitimate government of the United States
   (2) could not break its ties with the Union
   (3) could not develop an original plan for government and had to borrow ideas from the Union
   (4) never intended to remain separate from the Union but merely to make a statement
   (5) had a basic respect for the Union and its government

Answers are on page 371.

Reconstruction

Prereading Prompt

The end of the Civil War didn't bring an end to the nation's problems. How could the states that had seceded and been defeated rejoin the Union? What would become of the four million freed slaves? Who would be responsible for the solutions to these problems—the states or the federal government? These and many other questions remained unanswered.

Key Words

Reconstruction—the program to integrate the South back into the Union and give rights to freed slaves (1865–1876)
Jim Crow laws—laws passed in the South that legalized segregation
carpetbaggers—Northern whites who exploited business and politics in the South during Reconstruction

The period immediately following the Civil War—1865 through the 1870s—is known as Reconstruction. When John Wilkes Booth killed Lincoln just one week after the war's end, he also killed many people's hopes of an easy national recovery. The man who would take on the burden of putting the nation back together was Lincoln's vice-president-become-president, Andrew Johnson.

Johnson was a Democrat from Tennessee. He had been placed on the ticket with Lincoln in hopes of widening the Republican candidate's support. He hadn't supported the South's secession, but he was still distrusted in Congress because he was a Southerner. This, combined with his lack of leadership ability, made Johnson a weak president.

Johnson proposed plans for Reconstruction, but these were seen as weak and ineffective. The Southern economy was in a state of disaster, newly freed blacks needed protection and assistance, and the country as a whole needed help to heal its wounds. Congress decided to take matters into its own hands.

Under radical Republican leadership, several important measures were passed. In 1866 Congress enacted the Civil Rights Bill, overruling Johnson's veto. This bill guaranteed federal enforcement of equal rights for blacks and whites. Although slavery was ended throughout the country in 1865, when the Thirteenth Amendment was passed, the Fourteenth Amendment was needed in 1868 to guarantee African Americans citizenship and equal protection under the law. The Fifteenth Amendment was passed in 1870, protecting black people's right to vote. By 1870, all of the Southern states had agreed to these amendments and were readmitted to the Union.

Still, Reconstruction did not progress smoothly. Johnson was charged with defying an order of Congress, but was found not guilty. He served out his term and left office in 1869, replaced by General Ulysses S. Grant.

Despite the change in presidents, nothing much changed among the people. African Americans remained second-class citizens. Many became *sharecroppers*, working for white farmers who demanded the major share of their crops in payment for use of the land. Southern states found ways around the Fifteenth Amendment by making uneducated African Americans take literacy tests to be able to vote. Segregation was legalized by **Jim Crow laws** that provided for separate public facilities for African Americans and whites.

The corruption of Southern politics further complicated the problems. Southern Reconstruction governments were run by **carpetbaggers** and scalawags. Carpetbaggers were Northern whites who went South to exploit the region for business and political purposes. **Scalawags** were Southern whites who sought to control the African-American population by joining the radical Republicans and working within politics. The sham of Reconstruction lasted until 1876. By then African Americans were still treated like second-class citizens. Many were still poor, uneducated, and without basic rights.

Inferring the Main Idea of a Passage

In Lesson 2, you learned how to find the stated main idea of a passage. First you look at the topic sentences of all the paragraphs in the passage. Then you look for a statement that summarizes them. This statement is the topic sentence of the passage. Sometimes you can find a topic for the passage right away, and check the topic sentences of the paragraphs to see if they support it.

' Often, however, the main idea of a passage is not stated; there is no topic sentence for the entire passage. In this case, you have to find the main idea of each paragraph and put them together to come up with your own topic sentence for the passage. When you do this, you are inferring the main idea of a passage. You put together the details—the clues—to infer a meaning that is not stated.

Try this with the passage on Reconstruction that you have just read. First, reread the passage. What are the main ideas? It might help to jot them down on a piece of paper. Your notes might look something like this:

Reconstruction

- Lincoln's death kills hope of easy recovery
- Johnson a weak president
- Congress passes laws to help African Americans
- Segregation continues despite efforts to end it
- Southern Reconstruction governments are corrupt and hinder progress of African Americans

What you have done is write down the main idea of each paragraph. Now you can begin to formulate a summary of the passage: *After the Civil War, the nation had a long road to recovery. Its political, social, and economic health was poor. Despite the best efforts of Congress, the end of Reconstruction brought few solutions to the problems plaguing the nation.*

With this in mind, do the Practice exercise. Remember to test your main idea against the details of the passage.

Practice

The following item is based on the lesson.

Which sentence below best expresses the inferred main idea of the passage?

(1) Reconstruction would have been successful had Lincoln remained president.

(2) Reconstruction did little to change Southern politics, the Southern way of life, or conditions for African Americans.

(3) Life for African Americans improved during Reconstruction because of all the acts and amendments passed by Congress.

(4) Southerners were unable to accept assistance from the North because of their pride.

(5) Johnson was responsible for the failure of Reconstruction.

The only answer that works is (2). You can eliminate (1) and (5) because the last two paragraphs don't support them. Choice (3) is also incorrect because the last two paragraphs in the passage don't support it. Choice (4), perhaps true to some extent, is not really dealt with in the passage. The correct answer takes all the details of the passage and brings them together in one overall statement—the summary of its unstated main meaning, or inferred main idea of the passage.

Lesson 7 Exercises

1. The lesson would best support the statement that, during Reconstruction, Congress

   (1) wanted to turn the South into an industrial region like the North

   (2) favored African Americans over whites in its law-making

   (3) did not spend enough money to improve conditions for African Americans

   (4) worked to pass laws that would improve conditions for African Americans

   (5) ignored the North in its efforts to remedy problems in the South

2. The Civil Rights Bill of 1866, the Thirteenth Amendment, the Fourteenth Amendment, and the Fifteenth Amendment were all

   (1) attempts to legalize segregation in the South

   (2) attempts to improve conditions for African Americans

   (3) passed in the 1860s

   (4) passed despite President Johnson's vetoes

   (5) changes in the U.S. Constitution

Item 3 is based on the following passage.

Southerners after the war were a defeated people. Their fields lay untended and their cities in ruins. Families were left childless, women were widowed, and orphans roamed the streets seeking food and shelter.

In addition, Southerners were forced to live under Reconstruction governments that were established and protected by the North. African Americans held seats in every Southern state legislature. One response to this was the formation of the secret order of the Ku Klux Klan. The Klan's original purpose was to frighten African Americans away from the polls so they couldn't vote. Through this and other means, by 1877 Southern whites had regained power throughout the old Confederacy.

3. In response to their defeat in the Civil War, Southerners
   (1) used the sharecropping system to regain their wealth
   (2) refused to accept civil rights amendments that would readmit them to the Union
   (3) gradually changed their thinking to suit the new law of the land
   (4) worked with scalawags to undermine the North
   (5) used whatever means they could to deny African Americans their new rights

Answers are on page 371.

The Growth of U.S. Industry and U.S. Cities

Prereading Prompt

You know that America is a land of immigrants. Even the Native Americans, who were here before Europeans discovered the New World, are thought to have immigrated here from Asia. During the American Industrial Revolution and the period following Reconstruction, immigration soared. How do you think this new immigration and the Industrial Revolution changed the way Americans lived and worked?

Key Words

immigrate—to come into a country and settle there permanently from another country
immigrant—a person who immigrates

In 1869, the nation had its first transcontinental railroad. By 1893, five lines crossed the nation. Perhaps more than any legislation passed by Congress, the railroads united the nation. Flour ground from wheat grown in Minnesota was mixed with lard from Iowa cattle and made into pies that were baked in Ohio-made ovens used in New England.

With the growth of the steel and oil industries and Edison's invention of the electric light, American life was changed forever. The availability of energy from oil, steam, and electricity meant that more factories could be built. As factories were built, jobs became available, and the great move to the cities was on. In 1880, only one-quarter of all Americans lived in urban areas. By 1910, nearly half of America's population lived in cities. The chart on page 76 shows this flight to urban centers. The United States had shifted from a country of farmers to a country of factory workers.

However, this wasn't the only way America was changing. Immigration, which had always been a part of American life, was becoming a problem. Between 1860 and 1900, over 14 million immigrants joined the ranks of the American population. Fleeing Europe and Asia for political, economic, and religious reasons, they came to America's fertile farmland and made their living in activities that were familiar to them. But as less land became available, they too looked for employment in the cities. Germans, Irish, Swedes, Poles, Hungarians, Russians, Italians—all ended up in the factories and steel mills. The large cities felt the full impact of immigration. In 1900, almost 37 percent of New York's population was foreign-born.

Industrialists welcomed the immigrants as cheap labor for the factories. Because the immigrants were paid such low wages, they didn't have the money to afford much food or good housing. Large sections of the cities became overcrowded slums full of crime, disease, and hunger.

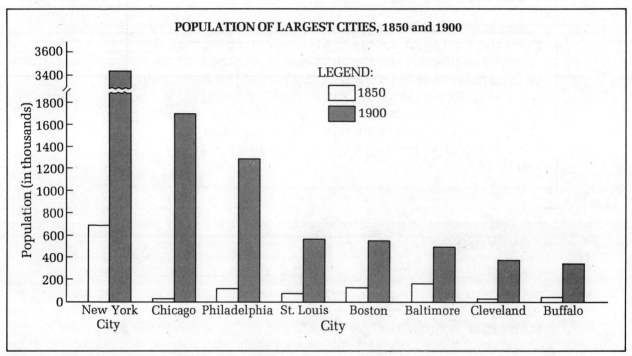

Fig. 2–6 Population of Largest U.S. Cities, 1850 and 1900. From Teacher's Resource Handbook, *The United States: A History of the Republic*, 2nd ed. (Englewood Cliffs, N.J.: Prentice-Hall, 1984), page 257. Used with permission.

Making Inferences from a Graphic

In Lesson 3 of this chapter you learned how to find specific details in graphic material. If you need to refresh that skill, go back and review that lesson now. Once you are comfortable with finding details in a graphic, continue with this lesson.

You will now go a step further and learn to infer details from a graphic. This means you will find answers to questions by finding information that is not stated directly on the graph. Just as you made inferences by putting together details in your reading, you will now find details on the graph and put them together to infer the information you want. Using the graph from the preceding lesson, let's look at an example of how this works. Here's the question: Of the three smallest cities on the graph in 1850, which one grew the most by 1900?

To answer this question, you first have to find the three smallest cities in 1850. The smallest were Chicago, Cleveland, and Buffalo. Now look at the size of these three cities in 1900—the blue bars. Which blue bar is largest? Chicago is by far the largest. Since Chicago's population in 1850 was the smallest (tied with Cleveland), its population experienced the greatest increase of the three smallest cities shown.

Try another question. Which city roughly tripled in size between 1850 and 1900? This question can be answered by eyeballing the graph, but you still have to compare the information given—in this case, the white bar of each city with the blue bar for that same city. Which blue bar is roughly three times larger than its corresponding white bar? The answer is Baltimore. The numbers bear this out. In 1850, Baltimore had a population of roughly 125,000. In 1900, that number was about 575,000—triple the 1850 figure. All of the other cities grew by more or less than three times.

Practice

This item is based on Figure 2-6 from this lesson.

Which city increased its population the most between 1850 and 1990?
(1) New York
(2) Chicago
(3) Philadelphia
(4) St. Louis
(5) Cleveland

This question is a little more difficult because you have more figures to compare. You might try eyeballing the graph, but you should check the figures afterward to make sure your answer is correct. A look at the graph suggests that Chicago's population might have increased the most. It started out the smallest (tied with Cleveland), and it ended up being second only to New York. Now, you can check your answer by comparing just New York and Chicago. In 1850, New York had a population of roughly 700,000. In 1900, it was almost 3,500,000. The population of New York in 1900 was five times what it was in 1850. Now look at Chicago. Its population was about 25,000 in 1850. By 1900 it was 1,700,000. That number is 68 times higher than what it was in 1850. So even though there were fewer people in Chicago in 1900 than in New York, Chicago's population had increased many more times than New York's. So the correct answer is Chicago, (2).

Item 1 is based on the following graph.

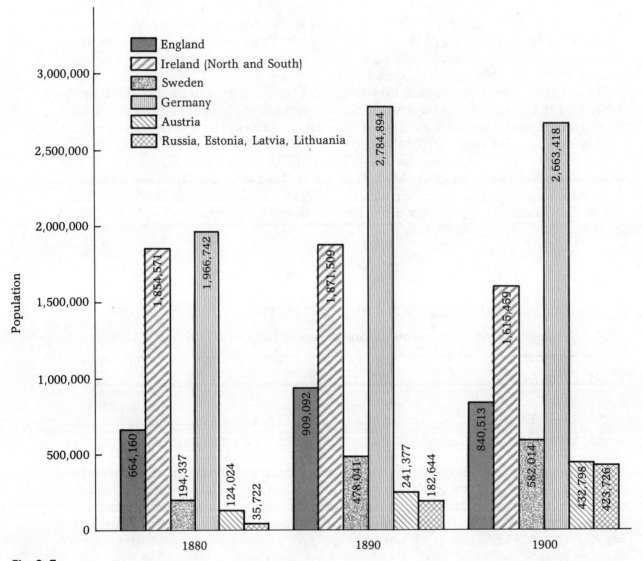

Fig. 2–7

1. According to the information in the preceding graph, the group in the U.S. population that increased the most between 1880 and 1900 was from
   (1) Ireland
   (2) Sweden
   (3) Austria
   (4) Russia and the Baltic nations
   (5) Germany

2. In Figure 2-6 on page 76, the cities in which regions grew the most because of immigration?
   (1) Northeast and Midwest
   (2) Northeast and Southeast
   (3) Midwest and West
   (4) Midwest and Southwest
   (5) Southwest and Southeast

3. Between 1880 and 1910, the number of Americans living in cities
   (1) doubled
   (2) tripled
   (3) quadrupled
   (4) was cut by half
   (5) was cut by a quarter

Answers are on page 371–372.

Reform Movements

Prereading Prompt

In the rapid industrial growth of late 19th-century America, business was left at first to develop without interference. The economy was healthy and people were working, so the government saw no need to step in. Big business, however, ignored its workers' needs. Greed corrupted honest business practices. What changes do you think were made in American business as a result?

Key Words

monopoly—complete control of one part of the economy by one company or one group; a company with such control

laissez-faire—a government policy of not interfering in any way in a nation's economy

Progressive Movement—a reform movement of the early 20th century intended to improve social conditions

The American government adopted a **laissez-faire**, or "hands-off," policy toward business during the late 19th and early 20th centuries. With business booming and the government looking the other way, there were huge fortunes to be made. J. P. Morgan and Andrew Carnegie made fortunes in steel, and John D. Rockefeller became the king of the oil industry. Power and money were concentrated in the hands of a few.

As big business got bigger, its morals got smaller. The giants of the big industries—railroads, steel, oil—grew even larger by forming *trusts* and *monopolies*. The reason for forming them was to own or control as many companies in a given industry as possible. This effectively eliminated competition. Once there was no competition, there was no limit to prices. With high prices, the rich got richer and the poor got poorer.

For the average city worker, living conditions were terrible, and working conditions were often worse. These were the days before overtime pay, minimum wage, and mandatory time off. The average worker put in 59 hours and made less than $10 a week, although many worked more than 70 hours and made even less. Through the efforts of Samuel Gompers, the American Federation of Labor was organized in 1886. Now in labor unions, workers were able to strike and negotiate for better pay, time off, and safer working conditions.

Politics became corrupt also. City politicians took advantage of the poor by offering jobs in exchange for votes. Local governments, particularly in large cities like New York and Chicago, were controlled by small groups of people who used the government for profit.

The **Progressive Movement** developed during the early 20th century in response to the corruption in business and politics. Reformers passed major legislation such as the Sherman Anti-Trust Act, which outlawed monopolies. Child labor laws made it illegal for children to work. Agencies were established to regulate trade and commerce, inspect food and drugs, and protect workers. Compulsory education was established so the working classes could attend school and improve their position in life. Women gained the right to vote with the passage of the Nineteenth Amendment to the Constitution. In 20 years the government's policy had changed from laissez-faire to regulation. American government would never be the same again.

(Credit: Spencer in *The Commoner.*)

Inferring the Main Idea of a Graphic

You can use your skill at inferring information from text to infer information from a graphic. Use the details in the cartoon to come up with an overall main idea.

Look at the political cartoon on page 87. What details do you see? The picture shows John D. Rockefeller standing next to an enormous rose. Written on the flower are the words "Standard Oil Company." At Rockefeller's feet is a pile of skulls with the word "competitors" written across it. Rockefeller is holding a pair of pruning shears in one hand and in the other a skull (one of his competitors).

You can infer the meaning of a cartoon by answering these three questions:

(1) <u>What are the main details?</u> The big rose, the rosebuds, Rockefeller.

(2) <u>What comparisons are made?</u> The rosebuds are shown as skulls, Rockefeller as a gardener, and the Standard Oil Company as a big rose.

(3) <u>What is the main action or situation?</u> Rockefeller has cut off his competitors so that the Standard Oil Company will grow large.

(4) <u>Which answer gives the meaning of the cartoon?</u> Look for the statement that connects the details (and the way they are pictured) to the main action to express the meaning you see in the cartoon.

Can you put all this information together to come up with the main idea? Try it in the Practice exercise.

Practice

The following item is based on the cartoon on page 87. This cartoon is based on a statement made by John D. Rockefeller's son about the way his father created the Standard Oil Company. By putting together the details of the cartoon, which statement do you think was made by John D. Rockefeller, Jr.?

(1) All money is as beautiful as roses.

(2) All roses have thorns, just as all men have faults.

(3) The most beautiful roses are produced by sacrificing other rosebuds.

(4) Rosebuds that are cut are more beautiful than big roses.

(5) The more rosebuds you cut, the more roses there will be.

Choice (3) is the correct answer. The cartoon shows Rockefeller as a gardener, holding pruning scissors and standing beside an enormous rose, the "Standard Oil Company." The rosebuds he has cut off are his competitors. The actual statement by John D. Rockefeller, Jr., was that the process of destroying competition and creating a monopoly was like cutting off rose-buds to grow the largest, most beautiful rose. The cartoon makes fun of this idea. If you put the details together, you see that (1) is not correct: a big rose labeled "Standard Oil Co." and rosebuds that look like human skulls do not suggest that money is as beautiful as roses. (2) is wrong because roses and thorns are not compared in the cartoon. The cut rosebuds look like human skulls, so (4) cannot be correct. Choice (5) is wrong because in the cartoon there is only one rose produced by cutting all the rosebuds.

Lesson 9 Exercises

(Credit: From PUCK, August 20, 1913)

1. The meaning of this cartoon is that
   (1) the banks want to overthrow the U.S. government
   (2) the U.S. government and the U.S. banks need to be replaced
   (3) politicians and bankers always work together
   (4) political power corrupts banking and banking power corrupts politics
   (5) political power hurts banking more than banking power hurts politics

2. Hostile attitudes toward the new groups of immigrant workers spread through American cities. A political party called the Know Nothings expressed these attitudes. The main idea of this Know Nothing cartoon is that immigrant Irishmen and Germans
   (1) are always fighting each other
   (2) are the main cause of city riots
   (3) show no interest in elections
   (4) refuse to fight for their rights
   (5) steal elections and corrupt politics

The Know-Nothings charged that Irish and German immigrants were stealing American elections and running the big city political machines.
(Note: The label on the barrel to the left reads "Irish Whisky" and the label on the barrel to the right reads "Lager Bier," i.e., Lager Beer.)
(Credit: New York State Historical Association)

3. A *stereotype* is an image, or a picture, of a group that describes them as all alike and all more or less bad. Often a few traits are used to describe the character of the whole group. This cartoon presents a stereotype of all Irish and German people as being

    (1) drunken, violent, and dishonest
    (2) fun-loving, childish, and irresponsible
    (3) illiterate, lazy, and stupid
    (4) cowardly, weak, and unreliable
    (5) emotional, unpredictable, and violent

Answers are on page 372.

The U.S. Becomes a World Power

Prereading Prompt

By the end of the 19th century, the United States had been free for about a hundred years. Soon it would have its own colonies off the mainland. It had already had two wrenching wars on home soil, and soon it would be fighting foreign wars. America was changing, becoming—almost against its will—a world power. What was the first foreign war America fought? How did America's foreign policy change after this war?

Key Words

imperialism—a nation's policy of extending control over other nations
isolationism—a nation's policy of avoiding involvement in international affairs
Fourteen Points—President Wilson's plan for peace after World War I

The Spanish-American War

Isolationism was the key word in American foreign policy for a hundred years. Since the Monroe Doctrine, the United States had been left alone to spread from sea to sea, and spread it did. By 1896, there were 45 states in the Union.

The first evidence that the United States might be ending its old policy of isolationism came with rapid growth of industry. Foreign markets were needed as places to buy raw materials and to sell finished products. One such market was Cuba, an island 90 miles off the tip of Florida.

Cuba was under Spanish rule. Newspaper publishers, eager to sell more papers, wrote exaggerated and sensational stories about the cruel and inhuman ways Spain treated its Cuban subjects. Such sensational reporting was called *yellow journalism*. Despite the outrage these reports generated, America maintained its noninterventionist foreign policy.

Then, in February 1898, the American battleship *Maine* was blown up near Havana, Cuba. Two hundred and fifty American lives were lost. The cause of the explosion was never discovered, but Americans, aroused by the yellow press, blamed Spain.

The Spanish-American War followed, lasting only four months. By the Treaty of Paris (1898), Spain gave Cuba its independence, ceded Puerto Rico and Guam to the United States, and sold the Philippine Islands to the U.S. for $20 million.

With the end of the Spanish-American War, the United States had won a war against a European nation. It also had accomplished its first act of **imperialism**: it acquired territory by military force, gaining colonies in the Caribbean and the Pacific. The United States was emerging as a world power.

World War I

Although it had become a world power, the United States still kept to its policy of isolationism after the Spanish-American War. Events in Europe, however, were making this policy increasingly difficult to follow. Imperialist ambitions caused constant conflict among the major European nations. In June 1914, the heir to the throne of the Austro-Hungarian empire was assassinated. By July, a full-blown war had broken out between the Central Powers (Germany, Austria-Hungary, Turkey, and Bulgaria) and the Allies (England, France, Russia, and some smaller European nations).

For three years the United States stayed neutral. American ships traded with both sides equally. More and more, however, German submarines attacked these ships to keep them from carrying supplies to England. In April 1917, the United States officially declared war on Germany and joined forces with the Allies. Americans rallied to Wilson's call to "make the world safe for democracy" and to fight "the war to end all wars."

But by 1918, Europe had been at war for four years. Her resources were dwindling and her armies were exhausted. With the help of American troops, the Allies finally defeated the Germans.

At war's end, President Wilson offered a plan known as the **Fourteen Points**, which proposed "peace without victory." The Allies, on the other hand, were determined to punish Germany and the other Central Powers. The Versailles Treaty of 1919 made Germany accept guilt for causing the war, give up much of her territory, and pay for all the damages done by the war. Wilson's Fourteen Points also provided for an international organization to settle disputes, the *League of Nations*. This was established, but was never effective.

(Credit: Imperial War Museum, London)

The total cost of World War I was over $350 billion. Ten million soldiers were killed, and twenty million wounded. In addition, millions of civilians died in the fighting and from famine and disease. Although they signed a peace treaty, the nations of Europe harbored hatred for their enemies. There was a new surge of nationalism as they rebuilt their countries.

Applying Information from Passages: Applying What You Read

To apply something means to use it. To apply information in social studies means to take what you have learned and use it in another situation. Let's see how this would work using the passage from the lesson.

You learned from the lesson that yellow journalism was a key factor in turning Americans against Spain in the late 19th century. Using what you know about yellow journalism, try to answer the following question: Which headline below is an example of yellow journalism you might see in a modern tabloid?

(1) Gorby and Bush Get Wet at Peace Talks
(2) Red Dracula Falls—Ceausescu's Last Bloodbath
(3) Thousands Party as Berlin Wall Crumbles
(4) Hundreds Die in Pan Am Crash—Bomb Blamed
(5) U.S. Seen as Bad Guy at U.N.

When you apply information you have learned from a passage, keep in mind the things about both situations that are similar. How is the new situation similar to what you have read? In this case, ask yourself this question: In what ways is yellow journalism today similar to the yellow journalism that turned U.S. sentiment against Spain in 1898?

To answer the question, you have to remember that yellow journalism distorts and exaggerates news to attract readers. It aims to get a strong, even violent, emotional response from readers. Finding the example of yellow journalism in a headline is hard because they all use everyday language with some emotional appeal. Which headline plays to emotions most strongly? Choice (1) refers to peace talks between Presidents Bush and Gorbachev that were held at sea. It may not be too respectful to call the Soviet president "Gorby" or to say the two leaders "get wet" (meaning their meeting was delayed by rough seas). The language does not whip up strong emotions, however, or distort the meaning of what happened. The same is true of (3) and (5). These headlines tell their stories in popular, or colloquial, language, but are not sensational. This is especially true of (5), in which the U.N. denounced U.S. policies in Central America. In (4), the event itself was sensational, but the headline is objective—it merely states what happened. This is not the case in (2), however. Ceausescu was a brutal Communist dictator of Romania, but to call him a "Red Dracula" is sensational. Transylvania, the home of the mythical vampire chief, Count Dracula, is in fact part of Romania, so the whole nation is being emotionally associated with superhuman evil from the world of romantic fantasy and horror movies. Calling the execution of the dictator his "Last Bloodbath" further plays up his association with vampires. Such a headline is really attempting to excite the reader with irrelevant images of violence while pretending to deliver a serious moral message. An objective headline would be: Ceausescu Falls—Cummunist Dictator Executed.

When you apply what you have learned to new situations, try to keep in mind the things that are similar about the situations. Remember this when you do the Practice exercise.

Practice

What event below reflects a similar foreign policy to that followed by the U.S. after the Spanish-American War?

(1) U.S. withdraws its troops from Vietnam in 1975.
(2) U.S. sends peace-keeping forces to the Persian Gulf.
(3) U.S. negotiates for freedom of hostages in Iran.
(4) U.S. sends aid to anti-Communist forces in Central America.
(5) U.S. waits until its territory is attacked to join the fighting in World War II.

To answer this question, you first have to know what the U.S. foreign policy was following the Spanish-American War. If you don't remember, reread the passage from the lesson. It tells you that after the war the United States returned to its policy of isolationism. During this time it attempted to stay out of foreign affairs whenever possible. Choices (1) through (4) are incorrect because they all reflect direct U.S. involvement in response to crises in foreign affairs. Choice (5) is correct because it reflects a policy of isolationism, broken only at the point that the United States was directly threatened. This is similar to the situation following the Spanish-American War and preceding World War I. The United States kept its distance while the war raged in Europe for three years. It didn't join the fighting until its own ships came under attack by German U-boats. By applying what you read in the lesson, you could answer the question correctly.

Lesson 10 Exercises

1. How did the growth of industry in the U.S. contribute to the new policy of imperialism?
   (1) Weapons were readily available and plentiful.
   (2) There were many immigrants to help fight a war.
   (3) The U.S. sought new markets for trade and raw materials.
   (4) Many ships could be built to fight the war because of the huge urban populations.
   (5) Industrial growth gave rise to yellow journalism, which pushed for imperialism.

2. Which one of the following headlines is an example of yellow journalism?
   (1) Wilson Calls on Americans to Fight "War to End War"
   (2) Versailles Treaty Dumps "Peace without Victory"
   (3) German Subs Hit U.S. Ships
   (4) Assassins Murder Austro-Hungarian Heir
   (5) Spanish Cuba—Hell on Earth

3. Which act below would be an act of imperialism by the U.S.?
   (1) The U.S. capture of Panamanian leader Mañuel Noriega.
   (2) The annexation of Hawaii as a state in 1959.
   (3) Fighting in the Persian Gulf in retaliation for terrorist acts against the U.S.
   (4) Sending U.S. troops to Vietnam to honor a treaty with an ally.
   (5) Lending money to Third World countries.

Answers are on page 372.

The Great Depression and the New Deal

Prereading Prompt

Who hasn't heard of Ford, Buick, and Chrysler? You probably are also familiar with United Artists, Paramount, and Metro-Goldwyn-Mayer. These are just a few of the companies that made it big during the decade known as the Roaring Twenties. The Roaring Twenties were followed by a decade of hardship for the American people. What event brought the Roaring Twenties to a grinding halt? Find out by reading the next lesson.

Key Words

stock market crash—October 23, 1929, a day of frantic selling on the stock market in which thousands of investors lost millions of dollars

Great Depression—the period of the 1930s in which millions were jobless, homeless, and hungry

welfare state—an economic situation in which people depend on government money for food, jobs, and shelter

America in the 1920s was a land of prosperity and growth. World War I had drained the economy, but after the war people returned their attention to making money. President Coolidge summed it up when he said that "the chief business of the American people is business." The economy soared.

Banks were eager to lend money. People bought cars, houses, and other expensive items on credit. Investors large and small bought stock in American companies. The economy grew even stronger. The American Dream became a reality for many.

However, a cycle known as *boom and bust* was coming full circle. The period of economic growth (boom) would soon be followed by financial *depression* (bust). In 1929, the **stock market crash** occurred, when people who owned inflated shares of companies began to lose faith in their value and sold them in huge quantities. These stocks rapidly became worthless, and the stock market crashed. The depression set in slowly, but as the 1930s unfolded, banks failed and sales and incomes fell. Unemployment, a key indicator of a healthy economy, told the real story. In 1929, there were about 1.5 million unemployed people in the United States In 1932, some estimate there were as many as 16 million. The Great Depression was on. The federal government, headed by Republican Herbert Hoover, stuck to its traditional laissez-faire policy, not interfering in the economy. After a brief economic surge early in the decade, the economy fell into an even deeper slump. It was just the opportunity the Democrats needed to regain the presidency.

(Credit: UPI/Bettmann Newsphotos)

In 1932, Franklin Delano Roosevelt won the election by offering Americans a *New Deal*. He launched America on a program of recovery marked by enormous government spending. The country became a **welfare state**: laws were passed to protect people's savings accounts; assistance programs for the elderly and unemployed were established; various federally funded public-works programs were launched. This was a new kind of American government, one that was much more actively involved in the lives of its citizens.

Applying Information from Passages: Applying What You Already Know

You have already learned how to apply information you learn from reading to new situations. On the GED tests, you will be expected to apply information you *already* know to what you read and to new situations. You will have to put your prior—knowledge you already have—into practice. For example, the preceding passage discusses the Great Depression of the 1930s. From your own experience you probably already know quite a lot about economic depressions. You may have relatives who lived through the Great Depression. Or you may have read books such as John Steinbeck's *Grapes of Wrath*, which deals with a family living through this era. You might even have seen the movie that was made from this book. Also, anyone who lived through the last few decades has experienced periods of minor economic depression. With all of this information, you probably know more than you even realized about economic depression—its effects on your bank account, your paycheck, you car loan, and the general cost of living. When you take the GED test, always bring your prior knowledge into play. Let's look at a specific question to see how your prior knowledge can help you.

The Social Security Act was one of the New Deal reforms. Which of the following would Social Security provide for?

(1) medical care for victims of accidents

(2) old-age and survivors insurance

(3) medical care for the needy

(4) educational loans for the unemployed

(5) benefits to disabled workers

What you already know—your prior knowledge—may help you a great deal in finding the correct answer to this question. The passage itself doesn't tell you what Social Security is. Take a minute to think about what you already know about Social Security. First, you may have a Social Security Card. Taxes are withheld from your paycheck to go toward Social Security. You probably know that you cannot get this money back until you retire. With this knowledge in mind, look at the choices and choose one.

A tax withheld for Social Security would not provide loan money for a voluntary activity such as education, which you could engage in before you retired from work, so (4) is wrong. Your prior knowledge also probably tells you that you cannot get money from Social Security for medical care. Did you ever know anyone who was not retired who paid medical bills with Social Security money? So (1) and (3) are wrong. Another reason for eliminating (3) is that you cannot get money from Social Security before you retire, no matter how needy you are.

A further reason for eliminating (1) is that—as you probably know—car owners must have automobile insurance, and many people have medical insurance from their jobs to provide them with aid if they have a serious accident or illness. In the same way, you can logically eliminate (5) by remembering that Social Security concerns aid people who have retired from work and therefore have nothing to do with benefits to disabled workers.

When you do the Practice question, remember to think about everything you know that pertains to the question.

Practice

Many people criticize the government today because it has created a welfare state. Which of the following situations would be typical of a welfare state?

(1) A mother hires a babysitter to watch her two-year-old while she goes to work.

(2) A pregnant teenager goes to a clinic for prenatal care.

(3) A father uses food stamps to buy groceries for his family.

(4) A college professor gets a federal grant to do research.

(5) A family gets a federal loan to buy a house.

To answer this question, you would have to use the information from the passage and also bring some of your prior knowledge to the situation. You know from the passage that a welfare state is an economic condition in which government money is used to give aid to citizens. You can also apply your prior knowledge to each of the choices. Choice (1) implies that the mother has used her own money to hire a private babysitter. No government money is involved, so (1) is incorrect. In Choice (2), you don't know whether or not the clinic is subsidized by government money. For this reason, it should be eliminated. To judge (4), it would help to know that private and government institutions often give grants to fund research that they consider worthy. This money is not welfare per se. It is more of a gift and has little to do with aiding the needy. In (5), the family is getting federal funds, but in the form of a loan. Your prior knowledge will tell you that a loan is meant to be paid back with interest. As such, it is not welfare. This leaves (3) as the correct answer. Food stamps are considered welfare. They are not paid back, and they enable people with little or no income to buy food to feed their families.

1. The American economy grew steadily during the 1980s. Many economists predicted that a bust would soon follow. Which events below suggest that they might be right?
   (1) high unemployment and drops in the stock market
   (2) increased foreign trade and low interest rates
   (3) high interest rates and low unemployment
   (4) high production rates and increased foreign trade
   (5) high rate of home-building and high mortgage rates

Items 2 and 3 are based on the following passage.

For many years, the farmers of the Great Plains of the Midwest abused the land. By allowing sheep and cattle to overgraze and then by farming the land, they destroyed the natural grass matting that held the rich prairie soil to the ground. This area was only semi-arid to begin with, not moist like the Mississippi Valley. By 1933 the Plains had been in a drought for 18 months. Massive dust storms plagued the area from Oklahoma to South Dakota. The region became known as the Dust Bowl.

2. The writer of this passage would agree with all the following statements *except*
   (1) Oil spills should be cleaned up quickly to prevent damage to land, water, and wildlife.
   (2) Acid rain should be stopped to save lakes and forests.
   (3) DDT and other toxic chemicals used on farm crops to fight insects should be banned.
   (4) Commercial fertilizers should never be used on soil in semi-arid areas.
   (5) Strip mining that causes severe soil erosion should be restricted.

3. During the Dust Bowl years, many farmers lost their farms to banks when they could no longer make payments on the loans they had taken to buy them. In John Steinbeck's novel *The Grapes of Wrath*, a despairing farmer watches as a tractor from a bank plows over his shack. "Who can we shoot?" he asks. The driver, a local farmer himself, says: "Maybe there's no one to shoot."

   In the 1980s, many people lost their savings when various savings and loan associations invested their money in risky and even illegal ways and then went bankrupt. In line with his previous remark, which of the following statements might the tractor driver say to people who lost their savings?
   (1) "You people who lost your savings have only yourselves to blame."
   (2) "All your money is lost, and there is nobody to pay you back."
   (3) "The S & L scandal is so big, there is nobody to pin the blame on."
   (4) "Your savings are lost, so it won't do you any good to punish the guilty."
   (5) "The S & Ls have so much power, nobody has the courage to attack them."

Answers are on page 372.

12 The Rise of Fascism and World War II

Prereading Prompt

In 1919, the Treaty of Versailles ended World War I. Some historians think it also planted the seeds for World War II, by dealing harshly with Germany. The German Nazi Party attacked the conditions of the treaty, thereby gaining support from the German people. What other factors gave rise to fascism in Europe? What started World War II?

Key Words

fascism—government headed by a dictator and characterized by aggressive nationalism
Axis—the forces of Germany, Italy, Japan, and other nations during World War II
genocide—a program of systematic killing intended to destroy a whole national or ethnic group

The effects of the Great Depression were felt throughout the world. One result was the rise of **fascism** in the Eastern Hemisphere. Fascist governments from Germany to Japan engaged in acts of aggression against other nations. In 1931, Japan invaded Manchuria; in 1935, Italy attacked Ethiopia; in 1936, profascists started a Civil War in Spain to gain control of the government; in 1937, Japan invaded China; in 1938, Germany invaded Austria. Through the end of the decade, acts of imperialism continued by these countries, unchecked by the rest of Europe or the United States.

European powers mistakenly believed that Hitler would stop invading countries after he had conquered one or two. Hitler believed that the Aryan people—non-Jewish (gentile), white Germans—were the master race and were born to rule the world's lesser peoples. His political movement, *Nazism*, was therefore based on racism, the idea that one race is superior to others, which the superior race has a right to dominate and exploit. It wasn't until German troops invaded Poland that Europe finally intervened. France and England, honoring treaty obligations with Poland, joined forces and declared war on Germany on September 3, 1939. World War II was underway.

During the late 1930s, the United States kept to its policy of neutrality. World War I and the Great Depression were still fresh in the minds of many Americans. Most watched events in Europe and the Far East with detached interest. By the 1940s, however, American popular sentiment was beginning to shift. France had fallen to the Germans and England was under attack. On December 9, 1940, President Roosevelt received an urgent message from England's Prime Minister Winston Churchill. Britain was in "mortal danger" and needed American arms and money. Congress passed measures to lend assistance.

Soon American ships were being attacked by German U-boats. Trouble was also brewing with Japan, which had joined Italy and Germany to form the **Axis** powers. Japanese aggression had caused Roosevelt to freeze all trade with Japan. On December 7, 1941, the Japanese retaliated by bombing Pearl Harbor in Hawaii. The United States was now an active player in World War II.

Joining the forces of England and France, the United States and the other Allies agreed to stop Hitler in Europe before turning their attention to Japan. In June 1944, Allied forces landed on the beaches of Normandy and fought their way through French countryside. Paris was reclaimed, and in September, after the allied forces crossed into Germany, the Nazis were forced to surrender.

With Europe back under control, it was time to deal with problems in the Pacific. President Roosevelt had died in April 1945, and America had a new leader, Harry S. Truman. Truman gave orders to drop the atomic bomb on Japan. Two nuclear bombs were dropped on Hiroshima and Nagasaki. The devastation was total, the destruction incomprehensible. Hundreds of thousands of people were killed. Japan surrendered a few days later, on August 14, 1945.

As with World War I, the cost of the war was staggering. Total military costs were over $1,100 billion, or more than a trillion dollars. Russia alone lost 30 million lives. Germany lost 3 million men and a million or more civilians. At war's end, it was discovered that Hitler's **genocide** had killed over 6 million Jews, a tragedy known as the *Holocaust*. He also killed millions of others—Eastern Europeans, gypsies, homosexuals, and members of religious and political groups. In hopes of preventing another such war, the United Nations was formed, to serve as a forum for discussion and negotiation of international issues. At times, the UN takes limited military action with forces from several nations.

(Credit: YIVO Institute for Jewish Research)

Applying Information from a List of Categories

On the GED test, there will be items that require you to fit a new piece of information into a list of definitions or categories. To do this, you first need to understand the definitions or categories in the list and then see how they apply to specific cases. The following is an example of this type of question.

World War II was a war of imperialism, but also a war of ideology. The powers involved had different ideas about how government should be run. Some different types of government are described below:

- **direct democracy**—all eligible citizens can vote directly on matters of public policy
- **representative democracy**—laws are made by representatives of the people, who are chosen in free elections
- **fascism**—the government is run by a dictator wielding personal and/or national power; characterized by aggression toward other nations
- **absolute monarchy**—the government is run by an absolute ruler whose authority to rule is often passed on through heredity
- **constitutional monarchy**—the constitution recognizes the royal family as head of government and an elected government actually governs the country

At the time of World War II England was ruled by King George VI, who became king in 1936 when his older brother Edward VIII abdicated the throne. Both George and Edward were sons of King George V, who ruled until his death in 1936. All three kings were merely figureheads; the actual affairs of government were handled by the prime minister and Parliament. Which type of government best describes England's government?

To answer this question, you first have to read and understand the definitions in the list of categories. Then you have to fit the information in the question with that list. The correct answer is constitutional monarchy. Rule of England was passed from father to eldest son to next elder son, in other words, through heredity. But the royal family in England plays a traditional and ceremonial role. The country is governed by elected representatives. Therefore, it is a constitutional monarchy. None of the other definitions fits this description.

Practice

Read these definitions and answer the following question.

- **racism**—one race believes it is superior to all others and has the right to dominate and exploit them
- **imperialism**—one nation takes control of other nations to dominate and exploit them
- **fascism**—glorifies national power and believes that "might is right"
- **Marxism-Leninism**—promotes communist revolution through revolutionary violence and dictatorship
- **totalitarianism**—uses propaganda and police force to totally control individuals in a "perfect" society

A group of young men form a club with the following rules: every member must never criticize the club or its leaders, avoid socializing with nonmembers, and report or physically punish anyone breaking a club rule. This club is an example of

(1) fascism
(2) Marxism-Leninism
(3) racism
(4) imperialism
(5) totalitarianism

Choice (5) is correct. The emphasis of the club is on total control of individual members. Nothing suggests that the club wants to exercise unlimited power over nonmembers, so (1) is not correct. Club members are not taught to dominate nonmembers, only to stay away from them, so (4) is wrong. No revolutionary activity is suggested, so (2) is also wrong. Choice (3) is wrong because nothing is said about race.

Lesson 12 Exercises

Below is a list of types of governments with brief descriptions of their characteristics. Read them and answer the questions that follow.

(1) representative democracy—government is run by a chief executive and legislators elected by the people in free elections; characterized by private ownership of property and high degree of personal freedom

(2) anarchism—society runs itself without a government or ruler; the economy works through voluntary cooperation

(3) oligarchy—government controlled by a few privileged persons, usually the wealthiest in the society

(4) dictatorship—government run by a dictator with absolute political and economic power; characterized by little or no personal freedom

(5) constitutional monarchy—government is headed by ceremonial monarch with limited power; government is run by legislative body or bodies and a prime minister

1. Certain enemies of the United States during World War II, such as Germany, had fascist governments. Japan, which attacked the U.S. at Pearl Harbor, was headed by an emperor who was the symbol of the state and the unity of the people. Ultimate power in government, however, rested with the people, who were represented by legislators in two houses: the House of Representatives and the House of Councilors. What system of government did Japan have?

(1) representative democracy
(2) anarchism
(3) dictatorship
(4) constitutional monarchy
(5) oligarchy

2. Italy was headed by a king and governed by a two-branch parliament and a cabinet appointed by the king. Due to political and economic instability, the king entrusted Benito Mussolini with the job of forming a new government in 1922. Gradually Mussolini eliminated his political opposition. By 1926 his power over Italian politics and economics was complete. All personal freedoms were abolished, and all political parties were banned. Mussolini's government was still in power during World War II. What kind of government existed in Italy from 1926 through 1943?

   (1) representative democracy
   (2) anarchism
   (3) dictatorship
   (4) constitutional monarchy
   (5) oligarchy

3. A group of people set up a community. They work as equals, share food and money, and settle disputes without appealing to laws or a leader. Their form of government is an example of

   (1) anarchism
   (2) direct democracy
   (3) representative democracy
   (4) oligarchy
   (5) constitutional monarchy

Answers are on page 372–373.

13 The Early Cold War

Prereading Prompt

World War II was over, but another war was just beginning. It wasn't an all-out war; it was fought without weapons and without loss of life. Only recently has it ended. Do you know the story of this war?

Key Words

satellites—nations under the control of another, larger power. The Soviet satellites after World War II were Bulgaria, Czechoslovakia, East Germany, Hungary, Poland, and Romania.

Marshall Plan—a plan to provide economic aid to Western European nations recovering from World War II

North American Treaty Organization (NATO)—a pact among European and Western nations to protect each other from attack

During World War II, the Soviet Union, under attack from the Nazis, fought on the side of the Allies. When the war was over, however, Russia reverted to its prewar beliefs: that the spread of communism was necessary for her security and that the triumph of communism over capitalism was inevitable. The communist **satellites** were drawn into the Soviet bloc, and the Western nations began to see Soviet expansion as a threat to democracy. The two superpowers became engaged in a **Cold War**—a war of strained relations, with bombs and armies that stand ready to fight but never do.

Believing that Russia intended to extend its influence over Greece and Turkey, President Truman issued the Truman Doctrine in 1947. Its purpose was to contain communism inside the Soviet bloc. This was followed in 1948 by the **Marshall Plan**, which offered economic aid to all European nations to help them recover from the destruction of World War II.

Russia denounced the Marshall Plan as an American ploy to gain control over Europe. In response, the Soviet Union cut off access to West Berlin. Truman ordered all United States planes in Europe to fly supplies to the West Berliners. For 321 days, United States planes flew coal, food, clothing, and other provisions into the city. The Berlin airlift was an unqualified success. Rather than driving the West out of Europe, Russia had brought the United States and Western Europe closer.

In 1949, England, France, Belgium, the Netherlands, Luxembourg, Denmark, Iceland, Italy, Norway, Portugal, Canada, and the United States entered into the **North Atlantic Treaty Organization (NATO)**. The NATO nations agreed that they would consider an attack on any one of them as an attack on all, and would come to the defense of the attacked nation with armed force if necessary.

While the Cold War remained a test of wills in Europe, it became a shooting war in the Far East. In 1945, Korea had been taken from Japan and divided at the 38th parallel. The north was occupied by Russian forces, the south by American. In June 1950, South Korea was attacked by Soviet-backed North Koreans. The UN Security Council recommended that member nations provide military assistance to South Korea. Under American General Douglas MacArthur, the UN forces drove the Communists up beyond the 38th parallel, almost to Korea's northern borders. In November, the North Koreans were joined by Chinese armies. MacArthur beat a hasty retreat, and by the middle of 1951, the battle line was drawn again at the 38th parallel.

America's effort to contain communism abroad soon found an outlet at home. Fear of communism became rampant when it was discovered that some American Communists had passed defense secrets to Russia. Headed by Senator Joseph McCarthy of Wisconsin, who claimed that the government was heavily infiltrated with Communist spies, a wave of investigations began. Many prominent Americans, particularly those involved in the creative arts, were either proved or believed to be Communists. Whether guilty or not, hundreds of careers were ruined. McCarthy was never able to prove, however, that the government was infiltrated, and he was finally condemned for his conduct by his fellow members of Congress. Irresponsible charges of treason or other political crimes came to be known as "McCarthyism." But America's fear of communism had not been lessened.

In 1952, Americans elected World War II hero Dwight D. Eisenhower to the presidency. He had campaigned to bring the war in Korea to "an early and honorable end." In 1953, this aim was achieved. Korea remained divided, but the war was over. Fifty-four thousand American lives were lost in the Korean War, which cost the United States $15 billion to fight. Today North Korea is still communist and South Korea is non-communist, and the tensions between the two remain.

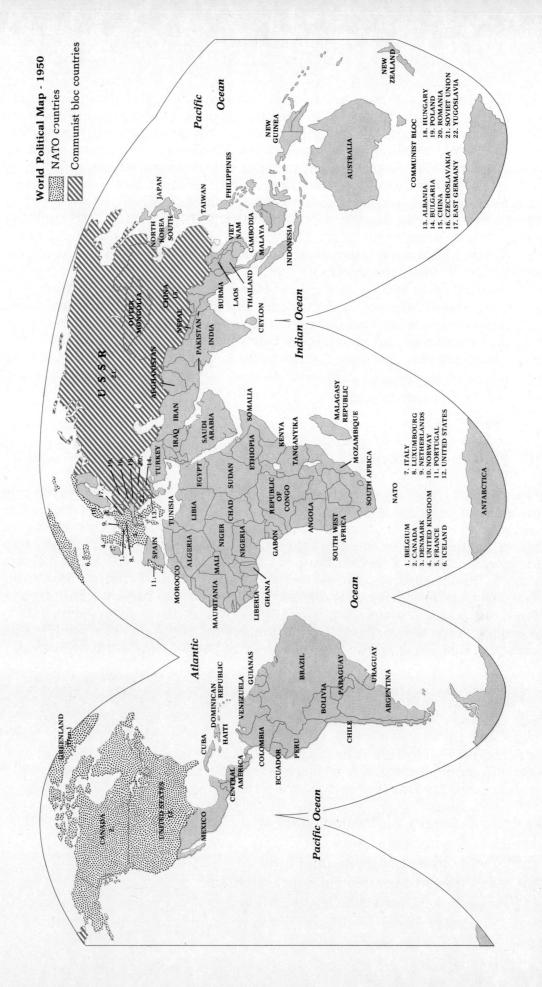

World Political Map - 1950

NATO countries
Communist bloc countries

NATO

1. BELGIUM
2. CANADA
3. DENMARK
4. UNITED KINGDOM
5. FRANCE
6. ICELAND
7. ITALY
8. LUXEMBOURG
9. NETHERLANDS
10. NORWAY
11. PORTUGAL
12. UNITED STATES

COMMUNIST BLOC

13. ALBANIA
14. BULGARIA
15. CHINA
16. CZECHOSLAVAKIA
17. EAST GERMANY
18. HUNGARY
19. POLAND
20. ROMANIA
21. SOVIET UNION
22. YUGOSLAVIA

Fig. 2–8

Applying Information from Graphics

On the GED, you will be asked to apply information from graphics such as maps and political cartoons. To answer this type of question, you first must be sure you understand the graphic. Look for the main idea—the important overall information the graphic illustrates. Then read the question and apply the information from the graphic. For these questions, as in all questions, use *all* the information you know about the topic. Brainstorm so that you use all of your knowledge to help answer the question.

Look at the map on page 103. It shows the NATO countries and the Communist bloc countries in 1950. Notice their locations in relation to each other. Think about what you already know and what you learned in the lesson. Now answer this question:

> In the early 1950s, as the Cold War grew ever more tense, the Communist bloc continued to feel threatened by non-Communist countries near its borders. Which countries would you expect the Soviet Union to have seriously considered conquering? Use the map.

(1) Portugal and Spain

(2) Greenland and Canada

(3) France and Italy

(4) Greece and Turkey

(5) Poland and Romania

The correct choice is (4). You know that the Soviet Union perceived any non-Communist country as a potential threat to the Communist bloc. The closer the country to its borders, the more of a threat it was thought to be. Looking at the map, you can see that Greece and Turkey share common borders with Russia. As non-Communist countries, they were seen as a direct threat to Soviet security. Russia believed the spread of communism to be necessary to her security; it is logical that Greece and Turkey would be perceived as threats. Choices (1), (2), and (3) are not as likely as (4) because they are farther from the borders of Communist bloc countries. Choice (5) is incorrect because these countries were already part of the Communist bloc.

Practice

The following question is based on the map in Figure 2-8.
Which Soviet action can best be explained by the Soviet fear of non-Communist countries near its borders?

(1) Soviet invasion of Afghanistan

(2) Soviet control of Cuba

(3) Soviet support of mainland China

(4) Soviet-backed invasion of South Vietnam

(5) Soviet aid to Nicaragua in the 1980s

To answer this question, you need to remember what information you are applying, both from the map and from what you've learned (and also what you already know). The map shows which countries belonged to NATO and which were part of the Communist bloc in 1950. It also shows the location of all the countries in the world and which ones are nearest each other. Since you know Russia's desire for the spread of communism and her feeling that she was threatened by non-Communist neighbors, you can use this information and the information from the map to answer the question. You are looking for a non-Communist country that shares borders with Russia or with Communist bloc countries or is very close to one of these countries. Cuba is in the Caribbean, closer to the United States than to the Soviet Union, so choice (2) is incorrect. South Vietnam is also thousands of miles away from the Russian border, so choice (4) is out. Mainland China, while a neighbor to Russia, is already Communist, eliminating choice (3). Choice (5) is not about a country on Russia's borders but one as far away from it as Cuba. This leaves (1), which is the correct answer; Afghanistan shares a border on the north with Russia.

Lesson 13 Exercises

Item 1 is based on the map on Figure 2-8.

1. John Foster Dulles, Eisenhower's secretary of state, despised communism and feared that it would one day take over the world. He championed the "domino theory"—that if one country falls to the Communists, its neighbor will fall, and then its neighbor, and so on.

   According to the domino theory, which group of countries in the Western Hemisphere would most likely turn Communist, if one went Communist?

   (1) Cuba, Haiti, the Dominican Republic
   (2) Cuba, Puerto Rico, Guadaloupe
   (3) Mexico, Peru, Bolivia
   (4) Venezuela, Colombia, Bolivia
   (5) Mexico, Costa Rica, Panama

Items 2 and 3 are based on the following political cartoon.

ONE OF THEM MUST BE WRONG

Source: Fitzpatrick in *The St. Louis Post-Dispatch*, October 29, 1952. By permission of *The St. Louis Post-Dispatch*. Courtesy State Historical Society of Missouri, Columbia.

The cartoon shows two sides of Dwight Eisenhower with regard to the Korean War: the World War II general studying the problems of the Korean War, and the presidential candidate offering solutions to the war like a salesman of cure-all medicine.

2. From the picture of Eisenhower in the cartoon, you would expect his approach to the economic problems of the country to be
   (1) basically conservative
   (2) basically liberal
   (3) neither conservative nor liberal but middle of the road
   (4) willing to give away national resources
   (5) not interested in economic solutions to problems

3. On the basis of his behavior in the cartoon, you might expect Eisenhower to react to McCarthy's charges of Communist infiltration of the government by
   (1) avoiding the issue and making irrelevant speeches
   (2) turning his back on the issue as unimportant
   (3) joining ranks with McCarthy to discover spies
   (4) applauding McCarthy as a national hero
   (5) attacking his accusations as unfounded

Answers are on page 373.

Postwar Reform Legislation

Prereading Prompt

By the late 1940s, problems that were 100 years old had begun to demand attention. The era of Reconstruction had failed to solve the problems of African Americans and whites; in the 1940s and '50s, the issue of civil rights became paramount. Big changes lay ahead, and future presidents would have many tough decisions to make.

Key Words

Fair Deal—Truman's extension of the New Deal, Roosevelt's program
New Frontier—Kennedy's program to promote civil rights, education, and welfare
Great Society—Johnson's social program, which continued Roosevelt's, Truman's, and Kennedy's

When Harry Truman inherited the presidency from FDR, he also inherited the New Deal. Truman wanted to extend the New Deal through his **Fair Deal**. The Fair Deal programs—government controls against inflation, an increase in the minimum wage, construction of low-income housing, civil rights legislation—were aimed at protecting people's welfare. Opponents attacked the program because they believed it would create a welfare state, and most of Truman's proposals were rejected. Civil rights, however, became an issue that wouldn't go away.

All across the nation, African Americans began turning to the Constitution to demand what was rightfully theirs—the right to live and work the way other Americans did. Since 1896, when the Supreme Court upheld segregation as long as facilities were "separate but equal," African Americans had been forced to live apart from whites. But in 1954, in the historic case of *Brown v. Board of Education of Topeka*, the Supreme Court ruled that separate but equal was inherently unequal. Some partial desegregation of schools in the border states occurred after this ruling, but three years later, at the beginning of Eisenhower's second term, not one child in the Deep South was attending a desegregated school. In 1956, a federal court ordered Little Rock, Arkansas, to begin integration. Armed forces were required to keep the peace, but when the doors of Little Rock's Central High School opened in September 1957, nine African American students entered the building.

(Credit: UPI/Bettmann Newsphotos)

A key force in the civil rights movement was the Reverend Martin Luther King, Jr., who warned that there would be neither rest nor peace in America until all African Americans received full rights. He was correct. Under President Eisenhower, two Civil Rights Acts (1957 and 1960) were passed to guarantee voting rights to *all* Americans. In the 1960s, the civil rights movement heated up, and Dr. King encouraged and organized many nonviolent protests, peace marches, and demonstrations. There were numerous violent confrontations between civil rights demonstrators, police, and anti-civil-rights demonstrators. Through the initiatives of Presidents Kennedy and Johnson, two more Civil Rights Acts (1964 and 1968) were passed, banning discrimination in voting, employment, and housing.

President Kennedy, in his brief term in office before his assassination, instituted many social reforms. He started the Peace Corps, which had the offical aim of at improving life for people in underdeveloped countries. He initiated many programs to end poverty, illiteracy, and disease at home. He didn't live long enough to see most of his **New Frontier** programs become law, but his successor, Lyndon Johnson, achieved many of them in his **Great Society** reforms. The Head Start program was aimed at urban preschoolers: it was believed that putting children in an enriched early environment would give them an advantage when they started school. The Job Corps and Upward Bound programs helped underprivileged youths get jobs and go to college. Medicare (for the old) and Medicaid (for the poor) were established to improve the health and quality of life for Americans. Legislation was passed to protect consumers, and direct federal aid was given to public schools. Other serious problems, however, were tearing the Great Society apart.

Analysis: Facts versus Opinions and Hypotheses, and Distinguishing Facts from Opinions

To analyze something means to look at the relationships among its parts—for example, the different roles economic, political, and social issues played in shaping the 1960s. Some analysis items in the GED will test your understanding of how separate ideas are organized within a passage.

One type of analysis item on the GED asks you to determine which of several statements are facts and which are opinions or hypotheses. You can use several strategies to tell facts from opinions and hypotheses. Ask yourself these questions about a statement:

(1) Is this something that can be proved by measurement or observation? If so, it is a **fact**.

(2) Is this someone's personal interpretation of the way things are—a view that cannot be proved right or wrong? If so, it is an **opinion**.

(3) Is this an educated guess or a theory developed to explain certain facts? Can it be proved or disproved over time and with more information? If so, it is a **hypothesis**.

Let's see how this works in the preceding passage. In the first paragraph, you are told that some people opposed Truman's Fair Deal because they felt it would create a welfare state. Truman's opponents believed a welfare state was wrong. Is this a fact or opinion? Put the statement to the test. Can it be proved that welfare is wrong? No. Some will argue that welfare protects people, and others will argue that it encourages people to rely on the state instead of on themselves. This statement is a belief—an opinion. One clue is the word *believed*. When you see words that indicate uncertainty, such as *believe, think, hope, wish,* or *want,* the statement is probably an opinion.

Now reread this sentence from paragraph four about President Kennedy:

"He started the Peace Corps, which had the offical aim of at improving life for people in underdeveloped countries." Is this fact, opinion, or hypothesis? This statement can be proved. Kennedy did start the Peace Corps, and its official, public purpose was to improve conditions in underdeveloped countries. How well it achieved this purpose is another issue. The statement is a fact.

Reread the statement on Head Start from paragraph four that says that "it was believed that putting children in an enriched early environment would give them an advantage when they started school." Is this fact, opinion, or hypothesis? Again, put the statement to the test. At first glance it might appear to be an opinion, because of the word *believed*. But the results of Head Start can be tested. The performance of students in Head Start can be compared to students not in Head Start. From this information, it can be determined if the program is successful. Therefore, this statement is a hypothesis.

Once you can determine if something is fact, opinion, or hypothesis, you are ready to apply this skill to a passage. Try it in the Practice exercise.

Practice

Read the following paragraph and answer the question.

The incredible power of the hydrogen bomb was demonstrated on November 1, 1952, when it destroyed an entire Pacific island during its first test. Within the next ten years, H-bombs would be made that were 15 times more powerful than this one. Humankind's existence on earth suddenly faced a new and great danger. In 1963, the superpowers signed a treaty to ban testing of nuclear bombs. With this treaty, it seemed less likely that man would blow himself off the face of the earth.

Which of the following statements is an opinion?
(1) An H-bomb destroyed an island in the Pacific.
(2) In 1962, H-bombs were more powerful than in 1952.
(3) The bomb threatened humankind's existence on earth.
(4) A treaty was signed to ban H-bomb testing.
(5) The treaty made it seem less likely that man would destroy himself.

The correct answer is (5). One clue is the word *seem*. This expresses uncertainty, which often indicates an opinion. Also, the statement cannot be proved or measured, so it is not a fact. It's not a hypothesis because it doesn't explain anything. It is simply a statement of opinion. Choices (1) through (4) are all facts. Each one can be proved or measured.

Items 1 and 2 are based on the lesson.

1. Which statement below is *not* an opinion?
   (1) "Separate but equal" is an unfair policy.
   (2) Kennedy would have been a great president if he had lived.
   (3) The Peace Corps has helped people in underdeveloped countries.
   (4) It is the government's job to provide for the needs of its citizens.
   (5) Blood would have been shed if armed forces hadn't been present at Little Rock when the African American students entered the school.

2. In 1956, African American students entered Little Rock High School because
   (1) armed forces were present
   (2) local people realized they had to change with the times
   (3) the federal court ordered integration
   (4) a majority of Americans believed segregation was wrong
   (5) it was a better school than the segregated school for African Americans in Little Rock

3. Dr. Martin Luther King, Jr., was only 39 years old when he was assassinated by a white man's bullet in April 1968. Shortly before his death, Dr. King gave his famous "I have a dream" speech. He spoke of a Promised Land where African Americans and whites were equal and lived together in harmony. At one point in the speech, King said: "I may not get there [to the Promised Land] with you. . . ." The lesson would support the belief that he said this because he
   (1) had probably received death threats
   (2) was 39 years old
   (3) thought the Promised Land was only a dream
   (4) was losing faith in nonviolence
   (5) thought the Promised Land of integration would never come

Answers are on page 373.

The Later Cold War

Prereading Prompt

You may remember the 1960s. It was an exciting time in America, full of paradoxes: peace/war, love/hate, flowers/guns. It was also a time of violence: the war abroad; the unrest at home; the assassinations of a president, a presidential candidate, and a civil-rights leader. What was going on in the White House during those years?

Key Words

Bay of Pigs—the 1961 invasion of Cuba by U.S.–backed Cuban exiles
Cuban missile crisis—a military face-off between the Soviet Union and the U.S. over Soviet missile bases in Cuba
détente—a relaxing of tensions between nations, specifically the U.S., the Soviet Union, and China

When John F. Kennedy became president in 1960, U.S. relations with Cuba were already strained. President Eisenhower had placed a trade embargo on Cuba in response to Cuban leader Castro's ties with China and the Soviet Union. In January 1961, U.S. diplomatic ties with Cuba were severed. In April 1961, Cuban exiles, trained in America and using American weapons, attacked Cuba in the **Bay of Pigs** invasion. They were no match for Cuba's troops, and the mission was a failure. Kennedy was heavily criticized for this incident.

In October 1962, Kennedy had another run-in with Cuba—the **Cuban missile crisis**. During the preceding summer, the Soviet Union had established missile bases in Cuba that directly threatened the security of the United States Kennedy ordered a naval blockade of Cuba. The two superpowers were at a stand-off, and during a tense week of negotiations between Kennedy and Soviet leader Khrushchev, it seemed likely that the two powers might start a nuclear war. American ships intercepted the Soviet ships delivering missiles. In the end, the U.S. gave up some bases in Turkey, and in return Khrushchev backed down and removed the missiles.

The Cold War continued on other fronts during this time. In a program started under Eisenhower, the United States was sending noncombat military advisers to aid South Vietnam, which was fighting a Communist takeover by North Vietnam. By 1961, the number of military advisers had increased from 800 to 1,800. Kennedy gave them the go-ahead to engage in combat alongside the troops they were training. In 1964, under President Johnson, the United States began air strikes against North Vietnam, and by June 1965, 50,000 U.S. troops were actively involved in combat. Johnson eventually raised the number of U.S. troops in Vietnam to 750,000. Weekly American death tolls soared. At home, massive antiwar protests occurred, in which students joined with others to condemn U.S. involvement in what seemed to them a senseless war. In the late '60s, some observers feared that civil war would break out over this issue.

In March 1968, President Johnson ordered a stop to the bombing of North Vietnam, and also announced that he would not seek a second term as president. Richard Nixon became the nation's 37th president. He was not popular with the younger generation, but under his orders a series of troop withdrawals began. U.S. bombing of Vietnam resumed, however, in 1972–1973, and heavy fighting continued. In 1975, a massive Communist offensive finally brought down the South Vietnamese government. The United States scrambled to get its last troops out, and the war was finally over. The Communists had gained control of South Vietnam, and the United States had sacrificed the lives of over 50,000 young men.

The main achievement of the Nixon administration was establishing **détente** with Russia and China. As tensions between the superpowers eased, Nixon became the first U.S. president to visit the People's Republic of China, in 1972. The two countries agreed to work for a "normalization of relations," resulting in official U.S. recognition of Communist China and the beginning of diplomatic relations between the two countries.

Distinguishing Facts from Hypotheses in Graphics

The information in graphics can be used to suggest hypotheses. Remember that a hypothesis is a possible explanation for a set of facts. On the GED, you will be expected to look at a set of facts (data) on a graph or chart and then identify a hypothesis that might explain the data. Some of the choices will be facts—verbal restatements of the data in the graphic. Other choices will be hypotheses. Your task will be to eliminate the facts, and then choose the correct hypothesis from the remaining choices. You can see how this works in the following example. First look at the chart.

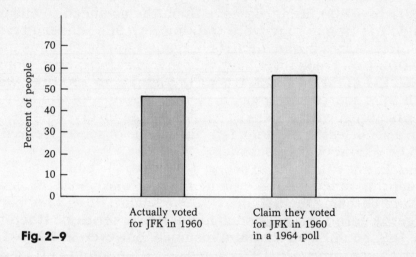

Fig. 2–9

Using the information in the chart, answer this question: Which of the following statements might best explain the information in the chart?

(1) People became confused about their opinion of JFK after the assassination.
(2) People do not always tell the truth in polls.
(3) Roughly 11 percent more people liked JFK in 1964 than in 1960.
(4) Public figures become more popular after they die.
(5) The assassination had a positive effect on people's perception of JFK's worth as a president.

To find the correct answer, first separate the facts from the hypotheses and then eliminate the facts. Choices (2) and (3) are facts and can be eliminated. Choice (1) is a hypothesis, but cannot be used to explain the information in the graph; if people were confused after Kennedy's death, their opinion of him could have changed for the worse or become mixed instead of positive. Choice (4) is a hypothesis, but it is not true. Public figures don't *always* become more popular after they die. It depends on the person and the situation. Choice (5) is correct. It is a hypothesis that could explain why JFK was more popular after his death than before.

Practice

Use the same chart to determine which of the following statements can also be a hypothesis that might explain the information.

People tend to idealize leaders who are killed in office.
Kennedy had a fairly low approval rating in 1960.
Many of Kennedy's enemies changed their minds about him.
There were more Democrats in the U.S. in 1964 than in 1960.
In 1964, almost two-thirds of the people said they had voted for JFK in 1960.

The correct choice is (1). It is often true that leaders who are killed in office become larger than life. In JFK's case, the tragedy seemed all the worse because he was a young man with a wife and small children. Time glossed over the negative memories, and the tragedy caused people to remember him as perhaps a greater president than he really was. Choices (2) and (5) are facts, not explanations, and should therefore be eliminated. There is no basis for (3) and (4).

Lesson 15 Exercises

Item 1 is based on the following table.

U.S. Deaths in Vietnam War			
Branch of Service	Number Engaged	Number of Deaths	Number of Deaths per Thousand Sent
Army	4,386,000	38,174	9 in 1,000
Navy	1,842,000	2,552	1 in 1,000
Marines	794,000	14,829	19 in 1,000
Air Force	1,740,000	2,580	1 in 1,000
Total	8,744,000	58,135	7 in 1,000

What might explain the great differences in "number of deaths per thousand sent" among the different branches of service?

It was most dangerous to be in the Marines.

More men were killed per thousand in the Army than in all branches combined.

The Navy was the least dangerous branch of service during the war.

Men in the Army and Marines were involved in more direct combat than men in the other branches of service.

The Air Force and Navy had better strategies for combat than the Army and Marines.

Item 2 is based on the following opinion poll.

A Gallup poll taken in December 1968 asked this question of 1,051 adult Americans: "Some people say that the U.S. should continue to send military supplies to South Vietnam but that we should let them take over the fighting and make all the decisions about peace and dealing with the Vietcong. Do you agree or disagree?"

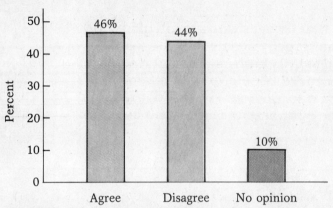

Fig. 2–10
[Source: *The New York Times*, December 18, 1968]

2. Which of the following statements would best explain the results of the poll?
   (1) A majority of Americans favored getting out of the war.
   (2) Most Americans had strong opinions about our involvement in the war.
   (3) Americans felt that the conflict in Southeast Asia was not their problem and that the U.S. had done enough for the South Vietnamese.
   (4) Americans thought North Vietnam was going to win the war so there was no point in continuing to fight.
   (5) The percentages that agreed and disagreed showed Americans were very divided about the war.

3. From the perspective of the U.S., the Vietnam War was
   (1) completely successful
   (2) moderately successful
   (3) slightly successful
   (4) moderately unsuccessful
   (5) totally unsuccessful

Answers are on page 373–374.

Carter and Reagan

Prereading Prompt

During the 1970s, the United States celebrated its 200th birthday. On July 4, 1776, the colonies ended a war and became an independent nation. Two hundred years later, in 1976, America was fighting different kinds of battles. Do you know what they were?

Key Words

recession—a moderate and temporary decline in economic activity characterized by low wages and limited production. It is similar to, but less serious than, a depression.

contras—the anti-Marxist forces that fought to overthrow the Marxist government of Nicaragua

START—Strategic Arms Reduction Talks between the U.S. and Soviet Union aimed at nuclear disarmament

In 1973, after his cover-up of a White House–planned burglary (the Watergate break-in) and other illegal operations, Nixon was driven from office, the first American president forced to resign. In 1976, disillusioned with the Republicans and Gerald Ford's brief administration, Americans elected Democrat Jimmy Carter. On Inauguration Day 1977, they watched the down-to-earth Carters walk the streets of Washington. It seemed that honesty and decency had returned to the White House. Carter, however, soon lost his popularity.

At home, Carter was blamed for the staggering inflation of the late 1970s, although the problem had been brewing for some time. High interest rates made it hard to borrow money; businesses couldn't expand, and consumers had little buying power. With the economy so weak, unemployment stayed high. Carter was unable to get his reform programs passed—among them a tax-reform bill—and he couldn't win the support of the nation.

Carter was more successful at foreign affairs. He was instrumental in bringing the leaders of Egypt and Israel together to talk about peace for their war-torn part of the world. Also during his administration, control of the Panama Canal was passed to Panama by a treaty to become fully effective in 1999. One issue of foreign diplomacy, however, became a symbol of his weakness as a president. In 1979, factions that had overthrown the Shah of Iran seized the American Embassy in Teheran and held 52 Americans hostage for more than a year. In a bungled military attempt to free the hostages, eight American servicemen died in the Iranian desert. Carter's popularity sank even lower. It is a bitter irony that the release of the hostages was finally announced by Ronald Reagan at his inauguration. Carter had worked hard to negotiate their release, but Reagan got credit for it.

The Reagan administration dealt with widespread unemployment and an economic **recession** by enormously increasing defense spending, while at the same time cutting taxes. As a result, the federal budget deficit doubled, and then tripled. And while the tax breaks lowered income taxes, many people faced higher local and state taxes to pay for local and state programs. Nevertheless, Reagan was extremely popular and was credited with economic reforms that eased inflation and eventually reduced unemployment.

In foreign policy, the major thrust of the Reagan administration was fighting communism. In 1983, the Organization of Eastern Caribbean States requested U.S. assistance in restoring order to the island of Grenada, where one Marxist group had overthrown another Marxist government. There were roughly 1,000 U.S. citizens on the island, many of them medical students. The United States succeeded in evacuating its citizens and deposing the Marxists. While members of the UN condemned the action, Reagan was given credit for protecting U.S. citizens and ousting the Marxists.

Under Reagan the United States also intervened in the ongoing civil war in Nicaragua between the Marxist Sandinista government and the antigovernment rebels, the **Contras**. The United States gave support to the Contras, but Congress ultimately cut off military aid because many Contras belonged to the dictatorship that had been overthrown by the Sandinistas. Secret and illegal efforts to supply arms to the Contras by members of Reagan's staff was exposed in the *Iran-Contra scandal*, which threatened to topple his presidency. At the end of Reagan's eight years, neither side had won. It wasn't until 1990, under President Bush, that the war ended and free elections resulted in a non-Marxist government.

Reagan also made headway in arms reduction with the Soviet Union. To help his near-bankrupt economy, Soviet leader Gorbachev wanted to reduce his enormous military budget, and was agreeable to drastic cuts in Soviet atomic weapons. The two superpowers engaged in Strategic Arms Reduction Talks (**START**). They signed a treaty that eliminated some ballistic missiles and also allowed for on-site inspection of missile-production facilities. Reagan shared the praise received for bringing the world one step closer to security and peace.

Identifying Unstated Assumptions in Passages

An assumption is an idea you take for granted. Suppose you hear on the evening news that a resident of a nearby town has been found to be an ex-Nazi. The unstated assumption of the reporter is that the man is guilty of all kinds of atrocities. Your reaction to the story will be based on this assumption, whether correct or not.

Authors too make unstated assumptions, and it's important to be able to recognize these. Otherwise you might think that what you're reading is fact, when it may be that the writer is trying to persuade you to share an opinion.

There are unstated assumptions in the lesson on Carter and Reagan. Can you spot them? Keeping in mind that unstated assumptions are not given in the text, see if you can answer this question:

An unstated assumption in the passage is that President Carter
(1) was weak in his domestic policy
(2) had foreign-policy problems that were easier to solve than his domestic problems
(3) was decent and honest but did not have some necessary qualifications of a good leader
(4) had trouble getting his programs passed because they were not what the nation needed
(5) was hurt politically because he was from the deep South

The correct answer is (3). The lesson states that Carter was honest and decent, generally well liked, but an ineffective president. There is much more to being a good leader than being honest and decent. Apart from the necessary qualities, it is important for the country to be behind its leader. This was not the case with Carter. Of the remaining choices, (1) is a restatement of a fact in the passage, so it is not an unstated assumption and therefore is incorrect. Choice (4) is an opinion. There is no basis in the passage for selecting (2) and (5).

Now try to find the unstated assumption in the Practice exercise.

Practice

Which statement below is an unstated assumption in the passage about President Reagan?

(1) Reagan was a "Teflon" president, getting credit for things he didn't do and not being blamed for things he did.

(2) Reagan was popular because his tax policies were so different from Carter's.

(3) Reagan had a good relationship with Congress and was therefore able to get his programs passed.

(4) Reagan resembled Franklin Roosevelt in the way he used government spending to bring the country out of a recession.

(5) If not for Reagan, START would not have been possible.

Did you spot the unstated assumption? It was (1). Reagan had a reputation for being a "Teflon" president—someone things didn't stick to. When things went wrong, he was not held to blame. When things went right, even if he was not instrumental in causing them, he was applauded by the public. Reagan was able to lead because he was good at getting people to believe in him. Whatever his other strengths and failings, this was his main gift as a leader. There is nothing in the passage to support (2) and (3). The passage states that Reagan used huge defense spending (and tax cuts) to bring the country out of recession; Roosevelt greatly increased spending for welfare programs in the Great Depression (and raised taxes). There is therefore no underlying assumption that Reagan's spending resembled Roosevelt's, so (4) is wrong. (5) is not accurate, because both Reagan and Gorbachev were responsible for START.

Lesson 16 Exercises

1. The best general statement about Reagan's policies would be that they
   (1) had good effects on domestic policy and bad effects on foreign policy
   (2) had bad effects on domestic policy and good effects on foreign policy
   (3) had good and bad effects on domestic and foreign policy
   (4) gave an illusion of being more effective than they were
   (5) had basically no effect on either domestic or foreign policy

2. Compared to his foreign policy in other matters, Carter's handling of the Iranian hostage crisis was
   (1) as ineffective as his other policies
   (2) more ineffective than his other policies

(3) more effective than his other policies

(4) typical of his military decisions in foreign policy

(5) the opposite of his policies toward Egypt and Israel

Item 3 is based on the following chart.

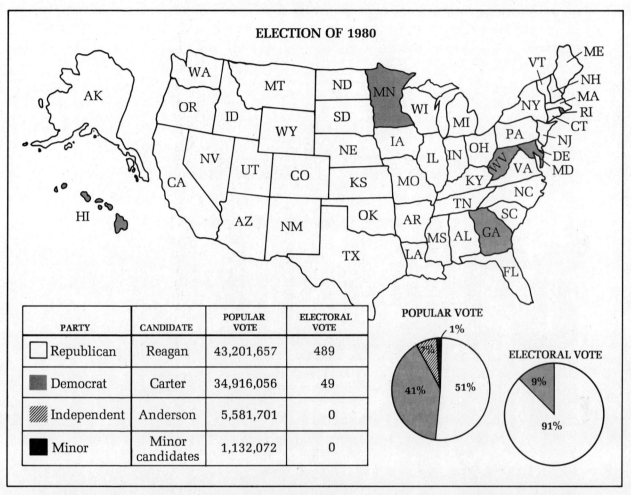

ELECTION OF 1980

PARTY	CANDIDATE	POPULAR VOTE	ELECTORAL VOTE
Republican	Reagan	43,201,657	489
Democrat	Carter	34,916,056	49
Independent	Anderson	5,581,701	0
Minor	Minor candidates	1,132,072	0

POPULAR VOTE

1% — 51% — 41%

ELECTORAL VOTE

9% — 91%

Fig. 2–11 Results of the 1980 U.S. presidential election. From Teacher's Resource Handbook. *The United States: A History of the Republic*, 2nd ed. (Englewood Cliffs, N.J.: Prentice-Hall, 1984), page 288. Used with permission.

3. Sometimes a candidate's chances of winning can be hurt by losing the votes that go to non-major-party candidates. Which statement accurately reflects what would have happened in 1980 if Anderson and other minor candidates hadn't run?

(1) Carter would have won by a small margin.

(2) Carter would have easily overtaken Reagan.

(3) The race would have been too close to call.

(4) Reagan would have won anyway, but not by much.

(5) Reagan would have won by a landslide.

Answers are on page 374.

CHAPTER 3

What is political science? It is the study of politics—the art and science of government. It is about the systems of rules people live by, the structures of the governments that keep order in society. When you hear a news commentary on an election, its content is political science. When you read an article about the new openness in the Soviet Union, you are reading about political science.

Brandenberg Gate, Berlin Wall (Credit: Presse-und Informationsamt der Bundesregierung)

Prereading Prompt

Government may seem abstract to you, but in fact all governments are made by people. Government is changeable. It is different from country to country and even within the same country. Sometimes change comes the hard way—through revolutions and coups—proving that governments are man-made structures, not abstract concepts.

Political Science

What Is Political Science?

Political science is about the political structure of society—**government**. Government refers to the way laws are made and executed in a society. **Laws** are supposed to provide security, order, and hopefully justice. Do they always? The study of political science will tell you that they do not. Throughout history many governments have provided far less than just and humane societies. Many still exist today. The 1990s promise to be very exciting for political scientists. Around the world, people are fighting for their freedom, and governments that have restricted freedom are falling left and right. The changes are so drastic and are happening so quickly that they are difficult to comprehend. Who would have thought a few years ago that we would watch the Berlin Wall crumble, and East and West Germany reunite? Who could have predicted that countries in the Communist bloc in Eastern Europe would hold free elections? And who foresaw the end of the Cold War between the United States and the Soviet Union? For those who grew up with air-raid drills and the constant threat of nuclear war, this new world is difficult to imagine.

There are many kinds of governments in the world. Certainly the one you are most familiar with is democracy. Without reading a sentence of political science, you already know a lot about how the United States government functions. If you are a conscientious citizen, you vote in local and federal elections. You elect people to represent you in government who have similar ideas to yours and who will fight for the issues you believe in. If your candidate doesn't win, you still can make yourself heard by writing letters to the people who are in office, by protesting peacefully, and by writing letters and articles in newspapers or magazines. In this country, you have the freedom to do these things.

Key Words

political science—the study of the various types of government and how they function

government—the political structure of a society

laws—the rules that govern a society and how it functions

You pay a price for your freedom, of course, for every freedom and right has a responsibility. Many of your responsibilities in a democracy fall under the general heading of paying taxes. Federal, state, and local taxes pay for many of the things you have come to expect from the government. Unemployment insurance, federal and state highways, national defense, public transportation, public parks, social security, the court system are all paid for with tax money. Taxes are the price you pay for living in a democracy.

Studying political science will tell you about other forms of government. You may either come to value democracy more after you survey the other types of government, or you may decide that another type of government is better. Either way, political science will help you make sense of this fast-changing world.

Types of Government

Prereading Prompt

Many of us in America never stop to think about our way of life. Yet there are many people throughout the world who would literally die to have a small portion of the rights and freedom we so often take for granted. How is our type of government different from others? Find out in this chapter.

Key Words

totalitarianism—government run by one party or person (dictator); almost no individual freedom; everything sacrificed to the goals of the state
republic—a representative democracy with no king or queen
federation—a unified group of states or countries governed by one central system

Governments are more different in theory than in reality. When you learn about types of government, you usually learn about them in their ideal state. This is partly because different countries practice the same type of government in different ways. It is also because government in practice operates much differently from government in theory.

One of the oldest types of government is the **monarchy**. In an *absolute monarchy*, the monarch has total, unrestricted power over the country. In a *constitutional monarchy*, the monarch's power is limited by a system of laws. This is the case in Great Britain, where the queen is actually a symbolic monarch.

The actual governing body of Great Britain is a **parliamentary democracy**. Its chief executive, the prime minister, is selected by the party that wins the election. This party has the most elected representatives in Parliament, the legislature that governs the country. The prime minister is selected by his party; he is not elected separately, as the U.S. president and vice-president are.

Like Britain, the United States is a **representative democracy**. Its national legislature of elected representatives is the Congress. (You might look back at Lesson 3 in American History for details about this system.) As you know, the ideal in a democracy is that all the people make all the decisions— the will of the majority becomes law. In a large country, however, it isn't possible for every person to vote on every issue. To solve this problem, we hold local, state, and national elections to elect people to represent us and our interests in government.

The opposite of democracy is **totalitarianism**. This form of government permits little or no individual freedom. The centralized state controls all facets of life—business and labor, religion, newspapers, TV and movies, science, the arts, the courts, the police, and the army. Totalitarian governments usually are controlled by one person, called a dictator. This form of government is also called a dictatorship. Often this type of government has an aggressive foreign policy. This was true of fascist Germany under Hitler, which sought to take over the world for the "master race." Other dictatorships are not so openly racist or imperialistic, yet they still exist for one purpose: to completely control the people of the nation. This was true of the Marcos regime in the Philippines and the old Duvalier regime in Haiti.

The term **republic** is often used as a reference to a form of government. A republic is any political system that is a representative democracy and has no monarch. Power in a republic is based on the citizens entitled to vote and the representatives they elect to govern the nation. In the U.S. pledge of allegiance, the United States is referred to as a republic, "and to the republic, for which it [the flag] stands. . . ." Once the United States declared its independence, it was no longer ruled by a monarch; it was a republic.

Another term you may have heard is **federation.** This is a union of states under one central government, in which the states give certain powers to a central government and keep others for themselves. The Soviet Union is in theory a federation; however, until recently, all power really was concentrated in a dictator who was head of a totalitarian central government. The United States is also a kind of federation. During the Civil War, the states that broke away from the Union were called "the Confederacy." The Confederacy was itself a federation, a union of states under a central government.

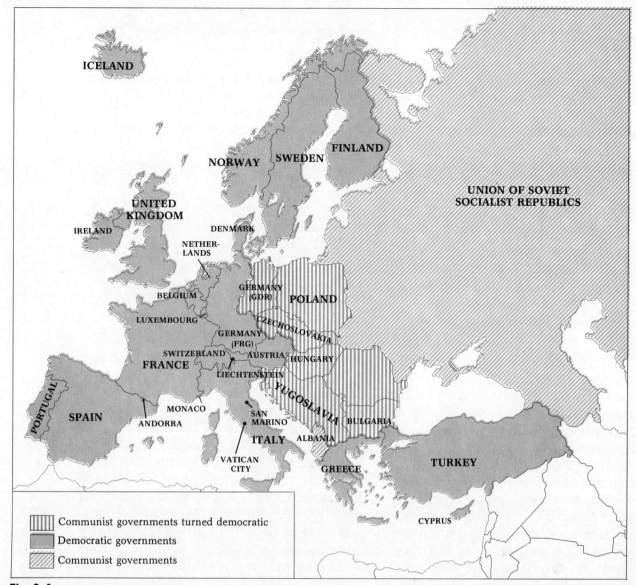

ICELAND

NORWAY SWEDEN FINLAND

UNION OF SOVIET
SOCIALIST REPUBLICS

UNITED
KINGDOM

IRELAND DENMARK

NETHER-
LANDS

BELGIUM GERMANY POLAND
(GDR)

LUXEMBOURG CZECHOSLOVAKIA

GERMANY
(FRG)

SWITZERLAND AUSTRIA HUNGARY

FRANCE LIECHTENSTEIN

YUGOSLAVIA

PORTUGAL

MONACO SAN BULGARIA
MARINO

SPAIN ANDORRA

ITALY ALBANIA

VATICAN
CITY

GREECE TURKEY

CYPRUS

Communist governments turned democratic

Democratic governments

Communist governments

Fig. 3–1

Identifying Unstated Assumptions in Graphics

You already know how to identify unstated assumptions in a passage. Now you have to transfer this knowledge to graphic material. When looking at a map or political cartoon, ask yourself this question: What is the unstated, underlying belief I am being asked to accept? Be sure not to confuse the unstated assumption with given facts, opinions, or hypotheses.

Look at the map on page 127. After studying the map, answer this question:

Which of the following is an unstated assumption of the map?
(1) The smallest communist nation shown is Albania.
(2) The Soviet Union is less communist than Poland or Hungary.
(3) More people prefer to be free than to have their freedom restricted.
(4) The world trend is for communist governments to become democratic.
(5) The size of the Soviet Union made it become communist.

Were you able to spot the unstated assumption? It is (3). The map shows that seven governments have recently gone from being totalitarian to being democratic. None is shown as having gone the other way. On the map only two nations—the Soviet Union and Albania—are totalitarian; all the others have democratic governments. The unstated assumption therefore is that more people prefer to live under democratic systems of government. (1) is a fact, not an unstated assumption. (2) is an opinion, unsupported by information on the map. The opinion is also not true. The Soviet Union in the late 1980s was undergoing a process of democratization, but is still controlled by a one-party Communist government, while Poland and Hungary are not. (4) is wrong because the map shows only part of the world. (5) cannot be the unstated assumption of the map because Albania is the other totalitarian country shown and is very small, so size cannot have made Russia turn totalitarian.

Practice

The following item is based on the cartoon in Figure 3–2.

Fig. 3–2

The cartoonist's unstated assumption about Nazi war criminals is that they

(1) should have no civil rights
(2) are often concerned with social issues
(3) have divided minds on social issues
(4) see themselves as victims of society
(5) are less important than social issues

(5) is the correct answer. The cartoon shows a person thinking about the issue of Nazi war criminals with one half of his brain, and thinking about social issues such as civil rights with the other half. The issue of war criminals is the only one under the heading "Things That Matter," while all the social issues are under the heading "Things That Don't Matter." The main idea of the cartoon is that it is ridiculous to think one issue is more important than nine other important issues. The joke of the cartoon is based on the unstated assumption that these social issues are more important than the issue of Nazi war criminals.

Remember it is important to identify the details of a cartoon accurately. (2) and (3) are based on the mistake of identifying the man in the cartoon as a Nazi war criminal. He is not; he is only thinking with half his brain about war criminals. (1) is wrong because the cartoon does not suggest Nazi war criminals should have no civil rights, but that rights are more important as an issue than they are. Nothing in the cartoon suggests (4).

Lesson 1 Exercises

Item 1 is based on the cartoon in Figure 3-3.

"Don't Mind Me—Just Go Right On Talking"

Fig. 3–3 "Don't mind me—just go right on talking"
——from *The Herblock Book* (Beacon Press, 1952)

1. The unstated assumption of the cartoon is that the atomic bomb
   (1) is being controlled by world leaders
   (2) keeps increasing in size
   (3) disturbs the meetings held by world leaders
   (4) will leave all but the North Pole uninhabitable
   (5) is beyond human control

Item 2 is based on the cartoon in Figure 3-4.

Fig. 3—4   (Credit: New York Public Library Picture Collection)

2. **An unstated assumption of this cartoon is that America**
   (1) is a friend to all immigrants
   (2) should accept no more immigrants
   (3) is being exploited by immigrants
   (4) is being undermined by war and famine
   (5) is an enemy of tyranny

3. **Which statement below is an unstated assumption of this lesson?**
   (1) Dictatorships always have the same characteristics.
   (2) Democracy is the most humane form of government.
   (3) A constitutional monarchy is basically a republic.
   (4) Parliamentary democracy is the best kind of representative democracy.
   (5) The governments of the U.S. and Soviet Union are similar because they are both federations.

Answers are on page 374.

The Constitution

Prereading Prompt

Government is changeable and adaptable, but the document that outlines the structure of the U.S. government has survived for over 200 years. Do you know how that structure has enabled this country to thrive for two centuries? Test yourself in the next lesson.

Key Words

Constitution—the document that details the structure and powers of the U.S. federal government
executive branch—the administrative branch of the U.S. federal government, consisting of the president and his administrative departments
legislative branch—the law-making body of U.S. federal government, the Congress
judicial branch—the Supreme Court of the U.S.

The U.S. **Constitution** is the supreme law of the land. No other laws—local, state, or federal—may conflict with it. The Constitution is limiting in that it grants government certain powers, and those are the only powers government has. Government actions that don't fall within the limits set by the Constitution are deemed *unconstitutional*. When the Supreme Court rules something to be unconstitutional, the action in question violates the limits set by the Constitution.

The limitation of powers by the Constitution is accomplished in three ways: (1) a separation of powers that defines three branches of government and their distinct authority and controls; (2) a system of checks and balances that allows each branch of government to oversee the others; (3) a federal system that divides the governing power between the federal government and the states. These three provisions act as a brake on the activities of the branches of government, making it almost impossible for one branch to gain control.

Each of the three branches of government has different responsibilities. These are listed in the chart below. The overall job of the **executive branch**, which consists of the president and his administrative departments, is to put the country's laws into effect. The president's *Cabinet* consists of all the heads of these departments, for example, the Secretary of State and the Secretary of Human Resources. The **legislative branch**, or Congress, is the law-making body of government. It consists of the Senate and the House of Representatives. Each state sends to Congress two senators, and also representatives, whose number is determined by the state's population. The **judicial branch**, which consists of the U.S. Supreme Court, sees to it that laws conform to the Constitution. The system set forth in the Constitution works well; it has governed this country successfully for over 200 years.

The System of Checks and Balances		
President	Congress	Supreme Court
Powers	Powers	Powers
1. Enforces laws. 2. Can veto bills. 3. Appoints judges and other officials. 4. Conducts foreign policy. 5. Commander in Chief of Armed Forces.	1. Make laws. 2. Can override a president's veto. 3. Can impeach president. 4. Approves president's appointments of judges and other officials. 5. Approves treaties. 6. Declares war.	1. Interprets laws. 2. Can declare laws unconstitutional.
Controls	Controls	Controls
1. Can be removed by Congress (impeached). 2. Congress can override veto. 3. Appointments must be approved by Congress. 4. Treaties must be approved by Congress.	1. President can veto a bill passed by Congress. 2. Laws passed by Congress can be declared unconstitutional by Supreme Court.	1. Judges appointed for life by president. 2. Appointments must be approved by Congress. 3. Judges can be removed by Congress for improper behavior.

Distinguishing Conclusions from Supporting Details in Passages

How can you tell the difference between a conclusion and a supporting detail in a passage? A *conclusion* is a final statement that summarizes the main idea. It gives the decision or opinion reached by the author. The conclusion is often based on several supporting details or facts. For example, if the number of car accidents and arrests for drunk driving goes down after the drinking age is raised, a logical conclusion is that raising the drinking age creates safer highways.

It will help you answer questions on the GED if you can tell the difference between conclusions and supporting details. To figure out which is which, ask yourself this question: is this one of several ideas the writer included to make his or her case, or is it the case itself—the main reason for presenting the information?

Look at the second paragraph in the preceding passage. It discusses the structure of the U.S. government. Some of the statements are supporting details and one is a conclusion. Can you tell which is which? See if you can answer the following questions:

The conclusion of the paragraph is that
(1) the Constitution sets limits on the branches of government
(2) the separation of powers defines the three branches of government and their functions
(3) the system of checks and balances gives each branch some power over the others
(4) the Constitution assigns some powers to the states and some to the federal government
(5) the Constitution is designed to prevent any branch of government from becoming too powerful

The correct choice is (5). It restates the last sentence, which summarizes the main idea of the paragraph. Choices (1) through (4) are details that support the conclusion in (5). Because (5) states the *purpose*, or reason, for all the limits on government power that (1) through (4) describe, it is the conclusion.

Often, the conclusion of a paragraph or passage can be found at the end. The preceding statements lead up to the conclusion. Sometimes, however, the conclusion may not be stated clearly, or may be found elsewhere. Don't automatically assume that a statement near the end of a passage is the conclusion. Always put it to the test.

Supreme Court Building (Credit: Photo by Horydczak)

Practice

The Practice item is based on the following passage.

Some residents of Salt Lake City have tried to sue the government. They claim that they got cancer as a result of government nuclear-weapons tests in the 1950s. Many Vietnam veterans have also tried to sue the government; they believe that a host of maladies they have contracted are directly related to Agent Orange, a chemical many of them came into contact with during the war. Nevertheless, in New York, courts have upheld that dangerous and harmful military activities are protected against lawsuits. They ruled that even if injuries are a result of government misjudgment, the government cannot be sued without its consent.

The conclusion of the passage is that
- (1) military activities have provoked federal lawsuits
- (2) the government cannot be sued without its consent
- (3) the government takes no responsibility for nuclear-weapons tests or chemicals used during warfare
- (4) individual citizens have lost court battles in trying to sue the government
- (5) the government should be more careful about the dangerous chemicals to which it exposes its citizens

Choice (2) is correct; it is the conclusion to which all the other statements are leading. Choices (1) and (4) describe what happened in the two lawsuits discussed, not why they failed, which is the purpose or reason they are discussed—to show that even in extreme cases "the government cannot be sued without its consent." This does not mean that the government is completely irresponsible about the use of chemicals and nuclear-weapons tests, so (3) is incorrect. (5) is an opinion you might have after reading this paragraph, but it is not its conclusion, which is about lawsuits against the federal government.

Item 1 is based on the following passage.

If you're planning to drive in a foreign country this summer, you should be aware that different governments have different auto-insurance requirements. Canada will accept a U.S. auto-insurance policy, but you will need a card from your insurer guaranteeing that it will meet Canadian requirements in case of an accident. Mexico, on the other hand, will not accept a U.S. policy. Travelers to this country must buy a short-term tourist policy. Since different governments have different requirements, it's a good idea to find out before you travel what a particular country's requirements are.

1. The conclusion of the passage is that U.S. travelers will find that
   (1) some countries place unreasonable restrictions on travelers
   (2) Canada accepts U.S. policies because their government is so similar to ours
   (3) they can buy short-term car insurance in Mexico
   (4) they will face similar car-insurance problems in Canada and Mexico
   (5) they should find out about car insurance before they leave on their trip

2. According to this lesson, the Constitution has worked for 200 years because
   (1) it has stood the test of time
   (2) it sets limits on the power of all the branches of government
   (3) the Supreme Court will declare a law unconstitutional if it does not conform to the Constitution
   (4) no branch of the federal government has any power over another branch
   (5) the federal system divides powers between the federal government and the states

Item 3 refers to the chart on page 133.

3. An unstated assumption of the chart is that
   (1) Congress has more power than the other two branches
   (2) the Supreme Court should have more power than it does
   (3) every power in each branch is controlled by one of the other branches
   (4) the purpose of a good government is to keep any part from gaining too much power
   (5) the system of checks and balances works well

Answers are on page 375.

Amendments to the Constitution

Prereading Prompt

How has the Constitution remained workable for so long? The answer is that it is a flexible document, often called a "living" Constitution. Find out why in this lesson.

Key Words

amendments—additions to the original Constitution
ratify—approve officially and legally
Bill of Rights—the first ten amendments, part of the original Constitution, that protect the rights of individuals

Without changing the overall structure of government, the Constitution can be changed to reflect important changes in society. Changes to the Constitution are called **amendments**, which are made through an amendment process outlined in the original Constitution. There are two steps in this process: (1) an amendment is proposed by two-thirds of both houses of Congress or by a national convention requested by two-thirds of the states; (2) three-fourths of the states must **ratify**, or approve, the amendment. When this process is complete, the Constitution is changed.

To date, thousands of amendments have been proposed, but only 26 have been ratified. The first ten are known collectively as the **Bill of Rights.** They were part of the original Constitution, added by the Founding Fathers to protect the rights of individuals from a strong central government. The chart on page 139 shows exactly what rights are protected by the Bill of Rights.

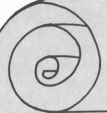

BILL OF RIGHTS

I. Guarantees freedom of religion, speech, and the press; guarantees the right of people to assemble peaceably and to petition the government

II. Protects the right of people to have weapons and form an emergency military service

III. Prohibits the government from housing soldiers in private homes without the homeowners' permission

IV. Prohibits the government from searching or seizing property without a warrant

V. Prohibits the taking of life, liberty, or property without due process of law; requires compensation if private property is taken for public use; guarantees the right of an individual to remain silent if accused of a crime; prohibits being tried twice for the same crime

VI. Guarantees an individual accused of a crime a speedy and fair trial; guarantees the right to legal counsel

VII. Protects the right to a trial by jury

VIII. Prohibits excessive bail and fines; prohibits cruel and unusual punishment

IX. Guarantees that rights listed in the Constitution must not interfere with other individual rights not listed in the Constitution

X. Grants all powers that are not specifically denied in the Constitution to the States and to individuals

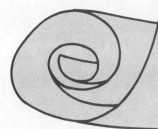

You have already learned about some of the remaining 16 amendments. In 1865, the 13th Amendment prohibited slavery. In 1870, the 15th Amendment was passed to protect the right of African Americans to vote. In 1920, women were guaranteed the right to vote by the 19th Amendment. In 1971, the 26th Amendment lowered the voting age to 18. Other amendments have given Congress the right to collect income taxes; limited the president to no more than two terms in office; prohibited alcohol; and repealed (took away) the prohibition of alcohol.

Distinguishing Conclusions from Supporting Details in Graphics

You already know how to distinguish between the conclusion and details in a passage. Now you have to apply this skill to graphic material. Remember that supporting details are the pieces of evidence a writer uses to support the main idea. The conclusion is the overall idea the writer wants to leave you with. It expresses his or her basic judgment on the information presented.

In graphics, the information and facts given in the chart or map are the supporting details. From this information you draw a conclusion. Hints as to what the conclusion is can occasionally be found in the title. For example, you might find a chart entitled "Amendments to the Living Constitution." The chart lists all 26 amendments, the dates they were ratified, and what each provides for. The amendments, and information about what they provide for, are supporting details. The conclusion might be that the Constitution can change in response to the needs of society.

Look at the Bill of Rights on page 139. It lists each of the first ten amendments to the Constitution. Read them and then answer the following question:

Which statement best represents the conclusion of the chart?
(1) There are ten amendments in the Bill of Rights.
(2) The Bill of Rights were designed to protect the rights of individuals from a strong central government.
(3) The Bill of Rights protects the freedoms of speech, religion, and the press.
(4) Some amendments were a direct result of government infringement on people's rights during the Revolution.
(5) The right to a fair trial is protected by the Bill of Rights.

The correct answer is (2). It states the overall idea of the chart, which is that *all* of these amendments were specifically designed so that people's rights would not be taken away by a strong federal government. Choices (1), (3), and (5) are supporting details—facts taken directly from the chart. While there is some truth to (4), the information in the chart gives you no reason to select this answer.

Practice

The Practice item is based on the following graph.

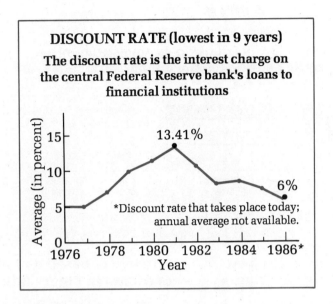

DISCOUNT RATE (lowest in 9 years)

The discount rate is the interest charge on the central Federal Reserve bank's loans to financial institutions

13.41%

6%

*Discount rate that takes place today; annual average not available.

The best conclusion from the information given in the graph is that the discount rate
(1) declined most rapidly from 1981 to 1983
(2) rose steadily from 1977 to 1981
(3) declined steadily from 1981 to 1986
(4) changed more gradually after 1983
(5) was the lowest in 1986 that it had been in nine years

Choice (5) is the correct answer. Here, the conclusion is given in the title of the chart: the discount rate in 1986 was the lowest it had been in nine years. Even if you didn't notice the name of the chart (you should always make a point of reading the names of maps and charts—they can contain important information), you could still choose this statement as the conclusion. Choices (1) through (4) are all supporting details. They describe parts of the overall pattern of rise and decline; the purpose of showing this pattern is the conclusion stated in (5).

Item 1 is based on the following graph.

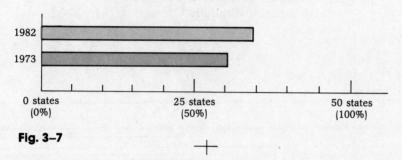

**Ratification History of Equal Rights Ammendment
(75% needed for ratification)**

Fig. 3–7

1. On the basis of the chart, the best conclusion about the Equal Rights Amendment is that
    (1) 30 states had it by 1973
    (2) 35 states had ratified it by 1982
    (3) it has not been added to the Constitution because it has not been ratified by 75 percent of the states
    (4) it was ratified and added to the Constitution in 1982
    (5) by 1993, enough states will have ratified it to make it the 27th amendment to the Constitution

Item 2 is based on the chart of the Bill of Rights in Figure 3-5.

2. Which statement below is an unstated assumption of the Bill of Rights?
    (1) People should have the right to defend themselves.
    (2) A fair and speedy trial is a right that must be protected.
    (3) Government should use its powers to protect the rights of its citizens.
    (4) Individual citizens must be protected by law against government power.
    (5) Governments may inflict cruel and unusual punishment on their citizens unless prevented by law.

Item 3 is based on the following chart.

Categories of Amendments (not including Bill of Rights)			
Voting rights/ Elections	Prohibitions	Citizenship	Other
XII, XV, XVII, XIX, XXII, XXIII, XXIV, XXVI	XIII, XVIII, XXI	XIV	XI, XX, XXV, XXVI

3. Which statement below is a conclusion of this chart?
   (1) The amendments about voting rights and elections cover the amendments in "Citizenship" and "Other."
   (2) The amendments about voting rights and elections cover the most important democratic rights.
   (3) The citizenship amendment is the least important.
   (4) The three amendments regarding prohibitions—of slavery, liquor, and repealing the prohibition of liquor—are less important than those in "Other."
   (5) The "Other" amendments are the last amendments that have been passed.

Answers are on page 375.

The Federal System– National, State, and Local Government

Prereading Prompt

You learned earlier that many compromises were made at the Constitutional Convention. One result of these was the creation of a system in which power is shared by the federal and state governments. How were these powers divided? Read this lesson to find out.

Key Words

federal powers—powers specifically granted to the federal government by the Constitution

residual powers—powers not granted to the federal government and not denied to the states; state powers

concurrent powers—powers shared by the states and the federal government

The Constitution gave certain powers to the federal government and denied them to the states. These are called **federal powers**. Powers not specifically given to the federal government nor specifically denied to the states are called **residual powers**—powers that remain with the states. Some powers are shared by both the federal and the state governments; these are called **concurrent powers**. The chart below lists which powers lie with which government.

The Division of Powers under the Federal System		
Federal powers	Residual powers	Concurrent powers
• Coin money; regulate value of money • Regulate interstate commerce • Regulate foreign commerce • Establish post offices and post roads • Grant patents and copyrights • Declare war • Raise and support an army • Control the seat of government • Control all federal property	• Regulate intrastate commerce • Establish local police forces • Regulate marriages • Provide education	• Levy and collect taxes • Borrow money • Build roads • Set up court systems • Provide social welfare

Besides specifying what powers are granted, the Constitution specifies what powers are denied. The federal government may not favor one state at the expense of another, grant titles of nobility, or interfere with the civil liberties of the people. The state governments may not coin money, enter into foreign treaties, levy taxes without permission of Congress, engage in war, maintain troops during peacetime, or interfere with the civil liberties of the people.

The Constitution also provides for a system of justice, known as the federal court system. Cases tried by the federal courts are those that concern violations of federal laws and treaties; are interstate in nature (that is, involve two or more states); involve representatives of foreign countries; or question the constitutionality of federal and state laws. The average crime or illegal action committed by a citizen, such as burglary or rape, is handled by state and municipal courts, not the federal courts. The lowest level of the federal courts is the *District Courts*. They are the first to hear and try cases. If the judgment of a District Court is challenged, the case moves up to a *Circuit Court of Appeals*, where a new trial determines whether justice was served by the District Court. Above the Circuit Courts is the *Supreme Court*, the highest judicial authority in the United States, and its decisions are final. The Supreme Court consists of nine justices and rules by majority. The primary responsibility of the Supreme Court is to decide whether laws and actions are in accord with the Constitution, the supreme law of the land.

How is all this government business paid for? Taxes. Depending on how much money you make, you may pay as much as 33 percent of your income to run the government. You pay federal, state, and local taxes on all money you earn. Federal money is used to fund federal projects: national defense, social programs, interstate highways, federal prisons, and national parks.

State money is used for state programs: state police, state highways, state parks, and state government. Local taxes pay for city services: garbage collection, police, fire and first-aid units, town parks, snow removal, and so on. In most states, you also pay a sales tax on many of the items you buy. If you own a home or land, you also pay property taxes, some of which goes to your local government and some to the state.

Identifying Cause-and-Effect Relationships in Passages

You may be familiar with the law of cause-and-effect. For example, if ten inches of rain fall in three hours, the river overflows and floods the area. Cause and effect—it rained ten inches in three hours (cause), and the river overflowed (effect).

It will help you answer questions on the GED if you can identify cause-and-effect relationships. One clue that you are reading a cause-and-effect relationship is the presence of certain words and phrases: *therefore, because, since, as a result, consequently, if . . . then.*

In reality, a cause must come before an effect. It rains, so you get wet. You hit the light switch, and the light comes on. In writing, however, the cause is sometimes placed after the effect. Take the example about the rain and the flood. In the sentence "The river overflowed because ten inches of rain fell in three hours," the cause still occurs before the effect, but the effect is written before the cause in the sentence. Try to identify the correct cause-and-effect relationship in the following question.

If your town needs more money to give teachers a raise and improve the condition of its schools,

(1) the mayor writes to the Senate for more money
(2) an amendment to the Constitution is made
(3) your property taxes go up
(4) the schools hold a fund-raising bake sale
(5) your federal income tax goes up

The correct answer is (3). The passage states that money for local government comes primarily from local taxes, largely in the form of property taxes. The cause is: your town needs more money. The effect is: your property taxes go up. You should be able to put the cause and effect together in one sentence that makes sense: "Your town needs more money, so your property taxes go up." (1) is incorrect because a municipality would not write to the Senate for money. (2) is incorrect because an amendment to the Constitution would not be made to solve local problems. A bake sale wouldn't raise enough money and is not dealt with in the passage, so (4) is incorrect. (5) is incorrect because federal income taxes are not used directly for municipal projects.

Practice

The Practice item is based on the following paragraph.

For many years, women in the United States struggled to win the right to vote. Often the women fighting for their rights, called suffragettes, were involved in other issues as well. In the early years of the suffrage movement, many were abolitionists working to end slavery. With their help, the 13th Amendment was passed in 1865, prohibiting slavery in the United States. The 15th Amendment granted African American men the right to vote in 1869, but women—African American and white— were still not allowed to vote. In the early 1900s, suffragettes again became involved in other political movements. Temperance—not drinking alcoholic beverages or drinking only small amounts—was a popular cause of theirs. In 1919, again with the help of suffragettes, the 18th Amendment was passed, prohibiting the sale or manufacture of liquor. Finally, in 1920 the suffragettes achieved their main goal: the 19th Amendment was passed, giving women the right to vote.

In 1920, women finally gained the right to vote because of
- **(1)** the 18th Amendment
- **(2)** the hard work of suffragettes
- **(3)** abolition
- **(4)** the help of African Americans
- **(5)** a law passed by Congress

(2) is correct. In this case, the cause and effect are reversed. The cause is: suffragettes worked hard for many years. The effect is: women finally gained the right to vote. Put the sentence together: "Suffragettes worked hard for many years, so that women finally gained the right to vote." (1) is incorrect because the 18th Amendment dealt with the prohibition of liquor. (3) is incorrect because the abolition of slavery did not give women the right to vote. (4) is incorrect, even though African American women were among the suffragettes, because African American people did not cause women to get the right to vote. There is no basis for (5).

1. The division of power between the federal and state governments is the result of
   (1) compromises made at the Constitutional Convention in 1787
   (2) an amendment to the Constitution
   (3) the system of checks and balances
   (4) residual powers
   (5) the need for more tax money

2. New York and New Jersey have a dispute over the size of trucks traveling between the two states. The case is tried in a federal court because
   (1) individual rights are involved
   (2) the case might have to go to the Supreme Court
   (3) trade within a state is a federal matter
   (4) the civil courts can't reach a decision
   (5) two different states are involved

Item 3 is based on the chart below. In a survey of 5,000 households, Americans rated the efficiency of various institutions as indicated on the chart.

3. A conclusion that can be drawn from this chart is that Americans believe
   (1) other businesses should be organized like supermarkets
   (2) department stores and credit card companies are equally efficient
   (3) police and airlines are a little more efficient than the post office
   (4) travel by private car is more efficient than commuter rail travel
   (5) no part of their government is very efficient

Answers are on page 375–376.

Percent Saying High or Very High Efficiency			
Supermarkets	51	Business	26
Banks	48	The Press	22
Department Stores	38	Public Schools	21
Credit Card Companies	38	Space Agency	19
Insurance Companies	33	Local Transport	17
Electric Utilities	30	Commuter Rail	12
Police	29	Trade Unions	12
Airlines	29	Pentagon	10
Post Office	28	Congress	8

Fig. 3–8 Source: The Conference Board, Survey of 5000 U.S. Households, reprinted from *Newsweek*, August 4, 1986, page 4. Reprinted by permission of The Conference Board, Inc., NYC.

Lesson 5

The United States Political Process— The Voting System

Prereading Prompt

Did you know that when you cast your ballot for president you are not voting directly for your candidate? When you vote for the mayor of your town, however, your vote is counted directly. How does the voting system work in our representative democracy?

Key Words

congressional district—divisions of 500,000 people each in a state; one representative from each district is elected to serve in the House of Representatives

electoral system—the system whereby voters choose an elector to vote for president; all electoral votes from a state go to the candidate who wins the popular vote

primaries—pre-election political races that determine which candidate will represent a given political party

Any citizen 18 years or older may vote in the United States. Sometimes when you cast your ballot, your vote is counted directly for your candidate. In state and local elections (that is, elections for mayor, governor, and the members of the state legislature) every time a voter pulls the lever in the voting booth, a candidate receives one vote.

Often when you go to the voting booth you also find a number of issues to vote "yes" or "no" on. Some are bond issues, designed to raise money for specific projects. For example, your town may want to build a housing complex for senior citizens. The residents vote whether or not to use local tax money to build the complex. In addition to bond issues, there are propositions that you vote for directly. These include such issues as protecting the environment and the use of public land. On these types of issues, one person equals one vote.

You also directly elect the people who represent you in the United States Congress. Members of the House of Representatives are elected every two years. Each representative is elected from a **congressional district** of about half a million people. The total number of representatives, 435, is set by constitutional law. The number of representatives from a given state depends on the population of the state. The chart below shows how the number of representatives changes according to changes in the population. U.S. Senators are elected for six-year terms. The Constitutional specifies that every state has two senators, regardless of its population, for a total of 100 senators. About one-third of the Senate is up for election every two years.

Congressional Apportionment
(determined by state population)

	1980	1970		1980	1970		1980	1970		1980	1970
Ala....	7	7	Ind. . . .	10	11	Neb....	3	3	S. C. . .	6	6
Alas. . .	1	1	Ia.	6	6	Nev....	2	1	S. D. . .	1	2
Ariz. . .	5	4	Kan. . .	5	5	N. H. . .	2	2	Tenn...	9	8
Ark....	4	4	Ky. . . .	7	7	N. J. . .	14	15	Tex....	27	24
Cal. . . .	45	43	La.	8	8	N. M. . .	3	2	Ut.	3	2
Col. . . .	6	5	Me. . . .	2	2	N. Y....	34	30	Vt.	1	1
Conn. .	6	6	Md. . . .	8	8	N. C. . .	11	11	Va.	10	10
Del. . . .	1	1	Mass...	11	12	N. D. . .	1	1	Wash. .	8	7
Fla. . . .	19	15	Mich...	18	19	Oh. . . .	21	23	W. Va. .	4	4
Ga. . . .	10	10	Minn...	8	8	Okla...	6	6	Wis....	9	9
Ha. . . .	2	2	Miss. . .	5	5	Ore....	5	4	Wy. . . .	1	1
Ida. . . .	2	2	Mo. . . .	9	10	Pa.	23	25			
Ill.	22	24	Mon. . .	2	2	R. I....	2	2	Totals	436	436

The president is elected every four years. Your vote does not count directly for your chosen candidate. To guard against "the excesses of too much democracy," the Founding Fathers devised the **electoral system**. When you vote for president, you are actually voting for members of the electoral college, who then vote for the president. Each state has one elector for each of its senators and representatives. By the electoral college system, the candidate with the most popular votes receives *all* of a state's electoral votes, even if his or her winning margin is only a few votes. The candidate who receives the most electoral votes wins.

For the last 30 years or so, **primaries** have been held before all presidential elections. Their purpose is to narrow the field of candidates down to one or two in each political party. When you vote in a primary, you select one candidate from the party to which you belong. Each party chooses its candidate at its nominating convention. On election day, you can vote for any of the candidates, regardless of what party you belong to. If you don't like the official party candidates, you can write in a vote for the candidate of your choice.

Since people don't vote directly on issues that come up in Congress, special-interest groups often try to influence representatives to favor their cause. Such efforts to influence law-makers are known as **lobbying**. Some of the more influential lobbying groups are the National Organization of Women, the National Education Association and the National Rifle Association, groups on both sides of such issues as abortion and prayer in the schools, and various environmental groups. Lobbying groups attempt to influence politicians and public opinion with TV and radio ads, telephone calls, and mailings. Some special-interest groups are powerful enough to influence voters to elect candidates who are sensitive to their particular issue. They can have a significant impact on the outcome of an election.

Identifying Cause-and-Effect Relationships in Graphics

In Lesson 4 you learned how to identify cause-and-effect relationships in passages. Now you can apply this skill to graphic material. Look at the chart of congressional apportionment on page 150. It shows the number of representatives from each state for the last two completed census years. Study the chart and then answer the following question:

The U.S. Constitution provides for a census to count the U.S. population every ten years. The number of congressional representatives from California, Florida, Texas, and Washington changed from 1970 to 1980 because

(1) the population of these states decreased

(2) the population of these states increased

(3) the population of other states remained the same

(4) the census-takers computed population differently

(5) the population count was adjusted to meet requirements in the Constitution

Looking at the chart, you should be able to complete the cause-and-effect relationship. Your knowledge from the lesson will also help. The correct answer is (2). The number of representatives is based on population; when a state's population increases (cause), the number of representatives from that state increases (effect). (1) is incorrect because the wrong reasoning was applied—an increase in representation on the chart would not be caused by a decrease in population. There is no basis for any of the other choices.

The Practice item is based on the following map.

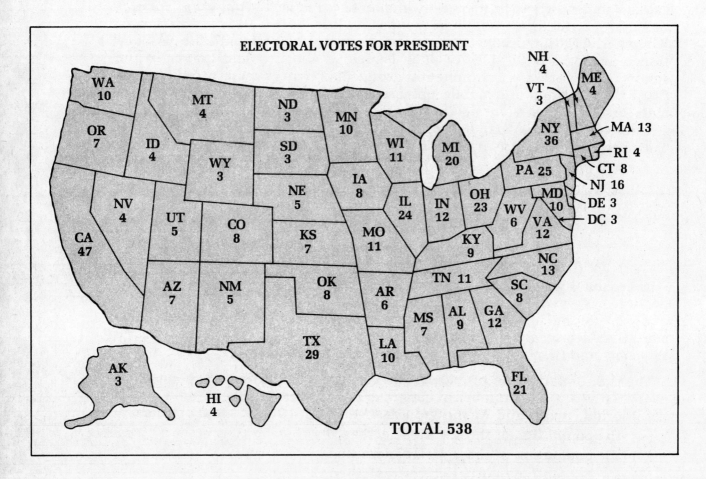

ELECTORAL VOTES FOR PRESIDENT

TOTAL 538

In a national election, winning small states in the eastern half of the country can be as important as winning the two huge western states of Texas and California. How do you explain this?

(1) What matters is how many states a candidate wins, not how large the states are.

(2) The eastern states are considered a good indicator of how the rest of nation will vote.

(3) Many of the eastern states are small but densely populated, and so have a high number of electoral votes.

(4) The nation's major cities are concentrated in the East; these are valuable votes to a candidate.

(5) Because of the time zones, voting results in the East are known early and may affect voting in the West.

Looking at the map, you can see that physically small states like New York, Pennsylvania, Ohio, and Illinois have many electoral votes. As you learned earlier, this is because they are densely populated. A candidate who can carry many of the small but vote-packed eastern states can afford to lose at least one of the two giants in the West. To answer this question, you need to know the cause-and-effect relationship from the lesson: the larger a state's population, the higher the number of its electoral votes. With this in mind, you had to identify which of the five choices made sense. It was (3). You know from the map and the lesson that (1) is incorrect. Nothing in the lesson or on the map supports (2). (4) is not true; there are major urban centers all across the U.S. Experience or common sense may have told you to eliminate (5): actual voting results are not tabulated until *all* of the polls are closed.

Lesson 5: The United States Political Process — The Voting System   **153**

Items 1 and 2 are based on the following chart.

Party Representation in Congress

	Senate			House of Representatives		
Years	Total	Demo-crats	Repub-licans	Total	Demo-crats	Repub-licans
1967–69	100	64	36	435	248	187
1969–71	100	58	42	435	243	192
1971–73	100	54	44	435	255	180
1973–75	100	56	42	435	242	192
1975–77	100	61	37	435	291	144
1977–79	100	61	38	435	292	143
1979–81	100	58	41	435	277	158
1981–83	100	46	53	435	242	190
1983–85	100	46	54	435	269	166
1985–87	100	47	53	435	253	182

Sources: Clerk of the House of Representatives; Secretary of the Senate.

Fig. 3–10 Sources: Clerk of the House of Representatives; Secretary of State, from *World Almanac 1986* (New York: Newspaper Enterprise Association), p. 231.

1. **From 1967 to 1987, the Democrats kept a majority in the House of Representatives while the Republicans have held a majority in the Senate since 1981. From 1980 on, Reagan was a popular Republican president. From this fact, and from your knowledge of the U.S. voting system, which of the following statements would NOT be a logical explanation of these effects?**

   (1) Republicans gained control of big states and increased the number of senators from each of them.

   (2) Representatives deal more with local politics, which are less affected by who is President.

   (3) Reagan's popularity as president carried some Republicans into the Senate as a side effect.

   (4) Republicans gained votes in states that normally elected Democrats to the Senate.

   (5) Democrats re-elected representatives by cooperating with President Reagan.

2. The number of representatives from a state is determined by the population of that state. Yet the total number of representatives in the House has remained at 435 since the 1910 census. What might be the reason for this?

(1) The populations of the various states have increased at about the same rate.

(2) The number of representatives is fixed at 435, although the number from each state is determined by population.

(3) Representatives are elected every six years, so it takes a long time for shifts in political party popularity to show up in the numbers.

(4) The overall population of the U.S. has increased and decreased at regular intervals, so overall representation has not changed.

(5) The number of representatives is based on the number of electoral votes, which has not changed since 1910.

3. In the electoral system, the number of electors is determined by the population of the state; there is one elector for each senator and representative. This should mean that the candidate with the majority of the popular vote will win. But it has happened that the candidate with the majority popular vote did not win the majority of electoral votes, and therefore did not win the election. This can happen if the candidate

(1) wins only the most populous states

(2) wins only the least populous states

(3) loses all states but Texas and California

(4) loses the small states by a large margin but wins by a slim margin in the big states

(5) loses one or more large states by a slim margin, but wins by a large margin in smaller states

Answers are on page 376.

Political Science Statistics

Prereading Prompt

Often it seems that everything we do is reduced to statistics—numbers that group us together, without names or faces. Statistics, however, are one of the main tools for political scientists. Find out how they are used in the following lesson.

Key Words

opinion polls—surveys to find out how people feel about a given person or issue

exit polls—surveys taken immediately after people have cast their ballots to see how they voted

statistics—information in numerical form

America has become "poll-happy." Months before every election, pollsters gather information by conducting telephone surveys and asking people on the street which candidate they favor. These **opinion polls** are used by the candidates to guide them in their campaign strategies. Political scientists also use the information to keep track of trends in American society.

It's difficult to know if opinion polls change the way people feel about a candidate when the election is still months away. But another kind of poll, known as an **exit poll**, can affect voters more directly. In an exit poll, people are asked how they have voted as they leave the voting area. The news media use exit polls to predict winners. When the results of these polls are publicized before all ballots are cast, this information can affect the outcome of the election. Suppose it's election night, and you're home after a hard day at work. You know you should vote, but it's raining and you're too tired to drag yourself down to the school. You turn on the evening news. You're relieved; your candidate is winning by a good margin. Since your candidate doesn't really need your vote, you don't have to go out in the rain. Meanwhile, on the other side of town, a person who favors the other candidate sees the news too. Her candidate is losing. She doesn't want to go out in the rain either but decides she'd better cast her vote to help her candidate win. In the morning, you discover your candidate has lost the election. What happened? It's likely that too many people who favored the candidate who *was* winning decided they didn't need to go out in the rain and vote. And many who favored the other candidate decided they'd better get out and vote. Because this has actually happened, many people argue that the results of exit polls should not be made public until *after* all the polls close.

Opinion polls are also used to find out how people feel about an issue. They survey matters of public interest and are often published in magazines and newspapers. The poll on this page is an opinion poll that was taken to find out how people feel about plans to reduce the federal budget deficit.

The numbers that come out of opinion polls are called **statistics**. Statistics are information in numerical form. Political scientists use statistics for more than just opinion polls. Studies of population shifts, trends in political beliefs, occupational changes, and religious affiliations are all reported with statistics. Look at the table showing estimates of job growth in major cities in the United States by the year 2000. The information is reported in statistical form. A political scientist might use these figures to help predict how government will change in major urban areas by the end of the century.

Projected Job Growth in Metropolitan Areas: 1985–2000					
Following are the top 30 metro areas for employment growth:					
City	Year 2000 job totals	1985–2000 increase	City	Year 2000 job totals	1985–2000 increase
Los Angeles	5,306,000	1,032,000	Minneapolis-St. Paul	1,652,800	352,000
Boston	3,056,800	754,700	Detroit	2,177,300	328,500
Anaheim	1,849,900	701,500	Nassau-Suffolk, NY	1,498,500	318,500
San Jose	1,453,600	539,200	Orlando	773,700	308,600
Phoenix	1,453,700	537,000	Fort Lauderdale	796,400	299,400
Washington	2,622,100	509,000	Miami	1,198,400	284,100
Houston	2,191,500	497,700	Oakland	1,149,000	277,700
Chicago	3,627,700	493,500	Seattle	1,202,500	268,400
Dallas	1,853,700	485,000	Baltimore	1,445,800	249,000
Atlanta	1,875,900	462,700	Middlesex Cty, NJ	736,000	206,100
San Diego	1,438,200	422,400	Riverside, CA	816,500	200,500
Tampa	1,245,400	421,500	West Palm Beach	534,200	196,400
Philadelphia	2,700,000	406,100	Newark	1,232,300	195,300
New York	4,700,800	383,600	Hartford	844,800	190,200
San Francisco	1,435,700	360,400			
Denver	1,283,700	354,800	United States	140.1 mil.	26.1 mil

Fig. 3–11 (Source: National Planning Association, *Regional Economic Growth in the United States: Predictions for 1985–2000* by Nestor E. Terlecky, 1985. Reprinted with permission.)

Evaluating the Adequacy of Information in Graphics

To evaluate something means to judge it. Some evaluation items on the GED will test your ability to judge whether information is adequate to support a given conclusion, hypothesis, or generalization. The only way you can know if the information is adequate is to understand it; you must carefully examine the graphic material, keeping in mind the details and the main idea. Only then will you be able to tell if the information in the graphic can support a given statement. Look at the chart on page 159 entitled "Reducing the Deficit." Read through all the figures and think about the chart.

Then answer this question: Which information from the chart supports the hypothesis that most of the people polled were in the middle and lower income brackets?

(1) 74 percent favored raising the highest tax bracket to 33 percent.

(2) 74 percent favored raising taxes on alcohol and cigarettes.

(3) 71 percent favored reducing defense spending.

(4) 26 percent favored raising the tax on gasoline.

(5) 26 percent favored a partial freeze of social security payments.

The correct answer is (1). The majority of those polled favored raising the taxes of those people who make the most money. Since people usually don't support raising their own taxes, you can assume that most of those polled were not in the highest tax bracket; they were in the middle and/or lower brackets. (2) doesn't address the issue of income, so it can be eliminated. The same goes for (3) and (4). As for (5), everybody, rich and poor, receives Social Security benefits after 65 if no longer employed. Therefore, you can't judge the income bracket of the people polled from this piece of information.

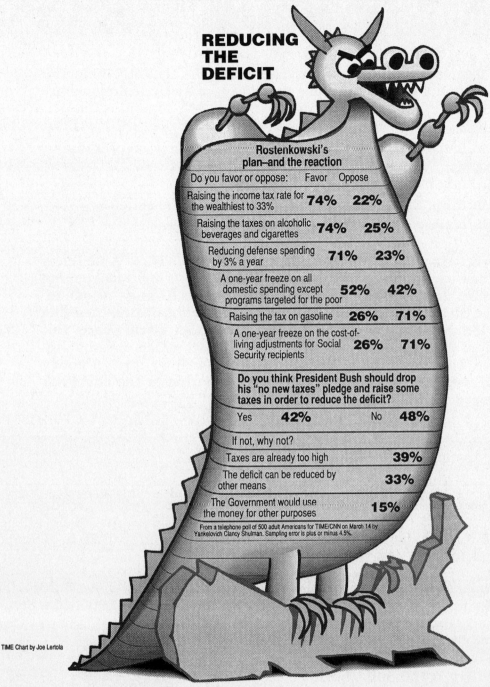

REDUCING THE DEFICIT

Rostenkowski's plan—and the reaction

Do you favor or oppose:	Favor	Oppose
Raising the income tax rate for the wealthiest to 33%	74%	22%
Raising the taxes on alcoholic beverages and cigarettes	74%	25%
Reducing defense spending by 3% a year	71%	23%
A one-year freeze on all domestic spending except programs targeted for the poor	52%	42%
Raising the tax on gasoline	26%	71%
A one-year freeze on the cost-of-living adjustments for Social Security recipients	26%	71%

Do you think President Bush should drop his "no new taxes" pledge and raise some taxes in order to reduce the deficit?

Yes	42%	No	48%

If not, why not?	
Taxes are already too high	39%
The deficit can be reduced by other means	33%
The Government would use the money for other purposes	15%

From a telephone poll of 500 adult Americans for TIME/CNN on March 14 by Yankelovich Clancy Shulman. Sampling error is plus or minus 4.5%.

TIME Chart by Joe Lertola

Fig. 3–12 Source: Chart by Joe Lertola, *Time*, March 26, 1990, p. 17. Copyright 1990 The Time Inc. Magazine Company. Reprinted by permission.

Practice

The Practice item is based on the chart "Reducing the Deficit." Which information from the chart suggests that Americans may be feeling secure about world peace?

(1) 48 percent don't want higher taxes.

(2) 52 percent favor a freeze on domestic spending except on programs for the poor.

(3) 71 percent favor a reduction in the defense budget.

(4) 42 percent think taxes should be raised to reduce the deficit.

(5) 23 percent oppose a reduction in the defense budget.

(3) is the correct answer. (1) doesn't address the issue of how Americans feel about world peace. It merely confirms that most people don't like paying taxes. (2) could be possible if not for the word *domestic*. If most people favored a freeze on *all* spending, including money for foreign affairs, then this could support the idea that Americans feel secure about world peace. But the statistics deal specifically with *domestic* spending, which does not address the issue. (4) doesn't address the issue of defense or foreign policy either. (5) is an incorrect restatement of the information in the chart; 23 percent *oppose* reducing the defense budget.

Lesson 6 Exercises

Items 1 and 2 refer to the table on page 157, "Projected Job Growth in Metropolitan Areas: 1985–2000."

1. Which statement supports the hypothesis that, in the 1990s, you might have a slightly better chance of finding employment in New York than in San Francisco?

   (1) There will be 4,700,800 jobs in New York by 2000.

   (2) There will be 1,435,700 jobs in San Francisco by 2000.

   (3) 383,600 more jobs will become available in New York by 2000.

   (4) 360,400 more jobs will become available in San Francisco by 2000.

   (5) New York will have 3,265,100 more jobs by 2000 than San Francisco.

2. The data provided in the table support the hypothesis that the biggest growth area will be

   (1) the western U.S.

   (2) the eastern U.S.

   (3) the southern U.S.

   (4) the northern U.S.

   (5) the central U.S.

Use the following timeline and graph
to answer *item 3.*

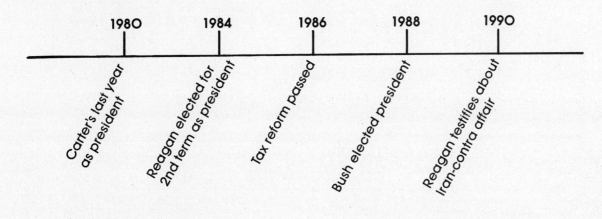

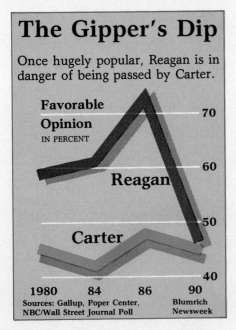

Fig. 3–13 Source: *Newsweek*, April 2, 1990, graph by Blumrich. ©1990 Newsweek, Inc. All rights reserved. Reprinted by permission.

3. According to the graph and timeline, Reagan's popularity fell sharply after his presidency because of
   (1) former President Carter's rise in popularity
   (2) President Bush's popularity
   (3) the failure of Reagan's tax-reform package to bring real tax relief
   (4) his poor performance at the Iran-Contra hearings
   (5) the fact that he has been out of office for a few years

Answers are on page 376–377.

Contemporary Issues

Prereading Prompt

You have been reading about what makes America the great country it is. But America has its problems, and in the 1990s many have come to a head. What has happened to America's moral structure? Why are so many children failing to enter the mainstream and lead productive lives? Do you see any solutions to these problems?

Key Words

inner city—sections of a large city in or near its center characterized by poverty, overpopulation, and crime
ghetto—any section of a city where members of a minority group are forced to live because of economic pressure and racial or religious prejudice; originally, the name for Jewish sections of European cities
Third World—the underdeveloped, nonindustrial countries of the world

For millions of people, the American dream is a figment of someone else's imagination. The American government, great though it may be, has failed to solve some key problems in the 1990s so far. Perhaps because of the sheer density of the urban population, America's cities seem to have more than their fair share of these problems. Millions of homeless people wander the streets. The poor live in their own separate sections, the **ghettoes**. The uneducated have little hope of getting work. Even the average middle-class person is being squeezed by taxes, high rent, and the general high cost of living.

(Credit: National Archives)

Chief among urban menaces is the drug problem. While certainly not limited to cities, urban drug use has become a major problem. **Inner-city** youths learn early that there is big money to be made selling drugs—more than most would probably make if they stayed in school and entered the workforce. What these children don't realize is that using and dealing drugs is a dead end. If they manage to stay alive—and many don't—they are destined for lives of crime and violence. By shunning school, they are shut out from gainful employment and a better life.

A problem that plagues rural as well as urban areas is the crisis in education. America has fallen far behind other countries, notably Japan, in virtually every school subject. One hundred percent of Japanese people can read and write. Ninety-nine percent of Soviet people can read and write. In the U.S., the number is 95 percent. Many American children don't even finish school. Those who do, do poorly in math and neglect science. In today's technological economy, Americans can't afford to lag behind in such important areas as math and science. Already American products are having difficulty competing with foreign products. The quality of education isn't the only problem. College tuition has more than quadrupled in the last 20 years. Many Americans can no longer afford a college education. The government has cut back on the money available for student loans, and there are precious few scholarships for the number of needy and eligible students.

A related issue is teenage pregnancy. While the argument rages over whether to teach sex education in the schools, America posts the world's highest rate of teenage pregnancy. Young, unmarried mothers often drop out of school and go on welfare. Feminism and religion offer no sure solutions: for many, abortion is not acceptable, and religious guidance has not greatly lessened the problem. The government and private institutions will have to deal with these issues if the United States is to reach its full potential and compete in a global economy.

Evaluating the Adequacy of Information in Passages

This skill is essentially the same as that discussed in Lesson 6. The difference is that you are evaluating the adequacy of written rather than graphic material. On the GED, you will be asked to judge whether written information is adequate to support a hypothesis or conclusion. To do so, ask yourself these questions: (1) Is there enough information to support this statement? (2) Is the information the right kind to support this statement? Put these questions to the test with the following exercise.

The information in the lesson supports most adequately which *one* of the following statements?

(1) The U.S. will cease to be a world power if it does not solve its drug problem.

(2) The greatest threat to the U.S. as a world power is the failure of U.S. education.

(3) Teenage pregnancy is the most explosive problem confronting society.

(4) Reductions in student loans and scholarships have made young people overcompetitive.

(5) Lack of education is the major cause of the homeless population in the U.S.

(2) is the correct answer. We are told that the drug problem and teenage pregnancy stop education for great numbers of (mostly urban) youth, that the United States lags behind in levels of literacy and in math and science study, and that college education is becoming too costly for more and more Americans. More information supports (2) than any of the other choices. Drugs are called "chief among the urban menaces" and "a major problem," but failures of education are more clearly tied to decline in U.S. power to compete worldwide, so (1) is not correct. The cause of the large homeless population is not even suggested, so (5) is wrong. Nothing suggests (4). It is not suggested that teenage pregnancy is more explosive than drugs—or any other problem discussed—so (3) has no support.

Practice

The Practice item is based on the following passage.

A major goal of Iran's revolutionary Islamic government has been to expand trade with the non-Western world. Recently, Iran's commerce minister reported that his statistics showed his government had successfully shifted most of its trade away from the West toward the Islamic world. A reporter pointed out, however, that Iranian government statisticians have moved Turkey, one of Iran's largest trading partners, out of the West and into the Third World.

Which of the following conclusions is supported by the passage?

(1) Iran has successfully shifted its trade away from the West toward the Islamic world.

(2) Turkey has left the West to become a Third World nation.

(3) The Iranian government has misrepresented statistics to support its policies.

(4) Iran's economy cannot survive without Western trade.

(5) The government is covering up its trade figures.

(3) is correct. Iran did not actually achieve its goal of shifting its focus of trade from the West to Islamic countries, but it felt it was important to say that it did. (1) is incorrect because the conclusion of the passage is that Iran did not actually achieve its goal. (2) is an incorrect statement: Turkey is not a Third World nation. There is no evidence to support (4) or (5).

Lesson 7 Exercises

Item 1 is based on the following passage.

Japanese students, like American students, vary greatly in economic background and in ability. Mixing students of differing ability in the same class and requiring them all to cover the same material have resulted in Japan's educational success.

Two researchers carefully studied several early-grade classes in Chicago schools. Teachers placed students in three reading groups according to achievement and ability. Not surprisingly, the group that was given the fewest vocabulary words to learn learned the fewest words. If members of the "low" group had been in the "high" group, very probably they would have learned more words.

1. Which of the following statements does the information in the passage support?
   (1) Children learn in similar ways, whether they are Japanese or American.
   (2) Students in higher groups resent having to learn more and therefore learn less.
   (3) Children who are given less to learn, learn faster.
   (4) American students separated according to different abilities have to work harder than Japanese students.
   (5) American students of different abilities would learn more if they studied in the same classes.

Item 2 is based on the following passage.

America is in the midst of a pollution crisis. Solutions abound; car-pooling, smokestack scrubbing, and improved solid-waste disposal all have some effect. Yet pollution still threatens the environment. One new proposal is to give all companies a certain number of pollution "points." A company may pollute up to the level of its points. Companies that pollute less can sell their unused pollution points to companies that are "overspending" theirs. In this way, companies that pollute too much will pay a price.

Opponents say this plan will lead to unacceptable levels of pollution. These critics argue that so long as companies can afford to buy unused points, they will continue to pollute.

2. The passage provides support for the belief that the "new proposal" described is
   (1) unnecessary
   (2) better than the other "solutions" listed
   (3) too expensive for most companies
   (4) too easy to get around
   (5) too complicated to work

Item 3 is based on the following table.

Ten Most Prominent Native Countries of Taxi Drivers	
Country	Percent
Haiti	25
Dominican Republic	6
Egypt	5
South Korea	5
Afghanistan	4
Colombia	4
India	4
Pakistan	4
Rumania	4
Soviet Union	4

Mean age	33.5 years
Two or more years of college	47%

Fig. 3–14 Source: Dr. Anne G. Morris, Center for Logistics and Transportation, City University Graduate Center, New York. Reprinted with permission.

3. The table shows figures from a survey of 4,369 people who applied for taxi licenses in New York between October 1984 and May 1985. The data in the table support the conclusion that most of the recent New York taxi drivers
   (1) have more than two years of college
   (2) are from countries in Europe
   (3) are from countries outside Europe
   (4) are about 33.5 years old
   (5) have two or more years of driving experience

Answers are on page 377.

Lesson 8

International Politics

Prereading Prompt

With all the different countries and types of government in the world, it sometimes seems amazing that they communicate and cooperate as well as they do. What are the forums for international communication? What systems and structures exist to keep peace in the world? You will learn the answers to these and other questions in this lesson.

Key Words

United Nations—a world forum for keeping peace, formed in 1945 and consisting of about 180 member nations

Common Market—also known as European Economic Community; an organization of Western European countries for economic unity

North Atlantic Treaty Organization— pact signed in 1949 by U.S., Canada, and Western European nations to protect themselves against military aggression from the Soviet Union

As long as there are different nations with physical and political boundaries to protect, governments will feel threatened by other countries. One way government protects its interests is by keeping a trained army ready to fight if necessary. Fortunately, most governments prefer to settle their differences through *diplomacy*—through peaceful negotiations rather than weapons. There have been many wars since 1945, but none on the scale of the two world wars. More and more countries have joined the peace-keeping efforts of the UN, and today, there are about 180 member nations. Each country, in addition to participating in the General Assembly, also participates in the UN's special agencies, which include the United Nation's International Children's Emergency Fund (UNICEF), the International Labor Organization (ILO), and the World Health Organization (WHO).

Besides the UN, nations also use their own diplomatic relations as a means of keeping peace. Most governments maintain embassies in foreign countries, with diplomats who serve to represent the government and maintain cordial relations between the governments in question.

Throughout this book, you have also learned about many treaties that countries have made to keep peace. *Treaties* are formal, legal agreements between countries, and can be economic or military. The Common Market is primarily an economic association. It consists of ten full members, including Great Britain, France, West Germany, Italy, the Netherlands, and other Western European nations. Among the purposes of the Common Market are the removal of trade barriers among member nations and the eventual coordination of transportation systems, agricultural policies, and general economic policies.

An example of a military treaty is the North Atlantic Treaty Organization (NATO), which exists between the U.S. and its European allies. You may recall that NATO was established after World War II as protection against aggression. In the 1990s, NATO may have outlived its usefulness. With Communism collapsing throughout Eastern Europe and the end of the Cold War, there is much less need to have a large military defense against possible Communist aggression. Moreover, by 1992 Western Europe is to be a union with no trade barriers and one currency. It will be much less attached to the U.S. and will form new alliances with Eastern European nations that are no longer Communist.

Identifying the Effect of Values on Information in Passages

We all have things that are important to us, things that we value. The ideas and beliefs that are important to us are called values. We may believe deeply in human rights, or family relationships, or the rights of animals. The things we believe in—our values—affect how we think and what we do. For example, a person who believes in animal rights may lobby for legislation prohibiting testing of cosmetics and drugs on laboratory animals.

The way authors write is often colored by their values. It will help you answer some questions on the GED if you understand how the information in a passage is influenced by the writer's treatment of the subject. Such understanding will help you answer questions about the writer's attitude toward the topic.

While reading, ask yourself how the writer's values affect the way he or she presents the information. Is the writer being objective—simply telling the facts—or are the facts being slanted by the writer's values? To answer this question, it helps to know about the source of the information you are reading. Are you reading something from a well-respected newspaper or magazine? If so, chances are the writing is fairly objective. Are you reading an opinion column or letter to the editor? These are, by nature, affected by the values of the writer.

Next, ask yourself what the writer would like you to believe. Is the writer for or against the issue in question? Look to see if the writer has used emotional appeals to support his or her belief, for instance, the language the writer has used. It can give you clues to the writer's point of view. Words and phrases like "unfortunately" or "it's a good thing that" can tell you where the writer stands on an issue.

When looking for the viewpoint of a passage, you also should look for what it emphasizes, and what it does not emphasize. The writer may mention something, or suggest an idea, but not stress it, or stress it much less than other things. These differences in emphasis show how the writer values different parts of his subject, presenting them as important or unimportant, positive or negative.

Reread the first paragraph of the preceding passage on international politics. Then answer the following question:

The point of view of the author of this lesson is that in international politics since 1945

(1) no government can be trusted to stay within its borders, so a well-trained army is the best defense
(2) the UN is not worth much as a peace-keeping body because there have been many wars since 1945
(3) it's better to settle disputes by peaceful means than through war
(4) the UN isn't effective because not enough countries belong to it
(5) war is an inevitable fact of life

(3) is correct. The writer emphasizes the peace-keeping efforts of the UN and the use of diplomacy by nations in the first two paragraphs, and the use of treaties to keep peace in the third paragraph. Even the discussion of the military alliance of NATO stresses its defense against aggression and points out the reduced need for its large military presence. The word "fortunately" in the third sentence of the lesson also lets you know the writer thinks it is a good thing that most feuding nations would rather talk than shoot. This writer therefore emphasizes (3) more than all the other choices. (4) is not even mentioned or suggested. The writer stresses that none of the wars since 1945 has been "on the scale of the two world wars," and therefore does not blame, but praises, the UN as a peace-keeping body, so (2) is wrong. The discussion of NATO might suggest (1), and the discussion of all the peace-keeping efforts might suggest (5), but the writer gives no emphasis to these suggestions.

(Credit: Official Marine Corps Photograph)

Practice

The Practice item is based on the following passage from a news magazine.

> Don't let [anyone] intimidate you into shrinking from reporting on one of the most important stories of our time: the Soviet [murders] in Afghanistan. . . . It is . . . a campaign to exterminate another nation. The [West] holds in [its] hands the Afghan people's only chance of survival.*

*Adapted from *World Press Review*, February 1987, page 4, Used with permission.

The writer of this letter is most likely
(1) a member of the Soviet army
(2) a Soviet sympathizer
(3) an American reporter
(4) an Afghan reporter
(5) a supporter of Afghanistan

Clearly, this writer sides with the people of Afghanistan. It is unlikely that he or she is a reporter because the writing is emotional; words like "murder" and "exterminate" are highly emotional and would usually be used only by a reporter in an opinion column. Therefore, you can eliminate (3) and (4). This person definitely doesn't side with the Soviet Union, so (2) is out. A case could be made for (1) if the writer were a Soviet soldier who wasn't loyal to his country, but you have no way of knowing if this is true. Choice (5) is the more logical and correct answer. This passage was a letter to the editor, which is why it is so opinionated.

Lesson 8 Exercises

Items 1 and 2 are based on the following passage.

The lessons of history can be hard to learn. After every major war America has fought, we have let down our defenses by decreasing our military strength. After World War I we pulled out of Europe; fascists took over, giving us World War II. After World War II, we again withdrew our troops—most of them, anyway. Instead, we kept the Communist world at bay with nuclear weapons. We didn't use them, and Communism spread throughout Eastern Europe, and China and Indochina. Now the Cold War is ending, and once again we are talking about disarmament. From what corner of the globe will the next threat come? No one knows, but shouldn't we be prepared?

1. Which statement best represents the viewpoint of the writer?
   (1) America shouldn't have withdrawn its troops after World War I.
   (2) The Cold War is not really over.
   (3) America cannot afford to let its guard down.
   (4) The spread of Communism must be stopped.
   (5) We always pay a price for peace.

2. What this writer seems to value most is
   (1) military security
   (2) trust among nations
   (3) military aggression
   (4) peaceful negotiations
   (5) the lessons of history

Item 3 is based on the passage in the lesson on international politics.

3. The passage supports the conclusion that
   (1) the world has never been closer to peace
   (2) the world is now closer to war
   (3) economic treaties are the best way to keep world peace
   (4) world peace will be attained when the Communist countries join the United Nations
   (5) diplomacy is a desirable, if uncertain, way of maintaining world peace.

Answers are on page 377.

CHAPTER 4

Economics has to do with the way products are made, distributed, and used. Products are called **goods**. When you buy a TV set, go grocery shopping, or pick up a newspaper, you are buying goods. Economics also has to do with services. When you get your TV or car repaired, the repair person is performing a **service**. Thus, economics also concerns the workers who make the products and deliver services to consumers.

Wall Street and New York Stock Exchange
(Credit: New York Convention and Visitors Bureau)

Prereading Prompt

Many people feel intimidated by the word "economics." But matters of money and finances need not be something to be feared. As with anything, understanding is the key. This chapter will help you become more comfortable with the subject of economics.

Economics

What Is Economics?

On some level, you are already familiar with **economics**. You know how much money you earn, and how much of that you spend on various goods and services: rent or mortgage, car payments, food, utilities, and other necessities. Perhaps you have drawn up a *budget*—a plan that lists all of your expenses and income, and tells you how much you can spend on what.

You may not realize it, but the amount of money you earn and the amount you spend are determined by a complex economic system. The availability of **goods** and services, the cost of raw materials, the cost of labor, the mood of the business community, and the world economic picture all affect the cost of living in America in the 1990s.

For many people, it always seems that there is never enough money to pay for everything. If there are things you really want or need but can't afford, you may overspend, running up bills on your credit cards. The amount you spend beyond what you have is called a **deficit**. The U.S. government has incurred just such a deficit, spending hundreds of billions it doesn't have. In 1990, the deficit is expected to be anywhere from $150 billion to $350 billion.

In recent years, reducing the U.S. budget deficit has become a major political issue. Some people argue that everything comes with a price, that if Americans want continued defense spending and social programs, they will have to pay more taxes. Most people, however, feel their taxes are already too high, and politicians who favor raising taxes risk not being elected. In 1988, George Bush campaigned and won with the slogan, "Read my lips: No new taxes." When as President he said he might raise taxes after all, he caused a political storm. Both parties must struggle with the question of how to cut spending and reduce the deficit.

A basic understanding of economics will give you a better perspective on the workings of the government and will also help you be more informed about your own financial situation.

Key Words

economics—the study of the production and distribution of goods and services

goods—products that are made, distributed, and sold

deficit—the amount by which a sum of money falls short of what is needed

Modern Economic Systems

Prereading Prompt

America's economic system, capitalism, is just one type of system. Other countries have other systems, each with its advantages and disadvantages. How do these systems work? What are their strengths and weaknesses?

Key Words

capitalism—an economic system based on free enterprise and private ownership
communism—an economic system based on state ownership and control of all aspects of business and property
socialism—an economic system based on some private and some state ownership

Different governments have different economic systems. Economic systems are closely tied to political systems. There are three major economic systems in the modern world: capitalism, communism, and socialism. **Capitalism** is based on the idea that a country's economy works best when the government does not interfere much or at all with business. Businesses are privately owned with a minimum of government regulation. Capitalism is a *free-enterprise system*; businesses are free to produce as much as they want and charge whatever buyers are willing to pay. In theory, free enterprise is a self-regulating system. For example, suppose you own a shoe store. You receive shoes from the factory with suggested prices to charge. If you can sell them for more, you will make more of a profit. When you try to sell the shoes at that price, however, you may discover that people aren't buying, because they can get the same shoes across town for less. To compete with these other shoe stores, you will have to lower your prices to a level that customers think is reasonable. To offer products of good quality at a price people will pay is *competitive* in a free-enterprise system.

Under **communism**, there is no such thing as competition because private ownership of businesses is not permitted. Businesses are owned and regulated by the state. Prices of goods are set by the state and sometimes are kept low by having the government pay part of the cost. In addition, citizens don't have the freedom to choose what business they will go into or how they will run it. To use the example of the shoe store: the government might close down your store because it decides there are already enough shoe stores in your city. What the society really needs is more factory workers, so the state will train you to work in a factory where help is needed. Communism is, in theory, a classless system. Since there is no competition, there are no wealthy people and no poor people, and essential services are the same for all.

Socialism is based on the idea that it is good for society if the government owns some, but not all, businesses. Government ownership, it is argued, yields more efficiency in certain basic industries. Citizens benefit because the cost and quality of products are regulated by the state. In most socialist states, only the major elements of the economy are owned by the state—the banks, transportation, heavy industries such as ship-building and natural resources. To use the shoe store example again: you probably would own your store, but some of the raw materials used to make the shoes might be state-owned. This means the state would make money off every pair of shoes you sold. In addition, you would pay high taxes. In return, you would often get some important benefits: free health care, decent and inexpensive housing, free quality education, free care for the old, free day care. The high taxes pay for a quite high minimum standard of living for all. Sweden, Denmark, and Great Britain are examples of this type of socialism.

The economies of all modern countries are really a mixture of different economic systems. In capitalist systems, such as the U.S., there is some government regulation of business. The government sets quality standards for products, monitors business practices, and regulates interstate trade, among other things. In communist systems, such as the Soviet Union, there is a trend today toward more private ownership, even toward a full free-enterprise system. Socialist systems also vary tremendously from country to country, so that some have many privately owned businesses and others have few.

Identifying the Effect of Values on Information in Graphics

From your study of American history, you already know how to comprehend details and main ideas in cartoons, both details and ideas that are stated (Lessons 3 and 4) and those that must be inferred (Lessons 8 and 9). Remember the four main questions you should ask yourself when looking at a cartoon:

(1) What are the main details? (people, things, clothes, facial expressions, gestures)

(2) What is the main action? (What is happening? What are they doing or saying?)

(3) What are the comparisons? (What are the things or people made to look like? What does this mean?)

(4) What is the main idea? (What is the main point or joke of the cartoon?)

After you find the main idea you might ask yourself: What is the viewpoint of the cartoonist? You can figure it out by using the skills you learned in the last lesson. Look at the details, action, and comparisons to see what the cartoonist is emphasizing, and giving emotional meaning to. For example, what is being exaggerated? What words are used, in the caption or in the dialogue balloons, to make the people, things, or action seem funny? Use these guidelines with this question.

Fig. 4–1 Source: Cartoon by Walt Handelsman. Reprinted by permission: Tribune Media Services.

The cartoonist's basic belief is that, as the form of government that responds to the needs of the people, democracy

(1) is failing under Gorbachev in Russia
(2) is inspirational
(3) is not being practiced in the U.S. government
(4) is Gorbachev's idea
(5) is catching on in Congress

(3) is correct. This cartoon created in 1990 makes its point mainly through words. The dome of the U.S. Capitol Building tells us that the two men are members of Congress. In the left-hand picture they seem to be praising Gorbachev and the changes from dictatorship to democracy he was making in the Soviet Union in the late 1980s. The right-hand picture shows us, however, that they don't really like democracy because one says, "Let's hope it [democracy] never catches on here." The joke is that elected members of Congress fear democracy. (5) is therefore false. The joke would not work if Gorbachev's changes for democracy were failing in 1990, because then the congressmen would have nothing to fear; so (1) is incorrect. (2) is only a detail, something that one insincere congressman says, so it cannot the be cartoonist's basic belief about democracy. (4) is false because Gorbachev obviously did not invent the idea of democracy.

Fig. 4–2 Source: Cartoon by Dana Summers. ©1989, Washington Post Writers Group. Reprinted with permission.

The cartoonist seems to value most an economic system that
- **(1)** remains a giant producer
- **(2)** constantly increases its wealth
- **(3)** invents products for changing markets
- **(4)** protects its environment
- **(5)** builds large, modern structures

(3) is correct. The main details in the cartoon are the large white bones that the men in uniforms have discovered. These men are explorers. The dialogue balloon identifies the bones as those of a dinosaur or other "giant lumbering creature that couldn't adapt to the changing environment." The cartoon makes the bones look like the hammer and sickle symbol of the Communist Party. The balloon's words and this comparison suggest that Communism died out because it could not adapt to change. The cartoonist must value most highly an economic system that *can* adapt to change, such as is described in (3). An economy that (1) remained a giant producer or that (2) constantly increased its wealth might still, like Communism, fail to adapt and die out. (4) is about protecting the environment, not adapting to it. (5) refers to the giant bones as if they were tall modern buildings, and therefore makes no sense.

Item 1 is based on the cartoon in Figure 4-3.

Fig. 4–3 Source: Cartoon by Clifford Berryman, January 4, 1937. Courtesy of the Library of Congress.

1. This cartoon is based on the belief that it is better to
   - (1) be independent than deal with government
   - (2) deal with government than be independent
   - (3) be a U.S. citizen than have Social Security
   - (4) bully people in authority than to be without security
   - (5) bully U.S. citizens than to leave them without security

Item 2 is based on the cartoon in Figure 4-4.

©1990 THE PITTSBURGH PRESS
UNITED FEATURE SYNDICATE

THERE'S A CROWD GATHERING OUTSIDE TO PROTEST YOUR NEW BUDGET...

SHOULD WE CALL IN THE MILITARY?

IT _IS_ THE MILITARY.

Fig. 4—4 Reprinted by permission of UFS, Inc.

2. The cartoonist apparently believes that the military budget
   (1) has been cut too much
   (2) has made the military too strong
   (3) has made President Bush assert his power
   (4) has made President Bush approve of the military
   (5) has added to the budget deficit

Item 3 is based on the following paragraph.

An aggressive new lobby contends that the United States is experiencing a health-care crisis. It argues that many people cannot afford the high cost of medical care, and that these "have-nots" should be given free or subsidized care. Many of these people have simply failed to save enough to pay their bills, though some may be victims of inflation or bad luck. Some people are even pushing for a national health-care system, similar to the costly ones in Sweden and Great Britain, where the government pays for almost all medical care. What they don't want to face is that this is the first step toward living in a welfare state.

3. What does the writer of this paragraph value?
   (1) communism
   (2) socialism
   (3) lobbies
   (4) the free-enterprise system
   (5) health care

Answers are on page 377–378.

The Free-Enterprise System: The Law of Supply and Demand

Prereading Prompt

The economic system in most free countries is based on competition. But what factors determine how much you pay for a product? What happens when a supplier overestimates how much demand there is for this product? Read on to find out.

Key Words

supply—goods and services that are available

demand—the immediate market for goods and services

law of supply and demand—when demand increases, supply increases; when demand decreases, supply decreases

market price—the price determined by the point where demand and supply meet

equilibrium—when supply equals demand

surplus—when the supply of a product exceeds the demand for it

The free-enterprise system is based on the **law of supply and demand**. **Supply** refers to the goods and services that are available. **Demand** refers to the immediate market for those goods and services. The relationship between supply and demand is what determines the cost and availability of a product or a service.

Normally, in a free market, when the demand for a product increases, the supply of that product increases; suppliers work to make sure there is enough of the product for everyone who wants it. The more they sell, the more money they make. Think of hoola-hoops, a product that was a fad in the 1960s. Every kid had to have a hoola-hoop. Demand soared and suppliers stepped up production to meet the demand. After a few years, the hoola-hoop craze died down. Did it make sense for suppliers to continue producing hoola-hoops? Of course not. If they had, they would have been stuck with a product they couldn't sell. Suppliers and producers know that when demand decreases, supply must also decrease.

The hoola-hoop example illustrates the law of supply and demand: Supply is directly tied to demand. When demand is high, supply is increased; when demand is low, supply is decreased. But how does the law of supply and demand affect how much we pay for goods and services? To answer this question, we must consider a third factor—price, specifically **market price**.

The supply and demand curve in Figure 4-5 shows that when prices are high, consumers buy less of the product, and when prices are low, consumers buy more. Think about this from your perspective as a consumer. For example, if a pair of running shoes costs $70, you won't buy too many pairs. If they cost $20 a pair, however, you might buy an extra pair in another color because the price is low.

Fig. 4–5 The Supply and Demand Curve

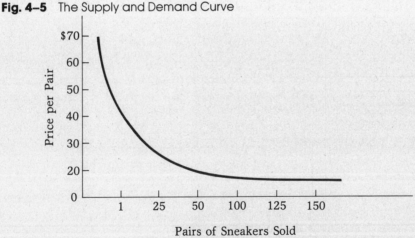

As demand increases, supply increases, and prices drop. Suppliers may even lower their prices to underprice each other as they compete for sales.

When supply and demand are equal, this is known as **equilibrium**. When the supply of a product becomes too great, there may not be enough buyers for the product. If supply exceeds demand, there is a **surplus**. Too much of a product on the market usually drives prices down. In some cases, it also drives some competitors out of business. Take the example of a shoe store. In a fairly small town, if there are five shoe stores, chances are there won't be enough business to keep all five going. The one that charges the most or has the poorest service probably will fail to thrive. In a free-enterprise system there are no guarantees. However, if people are trying to cut spending, businesses that give customers what they want at a good price are the most likely to succeed.

Identifying Faulty Logic in Graphics

Suppose you are car shopping with a friend who says, "I love the way the red car looks, but I'm not going to buy it because statistics show that more red cars are involved in fatal accidents than any other color." Is your friend's reasoning sound? No. While it may be true that more red cars are involved in fatal accidents, this doesn't mean your friend will die if she buys a red car. You have to look at the facts behind statistics. Also, it could be that people who buy red cars have "racy" personalities—they may drive less safely and therefore are involved in more accidents. There is nothing about a red car that makes it less safe than a green or a blue car. So your friend's reasoning, or logic, is faulty.

On the GED, you will be asked to identify faulty logic in written material and graphics. To do this, use the following guidelines:

(1) Is an overgeneralization or oversimplification being made? (*All* red cars are unsafe.)

(2) Is a false connection being drawn? (Red cars are inherently less safe than cars of other colors.)

(3) Is a misleading cause-and-effect relationship being stated? (The fact that a car is red causes it to be in an accident.)

(4) Are statistics being used in a misleading way? (The fact that so many red cars are involved in fatal accidents means that it is unsafe to drive a red car.)

(5) Is the original question really being answered? (Does the color of a car have any bearing on its safety?)

Asking these questions would have point up the faulty logic in your car-buying friend's reasoning. She used statistics in a misleading way; she drew a false connection; and she came up with an incorrect cause-and-effect relationship. See if you can find similar faulty logic in the following question.

The following item is based on the graph below.

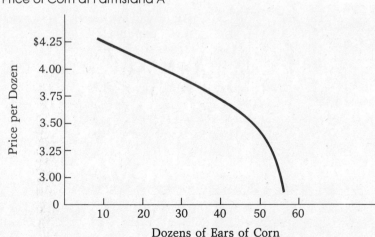

Fig. 4–6 Price of Corn at Farmstand A

The graph shows the price of corn at a local farmstand, Farmstand *A*. Early in the season, when corn isn't at its peak and little is available, supply is low and the price is high. At the peak of the season, when the corn is ripe and its supply plentiful, demand is very high and the price drops. Meanwhile, the farmer down the road at Farmstand *B* needs more cash to get one of his harvesters repaired. Which action below would probably *not* help him make more money at the peak of the corn season?

(1) sell corn for $3.50 per dozen ears
(2) sell corn for $2.75 per dozen ears
(3) sell a ''baker's dozen'' of 13 ears for $3.00
(4) sell single ears for $.30 each, or a dozen for $3.00
(5) sell 7 ears for $1.50

The correct answer is (1). Remember the relationship between supply and demand and price: When supply and demand are low, price is usually high; when supply and demand are high, the price drops. At the peak of corn season, supply and demand are high and consumers expect lower prices at the farmstand. If two competitors who are located near each other have similar produce (that is, good, sweet corn), usually the stand with the lower prices will sell more. Since there is a fairly high mark-up on produce, the farmer at Farmstand *B* could afford to drop his price a little in order to sell more corn and still make more money. All choices except (1) involve selling for a lower price. By selling for a higher price, as in (1), the farmer would probably lose business, and therefore make less money.

Practice

The Practice item is based on the following graphic.

Fig. 4–7 Source: *USA TODAY*, April 17, 1990. Copyright 1990, USA TODAY. Reprinted with permission.

Based on the graphic, which statement below shows faulty reasoning?

(1) People generally spend less of their salary on recreation than on other expenses

(2) People would spend more money on recreation if they didn't have to spend so much time working to pay the government

(3) People spend less time working to pay their taxes than they spend on all other expenses combined

(4) Increased housing costs account for the large amount of time people spend working to pay for a place to live

(5) People don't pay much more for food in a year than they do on medical expenses

(2) is the answer that shows faulty reasoning. If the government took a smaller bite of our annual income, we would not necessarily spend the extra money on recreation. Some people might, but others might use the money to buy a bigger house or get medical care they couldn't otherwise afford. This answer shows evidence of a false connection and is therefore illogical. (1), (3), and (5) are neither logical or illogical, but are restatements of information in the graphic. (4) is an hypothesis that would have to be proved true or false by supporting evidence, but it is logical that higher housing costs would take more work time to pay for.

Lesson 2 Exercises

Item 1 is based on the following table.

Labor Force Participation Rates by Sex (in Percent)				
	Female		Male	
Country	1987	1980	1987	1980
Canada	50.9%	46.2%	70.1%	73.0%
Japan	46.2%	45.7%	74.9%	77.9%
Sweden	61.6%	58.0%	71.0%	73.6%
United States	52.5%	47.7%	71.5%	72.0%

Source: *Statistical Abstract of the United States, 1989*

1. Which statement below shows faulty reasoning?

   (1) As women enter the labor force, fewer men will have to work.

   (2) Increasing numbers of women are entering the labor force to take the places of men who are leaving.

   (3) There is a slight trend toward higher unemployment among men in the countries shown.

   (4) The overall rate of unemployment is higher in Canada than in the United States.

   (5) Japanese women are entering the labor force more slowly than women in other countries.

Item 2 is based on the following chart.

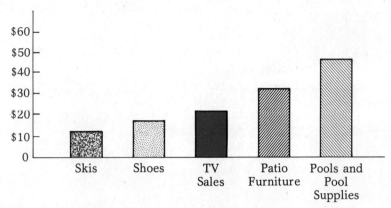

Fig. 4–8 Total Sales/Northeast Region: July-August 1990 (in millions of dollars)

2. A friend wants to open a retail store. To find out what type of product would sell well, he looks at the most recent sales figures. He notices that pools and pool supplies are by far the highest moneymaker. He does his research and finds that there is only one other supplier of pools in the area, a store ten miles away from where his will be. He also finds statistics that show increasing numbers of people putting pools in their backyards. He decides to open a pool and pool supply store, and looks forward to a year of heavy sales. Why is his reasoning flawed?

   (1) He hasn't counted on the increasing popularity of skiing.

   (2) The law of supply dictates that he must sell low when he first opens because it will take a while to get established.

   (3) The law of demand dictates that people won't want to pay much for a pool.

   (4) He hasn't taken into account the fact that pools are a seasonal item.

   (5) There will be a surplus of pools because supply will exceed demand.

Item 3 is based on the following cartoon.

Fig. 4–9 Source: *The Colorado Springs Gazette Telegraph*, May 30, 1990. Reprinted by permission of *The Colorado Springs Gazette Telegraph*.

3. This cartoonist believes that
   (1) demand is determined by supply
   (2) demand is determined by factors other than supply
   (3) price is determined by supply
   (4) price is determined by demand
   (5) supply is determined by factors other than demand

Answers are on page 378.

Business Organization

Prereading Prompt

Businesses, whether large or small, have rules and regulations that govern their operation. What are the advantages to owning a business? What are the disadvantages? Why are many large companies corporations? Learn the answer to these and other questions in this lesson.

Key Words

sole proprietorship—a business that is owned by one person

corporation—a business with one or more owners that is run by a board of directors

stockholder—a person who owns shares of a company

Small Business Organization

If you decided to go into business for yourself, you would have several choices as to how to organize your enterprise. Each has legal consequences. Your particular needs would determine which you would choose.

Over 75 percent of all U.S. businesses are **sole proprietorships**. If you owned a sole proprietorship, you would be the only owner or proprietor. As the sole owner, you would make all decisions about how the business would be run. You could, if you wanted, hire someone else to run the business for you. You would pay that person a salary, but you would still be the boss—the person who makes all the decisions. Small businesses, such as clothing shops, beauty salons, restaurants, and shoe stores, are commonly sole proprietorships.

Being the boss has its advantages, but also its drawbacks. If your business loses money, you, as the sole owner, are responsible. If you cannot pay off the debts, you can lose your house, your car, and any other valuable items you own. It's discouraging to know that the majority of small businesses that open each year fail. For these reasons, it can be difficult to get a loan from a bank if you are a sole proprietor.

Lower East Side (Credit: New York Convention and Visitor's Bureau)

Another business arrangement is the **partnership**. This is exactly what it sounds like—one or more partners go into business together. All partners share in running the business, and all share in the profits. They also share in the losses. Partners are bound legally by a written contract that spells out what each is responsible for. About 8 percent of U.S. businesses are partnerships. Many of these are professional practices, such as doctors, dentists, lawyers, and accountants. Each partner may specialize in a different area of the practice. This tends to draw more business and is a great convenience to the consumer.

The disadvantages of a partnership are several. Since there is more than one boss, it is more difficult to make decisions. The more partners, the harder this becomes. Also, if one partner causes the business to suffer heavy losses (a bad lawsuit, for example), all partners must pay the price, which may include their personal assets. Yet banks are more willing to lend money to partnerships than to sole proprietorships, because partnerships generally have more financial resources to draw on. This makes the loan safer from the bank's perspective.

Big Business Organization

About 17 percent of businesses in America are **corporations**. A corporation is a legally bound, self-governing organization set up to run a business. A corporation can have one or two owners, or thousands of owners who can also be on the board of directors. Ownership is divided into shares that are bought and sold. Each shareholder, or **stockholder**, owns shares of the company. When a person buys stock in a corporation, he or she is actually becoming an owner. The owners don't run the corporation directly. Each stockholder has a certain number of votes, depending on how much stock he or she owns. Stockholders elect a board of directors, who in turn appoint a president, treasurer, secretary, and other officers. Major stockholders can have a tremendous effect on the election of the board of directors, thereby controlling the company.

The money and assets of a corporation are separate from those of the owners. If a corporation goes bankrupt or into debt, the stockholders are not responsible. The value of their stock can go down, or may become worthless, but stockholders cannot lose their houses or their cars if the company gets into financial trouble. This is one advantage of a corporation over a partnership or sole proprietorship. For this reason, some small businesses may decide to incorporate, especially if they feel their business is risky and may lose a lot of money.

Another advantage of a corporation is that the owners don't have to be bothered with its day-to-day operation. This is left to the board of directors, whom the owners have elected. Also, corporations can usually borrow money fairly easily because they have so much financial backing.

Identifying Faulty Logic in Passages

Sometimes people use faulty logic in interpreting graphs or other visual representations such as cartoons. You may remember from the last lesson the case of the person who wouldn't buy a red car because he or she had read that red cars were involved in more accidents than cars of other colors. Writers can also use faulty logic. It will help you to answer certain questions on the GED if you can identify reasoning that is not sound. Remember the guidelines from the previous lesson on judging if faulty logic is being used:

(1) Be on the lookout for overgeneralizations or oversimplifications. These usually take the form of sweeping statements, such as: "Corporations are always a better form of business organization."

(2) Make sure that false connections, or cause-and-effect relationships, are not being made, as in the example of the person buying the car.

(3) Check that any statistics used actually support the reasoning. Again, the woman buying the red car used statistics illogically; they didn't support her conclusion.

(4) Make sure the original question is being answered. Politicians are especially good at appearing to answer questions without really doing so, as in this example: "Mr. Governor, will you be cutting back on aid to public education?" Reply: "All public services will be adequately funded."

Using these guidelines, read the following passage and answer the question.

Rick and Tony want to open a consulting business. They are aware that the majority of small businesses fail and consider the pros and cons of a partnership versus a corporation. Tony argues that a corporation would be better; if the business fails, they won't risk losing their personal assets. Rick argues that he doesn't like the idea of a corporation because he doesn't want other people telling them how to run the business; a partnership is the way to go.

Rick's logic is faulty because

(1) a partnership would leave them open to losing their personal assets
(2) they are taking no greater risk of failure than any other new business
(3) becoming a corporation doesn't mean they will lose control of the business; they can be the sole officers
(4) a corporation will not protect their personal assets
(5) their argument is beside the point; two people can't be a corporation

The correct answer is (3). A corporation can be as small as one or two people, who can be the board of directors and hold all the stock in the company. Rick's argument that they would lose control of the business is illogical. So (5) is wrong. (1) is true, and is therefore a logical reason against Rick's argument, but it is not a fault of his argument. (2) is a general statement of fact that does not support either man's argument.

Practice

The Practice item is based on the following passage.

One way investors make money is to buy stock in companies after the company has experienced some difficulty and the price of the stock has gone down. The hope of these investors is that the stock they bought cheaply will increase in value as the company corrects the problem. Then they can sell the stock for a profit.

With this in mind, let's look at this example. A new pharmaceuticals corporation claims to have found a cure for the common cold. The news is quick to get out and stock in the company soars. Unfortunately for stockholders, independent testing shows that the drug does *not* cure colds. Stock in the company tumbles. Some young investors, however, try to take advantage of the low prices and buy stock, hoping to sell it later at a higher price.

The faulty logic behind the investors' decision to buy stock in the corporation is that

(1) most investors know that stock should not be bought when its value is low

(2) the company's high value was built on this one drug; there's no reason to think the value of the stock will bounce back

(3) it is unlikely that a cure for the common cold will ever be found

(4) this strategy only works with large companies

(5) there would be no stock available to buy because stockholders would want to hold onto all their shares

(2) is the correct answer. Logic would lead you to conclude that the value of this company's stock will remain low until the company can prove that its other products are not like its failed cold cure. It's difficult for a new company to survive such a severe early failure. Since so many new businesses fold, the chances are better than ever that this company's stock will be worthless in the near future. Buying stock that has fallen this far in value is generally safe only when a company has a well-founded reputation that can be rebuilt. (1) directly contradicts other information given in the passage, so it is not correct. There is no basis for choosing (3) or (4). Logical reasoning would lead you to discount (5); while people who already own stock would lose money if they sell after the price drops, many would still want to sell in case the stock became worthless in the near future.

1. Since 17 percent of all businesses in the U.S. are corporations, corporations do 17 percent of the business in the U.S. What is the faulty logic in this statement?

   (1) More than 17 percent of all businesses in the U.S. are corporations.

   (2) Corporations hire a lot of people and produce a lot of goods.

   (3) Corporations are more productive than other organizations because the employees are owners of the business.

   (4) Corporations can afford to take more risks than other organizations because the owners cannot lose their personal assets if the business fails.

   (5) Corporations are sometimes very large businesses and might therefore do a higher percentage of U.S. business than 17 percent.

2. Sally got a Christmas bonus and decided to invest it by buying stock in a corporation. She didn't have much information, so she invested in a company that had many shares to sell, figuring there would be safety in numbers. Why was her reasoning faulty?

   (1) Only a stockbroker can know if stock is likely to go up or down.

   (2) The stock market is too risky for small investors; she could lose all her money.

   (3) The idea of "safety in numbers" is not relevant; the value of the stock could still go down.

   (4) She couldn't have gotten enough from a bonus to make it worth investing in the stock market.

   (5) She oversimplified the situation by assuming that people who invest in the stock market make money.

Item 3 is based on the following table.

THE TEN MOST DENSELY POPULATED STATES IN THE U.S.	
State	Persons per square mile
New Jersey	940
Rhode Island	780
Massachusetts	695
Connecticut	620
Maryland	399
New York	354
Delaware	289
Ohio	262
Pennsylvania	262
Illinois	202

Fig. 4–10   Source: U.S. Bureau of the Census, 1980 Census figures.

3. Wayne has decided to open a sole proprietorship—a print shop where he can make personalized stationery, business cards, and provide other printing services. He currently lives in a suburb of Chicago, but he thinks he'd do better in a place where there are more people. Since he doesn't like city living, he rules out moving to a place like New York or Chicago. Besides, he's afraid there would be too much competition in a large city. Observing that New Jersey has a high population density, he sets up in a small town in a central part of the state. What is faulty about his reasoning?

(1) State population-density figures don't mean that small towns provide big enough markets

(2) There probably wouldn't be more competition in a large city

(3) There isn't much need for print shops outside of large cities

(4) He won't be able to get the supplies he needs as easily as he would in a city

(5) Central New Jersey has a lot of farms

Answers are on page 378–379.

Banks and Other Financial Institutions

Prereading Prompt

What happens to the money we deposit in checking and savings accounts at banks? How do banks use our money? What services do we get in return? Test your knowledge of banks and the banking system in the next lesson.

Key Words

commercial bank—bank that makes its money primarily by lending to businesses

savings and loan association—bank that provides savings accounts and money for home and personal loans

credit union—nonprofit organization owned by depositors that offers many services of a bank but no more advantageous terms

Basic Elements of Banking

In the old days, many people kept their life savings in the home, maybe stuffed in an old mattress or under a loose floor board. Today, most of us keep our money in a bank. Banks are institutions that specialize in financial transactions. They take in money, lend money, and store valuables, such as jewelry and important papers, in a vault.

If you have a checking account at a bank, you deposit money into your account and then write checks against this money. You use checks to pay bills, purchase goods in a store, and to withdraw money from the account.

Some banks charge you a fee for every check you write or a monthly service charge to cover the cost of managing your account. With other accounts, if you keep enough money deposited, there is no fee because the bank is making money from your account in other ways.

When you deposit money into a bank, it doesn't just sit in a vault. The bank uses your money to make more money. One way it does this is by lending money to its customers. Many banks offer loans for different purposes. You can get a loan to buy a house, through an arrangement in which you promise to give your house to the bank if you cannot pay off the loan. This is called a *mortgage*. You can also get a loan to buy a car or some other expensive item. Other types of loans include home-improvement loans, for people who want to fix up their homes, and small-business loans, for people who are starting a business. When you take a loan, you pay back a set amount every month, with *interest*—a fee that you pay to the bank for the service of using its money.

(Credit: Wally Aaron)

Sometimes the bank pays *you* interest for the service of using *your* money. This is the case when you hold a *savings account* with a bank. The money you deposit into your account is used by the bank to make more money, and the bank pays you interest according to how much is in your account.

Many banks also offer customers bank *credit cards*. A credit card is essentially a loan, providing you with money you don't have. When you pay back the money, you pay it with interest, just as with a loan.

Types of Financial Institutions

The most common financial institution in the United States is the **commercial bank**. Checking accounts are held with commercial banks. Commercial, as in the word commerce, means that these banks make money primarily by lending to businesses. If you need money to start a business, such as a hairstyling salon, a commercial bank would be the place to go for a loan. Established businesses that need money for new equipment or wish to expand also go to a commercial bank for a loan. Businesses, like individuals, also have checking accounts with commercial banks.

Another type of bank is the **savings and loan association**, or S & L. The primary functions of these banks is clear from their name—savings and loans. S & L's provide a place for you to keep your money while earning interest on your account. They are also the main source of most home mortgages and home-improvement loans. S & L's charge you interest to borrow their money, and pay you interest when they use your money.

A third type of financial institution is the **credit union**. Credit unions are owned by their depositors and so are not run for profit. Their purpose is solely to serve their members; they are not open to the public. Credit unions are often established at large companies that have many employees. Because they are nonprofit, they pay higher interest on savings accounts and charge lower interest for loans than banks do.

1. Credit unions can offer their members better rates on savings accounts and loans because they
   (1) have so many members
   (2) are not in business to make money
   (3) are part of large corporations
   (4) are owned by their depositors
   (5) are not open to the public

2. Some banks issue credit cards that enable you to spend money you don't have at the moment. Banks can also issue debit cards. These enable you to draw on money already in your account. Using a debit card is most like using
   (1) a savings account
   (2) a checking account
   (3) cash
   (4) a credit card
   (5) a loan

3. Which conclusion is supported by information in the passage?
   (1) Banks are in business to make money.
   (2) Banks are in business to provide low-cost loans to businesses.
   (3) People should do their banking at credit unions rather than at banks.
   (4) Banks charge interest to cover the cost of handling your loan.
   (5) Banks can invest your money only for limited periods of time.

Answers are on page 379.

The Federal Reserve System

Prereading Prompt

You often hear on the news that "the Fed" has tightened or loosened its money policy. What does this mean? What determines how much interest you will pay on a loan? Where do banks get their money from? Find out the answers in this lesson.

Key Words

Federal Reserve System—system that regulates the nation's money supply
reserve ratio—the amount of money that banks are not allowed to lend out as loans; equal to a percentage of deposited money
discount rates—interest charged for borrowing money from the Federal Reserve

The argument over whether or not to have a central banking system in the United States is almost is almost as old as the nation. Without a centralized system, the government could not regulate the supply of money or its value. This would lead to a very unstable economy.

(Credit: Laima Druskis)

There are 12 Federal Reserve banks, not to be confused with the national and state banks at which we do our banking. These banks are run by a Board of Governors, appointed to 14-year terms by the President and approved by the Senate. The Federal Reserve Board makes the decisions regarding the nation's money supply.

One way the **Federal Reserve**, or Fed, regulates the money supply is by determining the **reserve ratio** for banks. Remember that banks use money on deposit to increase the money supply by issuing loans. The reserve ratio is the percentage of deposited money the bank is not allowed to lend out. If banks are required to keep a lot of money on hand, less is available for loans. There will then be less money in circulation to invest. Everyone from home builders to home buyers, both small and large businesses, will have trouble getting loans. Economic activity slows down when this happens. Another purpose of this so-called "tight money" policy is to prevent inflation.

Of course, the opposite is also true. If the Fed sets a low reserve ratio, the banks have more money available for loans. If loans are easier to get and there is more money in circulation, economic activity increases. Along with this "easy money" policy, however, sometimes comes inflation.

The Fed also regulates the money supply by fixing the *discount rate*. This is the interest rate that state and national banks pay to borrow money from the Federal Reserve banks. If your bank has to pay a lot of interest to borrow money, you will have to pay higher interest to your bank to take out a loan. If you hear on the evening news that the Fed has tightened its money policy, this is what they are referring to. Likewise, the opposite is also true. When the Fed loosens its money policy, the discount rate is low; banks can then borrow more money for less and charge their customers less for loans.

Item 1 is based on the following charts.

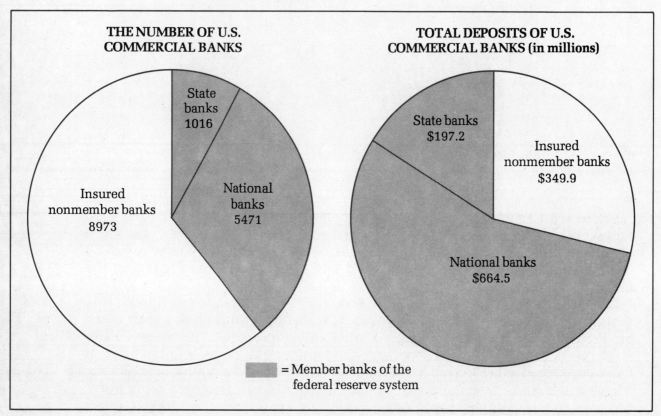

THE NUMBER OF U.S. COMMERCIAL BANKS

State banks 1016

Insured nonmember banks 8973

National banks 5471

TOTAL DEPOSITS OF U.S. COMMERCIAL BANKS (in millions)

State banks $197.2

Insured nonmember banks $349.9

National banks $664.5

= Member banks of the federal reserve system

Fig. 4–11

1. Which generalization can be supported by the information in the two charts?

    (1) There are disadvantages to banks and customers to belonging to the Federal Reserve System.

    (2) There are advantages to banks and customers to belonging to the Federal Reserve System.

    (3) National banks hold the most deposits because they are the only members of the Federal Reserve System.

    (4) Members of the Federal Reserve System hold the most deposits because they are the only banks that are insured.

    (5) Because there are so many of them, nonmember banks do almost as much business as national banks and state banks together.

2. A young family wants to get a home-improvement loan so they can make an addition to their house. They decide to wait until the Fed tightens its money policy. Is this decision based on sound reasoning?

    (1) Yes: there will be a lot of money available for loans at lower interest rates.

    (2) Yes: interest rates will be a little higher, but a lot of money will be available so the loan should be easy to get.

    (3) Yes: there won't be a lot of money available, but what money there is will be lent at a fairly low rate.

    (4) No: there will be little money available and the interest rates will be high.

    (5) No: it would be better to wait until the reserve ratio is raised.

3. Which of the following would be most likely to lead to an economic upswing?

    (1) lowering the reserve ratio and the discount rate

    (2) raising the reserve ratio and the discount rate

    (3) lowering the reserve ratio and raising the discount rate

    (4) raising the reserve ratio and lowering the discount rate

    (5) keeping the reserve ratio the same and raising the discount rate

Answers are on page 379.

The Role of Government in Business and the Economy

Prereading Prompt

As a consumer, what guarantees do you have that the products you buy are safe? Why don't car companies manufacture automobiles that emit high levels of pollutants? There are government agencies that watch almost every facet of business in America. Learn more about them in this lesson.

Key Words

Environmental Protection Agency—agency responsible for regulating pollution and use of the environment
Occupational Safety and Health Administration—agency that oversees safety in the workplace
Federal Drug Administration—agency that tests products for human use and consumption before they are released to the public
Equal Employment Opportunity Commission—agency designed to eliminate discrimination in the workplace

Regulation of Business Activities

Americans have always resented government intervention in their private and business affairs; our Constitution and Bill of Rights were designed to protect citizens from the power of big government. This hasn't stopped the government, however, from intervening in the name of the best interest of the people.

Aside from regulating the nation's money supply, the federal government also sets regulations on businesses. Antitrust laws were passed to keep businesses from becoming *monopolies*—businesses in a single industry so big that they effectively eliminate all competition. The telephone company is an example of a monopoly that was ordered by the government to break up. Before the break-up, AT&T (the American Telephone and Telegraph Company) handled all matters having to do with your phone, from installation and service to equipment and repairs. Today, regional companies provide local service, and you can choose from several long-distance phone companies that offer competitive rates. There are also a number of different brands of phones and accessories to pick from. Prohibition of monopolies helps keep the free-enterprise economy competitive.

The stock market is a major factor in the nation's economy, enabling shares in corporations to be bought and sold (see Lesson 3 of this chapter). In 1934, the **Securities and Exchange Commission (SEC)** was established to restore the confidence of investors after the stock market crash of 1929. The SEC prohibited certain practices that had contributed to the crash, such as purchasing stock without having enough money to pay for it. If many people do this and stocks decrease in value, as happened in the 1920s, the stock market and the economy can be weakened to dangerous levels.

The SEC also prohibits the use of nonpublic information in stock trading. This is a big issue today. In the mid-1980s, there was a rash of *insider trading*—the illegal use of secret, nonpublic information to make money on the stock market. The SEC investigated and brought charges against several big investors and traders who had engaged in insider trading. Many were convicted of violating securities laws.

The federal government has many other "watchdog" agencies whose job is to regulate business. The **Environmental Protection Agency (EPA)** was designed to keep businesses from destroying the environment. It sets limits on the amount and type of pollution that factories can release into the air and water; it limits where and how oil drilling and mining can proceed; it sets limits on the amount of pollution that cars can emit in their exhaust; and it oversees the dumping of toxic waste.

The **Federal Trade Commission (FTC)**, established in 1914, is another watchdog agency. It prohibits misleading or false advertising, spying on competition to obtain trade secrets, and imitating a competitor's product. Corporations need never hear from the FTC if they stay within their guidelines. Violators can be forced to change their business practices or close down. The courts have the final say in such matters.

Consumer Protection

Many restrictions placed on businesses are designed specifically to protect consumers from unsafe or unfair practices. The **Occupational Safety and Health Administration (OSHA)** sets standards for safety in the workplace. Among other things, it requires employers to provide adequate lighting and ventilation and protective clothing for people who work with hazardous materials.

(Credit: Courtesy of AEROVOX, INC., New Bedford, MA)

Another government regulatory agency is the **Food and Drug Administration**. The FDA inspects, tests, approves, and sets safety standards for foods, drugs, cosmetics, and chemicals such as pesticides and household cleansers. The **U.S. Department of Agriculture (USDA)** also protects consumers by inspecting and grading food products. The blue stamp you may have noticed on a piece of beef in a market shows that the meat has been inspected and approved by the USDA.

The **Equal Employment Opportunity Commission (EEOC)** was established to prohibit business from discriminating against workers on the basis of race or sex. A job applicant who feels that he or she has been passed over for a job solely because of race can lodge a complaint with the EEOC against the offending business. The EEOC will investigate and bring charges, if necessary.

Lesson 6 Exercises

1. The Food and Drug Administration will not release drugs until it tests them and is satisfied that they are safe and effective. People lobbying for the cause of AIDS patients, however, have convinced the FDA to make exceptions. Since FDA testing takes so long, many AIDS patients would die before drugs that might help them become available. In 1989, the FDA agreed to make dideoxyinosine (DDI) available for widespread use, even though testing was not yet complete. A report showed that of 8,000 people taking DDI under the FDA's "expanded access" program, 290 have died. With the release of this report, the FDA has come under attack for relaxing its standards. Which statement below expresses the apparent reason for the FDA's decision?

   (1) The risk involved in relaxing standards was worth it to save some lives.
   (2) The pressure from AIDS activists was so great that the agency caved in to their demands.
   (3) Drugs should never be released for widespread use until they have been adequately tested.
   (4) AIDS must be stopped before the entire population becomes infected.
   (5) The agency was quite convinced that the drug was safe, even without completing testing.

2. The CPSC is a government regulatory agency many of us know about indirectly. If you buy a toy for your child that is later found to be harmful in some way, the CPSC notifies toy stores, doctors' offices, and the press to alert people to the potential danger. It also sounds the alarm if electric shavers, hair dryers, and other kinds of products are found to be dangerous. CPSC stands for

   (1) Council on Prices and Standards of Commodities
   (2) Commission on Protection and Safety for Children
   (3) Consumer Product Safety Commission
   (4) Central Press Services Committee
   (5) Commercial Product Services Council

Item 3 is based on the following advertisement.

"The greatest health aid yet!"
That's what nutrition expert Heather Heath says about new Chop-a-Lot, the fabulous new, state-of-the-art food processor. It slices, it dices, it chops and grates, but it does much more than that! It makes the world's best-tasting and healthiest drinks from your own fresh fruits and vegetables. And best of all, you'll never have to worry about getting another cold!!

3. Which government regulatory agency would blow the whistle on this company?

   (1) SEC
   (2) USDA
   (3) FDA
   (4) OSHA
   (5) FTC

Answers are on page 379–380.

Measuring the Economy

Key Words

gross national product—total value of goods and services produced and sold in a given period
consumer price index—measure of change in the cost of goods and services

Two Economic Measures

If you follow the evening news, you often hear the term, "leading economic indicators." This refers to several figures that indicate the relative health of the economy. Perhaps the most important economic indicator is the **gross national product,** or **GNP**. It is the total value of everything produced and sold in the United States during a given period. If you buy a TV set or a hammer or a pair of jeans, this is part of the GNP. If you pay someone to paint your house or fix your washing machine, this is also part of the GNP. The GNP is computed four times a year.

The **consumer price index**, or **CPI**, is another economic indicator. The CPI measures changes in the cost of certain groups of goods and services—things the average person buys and uses, such as food, clothing, housing, transportation, and medical care. It is a measure of prices in a given year against prices in another year. All the figures are relative. The table below shows the CPI for March 1988 and March 1989. It uses prices in 1984 for comparison. Next to the heading "Food," you see that the average city dweller paid $123.5 in March 1989 and $115.9 in March 1988. The same amount of food cost only $100 in 1984. What this shows is that food cost almost 25 percent more in 1989 than in 1984.

Consumer Price Index for All Urban Consumers (1984 = 100)		
Group	March 1989	March 1988
All items	122.3	116.5
Food	123.5	115.9
Alcoholic beverages	121.8	117.4
Apparel and upkeep	119.3	114.3
Total housing	121.5	117.0
Rent	138.6	132.9
Gas & elec.	104.8	101.7
Transportation	111.9	106.5
Medical care	146.1	136.3
Entertainment	124.7	119.0

Source: Department of Labor, Bureau of Labor Statistics

Business Cycles and Unemployment

The GNP and CPI are used to gauge the health of the economy. As conditions change, so does the economy. It moves in cycles from prosperity (good health) to recession or inflation (poor health).

When there is **inflation**, prices of goods and services go up. Wages may go up too, but usually not enough to keep pace with prices, and so people are able to buy less with their money. With inflation, it costs you more to do or buy the same things today than it did a year or two ago. If you go to the movies today (in 1991), it might cost you between $6.00 and $8.00, depending on where you live. Five years ago, it probably cost you $3.00 to $5.00 at the same theater. Inflation caused the value of the dollar to fall. Sometimes, if inflation gets out of control, the government may "freeze" wages and prices to keep them from going any higher.

In a **recession**, production slows and unemployment rises. Low production causes a low GNP. With many people out of work, business is generally slow because people can't afford to buy much. The entire economy sags. If a recession becomes serious enough or goes on for too long, the government may try to give the economy a boost. One way it does this is by creating public-works projects to get people back on the payroll. Another way is by granting low-cost loans to businesses to encourage production and raise employment.

The rate of unemployment is also an indicator of economic health. Under normal conditions, the unemployment rate is generally around 4 percent. This means that of all the people who are willing and able to work, 4 percent cannot find jobs. In a recession, unemployment may go as high as 7 or 8 percent. During a depression, which is a severe recession, unemployment can skyrocket. During the Great Depression of the 1930s, unemployment was over 20 percent. Unemployment that is related to the normal cycles of economic health is called **cyclical unemployment**.

Another kind of unemployment is **structural unemployment**. This is caused by rapid changes that are not related to the normal economic cycle. An example of this is often found in "factory towns." If an entire industry declines (like the U.S. steel industry), or if the company that owns the factory either closes it or moves it to an area where labor is cheaper, structural unemployment is the result.

Lesson 7 Exercises

Item 1 is based on the following table.

Percentage changes in Consumer Prices In Selected OECD Countries % changes in consumer prices in						
Country	1979	1980	1981	1982	1983	1984*
United States	11.3	13.5	10.4	6.1	3.2	4.2
Japan	3.6	8.0	4.9	2.7	1.9	2.3
West Germany	4.1	5.5	5.9	5.3	3.3	2.1
France	10.6	13.6	13.4	11.8	9.8	8.9
United Kingdom	13.4	18.0	11.9	8.8	5.1	5.0
Italy	14.8	21.2	19.5	16.6	14.5	8.6
Canada	9.2	10.2	12.5	10.8	5.9	3.4

*Twelve month rate of change (not directly comparable with annual changes).

Fig. 4–12 Sources: *OECD Economic Outlook*, July 1984; *OECD Main Economic Indicators*, From 1985 *Britannica Book of the Year* (Chicago: Encyclopaedia Britannica 1985), p. 204.

1. Percentages of change in consumer prices are often considered a good indication of the rate of inflation. On that basis, which of the following generalizations is NOT supported by information on the table?

   (1) Japanese and German consumers consistently got the most for their money.

   (2) Italian consumers consistently paid more for less than any other nationality listed.

   (3) Nearly all these countries had their worst inflation in 1980.

   (4) Canadian consumers consistently got more for their money than consumers in the United States.

   (5) Consumers in the United States consistently got more for their money than consumers in the United Kingdom.

2. Oil has always been big business in Texas. But when the price of oil began to fall in the 1980s, many Texans found their main industry in ruins. Work was hard to find, and towns that had grown up around the oil industry became ghost towns. This is an example of

(1) inflation
(2) recession
(3) depression
(4) cyclical unemployment
(5) structural unemployment

Item 3 is based on the following cartoon.

Fig. 4–13 Source: Cartoon by Bruce Shanks. Reprinted by permission of *The Buffalo News*.

3. In 1958, the United States experienced a serious recession, so serious that some people talked of a depression. A popular joke was that recession is when you lose your job; depression is when I lose mine. The cartoon below is from the late 1950s. What is its main point?

(1) Business upturns are usually as steep as the recessions that precede them.
(2) The economy moves in cycles from poor health to good health.
(3) The hardship of recessions makes business upturns seem unlikely.
(4) Recession can snowball into inflation.
(5) The economy can be compared to the downward ride of a rollercoaster.

Answers are on page 380.

CHAPTER 5

Geography has two interacting parts. It is the study of the Earth and how it affects people, and it is the study of how people affect the Earth. In the 1990s, we are finally coming to appreciate just how critical our relationship with this planet is. We are at the mercy of natural onslaughts—earthquakes, hurricanes, floods, and droughts. The Earth is at the mercy of human on-slaughts—pollution, destruction of the rainforests, and misuses of the land. The relationship is delicate and precious; we cannot live without the Earth.

Rain Forest, Africa
(Credit: Charlotte Kahler/PIX, Inc., NY)

Prereading Prompt

Where is Panama? Iraq? The Amazon River? Studying geography will tell you. What will happen if the rainforests disappear? Studying geography will also tell you. In this chapter you will discover the many fascinating topics that make up geography.

Geography

What Is Geography?

There was a time when home for human beings was a cave, a hut, a log cabin, or a house. As travel became easier, we started to think of home as the city, the state, or the country where we lived. Now the Space Age has given us a new view of the world—a global view. We live on the planet Earth.

People who study **geography**—the relationship between the Earth and its inhabitants—know that the way people live is affected by where they live. The Portuguese, the Japanese, and the Eskimos, for example, all live near oceans, and so eat a lot of fish. Inland groups, such as Eastern Europeans and people in the central U.S., eat what is available—domestic farm animals and seasonal fruits and vegetables. The types of homes people live in and the building materials they use are also largely determined by where they live— their **environment**. In New England or the Pacific Northwest, forests cover much of the land; homes are made of wood. In the American Southwest, however, the hot, dry conditions don't support forests, and houses are often made of adobe, a sun-dried combination of clay and straw.

People are also affected by the Earth when natural disasters occur. People who live near large rivers know that too much rain can cause the river to spill over its banks and flood their homes and businesses. People who live in areas where earthquakes occur also feel the effects of the Earth. Residents of California live with the constant threat that the ground will suddenly start shaking.

Geographers also know that people affect the Earth. Unfortunately, much of what we do has a negative effect. Every time we drill for oil, mine for coal, or level forests for wood, we do some damage. However, we need the Earth's **resources** to live. People must find a way to get what they need from the Earth without destroying it. Geographers can help protect the planet by studying how the water, soil, and air change due to humanity's influence. They can also help protect people by studying weather and climate, patterns of natural disasters, and how the population is distributed across the globe.

Key Words

geography—the study of the relationship between people and the Earth

environment—everything that surrounds us, including animals, air, water, soil, plants, and people

resources—available supplies, such as oil, coal, water and metal ores, that can be drawn upon when needed

Maps and Globes

Prereading Prompt

When you drive to a place you've never been before, you probably use a road map to help find the way. There are hundreds of ways to represent the Earth's surface on paper, of which road maps are only one. Find out about some others in this lesson.

Key Words

political maps—maps showing man-made boundaries
physical maps—maps showing major land features and general elevations
latitude—distance north or south of the equator
longitude—distance east or west of the prime meridian

Kinds of Maps

Maps are the main tools of geographers. There are many different kinds, each used to show particular kinds of information. You are probably most familiar with **political maps**, which show the man-made boundaries between countries, states, counties, and towns. They also show the locations of cities and major bodies of water. Figure 5-1 on page 217 is a political map of the United States. Like most political maps, there is *a legend*, or scale of miles, that helps you figure out distances on the map. In this case, one inch equals 630 miles.

A **physical map** shows the natural features of the Earth, including rivers, lakes, oceans, deserts, mountains, and continents. Figure 5–1 is a physical map. It uses colored shading to show relief, or variations in the elevation of the Earth's surface. **Sea level** is the point against which elevation is measured. A physical map uses shades of colors to indicate the general elevation of whole areas, such as mountain ranges, deserts, and plains.

More specific details about elevation are shown on special kinds of physical maps known as *topographical maps*. These maps use contour lines to represent distances above or below sea level. They also often use colors, and shades of colors, to indicate differences in elevation. Such use of color on maps is called *relief*.

Many other kinds of information can be shown on special-purpose maps. These maps may present information on natural resources, climate and weather, population, land use, agricultural production, vegetation, soil groups, and so on.

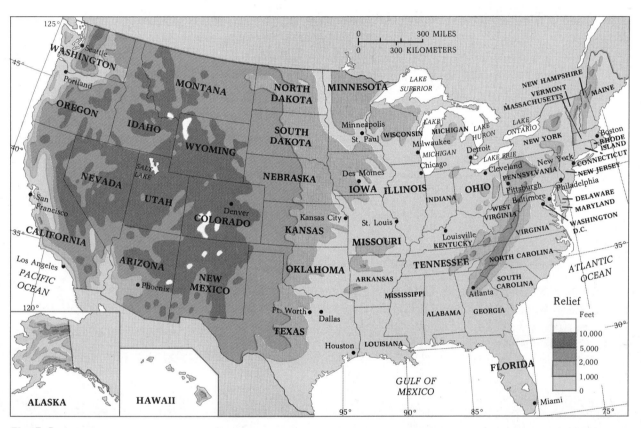

Fig. 5–1

Latitude and Longitude

You have probably heard of the **equator**—an imaginary line that divides the Earth in two. Areas north of the equator are in the Northern Hemisphere; areas south of it are in the Southern Hemisphere. How far north or south of the equator a region lies is measured in degrees of **latitude**. The equator is at 0° (zero degrees) latitude. Look at Figure 5-2 to see how the lines of latitude indicate distance from the equator. The United States (excluding Alaska and Hawaii) lies generally between 25° and 50° north latitude.

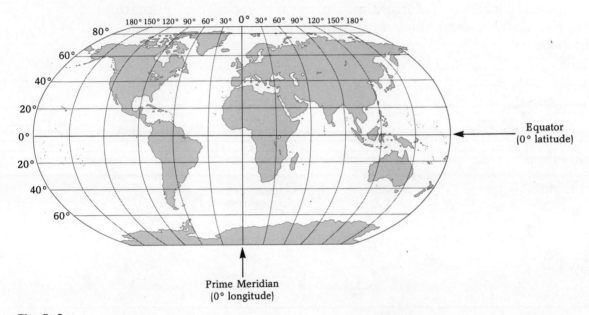

Fig. 5–2

Another imaginary line, called the **prime meridian**, divides the Earth in the other direction. Areas east of the meridian are in the Eastern Hemisphere; areas west of it are in the Western Hemisphere. Lines running parallel to the meridian measure distances east and west in degrees of **longitude**. The prime meridian is at 0° longitude. Look again at Figure 5-2. You can see that most of the U.S. (excluding Alaska and Hawaii) lies between 70° and 125° west longitude.

You can see that lines of latitude and longitude cross each other to form a grid on a map. The two numbers where the lines intersect are called **coordinates**. Coordinates are used to give the exact location of a given place. Look at Figure 5-1 to see how this works. Find Jacksonville, Florida. It is located at about 31° north latitude and 82° west longitude.

Item 1 is based on the following map and passage.

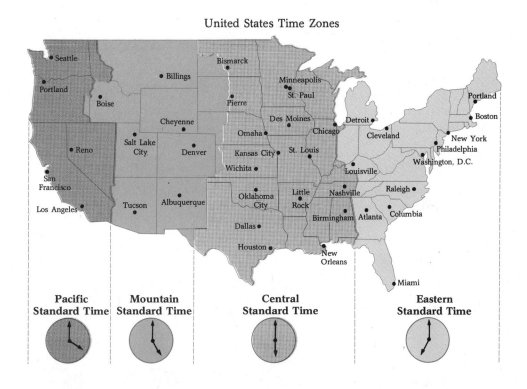

United States Time Zones

Fig. 5–3 Source: Reprinted with permission of *The New Book of Knowledge*, 1990 edition, © Grolier Inc.

If you have traveled, you know that there are different time zones throughout the world. There are 24 time zones in all. Because it takes the Earth 24 hours to rotate one full turn (360°), each zone is one hour away from the next. Also, each zone is the equivalent of 15° of longitude (360° divided by 24).

Within the continental United States there are four time zones. Each is one hour later than the one immediately to the west of it. This is because the sun appears to move from east to west relative to the Earth. Figure 3 shows the four different time zones. Notice that when it is 7:00 P.M. on the east coast, it is 4:00 P.M. on the west coast.

1. You are on a business trip to Washington, D.C. You want to call your family in Tucson. The best time to get everyone at home is around supper time, 6:00 P.M. What time should you place the call by your time in Washington?
   (1) 6:00 PM
   (2) 4:00 PM
   (3) 3:00 PM
   (4) 8:00 PM
   (5) 5:00 PM

Items 2 and 3 are based on Figures 5-1 and 5-2.

2. According to the map, which two U.S. cities are at the same longitude?
   (1) Pittsburgh and Salt Lake City
   (2) Pittsburgh and New York
   (3) New Orleans and Mobile
   (4) Memphis and St. Louis
   (5) St. Louis and New Orleans

3. In what country would you be if you were at 65° north latitude and 150° west longitude?
   (1) the United States
   (2) Canada
   (3) Mexico
   (4) the Soviet Union
   (5) Greenland

Answers are on page 380.

Topography

Prereading Prompt

As you know, the surface of the Earth is not flat. Representing its uneven surface on flat paper poses special challenges to cartographers (mapmakers). This lesson describes how these challenges have been met.

Key Words

contour lines—lines that show elevations of landforms on a topographical map
relief—colors and shades of color used to show elevations of landforms on a topographical map

Geographers use topographical maps to show elevation. Some topographical maps use **relief** to indicate elevation. Look at Figure 5-1 in the previous lesson.

You can see some of the features indicated in relief. The mountain chain extending down the western part of North America appears as the darkest area. The smaller white areas indicate the highest peaks. The highest altitudes below the mountain chains are shown in blue. Altitudes of 1,000 feet above sea leavel appear tan, and those at sea level as light blue.

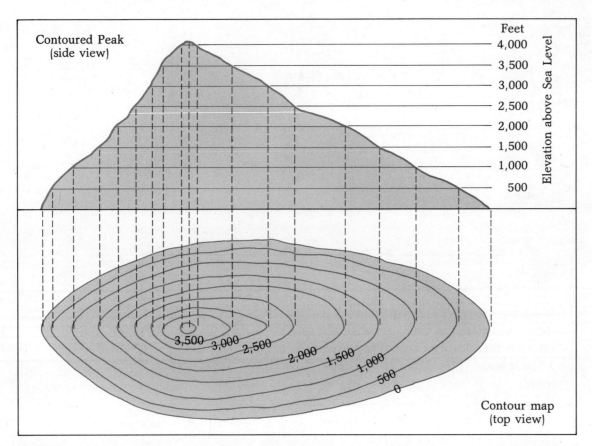

Contoured Peak
(side view)

Feet
4,000
3,500
3,000
2,500
2,000
1,500
1,000
500

Elevation above Sea Level

3,500 3,000 2,500 2,000 1,500 1,000 500 0

Contour map
(top view)

Fig. 5—4

Another way to show elevation is with **contour lines**. Contour lines give more precise information than relief maps. Look at Figure 5-4. The top figure represents a mountain. The numbers on the right show the elevation of the mountain at different points. Find 2,500 feet on the right. Follow the dotted line left to the mountain, then down to the contour map. The area within the ring is between 2,500 and 3,000 feet. The entire contour map represents the mountain shown above it, as if you were looking down on it from above. When the lines of a contour map are spaced closely together, they represent a steep incline. The farther apart they are, the more level the land they represent.

Lesson 2 Exercises

Item 1 is based on Figure 5–1.

1. Look at the east and southeast coasts of the United States. Find the contour lines that radiate out from the land into the ocean. These are shaded lightest blue right by the land, with each ring becoming a progressively darker blue as they extend into the water. From the map, you can see that the land below sea level that lies off the coasts
   (1) drops sharply
   (2) drops sharply and then levels off
   (3) drops gradually
   (4) drops gradually and then levels off
   (5) is level and then very uneven

2. Suppose you are looking at a topographical map with contour lines. The lines are widely and evenly spaced, and the elevations run between 10 and 100 feet. What is this a map of?
   (1) a mountain range
   (2) plains with gently rolling hills
   (3) plains with occasional plateaus
   (4) a hilly region
   (5) coastal plains with cliffs

Item 3 is based on the following map.

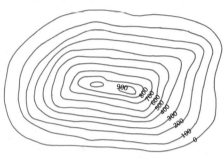

Fig. 5–5

3. The landform in Figure 5–5 represents
   (1) a steep hill
   (2) a gradual slope
   (3) a series of small hills
   (4) a steep hill that levels off into a plain
   (5) a gradual slope that levels off into a plain

Answers are on page 380.

Climate and the Seasons

Prereading Prompt

Suppose you wanted to get away to a place that's sunny and warm. Where would you go? If you're like most people in the United States, you head south, to the tropics. While there is no guarantee you'll have splendid weather, in general the tropics are always hot. Do you know why?

Key Words

tropical zone—the region around the equator, between the Tropics of Cancer and the Tropic of Capricorn, characterized by a hot, humid climate
temperate zones—two regions, one between the Tropic of Cancer and the Arctic Circle, the other between the Tropic of Capricorn and the Antarctic Circle, characterized by four distinct seasons
arctic zones—two regions, one north of the Arctic Circle, the other south of the Antarctic Circle, with an extremely cold climate

Seasons

You may know that the seasons are relative to where you are on the Earth. When it's summer in North America and Europe, it's winter in most of South America and Africa. Why is this?

The Earth rotates, or spins, on its axis. The axis is an imaginary line running through the middle of the Earth. The Earth's axis is tilted, either 23 1/2 degrees toward the sun or 23 1/2 degrees away from the sun. Figures 5–6 and 5–7 illustrate how the sun's rays hit the planet. When the north pole of the axis tilts away from the sun (Figure 5–6), the sun's rays hit the Northern Hemisphere less directly. The days are shorter and the weather is colder: it is fall and winter. When the north pole of the axis tilts toward the sun (Figure 5–7), however, the Northern Hemisphere receives the sun's rays directly. The days are longer and it is warmer: it is spring and summer.

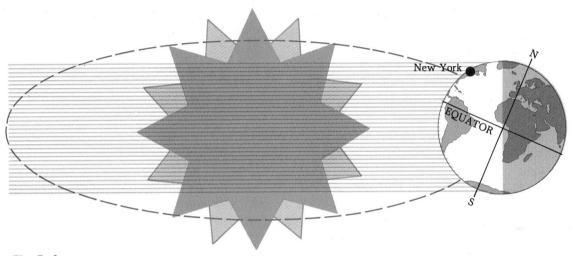

Fig. 5–6

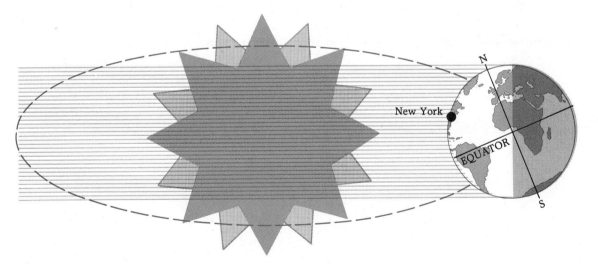

Fig. 5–7

The seasons change from summer to winter when the Earth has completed half its journey around the sun. On March 21st, day and night are the same length all over the Earth. This is the first day of spring in the Northern Hemisphere. Autumn begins on September 21 in the Northern Hemisphere.

Climate

People often talk about climate and weather as if they were one and the same. **Climate** is the general weather pattern in a geographical area. **Weather** refers to the specifics of temperature, wind, and precipitation at a given time.

The tilt of the Earth's axis has a lot to do with the climate of a given region. The region around the equator always receives a lot of sun because of the Earth's tilt. The **tropical zone** is defined by two imaginary lines: the Tropic of Cancer is 23 1/2 degrees north of the equator; the Tropic of Capricorn in 23 1/2 degrees south of the equator. Between these two lines the climate is tropical. Figure 5–8 shows the tropics and their climate. Most of the tropics are hot and humid, with heavy rainfall. The temperature changes little throughout the year. Thick jungle and rainforests cover much of this area, especially in South America.

There are two **temperate zones**, extending north and south away from the tropics. The northern region lies between the Tropic of Cancer and the Arctic Circle (66½ degrees north). The southern region lies between the Tropic of Capricorn and the Antarctic Circle (66½ degrees south). In the temperate zones, there are four distinct seasons. This is because the farther you go from the equator, the more the climate is affected by the tilt of the Earth's axis. Most of the United States lies within the temperate zone. Look at Figure 5–8 to see how many different types of climate occur in this zone. There are arid (dry) and semiarid regions, where little rain falls. There are mountainous areas, which have a climate all their own.

Moving outward from the temperate zones toward the poles, one finds two more regions—the **arctic zones**. These regions are characterized by extremely cold temperatures and are largely covered by ice caps, huge masses of ice hundreds of miles wide. The poles never receive direct sunlight, and because they are so cold, only certain kinds of plants and animals can live there.

Climates of the World

Cold Climates
  1 Ice Cap
  2 Subpolar

Cold Temperature Climates
  3 Subartic
  4 Humid continental short summer
  5 Humid continental long summer

Warm Temperature Climates
  6 Temperature marine
  7 Humid subtropical
  8 Dry summer subtropical

Dry Climates
  9 Arid mid-latitude
  10 Arid low latitude
  11 Semiarid mid-latitude
  12 Semiarid low latitude

Tropical Climates
  13 Rainy-and-dry tropical
  14 Rainy tropical

Highlands

Fig. 5–8

Items 1 and 2 are based on Figure 5–8.

1. Find the regions marked 10 in the United States. Which description below would you think best describes the plant life in these areas?

   very lush, dense, varied

   moderately dense, varied

   grassland and trees

   marshes and swamps

   sparse and limited

2. It's springlike in the area marked 7 in South America. At the same time, in the area marked 5 in North America the weather would be
   - (1) warm, with the days getting longer
   - (2) warm, with the days getting shorter
   - (3) cool, with the days getting longer
   - (4) cool, with the days getting shorter
   - (5) cold, with the days getting longer

3. In the phenomenon known as the midnight sun, the sun virtually never sets for six months. You would expect to witness this phenomenon
   - (1) above the Arctic Circle and below the Antarctic Circle
   - (2) between the Tropic of Cancer and the Arctic Circle
   - (3) between the equator and the Tropic of Cancer
   - (4) between the equator and the Tropic of Capricorn
   - (5) between the Tropic of Capricorn and the Antarctic Circle

Answers are on page 380-381.

Lesson 4

The Earth's Regions

Prereading Prompt

Most of us are aware of the weather patterns where we live. There is usually a wet and a dry season, a cool and a warm season. Many factors affect the weather patterns of the different regions of the world. This lesson will tell you more about them.

Key Words

precipitation—rain, snow, sleet, hail
prevailing winds—global wind patterns
continents—the seven great land masses
natural vegetation—wild plant life that is native to a region

Weather in the Earth's Regions

In the previous lesson, you learned about the broad climatic zones that radiate out from the equator. Look at Figure 5–8 again. You can see how different regions within the same zone have different climatic conditions. A major factor affecting climate is the oceans. Because large bodies of water take a long time to warm and to cool, their temperature remains fairly constant relative to the land. The oceans therefore have a moderating effect on the temperature of coastal regions. In the northeastern U.S., for example, winters along the coast are warm compared to the inland regions, particularly the mountains. It may be snowing a few miles inland, but raining near the water's edge. The same is true in the summer. When it is horribly hot inland, the shore areas tend to be cooler because the ocean temperature is cooler than the air temperature. Breezes off the water cool down the air.

Within the oceans are currents of warmer and colder water. These are like streams that carry water through the oceans around the continents. The Gulf Stream is fed by water flowing westward from North Africa, across the Atlantic to the Caribbean and into the Gulf of Mexico. This warm, equatorial water eventually finds its way back across the North Atlantic to England and Norway. Because of the Gulf Stream, the temperature in parts of Norway is extremely moderate during the winter even though the country is just south of the Arctic Circle. Likewise, in southwestern England, it is mild enough to grow vegetables and flowers—even subtropical lemon trees—in the winter.

Water in the form of **precipitation** is another major factor in the climate of a region. In the tropics, where the weather is always hot and the oceans provide plentiful water, rainfall is heavy and steady throughout the year. In the Arctic, even though there is plenty of water, it is too cold for much precipitation to fall. In the temperate zones, precipitation occurs in greater or smaller amounts according to the seasons and wind directions.

Windbelts and Latitudes

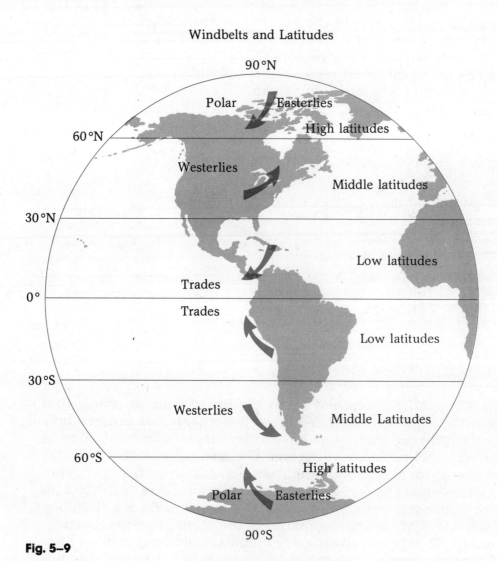

Fig. 5–9

Wind also affects weather. The interaction between the Earth's rotation and air currents sets up wind patterns around the globe. Figure 8–9 illustrates these **prevailing winds.** It is the rotation of the Earth that makes them blow in different directions in different zones. These prevailing winds influence the weather of these zones—both inland and on the coasts—more than other, more local winds.

Landforms and Vegetation in the Earth's Regions

There are seven great land masses—or **continents**—that cover the Earth: North America, South America, Europe, Asia, Africa, Australia, and Antarctica. While there are some very high places (Mount Everest in Asia: 29,028 feet above sea level) and some very low places (the Mariana Trench in the Pacific: 35,810 ft. below sea level), most of the Earth's surface is relatively level.

Landforms and natural vegetation vary greatly from continent to continent, and from region to region. The **tundra** of the polar regions consists of vast treeless plains where the ice caps have retreated. **Natural vegetation** is limited to a few grasses, mosses, and some flowering plants that can withstand the harsh conditions—little sunlight, strong winds, extreme cold, and frozen soil. On the ice of the glaciers, of course, nothing will grow.

In contrast to the tundra are the dense forests of the tropical zones. Here, the equatorial heat and abundant rainfall produce lush, green forests. **Rainforests** are found only near the equator, in Latin America, Africa, and Asia. Moist winds blow in from the oceans, constantly fed by the high temperatures. Conditions in the rainforest are similar to those in a greenhouse, so plant life is plentiful and varied.

Where moisture is blocked from reaching the land, deserts are formed. **Deserts** can be hot or cold, but they are always dry. Moisture can be blocked by high mountains, as in South America, where there is a desert on the eastern side of the Andes. In central Asia, the land has become desert because it is so far from the sea that rain-carrying clouds rarely reach the region. Great stretches of desert are found in the western U.S. and in Australia. A surprising number of plants have found ways to live in the arid conditions of the desert. Many, such as the cactus, have fleshy stems and leaves that store water. Other have waxy coatings and small leaves to minimize water loss.

In the temperate zones, there are **forests** and **grasslands.** The forests of the Northern Hemisphere are made up largely of deciduous trees, which shed their leaves in the fall. Temperate grasslands result where rainfall is too low to support forests and too high to cause a desert. Typically these are found in the interiors of large continents, particularly central North America and central Asia. Many grasses and flowers cover these vast regions.

Lesson 4 Exercises

Item 1 is based on the following passage.

Rimming the desolate tundra is a region known as taiga. While somewhat warmer and slightly brighter than the tundra, the taiga is still a dark and monotonous landscape. The growing season is somewhat longer and the average summer temperature is about 38°. Small numbers of spruce and pine trees live in the taiga, as well as willows, birches, and poplars in the better soils of river valleys and along forest lakes.

1. You would expect to find taiga
   (1) along the equator
   (2) in the outer reaches of the tropics
   (3) in the northern temperate zones
   (4) just below the Arctic Circle
   (5) in the southern temperate zone

2. A person who does not like extremes of temperature would do well to live
   (1) near the water in the tropics
   (2) well inland, away from the effects of the prevailing winds
   (3) in the mountains of the tropics
   (4) near a large inland lake surrounded by tundra
   (5) along the coast in a temperate zone

Item 3 is based on Figures 5–7 and 5–8.

3. The coast of a western portion of Africa is in two climatic zones. Some of it lies squarely within the tropical zone and some within the northern temperate zone. How can you explain the fact that the northern coast of this region is desert while the southern coast is either rainforest or rainy-and-dry tropical?

(1) The southern coast borders on an ocean and therefore receives plenty of rainfall.
(2) The prevailing winds blow off the water in the southern coast and off land in the northern coast.
(3) The northern coast is in a temperate zone, not in the tropics.
(4) The temperature is not warm enough to produce much rain along the northern coast.
(5) The prevailing winds blow off the land on both coasts, but the trade winds in the south contain more moisture.

Answers are on page 381.

World Population and Economic Growth

Prereading Prompt

The peoples of the world are separated by more than great land masses and bodies of water. Their ways of life, their customs, even their physical traits have been determined largely by where they live. What are some of these differences? How did they come about? Find out in this lesson.

Key Words

cultural geography—study of where different groups of people live and why
ethnic groups—groups of people sharing racial, religious, and social traits

Cultural Geography

Cultural geography deals with where different groups of people live in relation to the Earth's regions. The tendency to live in areas that readily support life partly explains why some areas are so densely populated and others are not. This is why most of the Earth's population lives within the temperate zones. People have always clustered along coastal and inland waterways, where water is a source of food (fish) and transportation. Once people learned to farm the land and domesticate animals, the fertile plains also became good places to live. Figure 5–10 shows how population is clustered throughout the world. Even with 5.3 billion people in the world, however, much of the land remains unpopulated.

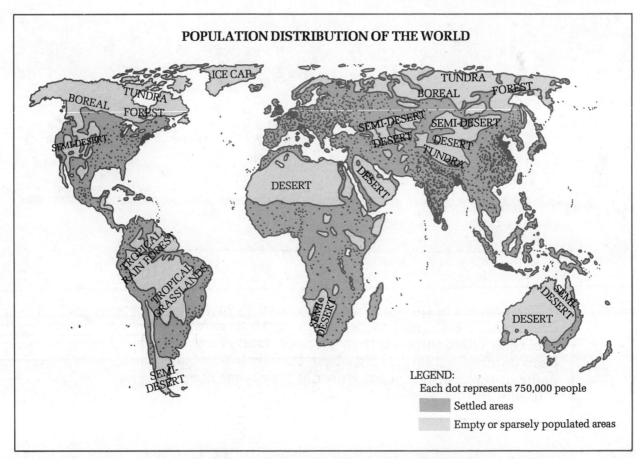

POPULATION DISTRIBUTION OF THE WORLD

LEGEND:
Each dot represents 750,000 people
Settled areas
Empty or sparsely populated areas

Fig. 5–10 Population distribution of the world.

In the developed nations, such as the U.S., Japan, and the nations of Europe, population is high because geographical and economic conditions make these desirable places to live. Population in these countries is increasing slowly, so the land will be able to support the population for a long time to come. This is not so in the developing nations, however. Many of these nations have undesirable climates where food is scarce, yet their populations are growing at alarming rates. India and countries in South America, Central America, Africa, and Asia have serious problems with poverty, hunger, and disease because of their enormous populations. These countries are not wealthy to begin with, and are only beginning to industrialize. The explosive growth of their populations will only make their problems more serious.

Races and Religions

Cultural geographers also study the ethnic composition of populations and how these ethnic groups are distributed throughout the world. People in **ethnic groups** have certain racial, religious, and social traits in common.

The world's population is divided into three broad racial groups. Each group consists of people with certain physical characteristics in common that include skin color, hair texture, and eye shape and color. The **Mongoloid race**, which originated in Asia, makes up 43 percent of the world's population. The Japanese and Chinese are members of this race. The **Caucasian race**, which originated in Europe, makes up 33 percent of the world's population. Europeans, Scandinavians, and Americans who emigrated from these countries are Caucasians. The **Negroid race**, which originated in Africa, makes up 24 percent of the world's population. Black Africans and Afro-Americans are members of this race.

Races contain many different **ethnic groups**. For example, the Italians and Irish are ethnic groups within the Caucasian race. Clusters of ethnic groups have emigrated from their homelands and established ethnic communities all over the world. Many have intermarried, thus softening the distinctions between groups. Often members of these groups marry among themselves but take on traits of the larger society around them. These ways of ethnic mixing have made the U.S. a **melting pot** of people. In countries that were colonized by world powers of the past, it is common for different ethnic and racial groups to live among each other. In India and South Africa, for example, large numbers of white people live among the black and Asian people who are native to the areas. In South America, where the population is largely of Spanish descent, many people are also Indians. Many have mixed Spanish and Indian ancestry, as well as African ancestry. If the human race manages to survive, it is likely that racial and ethnic intermingling will increase.

People who share racial and ethnic ties also tend to share religious beliefs. Of the world's **major religions**, more people belong to *Christian* denominations than to any other. Over 1½ billion Christians live throughout the world, on every continent and in almost every country. The next largest religion is *Islam*, with over 800 million followers (called Moslems) throughout the world. The Arab countries of northern Africa and the Middle East are largely Moslem, and there are large populations of Moslems in Asia and North America. Many African Americans follow Islam. The major religion of India is *Hinduism*. There are more than 600 million Hindus in India alone, with other large groups on other continents. Once the state religion of India, *Buddhism* is strong in Tibet, Mongolia, China, Korea, and Japan, with over 300 million members.

1. The passage states that developing nations are experiencing higher population growth than developed nations. High population growth in developing nations
   (1) ensures that more people will live
   (2) increases the available workforce and so increases the country's wealth
   (3) will eventually improve public health because more tax money will be collected
   (4) makes those nations potential military threats to world peace
   (5) overtaxes the economic and natural resources of those nations

2. Population growth in developing countries is affecting the United States. Many people from developing nations immigrate to the U.S. in search of a better life. Below is a table of the percentage of increase in four population groups in the U.S. from 1980 through 1988.
   If current trends continue, the most logical conclusion would be that
   (1) whites will no longer be in the majority in the United States
   (2) immigration laws will be changed
   (3) new immigrants will be forced to go to Canada or other countries instead
   (4) English will no longer be the main language of the U.S.
   (5) oriental religions will replace Christianity as the majority religion

Ethnic Group Increases in U.S., 1980–1988	
Asians and other	56%
Hispanics	34%
Blacks	13%
Whites	4%

Source: *Time* estimates, *Time*. April 9, 1990, p. 30.

Item 3 is based on Figure 5–10.

3. Population density—the number of people per square mile—varies from country to country. The population density of the United States is 60 persons per square mile. In Japan, it is only 5 persons per square mile.
   A cause of Australia's low population density is that it is
   (1) larger than the United States
   (2) largely uninhabitable
   (3) surrounded by water
   (4) so far south
   (5) a developed country

Answers are on page 381.

The World's Resources

Prereading Prompt

Whenever a crisis occurs in the Middle East, where much of our oil comes from, the world scrambles to find alternate sources of energy. Why are we still so dependent on foreign oil? What advances are being made in developing new means of power for our world? Read on to find out.

Key Words

acid rain—a condition caused by pollution from burning fuels that mixes with water vapor and falls with rain and other precipitation
solar energy—power derived from harnessing the energy of the sun
nuclear energy—power derived from nuclear, or atomic, reactions

Sources of Energy

In the 20th century, petroleum and petroleum products may be the world's most important natural resource. It powers our cars, heats our homes, and is used to make plastics, paints, soaps, asphalt, fertilizer, and other products. Petroleum is abundant in the Middle East, and is responsible for bringing great wealth to these otherwise poor nations. There are also oil fields in the southern United States and in the South American countries of Venezuela and Columbia, and in the North Sea off Great Britain.

Petroleum is a renewable resource, which means that its supply is constantly being replaced under the Earth's crust. It is derived from aquatic plants and animals that lived and died millions of years ago. Since it takes millions of years to make petroleum, however, the modern world is using it up faster than it can be replaced.

Petroleum also causes major environmental problems: oil spills pollute the world's waterways, and it contributes to **acid rain**. Acid rain is formed when by-products of burning fuel are released into the atmosphere and combine with upper-level water vapor. When it rains (or snows, sleets, or hails), these by-products fall to the ground polluting the rivers, lakes, and land.

Before petroleum became the main source of energy in the industrialized world, coal was widely used. It powered steam engines, fired huge furnaces in factories, and heated homes. Coal is still widely used. Like petroleum, it is a renewable resource, but it is also being depleted, and it too causes acid rain.

A cleaner fuel than both petroleum and coal is natural gas. Natural gas is a by-product of petroleum. It is used in gas stoves and ovens, and many people use it to heat their homes. Because it comes from petroleum, natural gas is also a renewable resource.

So far, water has proved to be only a limited source of energy. Only fresh water from rivers and waterfalls has provided enough power to be considered a real source of energy. People have been working on ways to harness the power of the ocean tides and waves, but with limited success.

New Sources of Energy

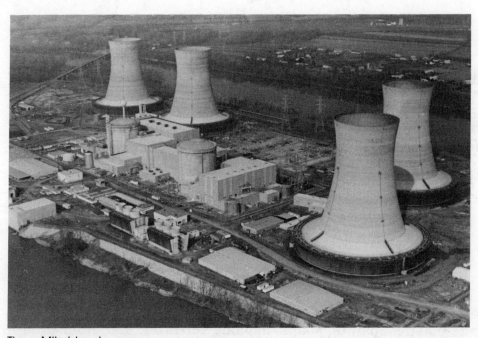

Three Mile Island
(Credit: AP/Wide World Photos)

Limited natural resources and pollution have prompted people to look for other sources of energy. One promising development is the successful harnessing of the sun's energy. **Solar energy** is clean because no fuels are burned, and is inexpensive, except for the initial cost of installing the energy collectors. The main drawback of solar energy is that it can be collected only on sunny days. Solar collectors can hold energy for just so long; the supply must be replenished by full days of strong sunlight.

Harnessing the power of the wind is another alternative source of energy. **Wind power** is clean, and the technology for harnessing it (windmills) has been around for centuries. Unfortunately, wind power, like solar power, is unpredictable, working only when it's windy.

The most controversial alternative energy source is **nuclear energy**. Nuclear power is clean in that it doesn't emit dirty by-products into the air. However, on many occasions, nuclear plants have released radioactive particles into the air and water, with devastating effects on plant and animal life.

Nuclear power presents another problem, for which there is as yet no good solution: the nuclear waste made by these power plants. Nuclear waste is dangerous. It must be stored in airtight, watertight containers that must not be disturbed for centuries, until the waste is no longer radioactive. Until the problems associated with nuclear energy are solved, nuclear power remains a risky alternative.

Items 1 and 2 are based on the following passage.

Geography determines a country's natural resources. Coffee, sugar, and rubber trees don't grow in the temperate zones. They do grow in the tropics, however. Likewise, there are relatively few oil fields in the tropics; there are many in the temperate zones. World trade makes it possible for countries to have things that are not native to their region.

World trade is important for developed and developing nations alike. Developing or non-industrial nations do not have the facilities to manufacture goods such as automobiles, housewares, and electronics. But they do have the raw materials—what the products are made from—such as rubber, tropical wood, and tin. Industrial nations, on the other hand, have the factories but not the raw materials. In some cases they have the raw materials, but they are less expensive to import from developing nations.

The imbalance of the world's natural resources has worked very much in favor of some Middle Eastern countries. Oil—so much in demand by the industrial world—is plentiful in the Middle East. Highly industrial countries, like Japan and those in Western Europe, have no oil of their own. They must rely solely on imported oil.

1. Which statement below is the unstated assumption of the whole passage?
   (1) Some natural resources are in greater demand than others.
   (2) Some countries are more fortunate than others in terms of the natural distribution of the world's resources.
   (3) World trade and the natural distribution of resources gives countries power over other countries.
   (4) Developed nations take advantage of developing nations in world trade.
   (5) The tropics have more natural resources than do the temperate zones.

2. Many oil-producing nations belong to OPEC—the Organization of Petroleum Exporting Countries. When the price of oil is high, the OPEC nations
   (1) have a trade surplus
   (2) have a trade deficit
   (3) decrease production
   (4) decrease exportation
   (5) buy more raw materials

3. Which item below is *not* a reason to find alternative sources of energy?
   (1) to stop polluting the environment
   (2) to find a less expensive source of energy
   (3) to stop depleting our natural resources
   (4) to not be dependent on other countries for oil
   (5) to find more efficient sources of energy

4. Solar energy would *not* be a good alternative source of power in
   (1) the southern U.S.
   (2) northern Canada
   (3) the Middle East
   (4) the midwestern U.S.
   (5) Western Europe.

Answers are on page 381–382.

CHAPTER 6

Behavioral science studies the behavior of people—how they think, act, react, and feel. Some behavioral scientists study individuals, their emotional life and personal relationships. Other behavioral scientists focus on how individuals fit into a social order. Still others focus on groups—their customs, beliefs and lifestyles.

(Credit: Stan Wakefield)

Prereading Prompt

You probably hear popular terms of psychology daily in conversation, or on TV or in the movies: "anxiety," "neurotic," "repressed." Every day you also may deal with problems concerning your relationships with groups that you belong to—families, clubs, churches. Such relationships are the subject of sociology. As we see the world gets smaller, we are more aware of the various life-styles and beliefs of people from all races and religions—which is the subject-matter of anthropology. Read about these three sciences in this chapter.

Behavioral Science

What Is Behavioral Science?

Psychology has the narrowest focus of the three fields of behavioral science. It is the study of the human mind—its thoughts and emotions—and how it affects behavior. Psychologists are interested in people's daily behavior as well as the more extreme and unusual problems that occur. What causes people to feel extreme fear or anger about certain things? Why can some people cope with stress and others can't? What makes some people shy and others bold? Why do people overeat or become addicted to drugs or alcohol? Why do some people continually engage in self-defeating behavior? These are just some of the many questions that interest psychologists.

While psychology studies the individual, **sociology** studies the individual within society. What relationships do people from different groups make with each other—that is, from different religions, races, socioeconomic classes? How does the organization of a family affect a person's behavior? What causes some people to obey society's rules and others to become criminals? How do people react in different environments—suburbs, big cities, rich or poor areas? Sociologists seek to learn the answers to these and many other fascinating questions.

Anthropology has the broadest focus of the three behavioral sciences. It studies the culture of entire societies or of groups within those societies. A *culture* is made up of all the patterns of behavior that are handed down from generation to generation in a group—customs, rituals, written and unwritten rules, and regulations. Anthropologists often find that living in a society is the best way to study its culture. Many anthropologists have spent years living among tribal groups, studying the similarities and differences between these cultures and ours.

Key Words

psychology—studies the mental and emotional life and how it affects behavior
sociology—studies groups in society
anthropology—studies the cultures of groups of people
scientific method—asks and answers questions about observed events by testing hypotheses and gathering information

Psychoanalysis

Prereading Prompt

People often say, "Oh, he's only rationalizing," or "That's just one of her defense mechanisms." What do we really mean when we say these things? How much do you know about the subconscious workings of the mind?

Key Words

psychoanalysis—study of and treatment for mental problems by uncovering unconscious memories and desires
id—unconscious part of the mind consisting of basic natural desires and appetites
superego—conscious part of the mind that acts as the conscience

The theory of psychoanalysis was developed in the late 19th century by Sigmund Freud, an Austrian physician. Freud worked with patients who suffered from paralysis, blindness, and other symptoms that had no physical cause. Freud deduced that memories of events in their childhood were causing their symptoms. The patients were not aware of these memories and the emotional effects they were having on their behavior. Part of the person's mind—the conscious mind—was not aware of thoughts and feelings in another part of the mind—the unconscious mind. From his work, Freud developed his theory—that much of human behavior stems from unconscious memories and feelings caused by events in childhood.

The human mind has three parts, according to Freud. The **id** is part of the unconscious mind, or the subconscious. The id is the home of the basic drives that keep us alive—the drives to eat, drink, have sex. The **ego** is part of the conscious mind. It keeps us in touch with reality and helps us adapt to our surroundings so that we can survive and do well in our lives. The third part of the mind is the **superego**. The superego consists of values we absorb from our parents and the world around us. From childhood on, these values shape our thinking, and control our moral decisions. The superego therefore can be thought of as the conscience.

Sigmund Freud (Credit: UPI/Bettman Newsphotos)

According to Freud, the ideal human condition is for the id, ego, and super-ego to work together to create a "normal," "balanced," "healthy" human being. Healthy people can be characterized as having drives for pleasure that are satisfied yet kept in check and acted on appropriately. Unhealthy people either do not control their impulses enough or check them too much.

People who satisfy their desires without any control or concern for others can be a threat to society and also self-destructive, by committing crimes and exploiting people. They have overactive ids and weak egos and superegos.

On the other hand, people who have too-powerful egos and superegos almost kill the basic desires of life contained in the id. These people are also self-destructive and can pose social problems—for instance, by trying to control other people's lives in the same way, or by escaping unhappiness in drugs, alcohol or violence.

According to Freud, these efforts to express, but control, emotions produces anxiety. *Anxiety* is a feeling of extreme uneasiness and tension that comes from a fear that the person will be unable to cope with his or her life. If the anxiety is extreme, the person may force the threatening feelings into the unconscious mind. This is called *repression*. Often, a person does not even know he/she is repressing the threatening emotions, which become completely hidden.

Other defenses against anxiety are more conscious. These are called *defense mechanisms*. One common defense mechanism is *rationalization*. Rationalizations are comforting but false reasons people tell themselves to explain their behavior. When a recovering alcoholic takes a drink, he may say it was because he got so nervous at the thought of asking for a raise that he *had* to have a drink. In truth, this was just an excuse to have a drink. The excuse is a rationalization.

Practice

People often use defense mechanisms to avoid feelings of anxiety. Defense mechanisms are usually not under a person's control; they click in automatically when certain situations are encountered. Which of the behaviors below might be an example of a defense mechanism?

(1) Laughing when someone pretends to get hurt in a slapstick movie.
(2) Calling a friend to talk about your drinking problem.
(3) Denying you have a weight problem when you are 5'4" and weigh 200 lbs.
(4) Staying up late to get some work done and smoking two packs of cigarettes.
(5) Working out at the gym two hours a day, five days a week even though you are in good shape.

Since a defense mechanism provides a way of avoiding anxiety, it usually entails keeping the truth from yourself, or at least distorting it. In choice (1), there is no need to get upset because you know the person is not really getting hurt. There is no defense mechanism at work here. Defense mechanisms are not operating in choice (2), either. This is actually a healthy response to a problem; the person is admitting that something is wrong and is reaching out for help. In the case of choice (4), while this is certainly not a healthy thing to do, there is no denial or distortion of truth. The person merely smoked too much in response to stress. Choice (5) is the case of someone who is fanatical about looking good. While he or she may be working out more than is necessary, the person knows he or she is in good shape and is working hard to remain that way. The person in choice (3) is the one using a defense mechanism. Denial of a problem is a classic example of a defense mechanism; the person is avoiding the truth because facing it causes tremendous anxiety.

Lesson 1 Exercise

Items 1 and 2 are based on the following information.

Psychologists and psychoanalysts use many professional terms in their practice. Some of these are defined below.

   (1) **psychosis**—severe mental disorder characterized by the breakdown of normal intellectual and social functioning and by partial or complete withdrawal from reality

   (2) **neurosis**—mental and emotional disturbance characterized by frequent, extreme anxiety and self-defeating behavior

   (3) **anxiety**—state of mind characterized by extreme uneasiness and tension and a sense that one is threatened and powerless

   (4) **repression**—the forcing of painful memories, ideas, and fears out of the conscious mind and into the unconscious mind

   (5) **sublimation**—the changing of "bad" natural impulses into socially acceptable behavior

1. A woman is being treated by a psychoanalyst for a personality disorder. In certain situations, her personality changes completely so that she actually assumes another identity. With each new identity, she assumes a different name, personality, and background. In the course of treatment, the doctor has encountered five distinct personalities in this one patient. The doctor diagnoses the patient as suffering from
   (1) psychosis
   (2) neurosis
   (3) anxiety
   (4) repression
   (5) sublimation

2. A 24-year-old man is seeing a psychologist because of "blackouts" in his daily living. From time to time, he seems to lose track of what he has just been doing, as if he has ceased to exist for a few minutes. When he comes out of the blackout, everything continues normally. In treatment, the young man tells the doctor that he once had a younger brother. The boy drowned one summer while the family was vacationing at a lake. The young man has no recollection of the actual incident, as if it were a blank. This patient is exhibiting a form of
   (1) psychosis
   (2) neurosis
   (3) anxiety
   (4) repression
   (5) sublimation

3. A person feels tremendous rage and anger toward a friend who has betrayed him. As many people do when they are angry, he feels as if he wants to kill his friend. Instead, he takes back everything the friend has ever borrowed from him, tells him what he thinks of him, and warns him never to come near him again. What is his person using to help him through his anger?

(1) a defense mechanism

(2) sublimation

(3) repression

(4) rationalization

(5) denial

Answers are on page 382.

Behaviorism

Prereading Prompt

Have you ever punished your dog for doing something wrong? Do you praise your child when he or she does something that pleases you? If so, you have used principles of behaviorism to teach acceptable behavior. Read about this interesting and controversial learning theory in this lesson.

Key Words

conditioning—changing behavior by using rewards to encourage some actions and punishments to discourage other actions

reward—something pleasurable, such as food or praise, given for desirable behavior

punishment—something painful or distasteful, such as a spanking or a scolding, given to discourage undesirable behavior

From birth, newborn infants show differences in personality. In the hospital nursery, some infants will react strongly to loud noises, perhaps by jerking their arms or legs, frowning, or crying. Others will act as if they scarcely notice the noise. This is a fairly strong argument for the idea that we are who we are because we are born that way. A whole school of psychological theory, however, argues that behavior is the result of the environment people grow up in. *Any* behavior, they argue, can be changed.

Through a method called **conditioning**, even physical responses can be changed. In a classic experiment performed in the early 1920s, the Russian scientist Ivan Pavlov trained a hungry dog to water at the mouth or salivate every time he heard a bell. Once the food was removed and only the bell remained, the dog still salivated when it rang. This led psychologists to the idea that behavior could be controlled by making people form associations.

(Credit: Ken Karp)

Influenced by Dr. Pavlov, the Harvard professor B. F. Skinner performed animal experiments using the principles of conditioning. Using **rewards**, Skinner was able to train pigeons, monkeys, and other lab animals to perform a whole series of complex tasks. When the animal performed the desired behavior, it would receive a bit of food. Thus rewarded, the animal would repeat the behavior to receive more food. In this way, new behaviors were learned. This is basically the technique that is used in obedience-training with dogs. Without realizing it, parents often use this technique. When a baby performs a desirable behavior such as smiling or finishing a meal, the parents reward the behavior by hugging, smiling, or telling the baby how good he or she is.

Likewise, **punishment** is used to *unlearn* behaviors. Through this method, certain behaviors come to be associated with undesirable consequences. For example, a mouse that attempts to cross its cage to get to food may receive a mild electric shock through the floor of the cage. After repeated attempts and shocks, the mouse will no longer try to cross the cage. Punishment in milder forms is often used by parents. A mother may spank or yell at her child for throwing food on the floor. She hopes that this punishment will stop the behavior.

Items 1 and 2 are based on the following passage.

One technique of modifying behavior is **successive approximation**. This is used to get a subject to perform behavior that he or she does not normally do. For example, successive approximation has been used to train pigeons to play ping-pong. First, the birds are rewarded for getting close to the paddles, then for picking up the paddles, then for hitting the ball, and so on. Each step closer to the ultimate goal of playing ping-pong is reinforced until finally the birds can hit the ball back and forth.

Another technique for shaping behavior is **differential reinforcement**. The technique is similar to successive approximation, but with one crucial difference—the action being taught must already be part of the subject's behavior. A good example of this is training a parrot to "dance" to music. Most parrots naturally move their heads back and forth and make their bodies sway in a sort of dancing motion. Often it is part of the mating ritual. It is not something they do, however, in response to music. Using differential reinforcement, the bird's behavior is selectively reinforced. When he moves his head or sways his body, each behavior is reinforced with food. When he does both together, both behaviors is reinforced. Finally, he will be reinforced only for "dancing" while music is on. The bird will eventually dance every time he hears music.

1. Which situation below is an example of successive approximation?
   (1) A 35-year-old dancer learns a new ballet routine.
   (2) A dog learns to sit on command.
   (3) A kitten learns to use the litter pan.
   (4) A five-year-old learns to tie his shoes.
   (5) A rat learns to go through a maze.

2. Which situation below is an example of differential reinforcement?
   (1) A baby learns to smile when others smile at him.
   (2) A monkey learns to draw a circle.
   (3) A two-year-old learns to brush her teeth.
   (4) A circus dog learns to "drive" a car (steer the wheel).
   (5) A 20-year old learns computer programming.

3. One important way that people learn is through **modeling**—watching the behavior and actions of others and then copying it. The more important the role model, the more likely it is that behavior will be copied. Which of the following is probably *not* the result of modeling?
   (1) teenagers dressing like their favorite rock star
   (2) a son smoking because he sees his father smoking
   (3) a daughter marrying a dark-haired man because her father is dark-haired
   (4) a four-year-old girl playing dress-up in her mother's clothes and shoes
   (5) youngsters talking like their favorite TV characters

Answers are on page 382.

Sociology: The Study of Society

Prereading Prompt

Why is there so much crime in America today? Why have so many young people turned to drugs? Why is the divorce rate so high? What effects does divorce have on families? Sociologists study these and other questions.

Key Words

stratification—the dividing of society into levels, or groups, according to social and economic standing
social mobility—the ability to move up or down among social or economic classes
socialization—the process by which members of a society come to follow the rules of that society

A society is a group of people who share a way of life and live in the same general area. All the people who live in the United States are the American society. We are loosely connected by the same rules, the same government, and many of the same customs and beliefs. This large society is divided into smaller groups whose members are more closely related. *Ethnic groups* share a common racial, language, or national heritage; *religious groups* share common religious beliefs; *peer groups* share a common age and way of life.

Social **stratification** divides society in yet another way. American society is usually thought to have three primary social and economic classes: working class, middle class, and the upper-middle or wealthy class. The members of each class are associated by similar income, standard of living, education, and level of occupation. In America more than in most other countries, classes are flexible; people can change their class by changing their economic and social circumstances. This is known as **social mobility**.

It is in the interest of societies for members to follow certain standards of behavior, or *norms*. Behavior that doesn't conform to these standards is said to deviate, or stray, from the norms. It is considered *deviant*. A child who steals or a mother who abandons her baby is exhibiting deviant behavior. **Socialization** is the process of transmitting a society's values to its members in the hope that they will follow certain rules of behavior. A number of social institutions, including schools, churches, and families, all play an important role in socialization. In school, children learn the history of their society, as well as how to get along with others and to become productive members of society. Churches also provide models for right and wrong behavior. Many sociologists believe that families are the most important factor in socialization. A child whose parents are good role models, and who has a strong and nurturing family, will learn right from wrong in a positive way. Such a child will not behave acceptably in society because he or she feels guilty or is afraid of punishment, but because such behavior is more satisfying and productive in the long run.

Items 1 and 2 are based on the following table.

Relation of Intelligence Levels to Crime Rate and Incarceration Drive		
Intelligence Quotient	Percent of Boys Convicted of Crimes	Percent of Boys Sentenced to Penal Institutions
Superior (IQ over 110)	26	0
Average (IQ 91–110)	46	16
Dull Average (IQ 81–90)	44	15
Sub-normal (IQ below 81)	35	19

Source: From William and Joan McCord *Origins of Crime*, (Columbia University Press, 1959: reprinted 1969 by Patterson Smith Publishing Corp.), page 66. Reprinted by permission.

The table is based on a study of 239 boys who took an IQ (intelligence quotient) test prior to the study. The lives of the boys were followed to see what percentage would commit and be convicted of crimes, and what percentage of those convicted went to jail or some sort of penal institution.

1. What conclusion can be drawn from the results of this study?
   (1) Low IQ is directly related to the tendency to commit crimes.
   (2) Low IQ does not lead to crime, but high IQ may prevent sentencing to a penal institution.
   (3) People of high intelligence commit almost as many crimes as those of sub-normal intelligence, but they aren't punished nearly as often.
   (4) There is no relationship between intelligence and being sentenced to a penal institution.
   (5) 151 of the boys in the study (more than 50 percent) committed crimes, regardless of intelligence.

2. According to the results of the study, judges apparently believe that high intelligence lessens the likelihood that a boy will pursue a life of crime. Which restatement of information on the graph supports this hypothesis?
   (1) Only 26 percent of the boys in the high-IQ groups were convicted of crimes.
   (2) More than 26 percent of the boys in the high-IQ group committed crimes, but they weren't convicted.
   (3) None of the boys in the high IQ groups was sentenced to penal institutions.
   (4) More boys of average intelligence were convicted of crimes than any other group.
   (5) A larger percentage of boys with subnormal intelligence were sentenced to prison than any other group.

3. Which of the following would be considered an example of deviant behavior in America?

 (1) a man wearing pants and long sleeves at the beach

 (2) a man not voting in several national elections in a row

 (3) a mother dressing a male infant in female baby clothes

 (4) a teenager driving a convertible with the top down when it is 45° outside

 (5) a woman going to the movies with her hair in curlers

Answers are on page 382–383.

The Study of Group Behavior

Prereading Prompt

Are you a member of a group—perhaps a company softball team or a group of friends with common interests and activities? Most of us belong to several groups. You may have noticed that you tend to behave differently when you are in the different groups. Why? Find out what sociologists have to say about the matter.

Key Words

nuclear family—a mother, father, and their children living the same household

extended family—the immediate family plus other blood relatives, such as grandparents, aunts, and uncles

primary group—a group with close ties and continual contact that has rules and standards for behavior

secondary group—a loosely associated group, less important than a primary group

peer group—people who are equals; members of a peer group usually share common age and interests

Over the years, the definition of family has changed. Traditionally, the word "family" conjured up the image of the **nuclear family**—the supposedly typical family of the 1950s and '60s, with husband and wife and their two or three children. Sometimes grandparents and other blood relatives were included, forming a family unit known as the **extended family.**

Today, however, family life is changing. Nontraditional families are becoming increasingly common. In today's economy, both parents often hold jobs outside the home. Children may be watched during the day by a babysitter, an aunt or other close family member, or may be sent to a day care center. Many families are headed by a single parent, usually the mother, who may or may not have been married to the father of her children. It is also becoming increasingly acceptable to live with a person to whom you are not married. Many couples even have children without being married. The stability of such relationships is widely debated; some people believe that legal and social ties make marriages more stable than a nonbinding live-in arrangement. Yet many unmarried couples remain together and have healthier relationships than some married couples.

The family is considered a **primary group** in society. Members of a primary group have close, personal contact with each other on a continuing basis. Primary groups such as families have their own rules and standards for behavior. What other groups do is often dismissed. If five-year-old Sammy comes home saying, "Tommy's mother lets him do that," Sammy's mother may say, "I don't care what Tommy's mother lets him do—we don't do that."

(Credit: AP/Wide World Photos)

Besides families, **peer groups** are also primary groups. As was mentioned in Lesson 3, peer groups consist of people who are equals. They may belong to the same age group, be involved in the same activities (going to school), and so on. For most adults, the peer group is a circle of close friends, or perhaps the people at the office. For children, the peer group may consist of classmates or the other kids in the neighborhood. As adults, we usually have no trouble accepting the different rules of the different primary groups we belong to. At work we behave one way, at home another. For children and adolescents, however, these distinctions can be difficult. Adolescents, especially, have conflicts between their desire for approval from their peers and approval from their parents.

Most of us also belong to **secondary groups,** which as the name implies, are not as important in defining behavior as primary groups. Relationships in secondary groups are characterized by limited and temporary contact. Certain rules and standards of behavior apply, but are of limited influence and tend to be related to tasks performed by the group. Examples of secondary groups are church organizations and professional associations of doctors, lawyers, and so on.

Items 1 to 3 are based on the following passage.

The Mormon religion was founded in the United States in 1830 by Joseph Smith, Jr. Among other things, Mormonism calls for a communistic lifestyle, in which people contribute what they can and receive what they need. One of the practices of Mormonism is polygamy, specifically polygyny, in which one man may have two or more wives at a time. Through the years, Mormons have clashed violently with other Americans over this practice. Mormons who lived in non-Mormon communities were often tarred and feathered, and many were killed. To escape persecution, Mormons established their own community in Utah in the mid-1800s. Salt Lake City was the result. In the 1880s, the Mormon church became involved in a serious conflict with the United States government over its practice of polygyny. Since then, Mormonism has adapted its teachings to the dominant marriage practice in the U.S.—one wife for one man, known as monogamy.

1. For Mormons, the church represents
   (1) a nuclear family
   (2) an extended family
   (3) a primary group
   (4) a secondary group
   (5) a nontraditional family

Which of the following is an unstated assumption of the passage?
(1) The standards of the larger society override those of groups within the society.
(2) Mormonism is an immoral religion.
(3) People have the right to live as they choose.
(4) The government is required to intervene to prevent immoral behavior.
(5) Mormonism cannot be practiced in the United States.

From the passage, you can infer about Mormons that they
(1) believed that the values of the larger society are correct
(2) believed it is more important to live in peace with your neighbors than to openly practice behavior that upsets them
(3) did not believe strongly in polygamy
(4) were not wealthy enough to fight all the legal battles needed to defend polygamy in the courts
(5) did not believe the U.S. government had the power to tell them how to live

Answers are on page 383.

Introduction to Anthropology

Prereading Prompt

The word "anthropology" comes from the Greek *anthropos*, meaning man or human, and *-logos*, meaning study of. Anthropologists study human beings—their physical characteristics, their origins, their way of life. This lesson will tell you some of what they've discovered.

Key Words

physical anthropology—the study of the racially determined physical characteristics of human beings
tribes—groups that share common beliefs, dress, and other aspects of culture
cultural anthropology—the study of the beliefs and customs of groups of human beings
rites of passage—rituals in which children become adults in the eyes of society
taboos—behaviors forbidden by a society

Physical Anthropology

Physical anthropology is the study of people as animals. How did human beings develop? What separates humans from other animals? What makes one person physically different from another? Slowly, anthropologists have assembled the record of human life to show where we have come from and to speculate about where we are going.

We are all aware of the physical differences among people. Scientists have categorized people into different races according to characteristics. Members of the Mongoloid race have pale yellow or light tan-colored skin, dark, often black straight hair, dark eyes, and a characteristic facial structure that includes high cheekbones. Members of the Negroid race have dark or light brown skin, dark hair, and dark eyes, and a tendency toward broad noses and lips. Members of the Caucasoid race have white—really pink or light orange-colored—skin and may have any combination of dark or light hair and dark or light eyes. The noses of Caucasians tend to be large, narrow, and with a high bridge.

Initially, the races were separated by enormous expanses of land and water. Mating among them was impossible. However, even if the races had had access to one another, it is doubtful that there would have been much intermating. Anthropologists believe that early man lived in clans, or groups whose members were biologically related. Clans were members of larger groups known as **tribes**. People within a tribe shared common language, dress, food, and ideas. Scientists believe that members of tribes had a basic distrust of other tribes. Since members of different races would not have belonged to the same tribe, there would have been little, if any, mating among the races.

Cultural Anthropology

Every society and group within society has its own values and beliefs. **Cultural anthropologists** study this aspect of human life. The fundamental belief that a group of people holds is called their *creed*. A creed may or may not be based on religion. In the United States, it is a basic creed of society that all people have equal political and legal rights and should have equal opportunities. Freedom of religious belief is a basic right of U.S. citizens, but the basic creed of the American people is not religious.

In some societies, however, religion and creed are inseparable. In the Dogon tribe of Africa, for example, almost every belief has a spiritual foundation. Many aspects of life, from a woman's menstrual cycle to the craft of the local blacksmith, are explained in spiritual terms, and the spiritual life of these people is even reflected in the physical layout of their communities.

Most modern societies have *monotheistic religions*—religions based on the belief in one god. Catholicism, Islam, and Judaism are all monotheistic. *Polytheistic religions* were more common in ancient times and can still be found among some primitive tribes. The ancient Greeks and Romans, for example, believed in many gods and goddesses. Whether worshipping one or several gods, most religions include the idea of an afterlife.

Many primitive religions believe in magic and the supernatural. The image of the witch doctor is an exaggerated form of a type of authority figure in these societies. These figures are known as *shamans*. Shamans are said to be able to heal the sick and communicate with the dead. Voodoo, a religious cult of African origin that is found throughout Central and South America, is especially well known for this kind of belief in the supernatural.

Sikh communal meal
(Credit: Eugene Gordon)

Most societies have **rites of passage**—rituals that children go through to cross the threshold into adulthood. Rites of passage are sometimes formal. In these cases, they are usually tied to religion, as in the Jewish bar mitzvah, a religious ceremony in which 13-year-old boys become men. In American society, most rites of passage are less formal and not tied to religion. These may include such milestones as getting a driver's license, taking one's first drink, and voting for the first time.

Just as societies have behavioral standards that are supposed to be followed, they also have behaviors that are **taboo**, or forbidden. Taboo behaviors often involve sexuality and other behaviors that are considered immoral. For example, almost every culture has taboos against incest—sexual relations between parents and their children, or between brothers and sisters.

Lesson 5 Exercises

Item 1 is based on the following passage.

The late Dr. Margaret Mead, world-famous anthropologist, studied three primitive societies in depth. The following is her summary of what she discovered.

"I found . . . in one [society], both men and women act as we expect women to act—in a mild, parental, responsive way; in the second [society], both act as we expect men to act—in a fierce, initiating fashion; and in the third [society], the men act according to our stereotype for women—are 'catty,' wear curls and go shopping, while the women are energetic, managerial, unadorned partners."

[From Margaret Mead, *Sex and Temperament in Three Primitive Societies*, copyright 1935, 1950, 1963 by Margaret Mead, reprinted by permission of William Morrow and Company, Inc./Publishers, New York.]

1. Which conclusion is supported by Dr. Mead's findings?
   (1) Differences between the sexes are inborn.
   (2) Many masculine and feminine characteristics are the result of cultural and societal influences.
   (3) People in primitive societies tend to reverse the typical male and female behaviors of Western society.
   (4) The more developed a society is, the less well-defined are the differences between the sexes.
   (5) Since each society studied was different, more societies will have to be studied before making a conclusion.

Item 2 is based on the following passage.

Hundreds of millions of years ago, long before people lived, dinosaurs ruled the Earth. For reasons not fully understood, they suddenly became extinct. Many other kinds of animals and plants also became extinct at this time. Scientists speculate that some major global catastrophe was responsible. Currently, the most popular theory is that the Earth was struck by a giant meteor whose impact sent tons of debris into the atmosphere. Sunlight was unable to penetrate the thick layer of dust, so millions of plants and animals died.

The earliest ancestors of man, *Australopithecus* and *Homo habilis*, appeared somewhere around 1.7 million B.C. These early hunter-gatherers bore more resemblance to apes than to modern man. About 500,000 B.C., *Homo erectus* appeared on the scene. These ancestors walked in a more upright position and used crude tools. By 35,000 B.C., *Homo sapiens* had evolved. With the use of fire and more advanced tools, "thinking man" had arrived.

2. Humans have existed only a fraction of the time that dinosaurs lived. Some scientists argue that humans will also become extinct. Why might this argument be faulty?
   (1) People can think and are more capable of controlling their environment than the dinosaurs were.
   (2) There is little chance that another giant meteor will hit the Earth and kill all human life.

(3) If not for the meteor, the dinosaurs would not have become extinct, so people will not become extinct either.

(4) Humans will probably have colonized other planets by the time another meteor hits the Earth, so the human race will survive.

(5) Humanity will continue evolving into some other form rather than become extinct.

3. The Alaskan Eskimos have black, straight hair, relatively flat faces, high cheekbones, and dark eyes. These traits are characteristic of people in China, Japan, and the Pacific islands. Which statement below best explains this?

(1) The cold weather and sparse sunlight of the arctic region have caused these physical adaptations.

(2) Many Chinese and Japanese people live in Alaska.

(3) The Eskimos are ancestors of members of the Mongoloid race who migrated to the area thousands of years ago.

(4) The Mongoloid race originated in North America and migrated to Asia.

(5) The American Indians, Mexicans, and South American Indians have similar physical features.

Answers are on page 383.

Lesson 6

The Study of Different Cultures

Prereading Prompt

We all tend to be aware of differences among people, even those we casually observe. Perhaps they dress differently or speak a different language. These are ways of identifying with a group. Can you think of other ways besides dress and language?

Key Words

cultural pluralism—a condition of society in which numerous distinct ethnic groups make up one culture

ethnocentrism—the point of view of one's ethnic group and the belief that it is superior

cultural relativity—a belief that cultures should be understood on their own terms, rather than judged by an absolute standard

Many of us remember the 1960s. "Flower power," drugs, rock music, Vietnam, hippies—all these stand out in our minds. The youth movement of the late '60s represented a **counterculture**—a culture with its own values and beliefs that clashed with the values of the dominant culture. War versus peace, sexual freedom versus sexual repression, drug use versus being "straight." The beliefs of members of the counterculture actually ran against those of the dominant culture.

In contrast to a counterculture is a subculture. **Subcultures** are groups within a society that adhere to the primary values and beliefs of the dominant culture, but also have their own particular beliefs and ways of life. In America, with all its ethnic influences, there are many subcultures. The Italians, Chinese, Japanese, African, and Hispanic people of this country maintain much of the culture from their homelands. This can be seen in their cooking, language, music, folklore, and customs. Yet their beliefs and values are not opposed to those of the dominant culture in America.

Often, aspects of the culture of one group spread to and become part of the culture of another group. This is known as **cultural diffusion**. American cuisine, for example, is a mix of cooking styles from all over the world: pizza, spaghetti and other Italian food; German food such as hot dogs, sauerkraut, potato salad; Chinese food; and more recently, Japanese, Thai and Vietnamese food. The influence of Mexican culture on border states such as Texas has led to the popular Tex-Mex cuisine.

There is so much cultural diffusion in the United States because it is a pluralistic society—a society made up of many ethnic and religious groups, each with a different culture. **Cultural pluralism** is the norm in the U.S. This means we are used to seeing people dressed in different ways who speak different languages and eat different foods. In many countries, however, the dominant culture consists of one basic group. Acculturation, or modification of one's culture to fit into another culture, is often the best way to survive in these countries.

Unfortunately, people still have a lot of distrust for people of a different culture or race. We tend to consider our way of doing things as *the* way; all other ways are inferior. This tendency is called **ethnocentrism**. You may recall the discussion of Eurocentrism, or a European-centered point of view, from the American history chapter. Ethnocentrism is the point of view of a certain ethnic group.

Anthropologists work to overcome ethnocentrism. Instead of judging cultures according to an absolute standard as good or bad, or "advanced" or "backward," they try to understand how cultures function. They study cultures as living organisms that take their shape in relation to certain environments and ethnic traits. This point of view is called **cultural relativity**, or cultural relativism. It is the most tolerant and reasonable way of looking at the many different cultures of the world.

1. From the 1920s to the early 1950s, there was a modest-sized and active Communist movement in America. American Communists believed that the Party had the answers to the problems of economic depression, mass unemployment, rampant homelessness, and an unresponsive government. Non-Communist Americans perceived Communists as immoral, indecent troublemakers—a threat to the foundation of the country's beliefs. The Communist movement within American society was an example of
   (1) a dominant culture
   (2) a counterculture
   (3) a subculture
   (4) cultural diffusion
   (5) acculturation

Item 2 is based on the following map.

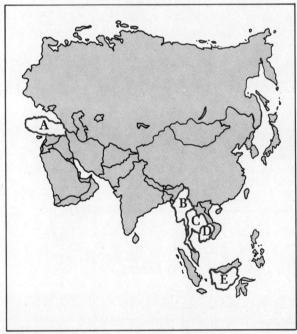

Fig. 6–1

The letters A through E on the map represent five different cultures. Which of those five cultures probably has the greatest influence on the others by cultural diffusion?
   (1) A
   (2) B
   (3) C
   (4) D
   (5) E

Which statement below would likely be made of an inexperienced anthropologist?
   (1) Fathers take tremendous interest in girl children from the time of adolescence; what a father considers a worthy male must be found for his daughter to marry.
   (2) A pig, a chicken, and a goat are slaughtered in ceremonial fashion and offered to the gods.
   (3) Courtship has begun when a girl allows a boy to serve her with an animal he has freshly killed.
   (4) The rites of passage include the rather cruel and painful practice of public circumcision.
   (5) Members of the tribe pay little attention to sex roles; each person performs whatever the tribe considers that he or she can do best.

Answers are on page 383–384.

CHAPTER 7

Now that you have studied the five branches of social studies, you can better appreciate how they are connected. History, economics, political science, geography, and the behavioral sciences are all *interrelated*: that is, they have two-way, or mutual, relationships. Economics can tell us how economic forces influence history and political science; political forces studied in those two fields also shape economic theory and practice. Behavioral sciences reveal things about the actions of people in all three fields; and economics and politics clearly influence behavior.

(Credit: AP/Wide World Photos)

Prereading Prompt

Pick a topic you hear about in the news. *Any* topic, such as the war in the Persian Gulf or the decay of U.S. cities. Which branches of social science relate to the topic? What insight or information about the topic do you get from each one?

Interrelationships among Social Sciences

How Are The Branches of Social Studies Interrelated?

On the GED you will be reading passages concerning **interrelationships** among the different branches of the social sciences. Let's look at an example. The stock market drops 150 points in one day. Since the stock market is at the heart of the economy, you know that economics is involved. But you would examine these, and many other relevant questions: What happened in the past when the stock market fell (history)? How will the dominant political mood in the country affect the market's recovery (political science)? How will investors react (psychology)? In the real world, the skills and knowledge of experts in many fields would be called upon.

It is unusual to find a person who is an expert in more than one field of study. There is simply too much information for most people to apply themselves to more than one area. However, a great anthropologist like Margaret Mead, about whom you read in the previous chapter, was extremely knowledgeable about geography, history, and sociology, in addition to anthropology. This knowledge enabled her to get the most out of her anthropological studies.

To answer some questions on the GED, you will also have to call on your skills and knowledge in more than one branch of social studies. This chapter consists of lessons that combine several of the social sciences in one topic. As you read each lesson, ask yourself which branches of the social sciences are involved. Think about the interrelationships and what impact they have on the topic. Doing this will help you to better understand the material.

Key Word

interrelationships—mutual relationships between different people, things, or areas of study

The New Europe

Prereading Prompt

Preview the lesson on the recent earth-shaking changes in Europe. What cleared the way for these changes to occur? What impact will a "new Europe" have on the rest of the world? Which branches of social studies would you expect this lesson to focus on?

Key Words

humanitarianism—a policy of respect for basic human rights and freedoms
glasnost—a policy favoring more democratic freedom in the Soviet Union, initiated by Soviet President Gorbachev
perestroika—a policy of economic reform in the Soviet Union, modifying Communism with elements of market capitalism

Changes in the Soviet Union

Over the years, Westerners formed images and impressions of Communist life in Eastern European countries: long lines outside food stores, shortages of essential goods, oppression of basic freedoms, low standards of living. The sudden changes of the late 1980s and early 1990s caught us all off-guard.

Soviet President Mikhail Gorbachev realized that Communism was leading the Communist bloc into ruin. The satellites, with their strangled economies, had drained the already poor Soviet economy. Perhaps more as a matter of survival than humanitarianism, Gorbachev began relaxing the grip of Communist rule. He allowed Eastern Europe to free itself of Soviet control. Policies such as **glasnost** and **perestroika** have brought a new openness to Soviet life and a reorganization of economic and political systems. An official policy of democratization and provisions for a limited market economy are allowing for freedom of expression, parliamentary government, and some private ownership of businesses and property in the U.S.S.R. For the first time, Soviet people are being allowed to openly criticize their government. Now some of the states within the Soviet Union are clamoring for independence. Estonia, Latvia, and Lithuania—the so-called Baltic states—were absorbed by force into the Soviet Union against their will through a Soviet agreement with the Nazis. Gorbachev's crushing of the Baltic states' rebellion has been strongly criticized in the Soviet Union and in Europe. He has turned to the military to keep the Soviet Union from splitting apart into separate republics. By 1991, the whole movement toward democracy and a market economy had slowed to near standstill.

Then, in August 1991 conservative old line Communist Party members of the Soviet government briefly overthrew Gorbachev. Strong opposition to this illegal seizure of power came from Boris Yeltsin, president of Russia, the largest part of the U.S.S.R. Faced with resistance throughout the country and in their own army, the hard-liners collapsed. The Communist Party lost control of the country and Gorbachev lost stature and power for remaining loyal to it. Glasnost and perestroika would go forward in a radically changed Soviet Union, with the Baltic states outside it, major parts of it independent of Moscow's control, and above all, with no Communist Party rule and with new structure of leadership.

Problems in the New Europe

The newly democratic countries of Eastern Europe are finding it difficult to adjust to the changes in their lives. They must form new governments based on new beliefs. They need new rules and laws to govern everything from taxes to trade with foreign countries. They must form a new economy, where workers work hard because they want to make more money. People in Communist countries have been accustomed to low pay, regardless of how hard they worked. Many therefore only did the minimum required of them. "They pretend to pay us, so we pretend to work" was a common saying. For many, adjusting to a competitive capitalist system has been painful. Some are even questioning the wisdom of their collective decision to adopt a democratic way of life and a market economy.

Questions also linger regarding the reunification of Germany. Twice, in two world wars, Germany has been an aggressive, imperialistic power. Will history repeat itself yet again if Germany is reunified? Many Europeans and Americans fear that it might. Others argue that Germany has changed, however, that the entire world picture has changed. Wealthy West Germany, like the rest of Western Europe and the U.S., must give aid to economically depressed Eastern Europe. Other questions remain unanswered. With whom will a reunified Germany ally itself? What will become of NATO?

Old conflicts in the New Europe are also surfacing. For example, tensions between Hungary and Romania have been revived now that these countries are free from communist control. After World War I, part of Hungary became Romanian territory. The Hungarians who lived in the region involved became Romanian citizens, even though they spoke Hungarian and followed Hungarian customs. In recent years, Hungarian Romanians have charged the Romanian government with attempting to destroy their cultural identity and heritage. Moreover, Communist leaders in 1991 are still largely in control of the Romanian government and also the Bulgarian government. The issue has become one of international concern. The whole world is watching and waiting to see what develops in the new Eastern Europe of the 1990s.

Lesson 1 Exercise

Items 1 and 2 are based on the lesson.

1. Which statement below is the main unstated assumption of those who fear German reunification?

   (1) The German people are naturally aggressive and cannot control their desire to rule the world.

   (2) The economy of Europe will buckle under the strain of an unstable German state after reunification.

   (3) NATO will become useless and Western Europe will have no means of defending itself against German aggression.

   (4) Germany will ally itself with the Soviet Union and the Cold War will begin again.

   (5) Germany will ally itself with Japan and increase the threat of another world war.

2. The newly democratic Eastern European states will experience tremendous economic instability as they struggle to form their new governments. What would *not* be a logical result of this economic instability?

   (1) Some of these states may revert to Communism.

   (2) Eastern Europe will become economically dependent on the U.S. or Western Europe and thereby come under their control.

   (3) These countries will experience a severe depression.

   (4) The Soviet Union will give large-scale assistance until their economies become stronger.

   (5) Eastern Europe will suffer through the transition and emerge as part of a stronger, new European community.

3. Hungarians living in Romania represent a

   (1) counterculture
   (2) dominant culture
   (3) subculture
   (4) clan
   (5) tribe

Answers are on page 384.

Lesson 2

The World Wars and Women's Liberation

Prereading Prompt

The title of this lesson suggests that the two world wars played a role in women's liberation. What do you think the connection is? As you read, pay attention to the different branches of social studies involved in this issue.

Key Words

women's liberation movement—a social movement begun in the 1950s and 1960s that seeks social, economic, and political equality for women
traditional role, conventional role—type of behavior forced on an individual or group by long-accepted ideas of a society

Women in the United States have always worked hard, but until recently their work was rarely recognized. This is because women have typically worked in the home, as housekeepers, mothers, cooks, and washwomen. As difficult as the job of homemaker is, it commands little respect from the outside world.

Before the 20th century, it was practically unheard of for women to work outside the home. Earning a living, smoking, drinking, and voicing one's opinion were considered extremely unfeminine. In the early 1900s some of this began to change. By the time of World War I, a sizeable number of women began working outside the home, often out of necessity; the factory and office jobs vacated by young men who went off to war had to be filled. Women filled the void.

During World War II, hundreds of thousands of women worked in defense plants producing guns, airplanes, warships, and ammunition. No longer was a woman's place in the home. Women were desperately needed to support the war effort. The popular image of "Rosie the Riveter" changed the way society saw women's ability to do a "man's job." Suddenly, it appeared that a woman could hold a blow torch and handle a rivet gun as well as a man could.

During World War II, women did more than produce weapons. They also joined the military. WAVES, WACS, and WAFS became common terms as more than 200,000 women joined the armed services. The WAVES were the women's reserve of the U.S. Navy—Women Accepted for Voluntary Emergency Service. WACS were the Women's Army Corps. And WAFS were Women in the Air Force.

When the war ended and the men came home, many women returned to their **traditional**, or **conventional, roles** of wife, mother, and homemaker. For many women, however, there was no turning back. They had gotten a taste of what it was like to be self-sufficient, to earn a living, to contribute in other ways to society and the economy. Nevertheless, most women stayed in their traditional roles.

The women's liberation movement began in earnest in the late 1950s and early 1960s with the publication of two books. *The Second Sex*, by Simone de Beauvoir, and *The Feminine Mystique*, by Betty Friedan, questioned women's traditional roles and encouraged women to seek personal and professional fulfillment outside of these roles. In the 1960s, many women joined consciousness-raising groups to discuss and ease the difficulty of this transition from traditional into nontraditional roles. By the 1970s, the women's liberation movement was in full swing. Women and men alike became aware that all jobs ought to be open to women and that women should receive equal pay for doing the same job.

In the 1990s, discrimination against women is hardly a thing of the past. Many women are passed over for promotions because their employers don't believe they can do as good a job as men. Others are passed over because their employers fear that they will leave if they become pregnant. The so-called *Mommy track* in business promotions routes women around the better-paying jobs with higher responsibility. Women may have come a long way, but they still have a long way to go.

Lesson 2 Exercises

1. What is the main conclusion that can be drawn from the lesson?
   (1) Major social changes usually come about from well-organized movements to promote change.
   (2) Wars often force people into traditional roles they avoid in peacetime.
   (3) Wars can have unexpected and radical effects on people's roles in society.
   (4) The jobs performed by women during the world wars gave them practical training for careers in the postwar years.
   (5) The women's liberation movement would not exist today if it weren't for the two major books by Simone de Beauvoir and Betty Friedan.

Items 2 and 3 are based on the following table.

Occupations and Median Earnings	
Occupation	Median Earnings (in dollars per week)
Industrial	
Machinists	356
Tool-and-die makers	433
Welders	334
Office	
Accountants	379
Bank officers	411
Bank tellers	189
Secretaries	229
Receptionists	200
Typists	213
Service occupations	
Cosmetologists	179
Firefighters	362
Food counter workers	141
Police officers	363
Constructions occupations	
Carpenters	325
Plumbers	404

Source: Bureau of Labor Statistics, U.S. Labor Department.

2. Which of the following statements is the conclusion best supported by the table?
   (1) Receptionists, secretaries, and typists make less money than accountants and welders.
   (2) Jobs that are typically held by women pay less than those typically held by men.
   (3) Women tend to choose jobs that don't pay as well as those that men choose.
   (4) Jobs typically held by men have to pay more because it is assumed that men have to support a family.
   (5) Women make as much as men when they work in a typically male job.

3. What is one implication of these statistics?
   (1) Jobs typically held by women will have to pay as much as those typically held by men, regardless of the work involved.
   (2) Jobs typically held by men will have to start paying less so that the pay of men and women can be equalized.
   (3) More men will hold lower-paying jobs as more women move into higher-paying jobs.
   (4) The cost of goods and services will increase because more people will be in higher-paying jobs.
   (5) Women will have to perform male-oriented jobs if they are to make more money.

Answers are on page 384–385

3 Famine in Africa

Prereading Prompt

The famine in Africa dominated headlines during the mid-1980s. Do you recall what the issues were? Did you participate by contributing money or food? Think about which branches of the social studies address this issue and then read the lesson.

Key Words

refugees—people who flee their homelands due to economic or political instability

terrain—the topography, or physical character, of the land

The dinner table is set, the steak sizzles in the pan, the potatoes are in the oven, and the evening news is on. The faces of starving children and adults in Africa, many with flies on their faces, invade the American home. Swollen bellies, distended from starvation, jab further at the heart. The TV set is turned off.

These images from the mid-1980s, when the American media seemed almost obsessed with the famine in Africa, were painful—so painful that many in positions of power and wealth tried to help. Hundreds of superstars like Michael Jackson and Bruce Springsteen worked to raise money to send food to the parched deserts of northern Africa. Millions sent whatever they could afford. What caused this disaster in the first place?

The first and most obvious cause was a drought of major proportion. As much as 44 percent of the total land area of the continent was affected; 27,000 square miles of land a year was turning into desert. This was further complicated by above-average damage to crops by insects and outbreaks of a severe infectious disease in cattle.

Another cause was the governmental policy of urbanization and industrialization. As farming was phased out in favor of industry, the nations of Africa were simply not producing as much food as they once did. Many African nations were also adversely affected by the high oil prices of the 1970s; conditions on the world market changed, causing a very unfavorable rate of exchange for developing countries. As a result, many poorer countries could not afford to buy fertilizer.

Political problems also contributed to the famine. Civil war in Ethiopia, for example, created great numbers of **refugees**—thousands of people who fled their homelands for safer areas. Farms were abandoned or destroyed by fighting troops. Areas that were unaffected became overpopulated and therefore increasingly unable to feed growing numbers of people. As the famine spread, more and more refugees roamed the countryside in search of food.

The generous outpouring of famine relief from the West had little real impact. Millions of dollars' worth of food that was sent to Ethiopia never reached the people who needed it because of the continuing civil war. The **terrain** further hindered the effort; access to remote areas was often difficult, and relief supplies could not be delivered to the areas where they were needed most.

Nomad refugees, Somalia
(Credit: UPI/Bettman Newsphotos)

In the 1990s, the situation improved somewhat; there was an unusually good harvest in 1989. But the drought continues in parts of Ethiopia, the Sudan, and Mozambique, threatening famine for upwards of 1.5 million people. Officials also warn of a spreading locust plague, the worst in 30 years. Clearly, the danger is not yet past.

Lesson 3 Exercises

1. Throughout history, when disease or famine has threatened the survival of groups of people, a common, seemingly instinctive, response has been to have more children. The reasoning behind this, presumably, is that having more children increases the likelihood that *some* will survive. In drought-stricken Africa, there has been a major population explosion; families are having more and more babies in the hopes that some will survive. Why is this reasoning flawed?

   (1) The same number of people will survive regardless of how many children people have.

   (2) There is no guarantee that any members of a family will survive.

   (3) Having more children takes food away from others who may need it more.

   (4) The government will be less likely to provide relief if it thinks that people are taking advantage of the situation.

   (5) Fewer people are likely to survive because there is already not enough food to go around.

2. The event that would probably have the most far-reaching impact on relieving the famine in Africa would be

   (1) several years of normal rainfall

   (2) an end to the locust plague and other insect infestations

   (3) government emphasis on—and support for—native agriculture

   (4) improving delivery of food so that supplies from other countries can reach those who need it

   (5) a greater emphasis on—and support for—democratic elections

Item 3 refers to the following passage.

One well-known comedian uses the famine in Africa as a topic for jokes in his routine. He familiarizes people with the situation: there are too many people and not enough food to go around; the soil won't produce crops because there is no rain; people wander from one part of the country to another searching for food and not finding it. Then he yells, as if trying to make the people in Africa hear, "Of course you can't find any food! You're living in a desert!"

3. The idea of the comedian's joke is that

   (1) the government should feed the starving people because they can't be expected to grow food in the desert

   (2) the situation is not all that serious

   (3) the people are feeling sorry for themselves

   (4) the people should know better than to try to live in a desert

   (5) the people have to find ways to make food grow in the desert

Answers are on page 385.

Practice

Introduction

When a theater group is about to open a new play, they have something known as a "dress rehearsal." During the dress rehearsal, the actors and stagehands run through the play as if it were a real performance, even though there is no audience. The dress rehearsal allows the group to judge how ready they are to open the play to the public. It allows them to realize the parts of the play that succeed, and discover areas that may need further work. The activities in this GED Practice section will be your dress rehearsal. The scores do not really count, but you can benefit a great deal from them. And come GED "show time," you will be able to obtain your best possible score.

This section is filled with GED-like test questions, or *items*. It provides valuable practice on the kinds of items found on the Social Studies Test. Arranged in two groups, the practice makes it easy to apply your knowledge to items based on content areas in social studies, as well as to a collection of items structured like the actual test.

On the pages that follow, you will find:

- **Practice Items** This practice contains 64 simulated GED test items, grouped according to the branches of social studies covered on the test. For example, you will find history items grouped together, geography items grouped together, and so on.
- **Practice Test** This is a 64-item test structured like an actual Social Studies Test. The passages are *not* grouped together according to content. Rather, the content varies from item to item.

As on the actual Social Studies Test, all the questions are multiple choice. By completing the Practice Items and the Practice Test, you will discover your strong points and weak points in social studies. And if you discover any weak points, *don't worry*—you will be shown how to strengthen them. The answer key not only provides the correct answer to each practice question, but it also explains *why* each answer is correct. The Performance Analysis Chart following each practice will direct you to parts of the book where you can review the skills or subjects that give you trouble.

You can use the Practice Items and the Practice Test in a number of different ways. The introductions that precede the practices will provide you with choices for using them to the best advantage. You may also wish to talk with your teacher to get suggestions about how best to make use of the Practice Items and Practice Test.

Practice Items

These Practice Items are similar to the real Social Studies Test in many ways, but there is one major difference. The items that follow are grouped according to the branches of social studies: history, geography, economics, political science, and behavioral science. As you work on the Practice Items, you will focus on one branch at a time. (The actual Social Studies Test presents passages from the various branches in mixed order.)

The whole group of 64 Practice Items is the same length as an actual test; the items are as challenging as the actual test items. Your results will help you determine which skills you have mastered and which you should study further.

Using the Practice Items to Best Advantage

You can use the Practice Items in the following ways:

- After you finish a chapter, you can test your ability by completing the section of the Practice Items that corresponds to the same branch of social studies. You can save the Practice Items until you've completed all the chapters. You can do the Practice Items one group at a time and then review the chapters for the areas in which you have difficulty.

- You can use the Practice Items as a practice test. To do this, complete the Practice Items in one sitting. Since the actual test allows you 85 minutes, you may want to time yourself. If 85 minutes elapse and you have not finished, circle the last question you answered, and then continue. This way, you can learn what score you'd earn within the time limit, as well as your total score counting the untimed portion of the practice. This will give you a rough idea of how you would perform on the actual Social Studies Test.

Keep an accurate record of your performance. Write your answers neatly on a sheet of paper, or use an answer sheet provided by your teacher.

Using the Answer Key

The answer key can be a very helpful study tool. Compare your answers to the correct answers in the answer key beginning on page 386, and check each item you answered correctly. Whether you answer an item correctly or not, you should read the explanations of correct answers in the answer key. Doing this will reinforce your knowledge of social studies and develop your testtaking skills.

How to Use Your Score

Regardless of how you use these Practice Items, you will gain valuable experience with GED-type questions. After scoring your work with the answer key, fill in the Performance Analysis Chart on page 312. The chart will help you determine which skills and areas you are strongest in, and direct you to parts of the book where you can review areas in which you need additional work.

Practice Items

Directions: *Choose the* one *best answer to each question.*

HISTORY ITEMS

Item 1 refers to the following map.

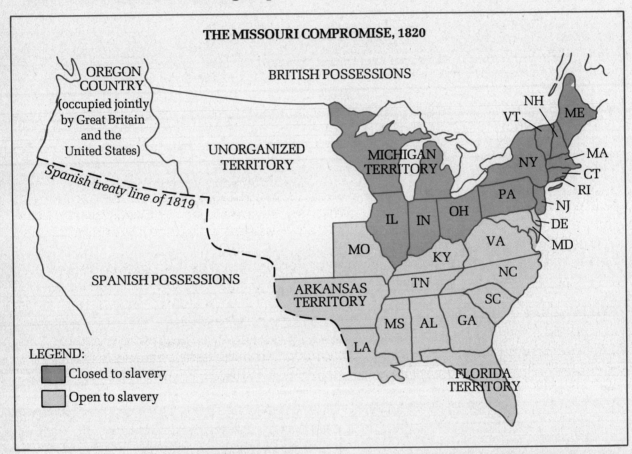

THE MISSOURI COMPROMISE, 1820

OREGON COUNTRY (occupied jointly by Great Britain and the United States)

BRITISH POSSESSIONS

Spanish treaty line of 1819

UNORGANIZED TERRITORY

MICHIGAN TERRITORY

SPANISH POSSESSIONS

ARKANSAS TERRITORY

FLORIDA TERRITORY

NH
VT
ME
NY
MA
CT
RI
PA
NJ
DE
MD
IL
IN
OH
MO
VA
KY
NC
TN
SC
MS
AL
GA
LA

LEGEND:
Closed to slavery
Open to slavery

1. The Missouri Compromise of 1820 created two new states, Maine and Missouri. Maine became a free state, while Missouri became a slave state. Based on the information provided in the map, which of the following is the best explanation for the adoption of the Missouri Compromise?

(1) It was the most convenient way to open the unorganized territories to new settlement.

(2) It maintained the balance between slave states and free states, allowing neither to control Congress.

(3) It divided the country between North and South, permitting separate federal legislation for each.

(4) It protected citizens in the new state against hostile Indian tribes in the unorganized territories.

(5) It pacified southerners who worried that the South would lose control of the Mississippi River.

Items 2 to 4 refer to the following passage.

During the 1950s and 1960s, numerous protests, legal decisions, political actions, mass marches, and government interventions brought an end to legal segregation in the United States. On December 1, 1955, Rosa Parks, a black woman, refused to give her seat to a white man on a bus in Montgomery, Alabama, and was arrested. In response to this event, blacks in Montgomery refused to use any buses. This boycott of the bus service led to an important decision by a federal court. The court ruled that a law that allowed buses to separate, or segregate, blacks and whites was not legal under the Constitution.

In 1957, President Eisenhower sent troops to Little Rock, Arkansas, to protect black students who were entering a high school that had been open only to white students. A previous decision by the U.S. Supreme Court had declared that segregated public schools were unconstitutional. In 1960, college students in Greensboro, North Carolina, began to protest segregation. In 1962, James Meredith became the first black to attend the University of Mississippi.

The civil rights movement received tremendous support on August 28, 1963, when 200,000 people came to Washington, D.C., to demand equal rights for blacks. On that day, Dr. Martin Luther King, Jr. delivered his famous "I have a dream" speech. The following year, the strongest civil rights bill in the history of the United States, the Civil Rights Bill of 1964, was signed into law.

2. According to the passage, which event touched off the movement to end racial segregation in the United States?

(1) James Meredith's entry into the University of Mississippi

(2) the Supreme Court's ruling to make segregated public schools illegal

(3) President Eisenhower's decision to send troops to Little Rock, Arkansas

(4) Rosa Parks's refusal to give up her seat on a bus in Montgomery, Alabama

(5) Dr. Martin Luther King, Jr.'s "I have a dream" speech in Washington, D.C.

3. Which of the following best explains why the civil rights movement was successful in achieving the laws that were set forth by the Civil Rights Bill of 1964?

(1) Dr. Martin Luther King, Jr.'s nonviolent actions convinced the southern whites to support civil rights.

(2) College-student protests gathered the backing of students everywhere to support civil rights.

(3) The United States Constitution guarantees equal rights for all.

(4) The national attention that was received by the march on Washington, D.C., raised American consciousness.

(5) The Supreme Court ruled in 1954 that segregation in public schools denied equality to blacks.

4. Court decisions on the civil rights cases that are mentioned in the passage were most likely based on which of the following amendments?

(1) the First Amendment, which guarantees freedom of speech, press, and religion

(2) the Tenth Amendment, which guarantees to the states all rights that are not prohibited by the federal government

(3) the Eleventh Amendment, which declares that no state shall be sued in a federal court by another state

(4) the Thirteenth Amendment, which abolished slavery in the United States

(5) the Fourteenth Amendment, which prevents states from denying equal protection of the laws to any person

5. In 1986, two authoritarian national leaders left office under pressure. One was Jean-Claude Duvalier, the "President for Life" of Haiti. The other was Ferdinand Marcos, president of the Philippines for twenty years. In both countries, there was widespread poverty and government corruption. Both leaders had been accused of stealing millions from their countries.

Which of the following statements would make the best newspaper headline for this passage?

(1) Dictator Duvalier Flees Haiti with Loot

(2) Marcos Falls—Accused of Theft

(3) Poverty Thrives in Haiti, Philippines

(4) Marcos and Duvalier Fall from Power

(5) Corruption King in Haiti and Philippines

Items 6 and 7 refer to the following illustration and text.

Brooks in The Birmingham News

"First things first!"

Charles Brooks in the Birmingham News.
Reprinted by permission.

The *Great Society* refers to a set of social programs that were designed by President Johnson and that were intended to end poverty and racism, to eradicate disease, to rebuild cities, to banish ignorance, and generally to help U.S. citizens live in harmony and abundance.

6. Based on the illustration, which of the following statements best describes the economic impact of the Vietnam War on the Great Society in the 1960s?

(1) American taxpayers were reluctant to spend more money on the war in Vietnam.

(2) President Johnson's Great Society had proved to be too expensive to support.

(3) The gas shortage was made worse by the need to supply the U.S. troops in Vietnam.

(4) Great Society programs were deprived of funds by the expense of the Vietnam War.

(5) The war caused a recession, which made it impossible to provide funds for domestic programs.

7. Which of the following statements is NOT supported by the illustration?

(1) President Johnson had no choice but to spend money on the Vietnam War that would have been spent on the Great Society.

(2) President Johnson's roles included head of the armed forces and domestic-programs legislator.

(3) Foreign-policy programs had a higher priority in the Johnson administration than domestic programs did.

(4) Funds for the war and for domestic programs were drawn from the same budget.

(5) More money was spent to achieve military aims than to improve social conditions.

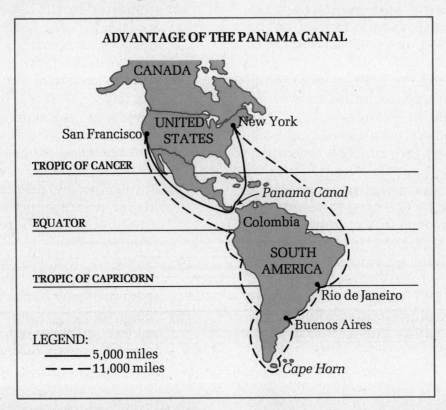

ADVANTAGE OF THE PANAMA CANAL

CANADA

UNITED STATES

San Francisco

New York

TROPIC OF CANCER

Panama Canal

EQUATOR

Colombia

SOUTH AMERICA

TROPIC OF CAPRICORN

Rio de Janeiro

Buenos Aires

LEGEND:
———— 5,000 miles
— — — 11,000 miles

Cape Horn

8. Based on the map, which of the following was the most likely benefit of the Panama Canal when it was built in 1914?

(1) It became cheaper to transport fruit and other produce from the west coast to the east coast.

(2) It opened new territories for American exploration and colonization.

(3) It increased U.S. trade with the countries of South America.

(4) It removed any obstacles to U.S. conquest of the Pacific Islands.

(5) It reduced the navy's difficulties in protecting U.S. coastal waters.

Items 9 to 11 refer to the following passage.

Before 1776, the Americans had been slow to settle the interior, which they called the "back-country." After 1800, the "back-country" became "frontier" in American speech, and the line of settlement advanced westward with astonishing speed. By its conventional definition, the "frontier" is commonly understood to be the outer edge of the area with a population density of at least two persons per square mile. Before 1783 that line was still largely east of the Appalachian Mountains except for a small settlement on the dark and bloody ground of Kentucky. Thirty years later, the great center of the continent was occupied. By 1820 the frontier had crossed the Mississippi. And by 1840, it had reached the 100th meridian. The plains beyond were subdued after 1865 with the aid of a new technology—the steel plough, the six-shooter, and the barbed-wire fence. After the census of 1890, the superintendent of the census observed that for the first time in American history, a single frontier line was no longer visible on his map. The frontier, in that sense, had come to an end.

From Geoffrey Barraclough, ed., *The Times Atlas of World History*, New York: Hammond, 1984, with permission.

9. Which of the following statements about the United States before 1800 is implied by the passage?
   (1) The population was moving steadily westward.
   (2) The population density was less than two persons per square mile.
   (3) Most Americans lived on or near the eastern seaboard.
   (4) The steel plough was used only in the East.
   (5) Most Americans lived in the "back-country."

10. Based on information that is provided in the passage, which of the following was the "frontier"?
   (1) New York in 1776
   (2) California in 1783
   (3) Kentucky in 1800
   (4) Kansas in 1820
   (5) Oregon in 1890

11. Which of the following statements is supported by information that is provided in the passage?
   (1) "Back country" is generally considered an area with a population density of two persons per square mile.
   (2) Unlike many colonial nations, the United States was fortunate to have an internal empire to conquer.

(3) The center of the continent was occupied as a result of the successful conquest of the "dark and bloody ground of Kentucky."
(4) The frontier advanced by pushing back the Native American tribes that it encountered.
(5) Improved agricultural tools were a cause of the frontier's rapid advancement into the plains.

12. As the United States expanded westward in the early nineteenth century, Americans felt that their country was destined to reach its natural boundary—the Pacific Ocean. This belief came to be called *manifest destiny*. Based on this information, which of the following is an action that was motivated by manifest destiny?
   (1) The development of the steel plough, the six-shooter, and the barbed-wire fence
   (2) The disappearance of a single frontier line in the west
   (3) The purchase of California from Mexico in 1848
   (4) The California gold rush in 1849
   (5) The annexation of Hawaii in 1898

Items 13 to 15 refer to the following passage.

On June 17, 1972, five men were arrested at the offices of the Democratic Party's National Headquarters in Washington, D.C. The offices were located in a hotel called the Watergate. The men, who were trying to steal private papers, all had connections to the White House.

President Richard Nixon denied knowledge of the Watergate crime, but newspaper reporters began to uncover proof that some of the White House staff members were involved in the attempted burglary. Other administration officials also denied participation, but further investigations implicated them in the use of secret funds and illegal wiretapping as well.

In July of 1973, it was discovered that President Nixon held secret tape recordings of conversations in the White House that concerned the Watergate scandal. President Nixon refused to turn over the tapes to the courts as he felt it was his right to withhold them. The Supreme Court ruled that he had to turn them over.

The Judiciary Committee of the House of Representatives began impeachment hearings, and in July 1974 the committee recommended impeachment. On August 5, 1974, President Nixon released the tapes that proved his involvement with Watergate and then resigned on August 9, 1974.

13. Many of those connected to the Watergate scandal were charged and tried by jury. With which of the following crimes are they LEAST likely to have been charged?
    (1) burglary
    (2) breaking and entering
    (3) treason
    (4) illegal wiretapping
    (5) illegal use of public money

14. Which of the following statements is best supported by the Supreme Court decision regarding the tape recordings?
    (1) The Supreme Court believed that President Nixon was guilty of a crime.
    (2) President Nixon was required by law to prove his innocence before the Supreme Court.
    (3) The Supreme Court may suspend the President's constitutional rights.
    (4) The President of the United States has the right to take the Fifth Amendment.
    (5) The office of the President is not above the law.

15. The Judiciary Committee recommended Nixon's impeachment because he
    (1) concealed stolen private papers in the White House
    (2) was involved in an attempted burglary
    (3) lied to federal investigators
    (4) knowingly interfered with the course of justice
    (5) had used secret tapes to implicate other administration officials in an attempted burglary

Question 16 is based on the following chart.

The Number of Days U.S. Workers Spent on Strike	
Year	Person-days Idle (in millions of days)
1930	3,320
1940	6,700
1950	38,800
1960	19,100
1970	66,414
1980	30,984

From Jack Abramowitz et al., *Economics and the Free-Enterprise System* (New York: Globe Book Company. 1983), page 292.

16. Which of the following conclusions can be supported by the table?

   (1) The desire to share in the high profits of corporations caused the high number of days workers spent on strike in 1950.

   (2) During the Great Depression of the 1930s, people couldn't afford to go on strike.

   (3) The high number of days spent on strike in 1970 reflects the general unrest of the late 1960s.

   (4) The numbers are higher in the last half of the century than in the first because more people are now members of labor unions.

   (5) There were fewer than half as many person-days spent on strike in 1960 than in the labor-troubled year of 1950.

Item *17* refers to the following graph.

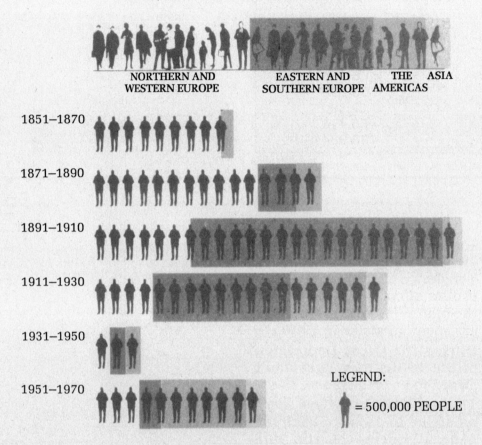

WHERE IMMIGRANTS CAME FROM
TOTAL, 1820–1970 = 45 MILLION PEOPLE

NORTHERN AND WESTERN EUROPE   EASTERN AND SOUTHERN EUROPE   THE AMERICAS   ASIA

1851–1870

1871–1890

1891–1910

1911–1930

1931–1950

1951–1970

LEGEND:

= 500,000 PEOPLE

17. Based on information that is provided in the graph, which of the following immigrants to the United States would you be least likely to find?

(1) a German in 1860
(2) an Italian in 1900
(3) a Mexican in 1925
(4) a Russian in 1954
(5) a Canadian in 1965

GEOGRAPHY ITEMS

Item 18 refers to the following maps.

TERRAIN AND POPULATION PATTERNS OF JAPAN

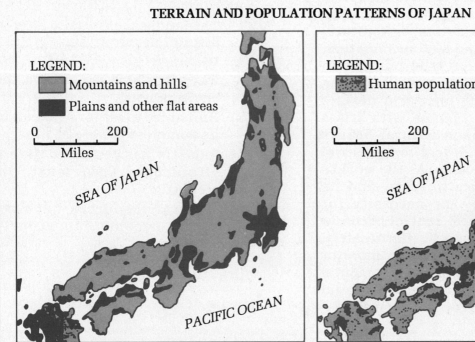
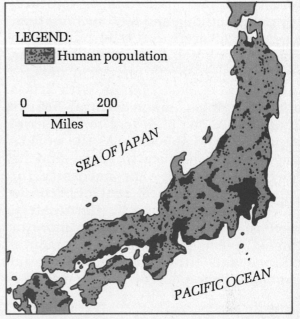

LEGEND:
- Mountains and hills
- Plains and other flat areas

0   200
Miles

SEA OF JAPAN

PACIFIC OCEAN

LEGEND:
- Human population

0   200
Miles

SEA OF JAPAN

PACIFIC OCEAN

18. Based on the information that is provided in the maps, which of the following is an explanation for the population distribution in Japan?

(1) No large urban population is more than 100 miles from another.

(2) The south is more densely populated than the north.

(3) The population is most dense on the Pacific coast.

(4) The population is concentrated where the farming is easiest.

(5) The mountains separate one part of the country from the other.

Item 19 refers to the following passage.

Humankind has had a great impact on the landscape. Through urbanization, forest clearance, irrigation, agricultural terracing, mining and land reclamation, we have altered our environment in many astounding ways, not all of them for the good. While once-arid deserts have been made to bloom with fruits and vegetables, much natural beauty and wildlife has been lost to industrial expansion and pollution. As the world's population continues to grow—and its needs to increase—the necessity for careful environmental control becomes more and more apparent. Fortunately, modern science enables us to monitor almost every aspect of environmental change and either to avoid potential problems or to plan for their solution.

19. Which of the following statements is the most accurate summary of humankind's relationship to the environment?
   (1) The landscape is easily altered to suit our purposes.
   (2) We must be cautious in the ways in which we change the environment.
   (3) Humanity must forge ahead in its conquest of nature.
   (4) Industry has destroyed the environment and must be stopped.
   (5) Natural resources have recently become dangerously scarce.

Items 20 and 21 refer to the following map.

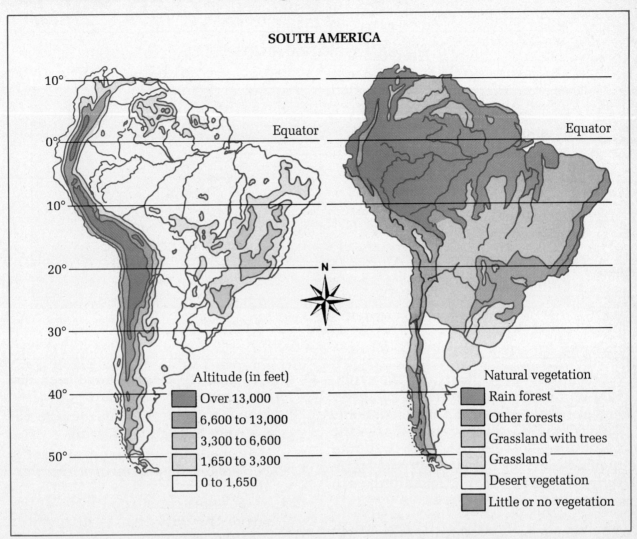

SOUTH AMERICA

Altitude (in feet)
- Over 13,000
- 6,600 to 13,000
- 3,300 to 6,600
- 1,650 to 3,300
- 0 to 1,650

Natural vegetation
- Rain forest
- Other forests
- Grassland with trees
- Grassland
- Desert vegetation
- Little or no vegetation

20. Typically, equatorial areas are covered with dense jungle. One area of all the regions below the equator shown on the maps has the least amount of plant life because it
- **(1)** has less vegetation than temperate regions
- **(2)** has grasslands without trees
- **(3)** is a desert
- **(4)** is not near rivers or oceans
- **(5)** is at very high altitudes

21. Amazon River Basin is the largest river system and the largest rainforest area in South America. On the map, you will find the largest network of rivers is in the largest rainforest area. Almost all of this area has an altitude of
- **(1)** 3,300 to 6,600 feet
- **(2)** 1,650 to 3,300 feet
- **(3)** 6,600 to 13,000 feet
- **(4)** 0 to 1,650 feet
- **(5)** over 13,000 feet

Items 22 to 24 refer to the following model.

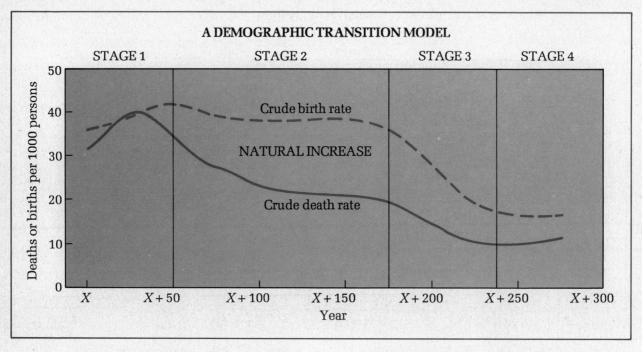

The model above illustrates the evolution of a typical society from an agrarian economy to an urban-industrial one. This transition, where *Year X* marks the beginnings of change, can be documented in terms of mortality and fertility rates, and their relationship to each other.

22. Which of the following stages will be marked by a high rate of population growth?
  (1) Stage 1
  (2) Stage 2
  (3) Stage 3
  (4) Stages 3 and 4
  (5) Stages 1 and 4

23. A country that is in Stage 4 is most likely to be one in which
  (1) health services are strong and family planning is encouraged
  (2) large families are regarded as status symbols

(3) health services have been disrupted by civil wars
(4) religious laws discourage the use of family planning
(5) medical facilities and family planning are only for the rich

24. A possible conclusion to be drawn from the data that is provided in the model is that
  (1) if the birth rate exceeds the death rate, population growth will increase
  (2) the population will grow when the death rate is below 30 per 1,000
  (3) a change in the death rate is affected by a change in the birth rate
  (4) the birth rate must exceed the death rate for the population to grow
  (5) it will require more than 250 years for any signs of change to become apparent

Items 25 and 26 refer to the following map.

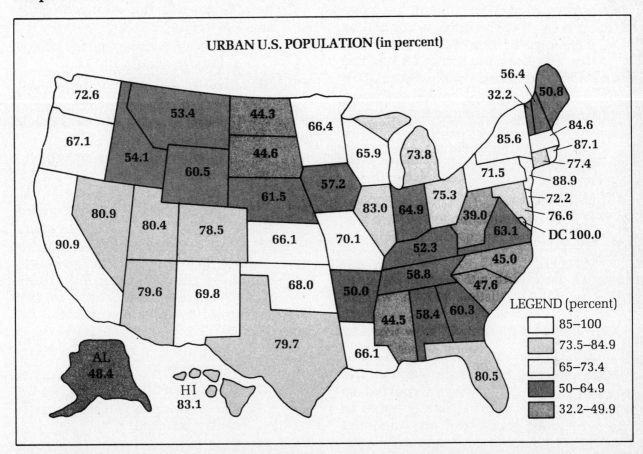

URBAN U.S. POPULATION (in percent)

LEGEND (percent)
- 85–100
- 73.5–84.9
- 65–73.4
- 50–64.9
- 32.2–49.9

25. Based on the map, which area of the United States has the largest number of the most highly urbanized states?

(1) the Southwest
(2) the Far West
(3) New England and the Northeast
(4) the South
(5) Upper Midwest

26. For which of the following applications would the data that is given in the map be adequate?

(1) to compare the percent of urban workers to the percent of agricultural workers
(2) to estimate the number of people per state who reside in urban areas
(3) to rank all the states in order of urbanization
(4) to determine whether urbanization patterns across the states relate to the presence of industry
(5) to predict changes in U.S. urban population percents

27. Money in a mattress or under a floor board is not protected if it is stolen. Money in a bank is, however, even if the bank is robbed or goes out of business. After the Great Depression of the 1930s, the government established the Federal Deposit Insurance Corporation (FDIC) to insure loss of savings up to $5,000 for each customer. Today each customer is insured for losses up to $100,000. What is this an example of on the part of the American government?

(1) tariff legislation
(2) imperialism
(3) economic intervention
(4) antimonopoly legislation
(5) business regulation

Items 28 and 29 refer to the following passage.

A balance of trade exists when the percent of goods that are exported to other nations is approximately equal to the percent of goods that are imported from other countries. A trade deficit occurs when the percent of imports is greater than the percent of exports. At present, the United States has a trade deficit.

Many factors affect the balance of trade. For example, a strong currency has more buying power; therefore, a country that has a strong currency tends to import more from countries that have weak currencies. When a country is at war, domestic industries are employed in defense production, and more manufactured goods and raw materials may be needed from other countries. In times of economic depression, fewer goods are imported. Inflation may also affect the balance of trade because it raises production costs and weakens the currency.

28. Based on the passage, which of the following strategies would be most helpful toward the elimination of the U.S. trade deficit?

(1) increasing the production of domestic goods
(2) raising tariffs on imported goods
(3) increasing the value of the dollar
(4) increasing the defense budget
(5) reducing inflation

29. A manufacturer in the United States wishes to increase its sales in France. Based on information that is provided in the passage, which of the following situations would be most favorable to the manufacturer's achievement of its goals?

(1) The United States experiences a depression.
(2) U.S. import tariffs are raised.
(3) The French economy is currently inflated.
(4) The French franc is strong compared to the American dollar.
(5) The U.S. economy is currently inflated.

30. A *mixed economy* is one in which private ownership and government ownership of industries exist side by side. The United States, for instance, has a capitalist economy in which private enterprise is the guiding principle; yet, the government owns and runs many industries, such as the postal service. Likewise, in many socialist countries, a good deal of property is privately owned.

Based on the passage, which of the following best describes a country that has a mixed economy?

(1) The government does not regulate business.
(2) All property is owned by the government.
(3) The government runs only the postal service.
(4) The government owns service-providing industries, but private citizens own profit-making businesses.
(5) Business and property are owned by both the government and private citizens.

Item 31 refers to the graph below.

31. In a time of economic inflation, the federal government decides to lower prices in an area of the economy that most affects the budget of the average wage earner. Which of the following government agencies would most likely be chosen to lower prices in the area of the economy under its control?

(1) the Department of Energy
(2) the Department of Agriculture
(3) the Department of Transportation
(4) the Department of Health, Education, and Welfare
(5) the National Parks Service

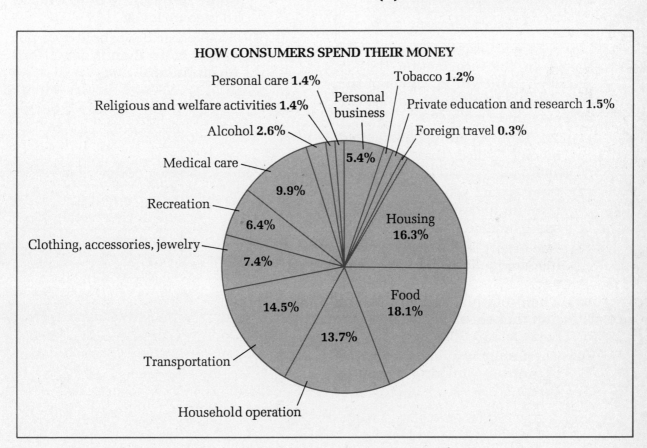

HOW CONSUMERS SPEND THEIR MONEY

Personal care 1.4%
Religious and welfare activities 1.4%
Alcohol 2.6%
Medical care
Recreation
Clothing, accessories, jewelry
Transportation
Household operation

Personal business
Tobacco 1.2%
Private education and research 1.5%
Foreign travel 0.3%

5.4%
9.9%
6.4%
7.4%
14.5%
13.7%

Housing 16.3%
Food 18.1%

Items 32 and 33 refer to the following graph.

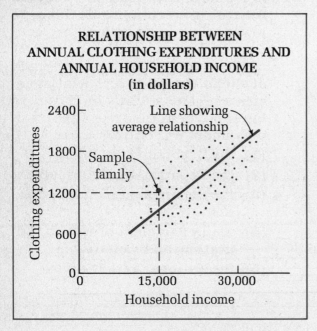

RELATIONSHIP BETWEEN
ANNUAL CLOTHING EXPENDITURES AND
ANNUAL HOUSEHOLD INCOME
(in dollars)

32. Based on the information that is provided in the graph, which of the following statements about the sample family is true?

  (1) The family's annual household income is less than the average.

  (2) They spend more on clothing than an average family of the same income.

  (3) The family's annual household income is more than the average.

  (4) Their clothing expenses are half those of a family whose income is $30,000.

  (5) The family is average in terms of annual clothing expenditures.

33. Which of the following statements is supported by information that is provided in the graph?

  (1) A family's annual clothing expenditure can be predicted based on its annual income.

  (2) A household that has two wage earners will spend twice as much on clothing as a household that has one wage earner.

  (3) Annual clothing expenditure is determined not only by a household's income, but also by the number of people that it comprises.

  (4) The average expenditure of clothing increases at a constant rate that is proportional to income level.

  (5) An average household does not spend more than it can afford on clothing.

Items 34 and 35 refer to the following passage.

The federal government has several means of intervening in the economy to assist vital or troubled industries, as well as, in many cases, unemployed workers or economically depressed regions. A *tax incentive* aids an industry by lowering, eliminating, or deferring certain taxes. A *subsidy* is a direct payment or credit given to a company or an industry. A new method has been proposed, in which the government could insure loans from private institutions, which may otherwise be reluctant to invest in risky projects.

34. Which of the following situations is an example of government subsidy?

(1) A hotel that is built in a depressed rural area in 1987 pays 10 percent of its property tax in 1987, 40 percent in 1990, and 100 percent in 2000.

(2) A steel mill in Pennsylvania does not pay sales tax on newly purchased processing equipment.

(3) An auto plant in Michigan obtains a federal grant to train displaced steelworkers to work on its assembly line.

(4) A company that makes computers gives word-processing training to welfare recipients, who are paid a salary by the federal government.

(5) A nonprofit environmental organization is not required to contribute to the unemployment fund.

35. Based on information that is provided in the passage, which of the following would be a benefit to the federal government of federal loan insurance compared to tax incentives and subsidies?

(1) It encourages the development of innovative technologies.

(2) It increases federal control over civilian industries.

(3) It is comparatively inexpensive for the government.

(4) It makes the government liable for private debts.

(5) It rewards the most profitable industries.

Items 36 to 40 refer to the following passage.

In the United States, there are several legal forms that a business organization may take. The three basic forms are proprietorships, partnerships, and corporations.

A *proprietorship* is a firm that is owned by a single individual and is usually a small business, such as a shop, a restaurant, a garage, etc. The advantages of a proprietorship are that its owner has complete control over it and that it is easy and inexpensive to establish. Disadvantages include the fact that the owner has unlimited liability for the business—if it fails, all of the owner's personal assets may be taken by creditors to cover its debts.

A *partnership* is a business in which two or more people agree to own and run the organization. Each partner contributes money and labor in return for a proportion of the profits or losses. One advantage of partnerships over proprietorships is that they can generally put together more financial resources and specialized skills. However, each partner remains personally liable for the bills of the firm—even if a partner owns only 30 percent of the firm, he or she must pay all of its debts if the other partners cannot do so.

A *corporation* is a form of organization that is considered by law to be separate and distinct from its owners. An owner in a corporation contributes money in return for stock, or shares. The greater the amount of money a person spends, the greater number of shares the person receives. Each share represents one vote in the corporation's management. It also entitles the stockholder to a proportion of the company's profits or losses. Unlike a proprietorship or a partnership, a corporation is run by directors who are hired by the stockholders. The advantages of a corporation are that it is able to raise large sums of money, and an owner's liability is limited to the amount of stock he or she holds; if the firm goes bankrupt, stockholders may lose only the value of their own stock.

36. Based on information that is provided in the passage, which of the following statements about business ownership is true?
  (1) Only owners of proprietorships and partnerships are liable.
  (2) A partnership is the best way to raise money for a business.
  (3) All owners are liable to a certain extent for their firms.
  (4) A stockholder is a partner in the corporation.
  (5) A business partner fully controls the company's finances.

37. Which of the following describes a situation that would occur in a partnership?
  (1) Six people own equal parts of a pizza parlor, in which they each spend one night a week behind the counter.
  (2) An executive owns a large department store and shares the responsibility of management with two other executives.
  (3) A business falls into debt, and its owner must sell the family car to pay back the creditors.
  (4) A farmer owns all of the equipment on the farm but rents the land from another farmer.
  (5) An oil company is run by twelve people, who are paid large salaries but do not share in its profits.

38. Which of the following statements best explains why someone would choose to invest in a corporation over other forms of business?

(1) A corporation is the most profitable form of business.

(2) If one goes bankrupt, liability for debts may be shifted to other owners.

(3) A person would be most likely to benefit from the skills of one's associates.

(4) A person's personal assets will be best protected.

(5) Less money is tied up in a corporation.

39. A shopkeeper declares that proprietorship is the best form of ownership. Based on the passage, which of the following arguments best supports this opinion?

(1) Unlimited liability can have little or no effect on one's life.

(2) Compromise amongst several owners may lead to weaker policies.

(3) No money can be made by investing in someone else's business.

(4) The greatest personal risks bring the greatest personal rewards.

(5) Owning your own business is the only satisfying way of life.

40. The passage provides evidence to support which of the following statements?

(1) The form that a business takes is determined by the number of people who own it.

(2) The amount of profit that a person makes is determined by the form of business that has been chosen.

(3) The type of personality that a person has determines the kind of business that he or she chooses.

(4) The amount of liability that a person has in a partnership is determined by the amount of money that she or he invested.

(5) The amount of influence that a person has in a corporation is determined by the number of stocks that she or he owns.

POLITICAL SCIENCE ITEMS

Items 41 to 45 refer to the following information.

The American judicial system is composed of many different types of courts to be found at three levels: federal, state, and local. Listed below are five different categories of courts and brief descriptions of the types of cases that are to be found in their jurisdiction.

(1) Federal Supreme Court: considers cases that are appealed from lower federal courts or from the highest state courts; also considers cases that involve ambassadors, foreign ministers, and consuls. Supreme Court decisions are final.

(2) Court of Appeals: considers appeals from individuals and from groups who seek to reverse the ruling of lower courts. Both the federal and the state court systems have courts of appeals.

(3) Federal District Court: tries cases that involve federal law and also those cases that involve persons or situations in more than one state.

(4) State Superior Courts: are distributed throughout the counties of a state; hear cases that involve state law, where all parties are residents of that state and the situation occurred in that state only.

(5) County or Municipal Courts: hear only those cases that involve persons and situations that are within the actual physical boundaries of their jurisdiction.

Each of the following cases would be decided by one of the courts that are described. Choose the category of courts that is most likely to try the case. The categories may be used more than once in the set of items, but no one question has more than one best answer.

41. The laws of a certain state declare that all school taxes must be based on local property taxes. The school board from a district where the property taxes are low contests this law on the grounds that its school will have less financial support. The school board takes the case to the
(1) Federal Supreme Court
(2) Court of Appeals
(3) Federal District Court
(4) State Superior Court
(5) County or Municipal Court

42. A New York City restaurant owner is arrested and taken to court for serving beer to a minor, who is a resident of Albany. The court rules that the restaurant's liquor license be taken away. The restaurant owner contests the ruling on grounds that the minor had presented a forged identification. The restaurant owner takes the case to the
(1) Federal Supreme Court
(2) Court of Appeals
(3) Federal District Court
(4) State Superior Court
(5) County or Municipal Court

43. In accordance with integration laws, white students from one high school are bused to another high school, which is in the same school district but in a black neighborhood some distance from their homes. The parents protest against the busing and take their case to the

(1) Federal Supreme Court

(2) Court of Appeals

(3) Federal District Court

(4) State Superior Court

(5) County or Municipal Court

44. A newspaper reporter writes an article that is sharply critical of a local politician. The politician sues the reporter for slander. The judge in the case rules that the reporter must pay damages, but the reporter contests the ruling on the grounds that her professional rights are being violated. After a series of legal battles, the case is finally settled in the highest court to which the reporter can legally appeal. This is the

(1) Federal Supreme Court

(2) Court of Appeals

(3) Federal District Court

(4) State Superior Court

(5) County or Municipal Court

45. A driver who lives in Muncie, Indiana, has an automobile collision on the Indiana state highway. The driver of the other car, a Chicago resident, is clearly at fault and is sued by the first driver in the

(1) Federal Supreme Court

(2) Court of Appeals

(3) Federal District Court

(4) State Superior Court

(5) County or Municipal Court

46. The Second Amendment to the U.S. Constitution gives all citizens the right to bear arms, claiming that a well-regulated militia is "necessary to the security of a free State." If a U.S. senator wished to have this amendment repealed, which of the following statements would be the best argument in support of the senator's position?

(1) A civilian militia is no longer necessary to our security.

(2) A truly free state does not need a militia.

(3) A well-regulated militia does not require weapons.

(4) The security of our country is no longer an issue.

(5) The Second Amendment is unconstitutional.

Items 47 and 48 refer to the following time line.

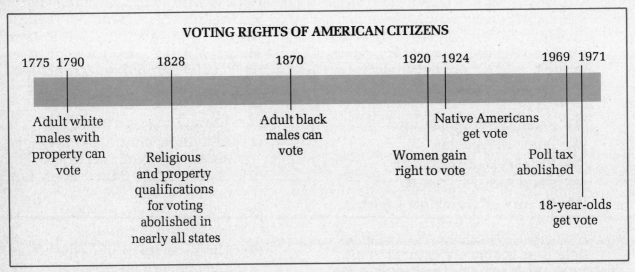

VOTING RIGHTS OF AMERICAN CITIZENS

1775 1790 1828 1870 1920 1924 1969 1971

Adult white males with property can vote

Religious and property qualifications for voting abolished in nearly all states

Adult black males can vote

Women gain right to vote

Native Americans get vote

Poll tax abolished

18-year-olds get vote

47. According to the time line, a person could have been prevented from voting in 1950 on the basis of which of the following?
   (1) sex
   (2) race
   (3) wealth
   (4) property
   (5) religion

48. Which of the following statements is supported by the time line?
   (1) As the population grows, more and more Americans have the right to vote.
   (2) More women have participated in elections since 1969 than ever before.
   (3) Since 1971, there has been no major group of citizens that does not have the right to vote.
   (4) A larger proportion of American citizens has the right to vote since 1971 than ever before.
   (5) Over the past 200 years the right to vote has been extended through a series of constitutional amendments.

49. In a factory that produces copper plumbing parts, a machine used for molding the copper into various shapes is very dangerous to operate. In the past, several workers have had hands caught in the machine and have been badly injured. The machine was redesigned so that both hands are now required to operate the machine, reducing the risk of injury. Which government regulatory agency would have been responsible for enforcing this measure?
   (1) The Equal Employment Opportunity Commission
   (2) The Environmental Protection Agency
   (3) The Food and Drug Administration
   (4) The Occupational Safety and Hazards Administration
   (5) The Federal Trade Commission

50. The United Nations is the largest international organization in the world, established as a forum in which all member nations may air their grievances and where disputes may be settled peacefully. However, many other international organizations exist in order to deal with more specific, regional problems. Some, like the North Atlantic Treaty Organization, are military organizations that were established to protect member nations from common enemies. Others, like the European Economic Community or the Association of Southeast Asian Nations, promote economic and cultural cooperation.

Which of the following statements is a conclusion that can be drawn from the passage?

(1) The United Nations is an arbiter in international affairs.

(2) International organizations serve a variety of functions.

(3) Military alliances serve to protect their members.

(4) International organizations contend with regional difficulties.

(5) The Association of Southeast Asian Nations is an economic community.

Item 51 refers to the following illustration.

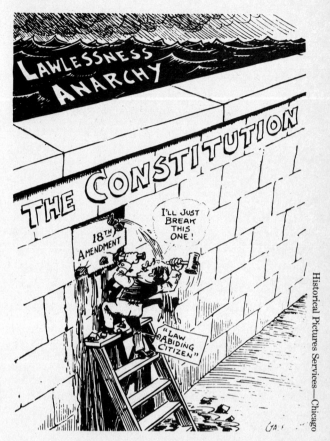

51. From 1919 to 1933, an amendment to the Constitution made it illegal to produce, sell, or transport alcoholic beverages in the United States. According to the illustration, the greatest danger from this law was that

(1) too many arrests would have to be made to enforce the law

(2) public disrespect for this law would encourage disregard for all laws

(3) the law would only result in more liquor being sold

(4) Congress would not be able to enforce it

(5) law-abiding citizens would vote against the amendment

52. Since the days of the Great Depression, the Democratic Party's strength has come from four major sources. The Deep South had been a traditional Democratic stronghold since the end of the Civil War. Big cities also were a traditional source of Democratic strength. The image of the Democratic Party as the party for the working class during the Depression gave the party great support among industrial workers and blacks.

Based on information provided in the passage, which of the following measures would be most likely to lose the Democratic Party a large portion of its support?

(1) decreasing the federal defense budget

(2) subsidizing farm crops and equipment

(3) increasing funds for national education programs

(4) decreasing federal funds for work programs

(5) passing strong affirmative-action legislation

BEHAVIORAL SCIENCE ITEMS

53. Reinforcement is one way to influence and to shape behavior. Reinforcement may be either positive or negative. That is, desired behaviors may be rewarded and therefore encouraged, while behaviors that are considered undesirable may be punished and therefore discouraged. Which of the following is NOT an example of reinforcement?

(1) The children in a family all finish their dinner and are given dessert.

(2) A debtor stops making payments on his credit card, and his account is cancelled.

(3) Several students in a class begin to make noise, and the teacher lectures in a louder voice.

(4) A dog snarls at a guest, and its owner yells at it.

(5) A baby smiles and her parents clap and smile back.

Items 54 to 58 refer to the following information.

Sociologists have classified social interaction into five broad types, which appear to be universal. These types are as follows:

(1) cooperation: people or groups work together to promote common interests or goals

(2) conflict: two or more people or groups struggle against each other in order to obtain something that both want

(3) coercion: one person or group forces its will on another

(4) exchange: one person assists another in order to receive something in return

(5) competition: two or more people or groups strive for the same goal under a set of mutually acceptable rules

Each of the following statements describes a social interaction. For each item, choose the one of the above types that most closely fits the interaction being described. The types may be used more than once in the set of items, but no one question has more than one best answer.

54. A group that colonizes an area makes the residents there clear land, build roads, and perform similar labor. The type of social interaction that is described is
  (1) cooperation
  (2) conflict
  (3) coercion
  (4) exchange
  (5) competition

55. A number of baseball clubs in a league play one another. Each is hoping to win the championship. The type of interaction described is
  (1) cooperation
  (2) conflict
  (3) coercion
  (4) exchange
  (5) competition

56. Two individuals are involved in a court case because each claims to be the rightful owner of a certain piece of land. The type of social interaction that is described is
  (1) cooperation
  (2) conflict
  (3) coercion
  (4) exchange
  (5) competition

57. A person lends his lawn mower to a neighbor on condition that the neighbor also mow the owner's lawn. The type of social interaction described is
  (1) cooperation
  (2) conflict
  (3) coercion
  (4) exchange
  (5) competition

58. A new supermarket opens across the road from an already established supermarket. It has a huge opening-day sale and advertises its everyday low prices. The type of social interaction described is
  (1) cooperation
  (2) conflict
  (3) coercion
  (4) exchange
  (5) competition

59. People often use defense mechanisms to avoid feelings of anxiety. The anxiety frequently comes from fear about an unpleasant part of someone's own character or behavior which the person finds difficult to face or to change. Defense mechanisms are usually not under a person's control; they click in automatically in certain situations. Which of the situations below might be an example of a defense mechanism?
  (1) Laughing when someone pretends to get hurt in a slapstick movie
  (2) Calling a friend to talk about your drinking problem
  (3) Denying you have a weight problem even though you are 5'4" and weigh 200 pounds
  (4) Staying up late to do work and smoking two packs of cigarettes
  (5) Working out at the gym two hours a day, five days a week even though you are in good shape

Item 60 is based on the following case study.

Jenny is a bright 13-year-old who lives with her mother and younger brother in Chicago. Her father left the family when Jenny was seven. When Jenny was eight, her mother met and fell in love with a man named Hal. They have been seeing each other exclusively for five years and are not married. Hal eats most of his meals with Jenny's family and often spends entire days in their apartment or taking Jenny and her brother to the park and the zoo. Hal does not spend nights at the apartment. The rules of the household are clearly delineated and usually obeyed.

Lately, Jenny has been acting withdrawn and stubborn. Even though she knows when she should be home, she has been coming home late. She seems to spend most of her time away from home with the same group of teenagers. Sometimes she smells of cigarettes, and a few times her mother has thought she smelled alcohol on Jenny's breath. Jenny occasionally talks back to her mother and has started fighting with Hal. She no longer wants to go with him on their outings.

60. The most likely cause of Jenny's changes in behavior is that
   (1) she has started smoking and occasionally drinking
   (2) the rules in her home are no longer clearly delineated
   (3) her stubborn and withdrawn behavior has intensified as she has grown older
   (4) the values of her teenage group conflict with her family's values
   (5) she resents the fact that her mother and Hal are not married

Item 61 is based on the following graph and passage.

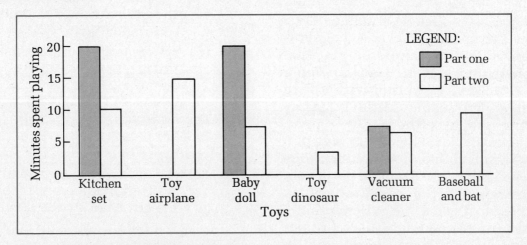

In Part One of an experiment, a sociologist noted the type of toys that a group of four-year-old girls played with. In Part Two, the sociologists observed the same girls playing with toys, but only let one girl at a time into the room. Sociologist's observations are recorded on the graph.

61. Which information supports the conclusion that the influence of the peer group is a strong determinant of play behavior?

(1) The kitchen set and baby doll were played with equally in Part One of the experiment.

(2) All toys were played with less during Part Two of the experiment.

(3) When girls played together they spent more time on one toy.

(4) The more masculine toys were played with only in Part Two of the experiment.

(5) The kitchen set and baby doll were most popular in both parts of the experiment.

Items 62 to 64 refers to the following article.

Psychologists Michele Paludi and Lisa Strayer asked 300 men and women to evaluate an article supposedly written by a man (John T. McKay), a woman (Joan T. McKay), an author with a sexually ambiguous name (Chris T. McKay) or an anonymous author.

The article was on a subject judged to be either masculine (politics), feminine (the psychology of women) or neutral (education). As the researchers expected, people rated the articles as better written, more insightful, more persuasive and higher in overall quality when they were told they had been written by a man.

"This pro-male bias was present even for articles in feminine and sex-neutral fields," Paludi and Strayer say.

. . . When the article was on a sexually neutral topic and either anonymously written or by Chris T. McKay, most thought that the author was a man. And they rated the article better than did those who thought the articles had been written by a woman.

Why the pro-male bias?

The researchers cite studies showing that "in North American culture the role of the male is more highly valued by both men and women than the role of the female. As a result, men's behavior is valued more even when their behavior is compared to the identical behavior exhibited by women."

62. Psychologists Paludi and Strayer found that when readers rated an article that was on a topic like education and supposedly anonymous, they generally

(1) thought the article was written by a man

(2) rated the article as better written than articles on the psychology of women

(3) gave the article an unfavorable rating

(4) thought the article exhibited a pro-male bias

(5) felt unable to rate the article fairly

63. According to the article, which of the following statements is the best explanation for the findings that were obtained in the study?

(1) Articles that supposedly were written by men are rated more highly than articles that supposedly were written by women.

(2) In American society certain fields have traditionally been—and still are—associated with men and certain fields with women.

(3) In American society men and, therefore, things that are done by men, are more highly valued than women and things that are done by women.

(4) The women's movement of the last few decades has produced significant changes in attitudes toward and beliefs about women.

(5) Readers were fooled by the sexually ambiguous name Chris T. McKay.

64. Which of the following conclusions is best supported by evidence that is presented in the study by Paludi and Strayer?

(1) Male authors generally have an easier time getting their writings published than do female authors.

(2) The sex of the author can influence readers' opinions of an article.

(3) Even when writing on similar topics, men and women tend to have significantly different writing styles.

(4) The feminist movement has had very little real impact on public opinion in the United States.

(5) The position of women in our society has changed less than people think.

Answers are on pages 386–393.

PRACTICE ITEMS

Performance Analysis Chart

Directions: Circle the number of each item that you got correct on the Practice Items. Count how many items you got correct in each row; count how many items you got correct in each column. Write the amount correct per row and column as the numerator in the fraction in the appropriate "Total Correct" box. [The denominators represent the total number of items in the row or column.] Write the grand total correct over the denominator, **64**, at the lower right corner of the chart. [For example, if you got 55 items correct, write 55 so that the fraction reads 55/**64**.]

	History (page 40)	Geography (page 214)	Economics (page 174)	Political Science (page 122)	Behavioral Science (page 242)	TOTAL CORRECT
Comprehension	2, 5, 6, 9, 15	19, 25	27, 30, 32, 36	47, 51	62	— 14
Application	10, 12, 14, 17	22, 24	31, 34, 37	41, 42, 43, 44, 45	53, 54, 55, 56, 57, 58	— 20
Analysis	1, 3, 8, 13, 16	18, 21, 23	28, 29 35, 38	49, 50 52	59, 63	— 17
Evaluation	4, 7, 11,	20, 26	33, 39, 40	46, 48	60, 61 64	— 13
TOTAL CORRECT	— 17	— 9	— 14	— 12	— 12	— 64

The page numbers in parentheses indicate where in this book you can find the beginning of specific instruction about the various fields of social studies.

Practice Test

Like the actual Social Studies Test, the items in the following Practice Test appear in mixed order. On the actual test, after completing items from one branch of social studies, you will be required to switch gears and answer questions from a different branch of social studies. This Practice Test is structured in the same way. It will provide you with two kinds of practice necessary for the GED: practice on the items themselves, and practice on switching from one branch of social studies to another.

This Practice Test is the same length (64 items) as the actual test, and it is equally challenging. By taking the Practice Test, you can gain valuable test-taking experience and you will know what to expect when you sit down to take the actual Social Studies Test.

Using the Practice Test to the Best Advantage

You can use the Practice Test in the following ways:

- To get hands-on, test-taking experience, you may wish to take the Practice Test under conditions similar to those of the actual test. To do this, complete the Practice Test in one sitting and try to answer all the questions within the 85-minute time limit. If time runs out before you finish, circle the last question you have answered. Then continue with the test. This way, you can learn your score within the time limit as well as your total score on the test.

- If you want, you can take the Practice Test in sections. For example, you can plan to answer ten items a day or complete a third of the test at a time. While this does not stimulate the actual testing situation, your results will still give you a pretty good idea of how well you would do on the real test.

When you take the Practice Test, write your answers neatly on a sheet of paper, or use an answer sheet provided by your teacher. If you don't know how to answer a question, skip it and come back to it later after you have answered the other questions. Remember that this is not the actual test, just some helpful practice. If your relax, you may discover that you actually perform better!

Using the Answer Key

Compare your answers to the correct answers in the answer key beginning on page 394, and check each item you answered correctly. Whether you answer an item correctly or not, you should read the information that explains each correct answer. This will help you reinforce your knowledge of social studies and enhance your testing skills.

How to Use Your Score

However you decide to take the Practice Test, your final score will point out your strengths and weaknesses in the subject of social studies. The Performance Analysis Chart at the end of the test will help you identify those strengths and weaknesses.

PRACTICE TEST

SOCIAL STUDIES

Directions: Choose the one best answer to each question.

Items 1 and 2 are based on the following chart.

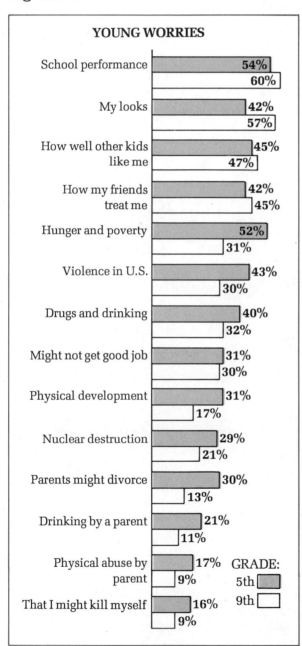

YOUNG WORRIES

Worry	5th	9th
School performance	54%	60%
My looks	42%	57%
How well other kids like me	45%	47%
How my friends treat me	42%	45%
Hunger and poverty	52%	31%
Violence in U.S.	43%	30%
Drugs and drinking	40%	32%
Might not get good job	31%	30%
Physical development	31%	17%
Nuclear destruction	29%	21%
Parents might divorce	30%	13%
Drinking by a parent	21%	11%
Physical abuse by parent	17%	9%
That I might kill myself	16%	9%

GRADE: 5th ▪ 9th ☐

Young Adolescents and Their Parents, a study conducted by the Search Institute of Minneapolis. Eight thousand students were asked which of several concerns worried them "very much" or "quite a bit." The chart contrasts the responses of fifth graders and ninth graders.

1. Which of the following statements is supported by the chart?
   (1) Few of the ninth graders would be upset if they failed a school examination.
   (2) It is likely that most of the fifth graders questioned will worry less as they mature.
   (3) Younger children tend to worry more about how their peers relate to them than older children do.
   (4) Younger children tend to worry more about general social problems than older children do.
   (5) As a child matures, he or she is less likely to be concerned about personal appearance.

2. Based on the chart, which book title do you think would be the most appealing to both a younger teenager and a younger child?
   (1) *How to Cope with a Problem Parent*
   (2) *Getting Along with Divorced Parents*
   (3) *Build a Stronger Body in Thirty Days*

(4) *How to Win Friends and Influence People*

(5) *Suicide: The Enemy Within Yourself*

Item 3 is based on the following map.

THE WESTERN STATES AND THE YEARS THEY BECAME STATES

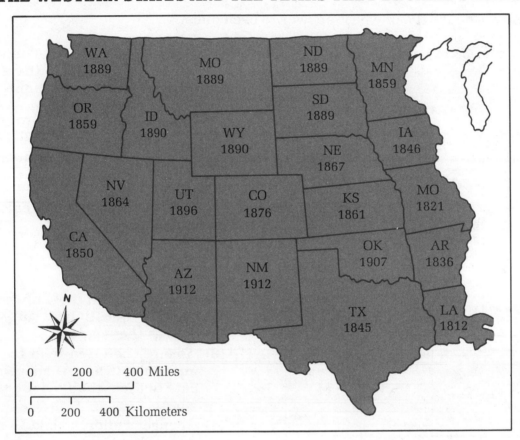

3. Which one of the following statements is supported by information given in the map?

(1) All the Northern states gained independence at approximately the same time.

(2) Statehood status for the territories that bordered Mexico spanned two centuries.

(3) All the states east of the Mississippi gained statehood before the Western states.

(4) Wyoming became a state before Arizona because it was easier to travel to from the East.

(5) Arizona and New Mexico were purchased from Mexico at the same time in the Gadsden Purchase.

4. Some insurance companies will lend money to those who hold life insurance policies with them. The policy itself is put up as collateral or security for the loan. The policyholder can borrow only up to the cash value of the policy, which is determined by the amount of money the holder has put into the policy. If the borrower does not repay the loan, the insurance is lost. Because risk to the company is low, the interest rate of the loan against the policy is low as well.

According to the passage, a borrower who defaults on a loan from an insurance policy is required to forfeit which of the following?
A. the life insurance policy
B. the cash amount of the loan
C. the low interest rate of the loan

(1) A only
(2) B only
(3) C only
(4) A and B only
(5) B and C only

Items 5 to 7 are based on the following chart.

HOW CONGRESS IS CHOSEN		
	HOUSE	SENATE
SIZE	435 members—in proportion to population	100 members—2 for each state
TERMS OF OFFICE	2 years—all members up for election at same time	6 years—one third of members up for election every 2 years
QUALIFICATIONS	1. At least 25 years of age 2. U.S. citizen for 7 years 3. Resident of state from which elected	1. At least 30 years of age 2. U.S. citizen for 9 years 3. Resident of state from which elected

5. Which of the following candidates would be eligible to run for senator from Florida?
   (1) a 25-year-old citizen of the United States and a resident of Florida
   (2) a 29-year-old Alabama resident who became a U.S. citizen in 1970
   (3) a 40-year-old resident of Florida who has been a U.S. citizen for four years
   (4) a 35-year-old citizen of the United States who has lived in Florida all her life
   (5) a 28-year-old resident of Florida who was born in the United States.

6. Now that the countries of Eastern Europe are no longer under Soviet control, many states within the Soviet Union are demanding independence. In 1990, Lithuania officially declared its independence from the Soviet Union. It seceded from the Union, just as South Carolina seceded from the United States in 1860. When South Carolina seceded, President Lincoln declared war on the newly formed Confederacy. His purpose was to preserve the Union. Few people today question the correctness of his actions. When Lithuania declared its independence, Gorbachev cut off its supplies of oil, natural gas and coal. Since then, he has sent the Red Army. Gorbachev has been condemned for his use of force to deny Lithuania independence.

Why? Gorbachev was merely trying to preserve the Union, as Lincoln did. Both South Carolina and Lithuania decided democratically to secede. The difference is that Lithuania never wanted to be part of the Soviet Union; it was conquered and annexed in 1940. South Carolina, on the other hand, joined the United States of its own free will. Also, Gorbachev is trying to preserve a dictatorial empire; Lincoln was protecting a democracy.

Some people argue that unlike South Carolina, Lithuania's declaration of independence was not really secession. On what would this argument be based?

(1) There has been no declaration of war, as there was when South Carolina seceded.

(2) Lithuania's original incorporation was illegitimate; it is merely attempting to recover its pre-existing independence.

(3) Secession is a democratic concept; a country cannot attempt to secede from a dictatorship.

(4) Lithuania cannot survive without the Soviet Union, whereas South Carolina could survive without the United States.

(5) Lithuania will have to form a new federation with Estonia, Latvia, and other neighboring nations—similar to the South's Confederacy—before it can really secede.

7. A statistician predicts a population growth for the United States of 10% during the next 50 years, with primary growth occurring in states along the Pacific coast. Based on this information, which of the following effects on state representation will most likely occur?

(1) Congressional representation in Oregon and Washington will increase.

(2) Congressional representation in Florida and Georgia will increase.

(3) Senate representation will increase in the Pacific coast states.

(4) House representation for the United States will increase in two-year increments throughout this period.

(5) Congressional representation will increase by 10% during the next 50 years.

Items 8 to 12 are based on the following passage.

Several factors seem to increase the risk of heart attacks. Smoking, obesity, a high-cholesterol diet, and lack of exercise are often contributing factors. Recently, it has been discovered that personality traits also play a part. Two behavior types are associated with high and low risks of heart attacks. They are known as Type A and Type B behavior.

Type A persons tend to be hard-working and competitive. They thrive under pressure and constantly drive themselves to succeed. Toward that end, they seek attention and advancement, and they take on many projects with deadlines to meet. Much of the time, they seem alert, efficient people who get things done. When put in a stressful situation that they cannot control, however, they often become hostile and impatient. For example, Type A persons may become angry with slow elevators or slow salespersons or with anything that might interfere with their tight schedule.

Type B persons are easy-going and relatively noncompetitive. They usually exhibit a calm and patient demeanor. Everyday problems do not seem to create much stress in their lives. Studies have shown that they are likely to live longer than people with Type A behavior.

8. According to the passage, which one of the following statements about heart attacks is true?
   (1) The likelihood of a heart attack is influenced by a combination of physical, life-style, and personality factors.
   (2) Type B persons are more likely to suffer heart attacks than Type A persons.
   (3) There is no way to predict who is more likely to suffer a heart attacks.

   (4) Smoking is not connected to heart attacks.
   (5) Behavior is not connected to heart attacks.

9. Which of the following situations would be most stressful to a Type A person?
   (1) a high-pressure job
   (2) preparing to run the New York marathon
   (3) a job promotion that requires meeting deadlines
   (4) a traffic jam
   (5) a social gathering where most of the people are strangers

10. According to the passage, which one of the following types of people would be the LEAST likely to get a heart attack?
   (1) a 40-year-old overweight smoker
   (2) a 60-year-old Type A nonsmoker
   (3) a Type B smoker
   (4) a Type B nonsmoker who exercises
   (5) an overweight Type B nonexerciser

11. Which one of the following statements is best supported by the information given in the passage?
   (1) Possible heart-attack victims cannot be identified.
   (2) We now know more about the causes of heart attacks than previously.
   (3) Smokers are most often Type A persons.
   (4) Type B persons are usually nonsmokers.
   (5) Exercise best prevents heart attacks.

12. All of the information in the passage is provided to support which of the following conclusions?

  (1) Type A persons are unlikely to suffer a higher risk of heart attacks because of their stressful life-styles.

  (2) A smoker is always more likely to suffer a heart attack than a nonsmoker.

  (3) Personality traits are now considered to be the primary factor in determining the risk of heart attack.

  (4) Type B persons have fewer everyday problems than Type A persons.

  (5) Life-style, as well as physical characteristics, affects the likelihood of heart attack.

13. Lines of longitude appear as north-south lines on a map. They show how far east or west of the prime meridian a place is located. Lines of latitude are east-west lines on a map. They show how far north or south of the equator a place is located.

  One way for someone to find out whether San Diego is farther north than New York City would be to

  (1) compare the longitude of San Diego with the latitude of New York

  (2) compare the longitude of San Diego with the longitude of New York

  (3) compare the latitude of San Diego with the longitude of New York

  (4) compare the latitude of San Diego with the latitude of New York

  (5) compare the distance of San Diego and New York from the prime meridian

Items 14 and 15 refer to the following passage.

All persons born or naturalized in the United States, and subject to the jurisdiction thereof, are citizens of the United States and of the State wherein they reside. No State shall make or enforce any law which shall abridge the privileges or immunities of citizens of the United States; nor shall any State deprive any person of life, liberty, or property, without due process of law; nor deny to any person within its jurisdiction the equal protection of the laws.

Fourteenth Amendment to the U.S. Constitution

14. Which of the following legal decisions would be most strongly influenced by the Fourteenth Amendment?

  (1) A state governor is impeached for accepting bribes.

  (2) The Supreme Court orders a state to desegregate its schools.

  (3) A state abolishes gambling within its jurisdiction.

  (4) An immigrant to the United States is denied citizenship.

  (5) A state lowers sales taxes on goods sold within its borders.

15. Which of the following most likely was an immediate effect of the ratification of the Fourteenth Amendment?

  (1) All immigrants automatically became United States citizens.

  (2) Slavery was abolished throughout the United States.

  (3) States had to obey federal law regarding citizens' rights.

  (4) All state laws became subject to federal authorization.

  (5) The residents of some states were granted special privileges.

16. Harvard College is the oldest college in the United States. It was built in Massachusetts 16 years after the Pilgrims first arrived. Most of the people at Harvard studied to become ministers. As ministers, they would become leaders of the New England colonies.

Which of the following conclusions is best supported by the passage?

(1) Church and state were closely linked in early New England.

(2) There were no ministers in New England before the construction of Harvard College.

(3) The purpose of college education in colonial times was to train people for the ministry.

(4) Most people in the early New England colonies went to college.

(5) Pilgrims were the predominant leaders of the early New England colonies.

Items 17 to 20 refer to the following information.

Defense mechanisms are mental processes that people use, often unconsciously, to protect themselves and to resolve conflicts. Psychologists have classified defense mechanisms into a number of types. Listed below are five types of defense mechanisms and brief descriptions of how they are used.

(1) Rationalization: An individual gives a false explanation of a threatening situation in order to protect feelings of self-esteem.

(2) Denial: An individual acts as though a particular upsetting situation never occurred or does not exist.

(3) Projection: An individual attributes to others negative characteristics and impulses that the individual possesses.

(4) Reaction formation: An individual displays behavior that is the opposite of all the individual's repressed unconscious attitudes.

(5) Sublimation: Impulses that are socially unacceptable (for example, aggressive impulses) are transformed into behavior that is socially acceptable.

Each of the following items describes the use of one of the defense mechanisms listed above. For each item, choose the type of mechanism that is being used. The categories may be used more than once in the set of items, but no one question has more than one best answer.

17. A person applies for a job but is turned down. She decides that she didn't want that job anyway. The type of defense mechanism that she uses is

(1) rationalization

(2) denial

(3) projection

(4) reaction formation

(5) sublimation

18. A person loses weight and shows many signs of serious illness. His friends are very concerned, but he refuses to see a doctor and insists that nothing is wrong. The type of defense mechanism that he is using is

(1) rationalization

(2) denial

(3) projection

(4) reaction formation

(5) sublimination

19. When a widower remarries shortly after his wife's death, he perceives that both his son and daughter are hostile to his new wife. His son is openly hostile. His daughter, in contrast, behaves as though she likes the wife while actually hating her unconsciously. The type of defense mechanism the daughter is using is
  (1) rationalization
  (2) denial
  (3) projection
  (4) reaction formation
  (5) sublimation

20. A person hates other people but is convinced that it is they who hate him. The type of defense mechanisms that he is using is
  (1) rationalization
  (2) denial
  (3) projection
  (4) reaction formation
  (5) sublimation

Items 21 and 22 are based on the following graph.

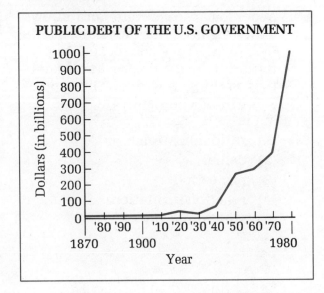

21. The graph offers adequate support for all of the following statements EXCEPT
  (1) In the first 30 years of this century the budget was most closely balanced
  (2) The first increase in the debt occurred during the period in which World War I took place—between 1910–1920
  (3) The first major increase in the debt occurred during the period in which World War II took place—1940–1950
  (4) The debt decreased during the period in which the Korean War took place—1950–1960
  (5) The greatest increase in the debt occurred during the period when the Democratic Party held the Presidency—1970–1980

22. As shown on the graph, which of the following statements is a fact?
  (1) The longest period in which the debt did not rise occurred in a time before the major wars of the century—the 1870s, 1880s and 1890s.
  (2) The New Deal spending of the 1930s for depression relief programs led to the heavy spending in the 1940s for World War II.
  (3) In the 1970s the rise in taxes failed to match the steep rise in spending for welfare programs.
  (4) The rise in spending for New Frontier and Great Society programs caused the debt to rise in the 1960s.
  (5) The slowing down of the debt in the 1950s was due primarily to Eisenhower's ending of the Korean war.

Item 23 is based on the following chart.

Comparison of the Quality of Life in Different Countries			
	Per Capita Income per Person per Year	Life Expectancy	Infant Mortality
Bolivia	$ 933	49 years	77 per 1,000
China	$ 250	68 years	not available
East Germany	$ 5,945	72 years	13 per 1,000
Japan	$ 8,627	76 years	16 per 1,000
Sweden	$12,831	76 years	8 per 1,000
Taiwan	$ 1,826	72 years	14 per 1,000
United States	$11,596	73 years	14 per 1,000
Vietnam	$ 113	53 years	not available
Zaire	$ 224	46 years	104 per 1,000

Source: Jack Abramowitz et al. *Economics and the American Free-Enterprise System* (New York: Globe Book Company, 1983), page 206.

23. Which of the following conclusions could you make from the information on the following chart?
    (1) the richer the country, the higher the infant mortality
    (2) the poorer the country, the faster its population grows
    (3) the poorer the country, the lower the infant mortality
    (4) the richer the country, the higher the life expectancy
    (5) the poorer the country, the higher the life expectancy

24. For which of the following hypotheses is there the strongest support in the information on the table?
    (1) Information on infant mortality is not available from China and Vietnam because they are Communist countries.
    (2) The countries with the lowest per capita income have the highest infant mortality rate because they have the highest birth rates.

    (3) The countries with the highest per capita income have the lowest infant mortality rates because they have the lowest birth rates.
    (4) Life expectancy tends to increase when greater wealth improves health conditions.
    (5) The wealthier countries do not spend enough on health care to reduce infant mortality as much as they could.

25. Although the water cycle keeps the world's water supply fairly constant, *quality* of water is a separate issue. In recent decades, water pollution has become a serious problem. Factories are major contributors to the problem, often spewing wastes directly into rivers and lakes. Chemical fertilizers and pesticides contribute to water pollution when washed from soils in sufficient quantities. Human wastes are also a factor, especially in urban areas.

Which of the following statements is best supported by evidence presented in the passage?

(1) Water pollution occurs through both direct and indirect means.

(2) Water pollution is a recent phenomenon.

(3) Factories are the main source of water pollution.

(4) Technology has provided a way to recycle water but not to purify it.

(5) Commercial sources of water pollution are a bigger part of the problem than noncommercial sources.

Items 26 to 28 are based on the following passage.

In its early days, the American labor movement was split into two major camps: reform unionism and trade unionism. The reform unionists rejected and sought alternatives to the factory system. Thus, they downplayed strikes against particular employers and were active in efforts to elect third-party (farm/labor) candidates to political office. The trade unionists, in contrast, accepted the factory system and sought, through strikes, to obtain better working conditions from employers. The most important of the reform-unionist organization was the Knights of Labor, which grew steadily until the "Haymarket Massacre" of May 1886.

Police broke up a protest by labor unionists, anarchists, and others in Chicago's Haymarket Square. Someone threw a bomb at the police, causing seven deaths and many injuries. Although the identity of the bomber was not discovered, eight anarchists were arrested and tried. The judge ruled that inciting a deed made a person as guilty as the one who perpetrated it. The jury then found the anarchists guilty. Some were executed; the others imprisoned. Several years later, the governor of Illinois, saying the trial had been unfair, pardoned those who were in prison. He was denounced as aiding and abetting anarchy.

Public anger at the anarchists was also turned against the Knights of Labor, although the union had in no way been responsible for the bomb. Membership declined steadily. The recently formed American Federation of Labor (A.F. of L.) soon became the main labor organization. Whereas the Knights were reform unionists, the A.F. of L. favored the trade-unionist approach.

26. Which of the following statements is a fact that is given in the passage?

(1) The anarchists were responsible for the murder of a number of policemen in Chicago's Haymarket Square.

(2) The governor of Illinois, in granting a pardon, was aiding and abetting anarchy.

(3) Inciting a deed is, for all practical purposes, the same as committing it.

(4) Members of the Knights of Labor, although not arrested, were involved in the bombing at the "Haymarket Massacre."

(5) The Haymarket incident had begun as a protest by anarchists, labor unionists, and others.

27. Which of the following is likely to have occurred during the labor movement of the 1890s as a result of developments that are discussed in the passage?

(1) The labor movement experienced a severe decline.

(2) The anarchists disassociated themselves from the labor movement.

(3) An increasing number of candidates who ran on the labor-party ticket were elected to public office.

(4) The movement shifted to focus on strikes and on better working conditions.

(5) The police were empowered to use more force in the event of demonstrations by labor.

28. Which of the following statements is best supported by evidence that is presented in the passage?

(1) Early labor leaders disagreed as to methods and goals.

(2) In the nineteenth century, public opinion tended to be hostile to labor.

(3) Most early labor leaders were often associated with anarchists.

(4) The A.F. of L. drew most of its early membership from the Knights of Labor.

(5) Police violence against union activists was common in the nineteenth century.

Item 29 is based on the following table.

This table reports the results of a poll of 1349 newspeople about which news organizations they considered most reliable.

Ten Most Reliable News Sources		
Organization	Rank	Percent of Vote
The New York Times	1	28
Associated Press	2	19
United Press International	3	13
Washington Post	4	10
Wall Street Journal	5	9
Los Angeles Times	6	5
Newsweek	7	5
Christian Science Monitor	8	4
Time	9	4
CBS News	10	3

Source: Johnstone, *"The Newspeople,"* page 224, © 1976 by the Board of Trustees of the University of Illinois. Reprinted by permission of the University of Illinois Press.

29. The newspeople polled in this table judged the various news sources listed on reliability according to their standards of value as reporters of the news. All of the value judgments listed below are reflected in the table EXCEPT

(1) television news is unreliable

(2) weekly newsmagazines such as *Time* and *Newsweek* are among the less reliable news sources

(3) newspapers with religious connections like the *Christian Science Monitor* are not adequate news sources

(4) conservative financial newspapers such as the *Wall Street Journal* are of only average reliability

(5) international news services are not reliable news sources

Item 30 refers to the following graph.

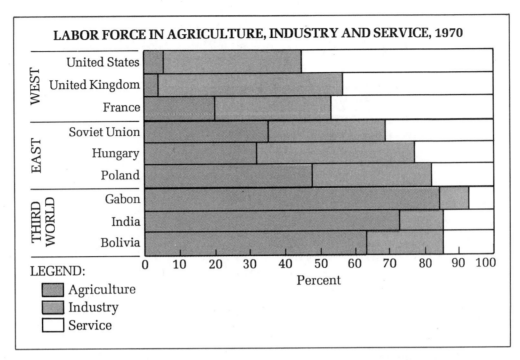

LABOR FORCE IN AGRICULTURE, INDUSTRY AND SERVICE, 1970

30. According to the information in the graph, the industrial sector is the largest sector, in terms of percentage of the labor force that is employed, in

(1) all and only the Western countries

(2) all the Western and the Eastern countries, but none of the Third World countries

(3) the United States and the United Kingdom only

(4) the United Kingdom and Hungary only

(5) Poland, Gabon, India, and Bolivia

31. The number of farms in the United States fell from more than 30 million in 1940 to 9 million in 1970, yet the United States continues to be the world's greatest supplier of food. Which of the following statements could best explain this phenomenon?

(1) The U.S. population has grown.

(2) Third World need for food has increased.

(3) Third World agriculture has become inefficient.

(4) U.S. agriculture has become very efficient.

(5) U.S. agricultural products are coveted worldwide.

Items 32 to 35 refer to the following passage.

By the early nineteenth century, the United States had already fought two major wars on its own soil—the Revolutionary War and the War of 1812. Conflicts such as these had led the young republic—which was still insecure and ill-defined as a nation—to mistrust the intentions of the European powers. As early as 1793, George Washington had proclaimed U.S. neutrality in the war in Europe, and in his Farewell Address of 1796, he recommended that the United States remain free of foreign alliances. Jefferson's policies reinforced this view; his Embargo Act of 1807 prevented United States ships from docking at any foreign port. Isolationism became official policy with Monroe's 1823 year-end congressional message—the Monroe Doctrine. He declared that European nations must halt both their colonization of the Western Hemisphere and their interference in its affairs. The United States would likewise stay out of European affairs and the affairs of their colonies. For nearly 100 years, isolationism was the basis of U.S. foreign policy and largely reflected the country's attitude toward the rest of the world.

By the 1890s, however, the situation had greatly changed. The Industrial Revolution had created the need for new sources of raw materials and for new markets for manufactured goods. Also, the expansion to the West was virtually complete, causing speculators to look outside U.S. borders for economic opportunities. In addition to this, the major European powers had embarked on a policy of imperialism by conquering much of Africa and Southeast Asia. The United States, fueled by these economic and political issues, felt the need to establish its position as a great world power.

In 1893, the United States annexed Hawaii, thereby gaining a valuable and strategic outpost in the Pacific. In 1898, it started Spanish-American War. American victory resulted in U.S. economic dominance of Cuba, as well as a military base there. It also gave the United States possession of Puerto Rico, Guam, and the Philippines. The U.S. foreign policy of isolationism had given way to that of imperialism.

32. Which of the following actions, if undertaken by the United States, would NOT be in accordance with principles of the Monroe Doctrine?
(1) defending the Caribbean Islands against Spanish invasion
(2) preventing British delivery of goods to the confederacy during the Civil War
(3) sending troops to help the Allies in World War I
(4) denying aid to the Allies in their fight against Napoleon
(5) declaring itself neutral early in World War I

33. Which of the following statements best explains the shift in U.S. foreign policy during the nineteenth century?
(1) There became fewer and fewer countries left to conquer.
(2) As the West was won, the people of the United States became more warlike.
(3) Latin America became less and less dependent on U.S. protection.
(4) European nations became increasingly hostile toward the United States.
(5) United States society experienced rapid economic and political growth.

34. Which of the following conclusions can be drawn from information that is provided in the passage?

(1) No U.S. ships docked at any foreign port during the nineteenth century.

(2) Increased European imperialism was a catalyst to U.S. imperialism.

(3) In the 1890s, the United States adopted a policy of belligerence toward Europe.

(4) Population growth compelled the United States to seek food supplies abroad.

(5) The Revolutionary War was the main reason that isolationism flourished.

35. Which of the following might have been the most likely effect that the Embargo Act of 1807 would have had on U.S. trading practices?

(1) Traders became more reliant on foreign merchant navies.

(2) Most sailors learned to disregard the laws pertaining to U.S. ships.

(3) Slave trade with Africa ceased.

(4) Foreign powers increased attacks on U.S. ships.

(5) Overseas trade was brought to a standstill.

Items 36 to 38 are based on the following illustration.

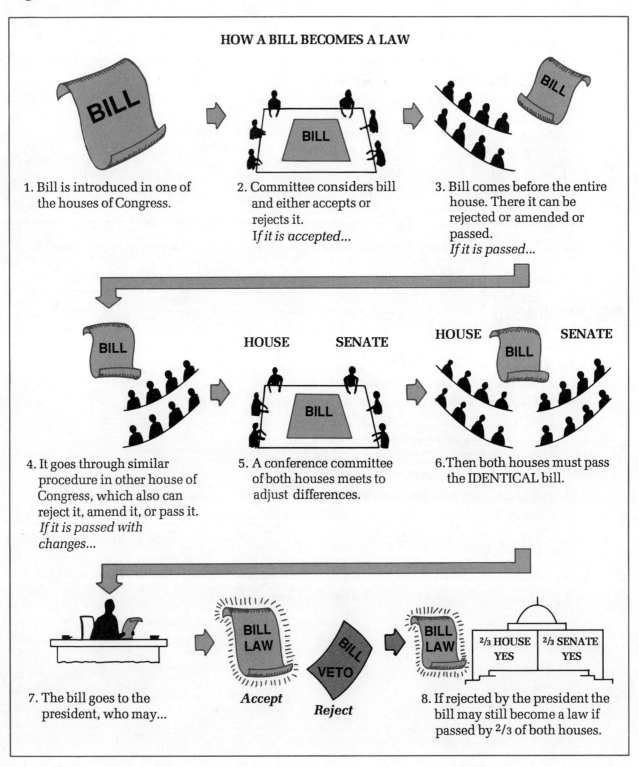

HOW A BILL BECOMES A LAW

1. Bill is introduced in one of the houses of Congress.

2. Committee considers bill and either accepts or rejects it.
If it is accepted...

3. Bill comes before the entire house. There it can be rejected or amended or passed.
If it is passed...

4. It goes through similar procedure in other house of Congress, which also can reject it, amend it, or pass it.
If it is passed with changes...

5. A conference committee of both houses meets to adjust differences.

6. Then both houses must pass the IDENTICAL bill.

7. The bill goes to the president, who may...

Accept

Reject

8. If rejected by the president the bill may still become a law if passed by 2/3 of both houses.

2/3 HOUSE YES   2/3 SENATE YES

36. A major benefit of the procedure for making a bill into a law is that

(1) it serves the primary goal of efficiency and speed in passing important legislation

(2) it is part of the system of checks and balances that keeps any given political party from controlling the country

(3) it ensures that all citizens vote via someone they elected to the Senate, the House of Representatives, or the presidency

(4) it is one of the ways to prevent a single branch of government from becoming too powerful

(5) it allows legislators to consider the consequences of their decisions after they have passed a bill

37. Based on the illustration, which of the following statements is true of the president's role in passing legislation?

(1) The president's veto cannot keep a bill from becoming law because Congress will override it.

(2) The president can only accept a bill that has been passed by both houses of Congress.

(3) The president's vote is only important when there is disagreement between the two houses of Congress.

(4) The president can accept the version of one house's bill and reject that of the other.

(5) After a veto, the president has the right to reject a bill that has been passed by two-thirds of both houses.

38. Which one of the following statements best summarizes the basic principles of democracy at work in the legislative process?

(1) The bill is introduced in one of the two houses of Congress.

(2) The president, who is elected by majority rule, can veto a bill that has been accepted by Congress.

(3) The people of the United States are given representation via their elected officials in Congress and the Presidency.

(4) The Senate, the House of Representatives, and the president all have equal say in the process.

(5) The committee that makes adjustments in a rejected bill is made up of members of both houses.

39. The last quarter of the nineteenth century saw fortunes that were made in railroads, oil, steel—any industry that could exploit the revolution in methods of production and distribution. The U.S. economy, which was based on free enterprise, was thriving. But by the 1880s, the people of the United States wanted Congress to pass legislation that would regulate commerce. The Interstate Commerce Act of 1887 restricted railroad commerce, and the Sherman Antitrust Act of 1890 aimed to destroy monopolies.

Which one of the following conclusions can best be supported by the passage?

(1) Many people sought to restrict free enterprise because they were unable to exploit the economic situation.

(2) The economy experienced a period of unchecked growth that ended because of the self-limiting nature of free enterprise.

(3) The people of the United States could not accept unlimited free enterprise and competition as the ultimate way of life in business.

(4) Government regulation is necessary for any system, economic or otherwise, to operate freely and fairly.

(5) Neither piece of legislation was effective, as evidenced by the huge increase in the pace of business consolidation in the 1890s.

40. *Society* is often defined as a complex of social relationships between individuals who are bound together by a common language and a common culture. Based on this definition of society, which of the following is NOT a society?

(1) a small tribe of Native Americans

(2) a confederation of English-speaking nations

(3) a nation where several languages are understood besides the native one

(4) The American colonies before the revolution

(5) the United States after the revolution

Items 41 and 42 are based on the following table.

Asian Immigration to the United States, 1820–1979	
China	540,000
Japan	411,000
Turkey	386,000
Philippines	431,000
Korea	276,000*
India	182,000
Indochina (Vietnam, Cambodia, Laos)	133,000*

* Nearly all since 1950

41. Which of the following statements can be supported by the information that is given in the table?

(1) More people can be expected to continue immigrating from Korea and Indochina than from the other countries.

(2) The fewest people have come here from India because more emigrating Indians go to Great Britain rather than the United States.

(3) Proportionate to each country's total population, a higher percent of China's population has immigrated than that of other countries.

(4) More than half of all Korean and Indochinese immigration occurred before 1950.

(5) The physical size and population of each country have little to do with the total number of people who have immigrated to the United States.

42. Based on information in the table, which is the most likely cause of immigration of the Koreans and Indochinese?

   (1) war
   (2) ideology
   (3) earthquake
   (4) high unemployment
   (5) famine and disease

Items 43 and 44 are based on the following passage.

The Cabinet is an informal body of executive officers, appointed by the president, that offers advice and opinions on how best to run the government. Although never specifically mentioned in the Constitution, it has by tradition evolved into an important council on which the president depends. It is composed of the principal officers of each executive department (for example, the Attorney General, the Secretary of the Treasury, and so on).

43. Which of the following statements best describes the Cabinet's relationship to the federal government?

   (1) It ratifies decrees that are made by the president.
   (2) It is responsible for controlling the federal budget.
   (3) It acts unofficially in the formation of government policy.
   (4) It offers advice that the president is compelled to follow.
   (5) It is the constitutionally decreed council on federal policy.

44. Which of the following actions is one that a member of the Cabinet would NOT be authorized to take?

   (1) The Secretary of Labor prepares a report on unemployment.
   (2) The Attorney General suggests possible amendments to the Constitution.
   (3) The Secretary of Transportation recommends that the president nationalize the railroads.
   (4) The Secretary of the Treasury orders the dollar to be devalued.
   (5) The Secretary of Defense proposes new aircraft carriers for the navy.

Items 45 to 49 are based on the following passage.

Maps are classified according to the type of geographical factor that they depict. Listed below are five different types of maps and brief descriptions of what they contain and how they are used.

   (1) **Topographical map:** Shows the natural features of Earth, including continents, oceans, rivers, mountains, plains, forests, deserts, and valleys.
   (2) **Contour Map:** Shows the elevation or depth of terrain, usually within a very small region; a contour map uses curve, or contour, lines that connect all points of the same elevation in a particular area.
   (3) **Political map:** Shows political boundaries of Earth—including borders between countries, states, and regions—and the locations of cities.
   (4) **Climatic map:** Shows weather patterns of particular areas; it often includes data on average temperature or rainfall.
   (5) **Geological map:** Shows formations and composition of Earth's crust and its interior; it will often include data on the locations of oil, coal, and mineral deposits.

Each of the following items describes a situation that calls for the use of a map. For each item, choose the type of map that would provide the appropriate information to solve the problem that is posed in the situation. Each map type may be used more than once in the set of items, but no one question has more than one best answer.

45. The Food and Agriculture Organization of the United Nations is asked to research the feasibility of rice production in parts of central Africa. To help to determine the areas that present the most favorable conditions for growing rice, the organization could refer to a
   (1) topographical map
   (2) contour map
   (3) political map
   (4) climatic map
   (5) geological map

46. A student is making a model of the United States for a school project and needs to know where to place the Continental Divide. The student could refer to a
   (1) topographical map
   (2) contour map
   (3) political map
   (4) climatic map
   (5) geological map

47. A company is building a factory in an area that is near a lake that experiences some flooding. The company wants to determine the pattern of flooding in the area. The company should refer to a
   (1) topographical map
   (2) contour map
   (3) political map
   (4) climatic map
   (5) geological map

48. A group of bankers is considering industrial investment possibilities in Mexico. A map that they might refer to in their decision-making is a
   (1) topographical map
   (2) contour map
   (3) political map
   (4) climatic map
   (5) geological map

49. A fishing group on Lake Superior is licensed to fish in the United States only. To be certain not to cross into Canadian territory, the group should refer to a
   (1) topographical map
   (2) contour map
   (3) political map
   (4) climatic map
   (5) geological map

50. *Status* is a ranked position in a social hierarchy. In our society, status is usually determined by several elements, including occupation, income, education, family background, and in some circumstances, age, sex, and ethnic group. For example, high income carries greater status than low income. *Status inconsistency* occurs when someone ranks high in one element of status and low in another.

   Based on the information given in the passage, which of the following is an example of status inconsistency?
   (1) a restaurant worker who has a modest income
   (2) a retiree who takes a part-time job
   (3) a self-made, self-educated millionaire

(4) a lawyer whose parents were both doctors

(5) a woman who is employed as a truck driver

Items 51 and 52 refer to the following passage.

The Dawes Act, which was passed in 1887, was a strong attempt to break up the Native American tribal system. Any Native American could become a U.S. citizen by giving up connections to the tribe and, therefore, rights to tribal ownership of the reservation. In this way, between 1887 and 1934, approximately 60% of Native American lands were lost. Yet the Dawes Act failed to destroy the tribes, in part because many Native Americans did not possess the skills or education to become fully assimilated into United States society and chose to remain on the reservations. The Indian Citizenship Act of 1924 sought to remedy this injustice by providing automatic citizenship for all Native Americans.

51. Which of the following statements about Native American life prior to the Dawes Act is suggested by information that is provided in the passage?

(1) Native American lands were vast, and their security against encroachment was ensured.

(2) Native Americans actively sought and were granted U.S. citizenship.

(3) The tribal system posed a threat to settlers' designs on Native American lands.

(4) Native Americans were encouraged to seek education and work skills.

(5) The tribal system was already on the verge of collapse.

52. Based on the passage, which of the following was a probable result of the Indian Citizenship Act?

(1) All Native Americans were assimilated into U.S. society.

(2) Native American lands lost between 1887 and 1934 were returned.

(3) The tribal system was broken up once and for all.

(4) Tribal power to lobby for political influence was strengthened.

(5) The Bureau of Indian Affairs was established.

Items 53 to 55 refer to the following table.

DISTRIBUTION OF ADULT AMERICANS BY TYPES OF HOUSEHOLD	
Heading single-parent families	16%
Other single, separated, divorced, or widowed	21%
Living in child-free or post-child-rearing marriages	23%
Living in extended families	6%
Living in experimental families or cohabiting	4%
Living in dual-breadwinner nuclear families	16%
Living in no wage-earner nuclear families	1%
Living in single-breadwinner nuclear families	13%

Source: News release, Bureau of Labor Statistics, March 8, 1977; reprinted in Juanita Williams, *Psychology of Women,* New York: Norton, 1983, p. 306.

53. According to the statistics provided, which of the following would find themselves in the smallest social minority?

   (1) a father who works while the mother manages the household

   (2) a mother and a father who both have jobs

   (3) a grandmother who lives with her daughter's family

   (4) a retired couple who have no children

   (5) a father and a mother who are both unemployed

54. Which of the following statements about the composition of United States society is suggested by the information provided?

   (1) Single breadwinner nuclear family households constitute the major portion of United States society.

   (2) Households that involve adults in a nonfamily structure are more common than family-based households.

   (3) Marriages that include children are less common households than marriages that do not include children.

   (4) Nonmarried households constitute a greater portion of United States society than married households.

   (5) No one type of household constitutes a majority in United States society.

55. Which of the following changes in percentage is most likely a result of an increase in the divorce rate?

   (1) Single-parent families would change to 20%.

   (2) Child-free marriages would change to 27%.

   (3) Cohabited households would change to 2%.

   (4) Dual-breadwinner nuclear families would change to 18%.

   (5) No wage-earner nuclear families would change to 3%.

Items 56 and 57 refer to the following temperatures and rainfall graphs.

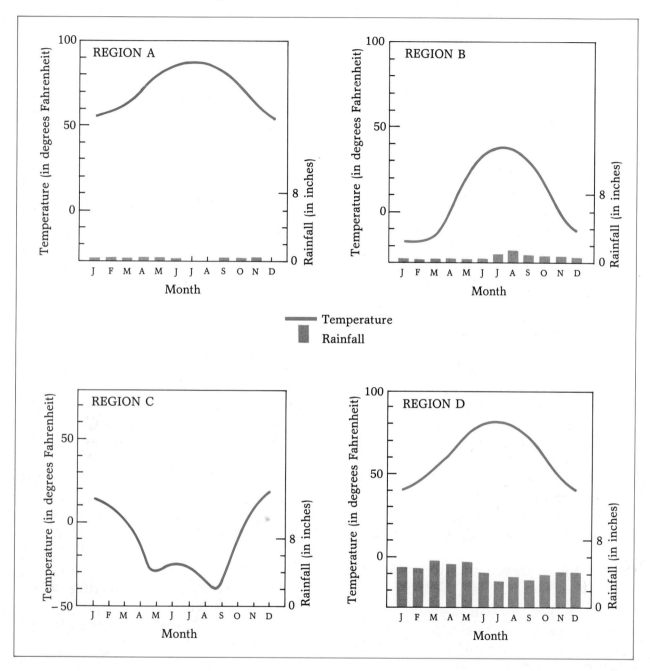

56. Which of the following regions would most likely be a desert?
   (1) Region A
   (2) Region B
   (3) Region D
   (4) Regions A and C
   (5) Regions B and C

57. Which of the following best explains the temperature variations of Region C?

(1) There is no rainfall or prevailing wind.

(2) It is far to the north near the North Pole.

(3) It is far to the south near the South Pole.

(4) It is far from an ocean.

(5) There is no indigenous vegetation.

58. In 1886, a new labor union, the American Federation of Labor (A.F. of L.), was formed. Taking a different approach to labor organization, the A.F. of L. admitted only skilled laborers. The A.F. of L. believed that these workers could strike with greater effect than unskilled workers. The most likely reason the A.F. of L. decided to organize only skilled laborers was that these workers would be

(1) more interested in joining a union than unskilled workers

(2) more difficult for employers to replace

(3) more willing to undertake long strikes

(4) more disciplined on a strike

(5) less likely to quit their jobs

Item 59 is based on the following passage.

The U.S. economy is basically one of free enterprise, but at times the federal government extends either direct or indirect influence over the production of goods and services.

Direct influence occurs when the government enters the economy directly. It may do this by producing goods or providing services—for example, providing postal service through the U.S. Post Office. It also can directly influence free enterprise by controlling the prices of certain products by setting price ceilings, to keep prices from going too high and causing inflation. It may also take over and direct production and distribution of certain things. During World War II, for instance, the government established agencies to adapt peacetime factories to war production, to set priorities for raw materials, to ration scarce consumer goods, and to settle labor-management disputes. Such direct action in the economy usually occurs only in times of crisis, such as deep depressions and wars.

More often, the government supports the workings of private industry through indirect methods. For example, it may use its indirect influence by establishing tariffs. Tariffs are taxes placed on imported foreign-made goods. The purpose of tariffs is to help U.S. manufacturers of the same kinds of goods compete against lower-priced foreign goods.

59. Which one of the following activities is an example of indirect government influence on the production of goods and services?

(1) a tax on imported electronic parts

(2) price ceilings for U.S. meat products

(3) government operation of a nuclear power plant

(4) nation-wide rationing of oil and gas

(5) federal settlement of a strike

Item 60 and 61 are based on the following passage.

Tariffs—taxes placed on imported goods and products—interfere with the natural laws of the marketplace. They protect a few economic special interests at the expense of the consumer. Tariffs do not even benefit the special interests in the long run, because they lead to "black markets," where the cheaper foreign goods—or stolen goods—are bought illegally by consumers. Even if there were no black markets, the tariffs would not save the special interests. Once tariffs eliminate foreign competition, these protected interests will have no incentive to produce quality goods and the consumers will reject their products, anyway.

60. A major assumption of the writer of the passage is that in the long run the real value of a product is determined by
   (1) special interests
   (2) cheaper foreign goods
   (3) consumers
   (4) tariffs
   (5) black markets

61. According to the writer's values, the main law of economics is that
   (1) consumers must be protected by fair market laws
   (2) consumers must organize against special interests
   (3) laws must be passed to control special interests
   (4) laws of the market must not be interfered with
   (5) quality goods must be provided illegally if need be

Items 62 and 63 are based on the following passage.

Without tariffs to protect the U.S. market against cheap foreign goods, thousands of American workers and American small businessmen are doomed. Neither can compete against goods made abroad by cheap foreign labor. This labor is paid "sweat shop" wages in Third World countries which are sometimes run by dictators or other governments that outlaw labor unions. Moreover, these so-called foreign goods are often made by American-owned companies. So American small businessmen are going bankrupt and American workers are losing their jobs to support big American corporations which are exploiting foreign labor.

62. According to this writer's values, the U.S. should be least concerned about
   (1) the working conditions of Third World labor
   (2) the wages of U.S. workers
   (3) to profits of American corporations
   (4) the profits of American small businessmen
   (5) the security of Third World governments

63. "Sweat shop" is used to describe the
   (1) climatic conditions in countries that make cheap goods
   (2) long work-hours of the Third World labor force
   (3) low wages of Third World labor force
   (4) small-scale industries of Third World countries
   (5) over-crowded workplaces of Third World industries

Item 64 refers to the following passage.

The Industrial Revolution greatly changed living and working conditions for United States laborers. Compelled to seek work where it was available, in the factories, displaced workers coming to the growing cities were put in a position that was easily exploited by their employers. Conditions were often crowded and dangerous; housing in the new cities was often inadequate and unhygienic; workers received low wages for long hours. Such conditions eventually led to the formation of labor unions.

64. Which of the following statements about working conditions prior to the Industrial Revolution is suggested by the information provided in the passage?

   (1) Most workers lived in the cities.

   (2) Factories were clean and safe.

   (3) People worked in their own homes or their own shops.

   (4) Employers were generous and concerned.

   (5) Labor unions safeguarded workers' rights.

Answers are on pages 394–400.

Practice Test

Performance Analysis Chart

Directions: Circle the number of each item that you got correct on the Predictor Test. Count how many items you got correct in each row; count how many items you got correct in each column. Write the amount correct per row and column as the numerator in the fraction in the appropriate "Total Correct" box. The denominators represent the total number of items in the row or column. Write the grand total correct over the denominator, **64,** at the lower right corner of the chart. (For example, if you got 54 items correct, write 54 so that the fraction reads 54/**64.**)

	History (page 40)	Geography (page 214)	Economics (page 174)	Political Science (page 122)	Behavioral Science (page 242)	TOTAL CORRECT
Comprehension	33, 51, 64		4, 21, 30, 59, 63	29, 43	8, 54	12
Application	32	13, 45, 46 47, 48, 49		5, 44	2, 9, 10, 17, 18, 19, 20, 37, 40, 50, 53	20
Analysis	16, 22, 26, 35, 42, 52	56, 57	31, 60	6, 15, 23 36, 38	12, 55	17
Evaluation	3, 27, 28, 34, 41, 58	25	39, 61, 62	7, 14, 24	1, 11	15
TOTAL CORRECT	15	9	12	12	16	64

The page numbers in parentheses indicate where in this book you can find the beginning of specific instruction about the various fields of social studies.

Simulation

Introduction

By this time, you are probably asking yourself, "Am I ready to take the GED Test?" Your score on the following Simulated Test will help you answer that question.

The test is as much like the real Social Studies Test as possible. The number of questions and their degree of difficulty are the same as on the real test. The time limit and the mixed order of the test items are also the same. By taking the Simulated Test, you will gain valuable experience and a better idea about just how ready you are to take the actual test.

Using the Simulated Test to Your Best Advantage

You should take the test under the same conditions as the real test.

- When you take the GED, you will have 85 minutes to complete the test. Though this will probably be more than enough time, set aside at least 85 minutes so you can work without interruption.
- Do not talk to anyone or consult any books as you take the test. If you have a question about the test, ask your instructor.
- If you have trouble answering a question, eliminate the choices that you know are wrong. Then mark the best remaining choice. On the real GED, you are not penalized for wrong answers. Guessing a correct answer will better your score, while guessing a wrong answer will not affect your score any more than not answering.

As you take the Simulated Test, write your answers neatly on a sheet of paper, or use an answer sheet provided by your teacher. When time is up, you may wish to circle the item that you answered last, and then continue with the test. When you score your test, you can see to what extent time played a factor in your performance.

Using the Answer Key

Use the Answers and Explanations (page 401) to check your answers, and mark each item you answered correctly. You should read the information that explains each correct answer. This will reinforce your testing skills and your understanding of the material.

How to Use Your Score

If you have 52 items or more correct, you scored 80 percent or better. This shows that you are most likely working at a level that would allow you to do well on the actual Social Studies Test. If you have a few less than 52 items correct, then you probably only need to do some light reviewing. If your score was far below the 80 percent mark, then you should spend additional time reviewing the lessons, so that you can strengthen the areas in which you were weak. The Skills Chart at the end of the test will help you identify your strong and weak areas.

SIMULATED TEST

TIME: 85 minutes
Directions: Choose the one best answer to each question.

Item 1 is based on the following cartoon.

PROGRESS OF HUMANITY.

Source: Fitzpatrick in the *St. Louis Post-Dispatch*. Reprinted with permission.

1. In this cartoon, "Progress of Humanity," the artist compares humanity to
   (1) a powerful army losing its biggest weapon
   (2) a losing army escaping from a powerful enemy
   (3) a big army building a giant weapon
   (4) a group of slaves pulling a giant weapon
   (5) a group of insects escaping extermination

2. In the past century, mass-produced goods have almost entirely replaced handmade goods in marketplaces worldwide. The main reason for this is that mass-produced goods, being manufactured on production lines, require less effort and fewer workers, are cheaper to make, and are therefore less expensive to purchase. A great advantage of mass production is that it makes many products affordable for consumers who might otherwise be unable to buy them.

   Which of the following statements about handmade goods is suggested by the passage?
   (1) They are of better quality than mass-produced goods.
   (2) They are no longer desired by consumers.
   (3) Many people cannot afford them.
   (4) They are often not produced worldwide.
   (5) There are no skilled workers left to make them.

Items *3 to 5* refer to the following graph.

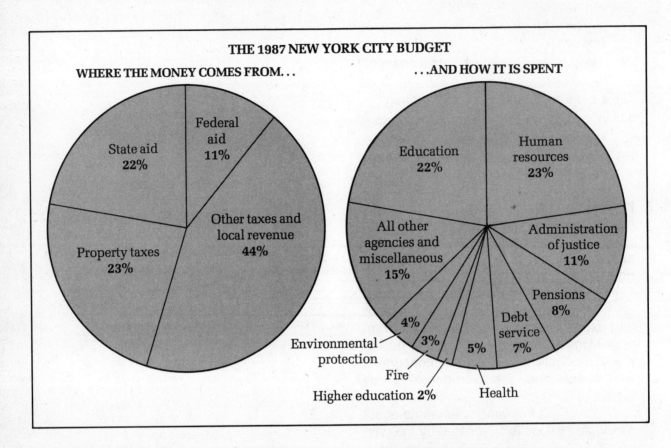

THE 1987 NEW YORK CITY BUDGET

WHERE THE MONEY COMES FROM...

...AND HOW IT IS SPENT

State aid 22%

Federal aid 11%

Property taxes 23%

Other taxes and local revenue 44%

Education 22%

Human resources 23%

All other agencies and miscellaneous 15%

Administration of justice 11%

Pensions 8%

Debt service 7%

4%

3%

5%

Environmental protection

Fire

Higher education 2%

Health

3. Based on information provided in the graph, which of the following form part of the second-largest expense item in New York City's budget?
(1) courts and jails
(2) health clinics and hospitals
(3) sanitation and clean air
(4) school maintenance and teachers' salaries
(5) pensions for city workers

4. Based on the graph, which of the following groups or agencies probably pays for the largest portion of New York City funding?
(1) the United States Treasury
(2) New York State residents and consumers
(3) the New York State Treasury
(4) New York City real estate owners
(5) New York City home owners

5. Which of the following statements is supported by information provided in the graph?
(1) Any population increase in New York City will add equally to the city's expenditures and revenues.
(2) New York City relies more heavily on municipal revenues to fund its services than any other city in the country.
(3) New York City's expenses are too high to be covered by its own city revenues alone.
(4) New York City's budget is too thinly spread to give adequate funding for all essential services.
(5) New Yorkers would stand to benefit from an increase in state and federal taxes.

Items 6 and 7 refer to the following passage.

As U.S. society evolves from an industrial into a service economy, the resulting increase in higher-status jobs has greatly affected upward mobility. People whose opportunities were once limited to factory work may now find that more jobs are available in which the pay is higher and the satisfaction greater, and in which better use is made of their abilities.

Other factors also affect a person's chances for advancement. Studies show that the three major factors are education, race, and sex. Of these, education is by far the most crucial. Three-fourths of all college-educated men move up socially, while only 12 percent of those who are not college educated do so.

6. According to the values implied in the passage, the author would favor which of the following?
   (1) reviving industry by retraining factor workers
   (2) increasing budgets of public colleges
   (3) lowering the requirements for high-status jobs
   (4) putting less emphasis on upward mobility
   (5) using race and sex for advancement

7. Based on information provided in the passage, which of the following government actions would be most likely to lead to an increase in upward job mobility?
   (1) reducing the funds for new adult literacy programs
   (2) lowering the national minimum wage rate
   (3) providing grants to minority scholarship funds
   (4) increasing welfare benefits for single mothers
   (5) subsidizing companies in the auto and steel industries

Items 8 to 10 refer to the following passage.

Before the beginning of this century, Sigmund Freud and Josef Breuer had recognized that neurotic symptoms—hysteria, certain types of pain, and abnormal behavior—are in fact symbolically meaningful. They are one way in which the unconscious mind expresses itself.... A patient, for instance, who is confronted with an intolerable situation may develop a spasm whenever he tries to swallow: He "can't swallow it." Under similar conditions of psychological stress, another patient has an attack of asthma: He "can't breathe the atmosphere at home." A third suffers from a peculiar paralysis of the legs: He can't walk, i.e., "he can't go on any more." A fourth who vomits when he eats, "cannot digest" some unpleasant fact. I could cite many examples of this kind, but such physical reactions are only one form in which the problems that trouble us unconsciously may express themselves.

Jung, Carl G. (Ed.), *Man and his Symbols*, Aldus Books, 1964; permission granted by the J.G. Ferguson Publishing Company, Chicago.

8. Based on information provided in the passage, which of the following is NOT a symptom of neurosis?
   (1) A person who is shy inevitably gets migraine headaches in social situations.
   (2) A person who fears challenges becomes dizzy when in tall buildings.
   (3) A person who has had a bad fright cannot talk.
   (4) A person who is overweight goes on a diet.
   (5) A person who finds life has become restrictive feels sick when in small rooms.

9. All of the following can be expressions of unconscious stress. Which differs from the way of expressing stress that is described in the passage?

    (1) limping
    (2) stuttering
    (3) dreaming
    (4) trembling
    (5) nausea

10. Which of the following statements is supported by information provided in the passage?

    (1) Hysteria and neurosis did not exist before the twentieth century.
    (2) Neurosis is a state of mind that can be overcome through psychoanalysis.
    (3) Asthma is generally a neurotic symptom brought about by a person's worries.
    (4) A person's neurosis can sometimes be diagnosed by the nature of its symptoms.
    (5) Physical symptoms of neurosis are usually accompanied by other types of symptoms as well.

Items 11 and 12 refer to the following passage.

There is no doubt that the world can now produce enough food for everyone. Yet many people in Africa and parts of Asia continue to starve or suffer from malnutrition, while vast surpluses of food are produced in the United States, Australia, Canada, and western Europe. The problem, above all, is one of distribution. One solution might be to ship food from rich countries to the hungry ones. But experience has shown that this can be costly, wasteful, and create a long-term dependency. The hungry nations might be able to make much of their poor soil fertile if they had the tools, irrigation systems, fertilizers, and modern agricultural technology. But they can't afford these things. Neither can they afford to buy food from the rich nations.

11. Which of the following actions would lead to the best long-term solution to the problem of world hunger?

    (1) Provide Third-World countries with low-interest loans to develop and to purchase modern agricultural technology.
    (2) Provide funds for an international relief agency to buy surplus food to be distributed among the hungry nations.
    (3) Encourage Third-World countries to relocate their hungry citizens to the large cities.
    (4) Encourage Third-World countries to repopulate the hungry regions with people from their large cities.
    (5) Provide tax rebates to American and European farmers who would be willing to donate part of their crops to starving countries.

12. Which of the following statements is supported by information provided in the passage?

    (1) The quality of a country's soil will determine whether it is prosperous or hungry.
    (2) The rich countries of the world are reluctant to waste their money helping the poorer ones.
    (3) There would be no starvation in the world if all the food was distributed evenly among the nations.
    (4) The poor nations are unwilling to spend money on agricultural technology and equipment.
    (5) The peoples of the West are more wasteful with their food than are the peoples of the hungrier nations.

13. In 1981, the U.S. national debt reached $1 trillion, an all-time high. The increasing rate of growth has alarmed many people who believe that the debt will be a burden on future generations. Others point out, however, that in terms of percentage of national output, the debt has declined steadily since 1945. In 1948, for example, the debt represented about 100 percent of national output. By 1981 it had declined to less than 40 percent.

Based on information provided in the passage, which of the following is the best explanation for the decline in the national debt as a percentage of the national output between 1945 and 1981?

(1) The Great Depression caused the government to borrow a lot of money, which it gradually paid off.

(2) Though the national debt continued to rise, the national output rose at an even faster pace.

(3) As the economy improved after World War II, the government was able to borrow more and more money.

(4) The national output is measured in terms of real dollars, whereas the national debt is measured in terms of interest.

(5) The U.S. dollar has grown stronger and stronger since the end of World War II.

Items 14 to 16 refer to the following passage.

From around 1800 through the Great Depression of the 1930s, the fertility rate in the United States was in constant decline. This meant that the average number of children born to each couple continued to decrease through those years, until World War II. Studies have shown a number of different possible explanations for this trend.

Some sociologists believe that the decline was caused by the desire for a higher standard of living. With fewer children, couples are able to devote more of their time and resources to leisure activities and material goods. Others believe, however, that the decline was caused by the economic shift from an agricultural society to an industrial one. Whereas large families are helpful to provide labor on a farm, they may often be a burden to industrial workers, who may often live in more cramped conditions than agricultural workers. Still others believe that the decline was caused by the increasing emancipation of women. As education became more available to women, they began to find new opportunities outside the home, which made childbearing seem less attractive. Further, as family planning and contraception grew to be more acceptable, more and more couples found themselves rethinking the advantages of large families, and the fertility rate was slowed even more.

14. Which of the following would be the most appropriate title for this passage?

(1) U.S. Fertility Rates: Past and Present

(2) Social Changes and Fertility Rates in U.S. History

(3) The Changing Social Order in America

(4) The United States: 1800 to 1940

(5) Fertility Rates and the Role of Women in U.S. Society

15. Which of the following statements about life in the United States before 1800 is implied by the passage?

(1) Family planning and contraception were not available to people who wished to limit the size of their families.

(2) Leisure activities and material goods were the privileges of the wealthy only.

(3) The American colonists had one of the highest fertility rates in the world.

(4) Industrial workers tended to have large families and to live in spacious housing.

(5) Women were expected to stay at home and to raise large families.

16. Which of the following is a likely explanation for the increase in the birth rate that occurred after the period described in the passage?

(1) Because the Great Depression threw many people out of work, more leisure time was available for having large families.

(2) The Great Depression caused more people to see the wisdom of having a large family.

(3) People who had postponed having children during the Great Depression now could afford to have a child.

(4) Many women were forced to go to work while the men were fighting in World War II.

(5) Women began to have larger families to replace their loved ones who were killed during the war.

17. A "victimless crime" is defined as the willing exchange of illegal goods or services between adults. Illegal gambling and prostitution are victimless crimes by that definition.

Which one of the following could be considered a victimless crime?

(1) burglary

(2) selling illegal drugs

(3) auto theft

(4) arson

(5) embezzlement

Items 18 to 22 refer to the following passage.

Intellectual property laws protect ideas, inventions, and products from being exploited by persons who have no right to profit from their use. These laws cover three main areas.

A *copyright* protects literary, dramatic, musical, artistic, or craft compositions from being copied, published, displayed, or performed by others without permission. Under the Copyright Revision Act of 1979, a work is automatically copyrighted as soon as it is completed. The creator gains additional protection by reg-istering the work with the Federal Copyright Office. Usually a copyright expires 50 years after the death of the creator.

A *patent* is granted only for original inventions, usually of a technical or scientific nature. Determining the originality of an invention is often a lengthy process. A United States patent, once granted, runs for 17 years.

A *trademark* is a word or symbol that a manufacturer places on a product to distinguish it from similar products offered by competitors. In the United States, trademarks are established through use. The first merchant or manufacturer to use a trademark automatically owns it. The owner gains additional protection by registering the trademark. A trademark registration runs for 20 years, under the condition that the trademark is used regularly.

18. Based on information in the passage, which of the following statements is the most accurate?

(1) A patent is automatically granted as soon as an invention is completed.

(2) A plaintiff may sue for copyright infringement even if the copyright is not registered.

(3) Trademarks, copyrights, and patents must be registered with the federal government.

(4) If a trademark is not renewed after 17 years, other companies may use it.

(5) A novel is protected by copyright law only if it is registered with the Federal Copyright Office.

19. Herman Melville, the author of *Moby Dick*, died in 1891. A publisher now wants to print a new edition of *Moby Dick*.

According to the copyright regulations, the publisher

(1) should get permission to publish from Melville's original publisher

(2) should publish the book and send part of the profits to Melville's family

(3) should not publish the book because it is protected by copyright

(4) can go ahead and publish the book because the copyright period has ended

(5) can go ahead and publish the book because there were no copyright regulations when *Moby Dick* was published

20. Which of the following explains why manufacturers use trademarks?

(1) They want to distinguish their products in the mind of the consumer.

(2) They want to prevent competitors from selling similar products.

(3) They want to use symbols in their advertisements.

(4) They want to be authorized to charge more for their registered products than their unregistered competitors can charge.

(5) They want to prove the originality of their creations.

21. According to the passage, which of the following reasons has NOT been a motivation for the establishment of intellectual property laws?

(1) preventing artists, writers, and inventors from stealing one another's ideas

(2) establishing legal ownership of ideas and creations

(3) maintaining a government record of ideas and creations

(4) recognizing the rights of writers, artists, scientists, and businesspeople to profit from their ideas and creations

(5) preventing unscrupulous business people from profiting from the ideas of others without their consent

22. For which of the following conclusions does the passage provide the strongest evidence?

(1) Copyrights, patents, and trademark registrations can be renewed.

(2) Copyrights, patents, and trademark registrations can outlive the people who created the protected material.

(3) Computer software cannot be protected under the current copyright regulations.

(4) Intellectual property laws stifle rather than stimulate technological advancement.

(5) Intellectual property laws are stronger in the United States than in other countries.

Items 23 and 24 refer to the following passage.

In 1980, 59 percent of all Americans voted in the national elections. Of those aged 65 to 74, 69 percent were voters, while of those aged 18 to 20, only 36 percent were voters.

23. Which of the following statements best restates the information provided in the passage regarding the 1980 elections?

(1) While barely one-third of those aged 18 to 20 voted, they still represented a larger group than those aged 65 to 74.

(2) The older citizens represented more than half the voting population, while the younger citizens represented barely a third.

(3) Less than half of those eligible to vote actually did, and of those, nearly two-thirds were over 65.

(4) The older citizens were more active participants than the younger citizens in an election where more than half the population voted.

(5) While more than half of the younger citizens and half of the older citizens turned out to vote, less than half of the population actually voted.

24. Which of the following is a conclusion that can be drawn from the information provided in the passage?

   (1) The older citizens are a more powerful voting group than the younger citizens.

   (2) More than half of all Americans are ineligible to vote.

   (3) The older citizens are a more reliable voting group than the younger citizens.

   (4) The voting age should be lowered so that more young citizens can vote.

   (5) Elected officials do not represent a true majority.

25. In recent years, cities in the developing countries have experienced enormous growth. Steady streams of impoverished rural workers have abandoned the land in the hopes of finding employment in the industrial centers. While many succeed, overburdened city services often cannot keep up with the growth. As a result, these migrants and other urban poor must often make do with minimal health care and extremely inadequate housing and sewage conditions.

Which of the following would NOT be relevant as a cause of the problems described in the passage?

   (1) the failure of crops in the rural areas

   (2) an inadequate transportation system between rural and urban areas

   (3) the high birthrate among the poor people in the cities

   (4) the inadequate government response to the problems

   (5) the low level of political organization among the poor

26. The U.S. Constitution grants certain specific rights to the legislative branch of the federal government. These powers include the drafting of all laws, taxation, the regulation of trade between states and with foreign governments, the raising of an army, navy, and air force, the printing of currency, and the prosecution and impeachment of federal officials.

Which one of the following actions is NOT assigned to the legislative branch by the U.S. Constitution?

   (1) passing a protective tax on certain goods imported from abroad

   (2) removing a president from office

   (3) reinstating the draft for military service

   (4) authorizing the issue of new Federal Reserve notes

   (5) vetoing a bill or signing it into law

Items 27 and 28 refer to the following chart.

Employment and Unemployment in the United States			
Year	Employed	Unemployed	Unemployment Rate in Percent
1970	78,678,000	4,093,000	4.9
1975	85,846,000	7,929,000	8.5
1976	88,752,000	7,406,000	7.7
1977	92,017,000	6,991,000	7.1
1978	96,048,000	6,202,000	6.1
1980	99,303,000	7,637,000	7.1
1981	100,000,397	8,273,000	7.6
1982	99,526,000	10,678,000	9.7
1983	100,834,000	10,717,000	9.6
1984	105,005,000	8,539,000	7.5

27. According to the chart, which of the following years experienced the largest change in the number of unemployed?
   (1) 1970 to 1975
   (2) 1976 to 1977
   (3) 1978 to 1980
   (4) 1981 to 1982
   (5) 1983 to 1984

28. According to the chart, the number of unemployed was lower in 1982 than in 1983, yet the unemployment rate was higher. This is best explained by the fact that
   (1) the overall population increased
   (2) the economy was weakened in 1983
   (3) the number of employed increased in 1983
   (4) the rate had been declining slightly for many years
   (5) the number of employed was less in 1983 than in 1984

Items 29 to 31 refer to the following passage.

The invention of the cotton gin by Eli Whitney in 1792 greatly changed the agricultural and economic structure of the South. In the eighteenth century, the main crop had been tobacco. Cotton was not grown because of the great labor and expense required to remove the seed from the lint. But with the cotton gin, this process was greatly simplified, and cotton became a profitable crop. In 1800 the United States produced less than 100,000 bales of cotton. This number had grown to 400,000 in the 1820s, 1,500,000 in the 1840s, and to nearly 4 million by 1860.

One important effect of the "King Cotton" boom was on the slave population of the South. As the demand for cotton grew, the need for cheap labor to pick cotton grew proportionally. In 1800 there had been fewer than 1 million slaves. By 1860 there were more than 4 million slaves, 60 percent of whom were employed in picking cotton. At the same time, the price for one slave more than tripled. Slave traders profited as much from the cotton gin as did the big plantation owners, and support for slavery became deeply entrenched in the South.

29. Based on information provided in the passage, which of the following statements about the cotton gin is true?
    (1) It had a deep impact on U.S. society in the eighteenth century.
    (2) Its use put many farm laborers out of work.
    (3) It revitalized the ailing cotton industry.
    (4) It helped to create the slave-trading industry.
    (5) It helped to provide a new source of U.S. wealth.

30. Which of the following was probably an effect of the cotton boom on Southern society?
    (1) It helped to concentrate wealth in the hands of the large plantation owners.
    (2) By raising the price of cotton, it helped the smaller, "one-horse" farms.
    (3) It destroyed the large tobacco farmers, who began to import tobacco from the Caribbean.
    (4) It encouraged "carpetbaggers" from the North to buy cheap Southern land.
    (5) It helped to dramatize the plight of the slaves to Southerners who had been unaware of their suffering.

31. Which of the following statements is the best explanation for the effect of the cotton boom on attitudes toward slavery in the South?
    (1) Whites began to resent slaves because of the added expense of keeping them.
    (2) Keeping slaves was profitable as never before, and those who benefited did not want to lose this bounty.
    (3) Increasing rebelliousness among the slaves caused fear among the slave owners.
    (4) Many abolitionists from the North and the South wanted the slaves to return to picking tobacco.
    (5) The slave population became larger than the free population, and people saw this as an indication that changes were needed.

Item 32 refers to the following graph.

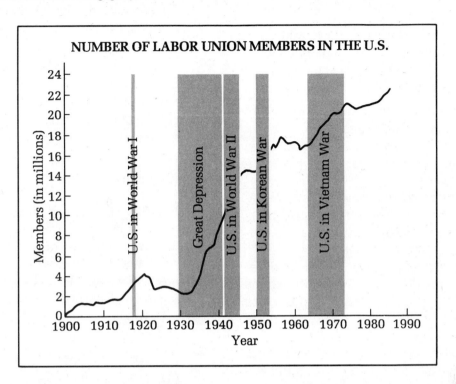

NUMBER OF LABOR UNION MEMBERS IN THE U.S.

32. Which of the following statements is supported by information provided in the graph?
    (1) Union membership declined from 1900 until the 1930s.
    (2) Union membership rises more slowly in times of prosperity than in times of crisis.
    (3) The major U.S. wars of the twentieth century had a devastating effect on union membership.
    (4) The rise in union membership is directly proportional to the increase in population.
    (5) U.S. labor unions profit most from a strong dollar and a healthy economy.

33. The number of American children who live in poverty rose steadily from 1979 to 1984. Many of these children live in urban areas; a good number of them end up becoming unwed parents and/or dropping out of school. In 1979, 16 percent of Americans under 18 lived in poverty. By 1984, 21 percent of Americans under 18 lived in poverty. These figures represent an increase from 10 million youths to almost 13 million youths in just 5 years.
Which one of the following statements is suggested by the passage?
    (1) Most poor people are children and live in inner cities.
    (2) Prior to 1979, childhood poverty was not a major social problem.
    (3) Teenage pregnancy is a major cause of teenage poverty.
    (4) Public and private poverty policies from 1979 to 1984 failed to reduce poverty among children.
    (5) The increase from 1979 to 1984 reflects a general increase of the population caused by "baby-boomers" having babies.

Items 34 to 38 refer to the following information.

Congress has a number of powers in addition to its main function of passing laws. Listed below are five types of nonlegislative powers entrusted to Congress.

(1) **Constituent powers:** powers related to changing the Constitution
(2) **Electoral powers:** powers related to the selection of the president and vice-president
(3) **Executive powers:** powers used to exert control over the administrative parts of the executive branch (such as departments, agencies, authorities)
(4) **Investigatory powers:** power to order and to conduct special investigations into alleged wrong-doing, as opposed to routine reviews of reports from parts of the executive branch
(5) **Judicial powers:** power to pass judgments and sanctions on certain individuals

Each of the following statements describes the use of one of the types of nonlegislative powers of Congress listed above. The types may occur more than once in the set of items, but no one question has more than one best answer.

34. In 1868, the House of Representatives impeached President Andrew Johnson, charging that he had violated the Tenure of Office Act. The Senate then acquitted Johnson, by a mere one-vote margin. In this example, Congress used its
    (1) constituent powers
    (2) electoral powers
    (3) executive powers
    (4) investigatory powers
    (5) judicial powers

35. In 1978, Congress proposed the Equal Rights Amendment, which stated that "equality of rights under the law shall not be denied or abridged by the United States or by any state on account of sex." In this case, Congress used its
    (1) constituent powers
    (2) electoral powers
    (3) executive powers
    (4) investigatory powers
    (5) judicial powers

36. In 1979, Congress divided the Department of Health, Education and Welfare into two separate departments—the Department of Education and the Department of Health and Human Services. In this case, Congress was using its
    (1) constituent powers
    (2) electoral powers
    (3) executive powers
    (4) investigatory powers
    (5) judicial powers

37. Most federal agencies are required to make annual reports to Congress, and members of Congress routinely call on agency heads for information and explanations. In so doing, Congress is using its
    (1) constituent powers
    (2) electoral powers
    (3) executive powers
    (4) investigatory powers
    (5) judicial powers

38. The Senate Watergate Committee decided that President Richard Nixon had committed certain crimes. It drew up articles of impeachment—a list of charges which would remove him from office if Congress voted to find him guilty of them. Their action caused him to resign. In doing this, the committee was exercising its

(1) constituent powers

(2) electoral powers

(3) executive powers

(4) investigatory powers

(5) judicial powers

Items 39 and 40 refer to the following passage.

The United States no longer has the highest standard of living in the world. Part of the reason is that American productivity—output of goods and services per worker—has declined. The reasons for this decline are complex, some reflecting short-term or even positive developments.

Other reasons for the decline appear more basic and troubling. One analysis links the decline in American productivity, especially in sectors such as the automobile and steel industries, to an emphasis on the present, rather than the future. Emphasis on *immediate* profitability has led to a failure to invest enough in modernizing equipment and processes. For example, statistics from the Organization for Economic Cooperation and Development reveal that the United States trailed behind all other Western countries and Japan in converting its steel plants into more up-to-date "continuous casting." The steel plants were profitable as they were, and the costs of converting them would have, in the short term, destroyed this profitability.

According to this analysis, the focus on the present is reflected not only in managerial decisions but also in consumer habits and business-government relations. Thus, in this view, the solutions to America's productivity problem will not be easy ones.

39. Which of the following statements best summarizes the main idea of the passage?

(1) The United States no longer has the world's highest standard of living.

(2) Some reasons for the decline in productivity are short-term or even positive, whereas others are more basic and troubling.

(3) The steel and auto industries are among the leading examples of the decline in American productivity.

(4) U.S. industry's focus on the present has been a major contributor to the decline in productivity and the standard of living.

(5) U.S. companies have not invested sufficient capital in industrial equipment and processes.

40. All of the following statements are supported by evidence presented in the passage EXCEPT

(1) there has been a sharp decline in U.S. productivity in the steel and auto industries

(2) the U.S. steel industry lagged behind its counterparts in other countries in switching to continuous casting

(3) the decline in U.S. productivity is linked to mistaken policies of industry decision-makers

(4) rising unemployment and inflation are central elements in the economic problems of the U.S.

(5) in the United States, productivity has declined for complex reasons

Items 41 to 43 refer to the following map.

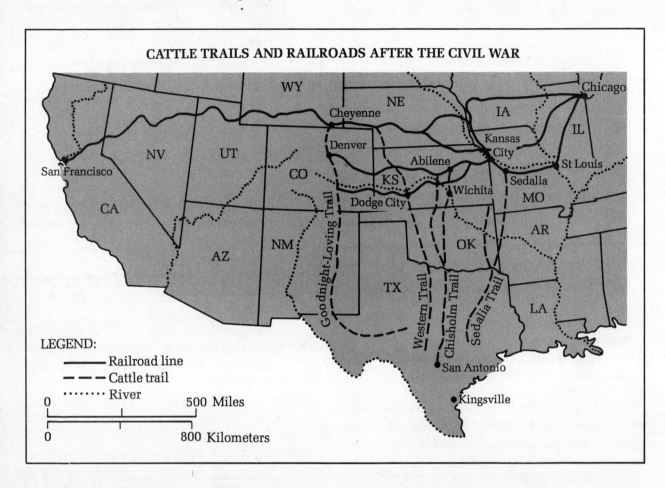

CATTLE TRAILS AND RAILROADS AFTER THE CIVIL WAR

LEGEND:
——— Railroad line
– – – Cattle trail
········· River

0   500 Miles

0   800 Kilometers

41. Based on the map, which of the following towns is most likely to have been one of the "cow towns"?

(1) Chicago
(2) San Francisco
(3) Kingsville
(4) Abilene
(5) St. Louis

42. Which of the following best explains the position of the cattle trails?

(1) They followed the deep valleys of the Great Plains.
(2) They brought cattle from the north to the ranches of Texas.
(3) They brought cattle from Texas to the railways for transportation.
(4) They avoided the desert areas farther west.
(5) They led north to avoid Native-American territories.

43. Which of the following hypotheses is supported by the information on the map?

  (1) Before the railroads, rivers were the best way for ranchers to get their cattle to market.

  (2) San Francisco became a major port only after the railroads connected it to the rest of the U.S.

  (3) Cattle trails did not go farther north than Cheyenne because of bitter feelings left over from the Civil War.

  (4) Ranching became a major industry only when railroads enabled ranchers to transport cattle to cities in the east and west.

  (5) As railroads multiplied, cattle trails multiplied and branched to connect with more railroad centers.

Items 44 and 45 refer to the following passage.

Between 1850 and 1930 more than 35 million immigrants came to the United States—anxious to escape poverty, hunger, political oppression, and religious persecution in their own countries, and drawn by the promise of America. Immigrants from the United Kingdom, Germany, and Scandinavia came in large numbers primarily during the early decades of this period. These were years of westward expansion, and many of these immigrants were lured especially by the rich lands of the prairies.

  By the 1880s the immigration pattern changed somewhat. Immigrants from southern and eastern European countries (for example, Italy, Austria, Hungary, Poland, and Russia), who had initially come only in small numbers, now poured into the United States. They settled primarily in urban areas, often working in factories at unskilled jobs. Moreover, the decades between 1880 and 1930 marked the peak of immigration. In the 1930s the number of immigrants to the United States dropped sharply.

44. Which of the following is the most likely explanation for the change in the settlement patterns of immigrants to the United States?

  (1) the significant increase in the number of immigrants

  (2) the change in countries of origin, as there was a tendency to seek areas geographically similar to the homeland

  (3) the fact that the early immigrants had generally been farmers in their countries of origin, whereas the later immigrants had generally been laborers

  (4) the westward expansion, which opened up rich farmland

  (5) the industrialization of the United States

45. Which of the following statements about immigration to the United States from 1850 to 1930 is best supported by the passage?

  (1) The largest number of European immigrants came from the northern countries of Europe.

  (2) Prior to 1850 the United States had been an essentially homogeneous society.

  (3) By 1870 immigration had substantially altered the ethnic composition of the American population.

  (4) Immigration from northern Europe declined during the peak of immigration.

  (5) By the end of the period, immigration declined because problems prompting immigration had become less pressing.

Items 46 to 49 are based on the following passage.

Although it is a little-publicized resource problem, the erosion of our soil is of great concern. Every year, soil is washed away into the sea or carried away with the wind.

Violent downpours rip the topsoil from the hillsides and carve great gulleys into the land. Windstorms blow across dry areas, turning topsoil to dust. Half of all countries suffer from severe soil-loss problems. One-third of U.S. cropland is now undergoing a marked decline in agricultural productivity because of soil erosion.

Human activity causes natural erosion rates to increase many times over. We plant on steep slopes without using the terracing method that helps save the soil. We allow animals to graze too long in the same places. We overwork the soil. Worst of all, we remove trees and don't plant new ones.

46. According to the passage, soil erosion has become a worldwide problem mainly because of
    (1) violent downpours and windstorms
    (2) terracing on steep slopes
    (3) overgrazing of animals
    (4) a combination of natural and human activity
    (5) removing trees and not replacing them

47. Based on information provided in the passage, which of the following environments is most likely to suffer from soil erosion?
    (1) a forest in the mountains
    (2) a river basin with dams for flood control
    (3) land used for grazing on an open plain
    (4) a tropical rain forest
    (5) a forest in a national park

48. Which one of the following statements is suggested by the passage?
    (1) There is little we can do to prevent natural soil erosion.
    (2) Soil erosion is less severe in the United States than in other countries.
    (3) Conservation can help cut down on soil erosion.
    (4) Events in nature increase the rate of soil erosion faster than human activities do.
    (5) More soil is blown away than is washed away into the ocean.

49. Which of the following conclusions follows logically from the passage?
    (1) Because soil erosion is such a pervasive problem, the national budget should include more money for conservation and less money for national security.
    (2) Countries with soil-erosion management programs will not undergo steep declines in agricultural productivity.
    (3) Soil-erosion management programs could be effective if there were better weather forecasts of windstorms and violent rains.
    (4) Erosion is not as much of a problem now as it was in the last century, because we now know more about how to prevent severe soil loss.
    (5) Part of the poor economic picture for today's U.S. farmers has to do with the problem of soil erosion.

Items 50 to 51 refer to the following map.

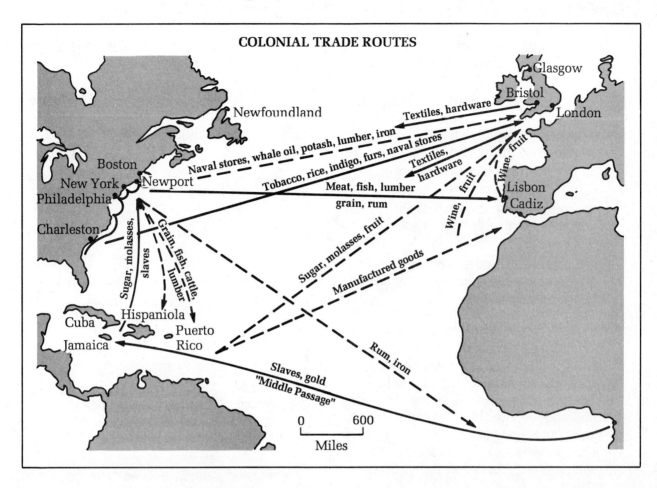

COLONIAL TRADE ROUTES

50. Based on the map, which of the following statements accurately describes an aspect of trade during the colonial period?
   (1) The American colonies imported goods from both Great Britain and southern Europe.
   (2) The American colonies exported lumber to both Great Britain and southern Europe.
   (3) The American colonies imported slaves from Africa.
   (4) The southern and northern colonies exported the same products to England and Europe.
   (5) The American colonies and the West Indies competed with each other in that their exports to Europe were similar.

51. Which one of the following acts passed by British Parliament with regard to the American colonies can be explained on the basis of the map?
   (1) act forbidding the colonies to establish furnaces to manufacture steel and hardware
   (2) act forbidding gold bullion acquired from Jamaica to be minted into coin
   (3) act imposing duties on colonial imports of luxury items
   (4) act requiring revenue stamps to be affixed to all commercial bills and other documents
   (5) act granting the East India Company a monopoly on all tea imported by the colonies

52. Which of the following statements is supported by information provided in the map?

(1) The complexity of trade routes ensured that countries which traded with one another were at peace.

(2) Great Britain imposed more restrictions on which countries the colonies could import from than on which countries they could export to.

(3) Great Britain favored a liberal trading policy with its colonies.

(4) The countries of western Europe enjoyed a profitable relationship with the British colonies in America.

(5) Repressive British trade policies ensured that the colonies would eventually revolt.

53. The writer [of a recent study] found that as one moves from middle-class urban centers in Britain to the rural lower-class islands, the distance between chairs at table decreases, so that in the outermost Shetland Islands actual bodily contact during meals and similar social occasions is not considered an invasion of separateness and no effort need be made to excuse it.

Based on the information above, which of the following is most likely to have been the subject of the study mentioned?

(1) the history of British table manners

(2) customs and rituals in the Shetland Islands

(3) the relation between social class and table manners

(4) the relation between social class and definition of personal space

(5) food and family in Great Britain

From Erving Goffman, *Interaction Ritual*, Pantheon Books. 1982, p. 63. © 1967 Erving Goffman.

Item 54 refers to the following chart.

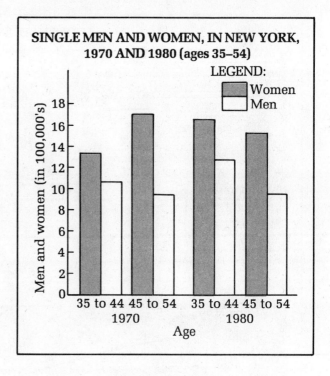

SINGLE MEN AND WOMEN, IN NEW YORK, 1970 AND 1980 (ages 35–54)

54. Which of the following statistics concerning New Yorkers can be determined by information provided in the chart?

(1) the percentage, in 1980, of all men and women between the ages of 35 and 54 who were single

(2) the change, in terms of percentage of total population, of single men, ages 35 to 54, from 1970 to 1980

(3) the change in the ratio between single men and single women, ages 35 to 54, from 1970 to 1980

(4) the number of single women, ages 45 to 54, who were married between 1970 and 1980

(5) the number of men, ages 35 to 54, who became single between 1970 and 1980

Item 55 is based on the following chart.

U.S. Immigration by Decades					
Years	**Immigrants**	**Years**	**Immigrants**	**Years**	**Immigrants**
1820–1829	128,502	1870–1879	2,742,287	1920–1929	4,295,510
1830–1839	538,381	1880–1889	5,248,568	1930–1939	699,375
1840–1849	1,427,337	1890–1899	3,694,294	1940–1949	856,608
1850–1859	2,814,554	1900–1909	8,202,388	1950–1959	2,499,268
1860–1869	2,081,261	1910–1919	6,347,380	1960–1969	3,213,749

Source: Kenneth Uva and Shelley Uva, *The United States in the Making*, vol. 2 (New York: Globe Book Company, 1986), page 35.

55. Which of the following statements is supported by the information on the chart?

  (1) Immigration increased until the Civil War period of 1860–1864 and then steadily declined until 1900.

  (2) Immigration increased from 1910 until the Great Depression of the 1930s, when it fell sharply.

  (3) Immigration decreased from 1890 until the end of the First World War in 1919, when it rose sharply.

  (4) Immigration steadily increased from the Irish Famine of the 1840s until just before the start of the Civil War in 1859, then decreased until 1890.

  (5) Immigration decreased from 1900 until the Great Depression of the 1930s, then increased from 1940 to 1950.

Items 56 and 57 are based on the following maps.

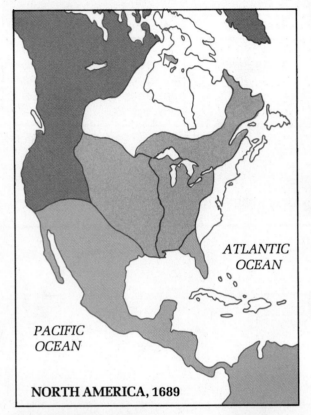

NORTH AMERICA, 1689

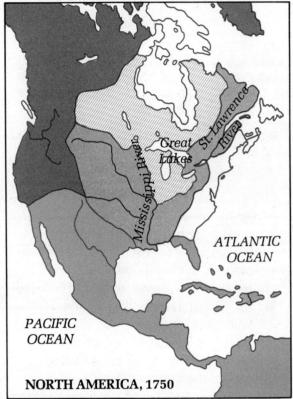

NORTH AMERICA, 1750

NORTH AMERICA, 1763

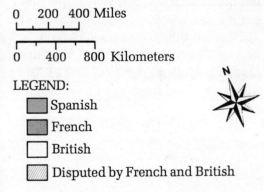

LEGEND:

Spanish

French

British

Disputed by French and British

56. Most of one area of today's United States was under continuous British control from 1689 to 1763. Which area is that?
    (1) the Northwest
    (2) the West Coast
    (3) the Midwest
    (4) the South
    (5) the East Coast

57. In 1732 King George II gave James Oglethorpe a charter to establish Georgia as the last of the thirteen colonies. One reason it was established was to serve as the king's only military outpost against the
    (1) French
    (2) Spanish
    (3) British
    (4) Indians
    (5) colonists

Items 58 to 62 refer to the following information.

Neuroses are disorders of the mind or emotions. Listed below are five types of neuroses.

    (1) **conversion neurosis:** repressed desires or fears find expression in physical symptoms (e.g., a repressed desire or fear causes illness)
    (2) **depressive neurosis:** fear and lack of self-respect causes a person to withdraw from others and from active life into passive behavior and a pessimistic state of mind
    (3) **dissociative neurosis:** the person's identity "splits" into two or more personalities, so that unwanted desires are expressed through one personality without the other personality knowing or admitting that this is happening
    (4) **obsessive-compulsive neurosis:** unwanted desires or fears find expression in repeated, obsessive actions which may be symbolic of the person's problem (e.g., repeated extreme dieting that expresses a fear of being rejected as unattractive, or an unadmitted desire to be perfect or to exert total control over the body)

    (5) **phobic neurosis:** abnormal, irrational fears (e.g., of open spaces, water, dirt) express underlying emotional conflicts that can prevent ordinary activities (e.g., self-hatred makes a person afraid to appear in public and therefore fearful of open spaces)

Each of the following situations involves one of the types of neuroses listed above. The types may occur more than once in the set of items, but no one question has more than one best answer.

58. A man feels that his sexual desires are "unclean." He represses his desires and instead spends much of his time keeping his house spotlessly clean. He vacuums the carpets several times a day. The man is suffering from a
    (1) conversion neurosis
    (2) depressive neurosis
    (3) dissociative neurosis
    (4) obsessive-compulsive neurosis
    (5) phobic neurosis

59. A woman cannot fly in airplanes and, in general, begins to panic whenever she finds herself in a confined space. The woman is suffering from a
    (1) conversion neurosis
    (2) depressive neurosis
    (3) dissociative neurosis
    (4) obsessive-compulsive neurosis
    (5) phobic neurosis

60. A business executive feels incompetent on the job and less intelligent than his coworkers. Instead of trying to improve his performance, he stops talking to his colleagues and gives in to feelings of self-hatred. The executive is suffering from a
    (1) conversion neurosis
    (2) depressive neurosis
    (3) dissociative neurosis
    (4) obsessive-compulsive neurosis
    (5) phobic neurosis

61. A woman's children have grown up; all but one have left home. Then this last child announces he's getting married. The mother's excited. She makes plans to move to an apartment and give the house to her son. She tells her friends about how much she's looking forward to being on her own. Then suddenly, several weeks before the wedding, she develops a paralysis of the legs. The woman is suffering from a
    (1) conversion neurosis
    (2) depressive neurosis
    (3) dissociative neurosis
    (4) obsessive-compulsive neurosis
    (5) phobic neurosis

62. In contrast to her brothers and sisters, a woman appears not to be too upset by her mother's death. Around other people she acts as before. But when she's alone she finds herself staring out windows. She's unable to concentrate and frequently bursts into tears. Time passes, but her feelings of sadness remain. The woman is suffering from a
    (1) conversion neurosis
    (2) depressive neurosis
    (3) dissociative neurosis
    (4) obsessive-compulsive neurosis
    (5) phobic neurosis

Items 63 and 64 are based on the following passage.

The American Revolution, also known as the War for Independence, was fought to give American colonies the right to elect their own leaders, make their own laws, and conduct their own trade without interference from Great Britain's king and Parliament. The American colonists had long enjoyed a certain degree of freedom, but they didn't feel secure in that freedom, as it was often just a result of negligence or oversight. The British government could, and did, appoint colonial governors, restrict colonial trade, and impose various taxes. Taxes, the colonists thought, should be levied by colonial legislatures, not by Parliament, in which they were not represented. The American Revolution was fought to enable Americans to determine their own destiny and to fully develop their own government.

63. Based on the passage, which of the following actions by the British government would have been most likely to anger the colonists?
    (1) repealing a tax levied on the colonies
    (2) sending soldiers to help suppress Indian rebellions
    (3) imposing import duties on goods entering American ports
    (4) making trade agreements with other powers
    (5) giving land grants to wealthy colonists

64. Based on the passage, which of the following statements might best reflect the feelings of many American colonists on the eve of the Revolution?
    (1) They were mostly concerned about British restrictions of their economic rights and freedoms.
    (2) They felt that Great Britain had too many interests worldwide and that the security of the American colonies was therefore in jeopardy.
    (3) They envied the greater freedom and democracy of French and Spanish colonies.
    (4) They felt their rights, needs, and freedoms could not be best served by an overseas power.
    (5) They did not want to keep their link to Great Britain because so many of them had come from countries other than Great Britain.

Answers are on page 401–408.

Simulated Test

Performance Analysis Chart

Directions: Circle the number of each item that you got correct on the Simulated Test. Count how many items you got correct in each row; then count how many items you got correct in each column. Write the amount correct per row and column as the numerator in the fraction in the appropriate "Total Correct" box. (The denominators represent the total number of items in the row or column.) Write the grand total correct over the denominator, **64**, at the lower right corner of the chart. (For example, if you got 54 items correct, write *54* so that the fraction reads *54/***64**.)

	History (page 40)	Geography (page 214)	Economics (page 174)	Political Science (page 122)	Behavioral Science (page 242)	TOTAL CORRECT
Comprehension	29, 41, 50, 51	46, 56	2, 3, 27, 39	18, 20, 23, 26	14, 15	—— 16
Application	63	47		19, 34, 35, 36, 37, 38	8, 17, 58, 59, 60, 61, 62	—— 15
Analysis	13, 30, 31, 42, 44, 51, 57	27, 48	4, 6, 7, 28	1, 21, 24	9, 53, 54	—— 19
Evaluation	32, 43, 45, 52, 64	11, 12, 49	5, 33, 40	22	10, 16	—— 14
TOTAL CORRECT	—— 16	—— 10	—— 12	—— 13	—— 13	—— 64

The page numbers in parentheses indicate where in this book you can find the beginning of specific instruction about the various fields of social studies.

Answer Key Chapters 1–7

Chapter 1: Introduction to Social Studies

Lesson 1

1. **(4)** *Comprehension/Behavioral Science.* We are told ''many poor and lower-income neighborhoods have been redeveloped into upper-middle class areas filled with expensive restaurants and fashionable shops. This trend toward gentrification. . . .'' The last phrase clearly is a *paraphrase* for the development of neighborhood described. Choices (2), (3), and (5) are things that happen as a result of gentrification; they are not gentrification itself. Nothing is said about prejudice against ethnic groups, so (1) is wrong. Many poor or low-income neighborhoods are inhabited by minority ethnic groups, but the passage does not say gentrification is motivated by prejudice; it suggests, rather, the economic motive of buying up cheap property to make money from it.

2. **(2)** *Comprehension/Behavioral Science.* ''This general movement toward gentrification'' in the third sentence is *parallel* to ''the trend toward gentrification'' in the first sentence. The last sentence refers to ''the trend toward gentrification,'' so ''trend'' and ''gentrification'' cannot be the same thing. Therefore, (3) is

wrong and so is (1), which is a vague definition of gentrification. Choice (4) makes no sense if you substitute it for the word ''trend'' in any statement. Choice (5) scrambles the references to fashionable shops in urban areas that gentrification brings.

3. **(4)** *Comprehension/Behavioral Science.* The list of landforms that are ''opposite extremes'' sets up a pattern of *contrasts.* The opposite extreme of ''low valley'' is ''steep hill.'' None of the other choices contrasts with valleys, but resembles them in being low, *unlike* ''high buttes.''

Lesson 2

1. **(5)** *Comprehension/American History.* The earliest event in the passage was 986, when Herjulfsson is said to have explored parts of the North American coast. The detail to remember is that on a timeline the earliest date is on the far left and the most recent date on the far right.

2. **(2)** *Comprehension/American History.* The passage states that there were two explorers who reached the New World before Columbus. None of the other choices is an accurate restatement of

information in the passage. Columbus was an Italian who sailed for Spain, and Ponce de Leon was a Spaniard, so (1) and (4) are wrong. Columbus landed not in North America but in the Caribbean in 1492, so (3) and (5) are wrong.

3. **(4)** *Comprehension/American History.* The passage states that he made three trips after his first successful voyage, a total of four.

Chapter 2: American History

Lesson 1

1. **(2)** *Comprehension/American History.* That Magellan and del Cano sailed all the way around the globe is the most significant thing about their voyage; (1) is a detail about their voyage. (4) is an important accomplishment of their voyage but is part of circling the globe. There is no basis for (3) and (5) in the paragraph.

2. **(2)** *Comprehension/American History.* (2) describes the only action that all the explorers after Columbus took. (1) is wrong because Cabot explored North America.

(4) is wrong because only Magellan and del Cano sailed both oceans. The paragraph says explorers found there was "at least one continent" in the New World, not that there was only one; so (3) is wrong. (5) says the opposite of what is stated in the paragraph.

3. (1) *Comprehension/ American History.* Columbus' distinction as the first person to land in the New World is the most important and convincing reason given for honoring him. The fact that he made four voyages (2) or that Magellan died before finishing his voyage (3) are not important reasons for honoring him. Likewise, (5) is not a solid reason for favoring Columbus: Columbus is honored for being the first to land in the Americas; Vespucci and del Cano would have been honored if they had been first. Nothing stated suggests that (4) was true of Cabot.

Lesson 2

1. (5) *Comprehension/ American History.* The most important, overall motive for the independence was the colonies' desire to govern themselves. (1) and (2) are parts of this overall reason; if they governed themselves they would not have to pay these taxes or pay off the English debt. The second paragraph tells us the colonists did not have the rights of English citizens, but nowhere does it say they rebelled to get these rights; therefore (4) is wrong. Nothing stated suggests (3).

2. (3) *Comprehension/ American History.* (3) is stated in the topic sentence for the first paragraph, which describes the debate; it covers all the other items, which state details about the debate. (2) and (4) are important details, but they are not as important as (3), which is the main idea of the paragraph.

3. (2) *Comprehension/ American History.* The main idea of the passage is stated in its first sentence; (2) is a restatement of it. The long process of signing the document can be considered part of the long and intense discussion. (1) and (3) are details that are not about the topic of the passage, which is the debate and signing of the Declaration; (1) and (3) are about its meaning in later history. (5) is not stated, only suggested, and is part of the main idea. (4) is a detail, certainly not the main point of the passage.

Lesson 3

1. (4) *Comprehension/ American History.* The chart about the Constitution indicates provisions for electing a national executive. None of the documents listed in (1), (2), and (3) provide for electing a president. Nor did the Federalists (5) provide for this.

2. (5) *Comprehension/ American History.* The basic idea of all the compromises was that they were fair to all the states, small and large, Northern and Southern.

3. (1) *Comprehension/ American History.* The South gained an edge in population representation, but the additional population would also be counted for taxation purposes.

Lesson 4

1. (1) *Comprehension/ American History.* What the Monroe Doctrine and Manifest Destiny have in common is acquiring land—keeping foreign countries out of the Western Hemisphere, so the land will be available for the U.S., and extending U.S. territory as far as the Pacific.

2. (5) *Comprehension/ American History.* The Monroe Doctrine was issued to keep foreign powers out of the Western Hemisphere. Uncle Sam, symbolizing the United States, was telling foreign powers to "keep out" of the Western Hemisphere.

3. (5) *Comprehension/ American History.* The Appalachian Mountains, the only mountains on the map, are in the first 15 states. (1) and (2) are incorrect because every state in the new territories is not larger than every one of the first 15 states. (4) is false; the map shows that the opposite is true. The map shows nothing about climate, so (3) is incorrect.

Lesson 5

1. (1) *Analysis/American History.* The Republican Party was founded on an antislavery platform. Founding a new party would have been neither

wise nor necessary if either of the other two parties had been antislavery.

2. **(3)** *Comprehension/ American History.* In the last sentence of the passage you are told that the Southern states feared a strong central government "particularly" because they were afraid of having the issue of slavery decided for them. (4) and (5) mention other probable reasons the Southerners might have feared a strong central government, but neither is as obvious or important as (3). (2) is not probable, since the South remained in the Union until Lincoln's election threatened slavery. (1) simply gives the name for the group opposed to strong central government, which is not a *reason* for their fear of such government.

3. **(3)** *Comprehension/ American History.* You can infer that the purpose of the taxes on foreign goods (tariffs) would be to keep their price high, so that the South and West would continue to buy Northern goods instead. None of the other choices is a logical result of tariffs.

Lesson 6

1. **(5)** *Comprehension/ American History.* Since the Emancipation Proclamation only freed slaves in the Confederacy, you can infer that his primary motive was to help the North win.

2. **(2)** *Comprehension/ American History.* We were told that The "primary difference" between the U.S. government's structure and the structure of the Confederate government "was that fewer powers were given to the central government." That is, the Southerners gave more power to individual states in the Confederacy than the U.S. government gave to the states in the Union. The South believed strongly in states' rights and structured the Confederate government to reflect this.

3. **(1)** *Comprehension/ American History.* We are told the Confederates thought their constitution was closer to the original principles of the U.S. Constitution than the Union government was. This was the main belief behind their choice of flag and form of government. Many in the Confederacy saw their government as the legitimate government of the U.S. and the North as the "rebellion." You can infer this from the fact that they modeled their government after the government outlined in the U.S. Constitution, and even considered using the same flag.

Lesson 7

1. **(4)** *Comprehension/ American History.* Congress passed a lot of legislation during Reconstruction to improve conditions for blacks. The passage supports none of the other choices.

2. **(2)** *Comprehension/ American History.* All four pieces of legislation sought to improve conditions for blacks by protecting and guaranteeing their rights and freedom. Johnson vetoed only the Civil Rights Bill of 1866, so (4) is wrong (Presidents cannot veto amendments). The Fifteenth Amendment was passed in 1870, so (3) is wrong. (5) is incorrect because the Civil Rights Bill did not change the Constitution—it wasn't an amendment—and (1) is obviously false.

3. **(5)** *Comprehension/ American History.* After the Civil War, the South used indirect and even illegal means to undermine the new civil rights laws for blacks, in order to restore prewar white supremacy. (2) and (3) are false. Nothing suggests that sharecropping or tenant dirt-farming would enable the South to regain the wealth it had with the plantation system; so (1) is wrong. (4) is incorrect because scalawags worked with, not against, the Reconstruction governments in the South.

Lesson 8

1. **(3)** *Comprehension/ American History.* Between 1880 and 1900 the number of people in the U.S. whose families came from Austria increased more than 450 times. Next came those from Russia and the Baltic nations (nearly 300 times) and Sweden (over 160 times). Americans deriving from Germany and Ireland were the first

and second largest groups in total numbers of new members in the U.S. population, but neither group increased at the rate of the other three groups mentioned. Americans deriving from England likewise increased in high numbers but not at a high rate of increase (their rate actually fell from 1890 to 1900). Note that the graph is about *rate of increase* in population, not amount of population among these groups; Americans of English descent probably were still the largest single ethnic group in the U.S.

2. **(1)** *Comprehension/ American History.* The graph shows the largest cities in the U.S. in 1900. All the cities are in the Northeast and the Midwest.

3. **(1)** *Comprehension/ American History.* The passage says that in 1880 one-quarter of Americans lived in cities. In 1910, half of them did. The number of Americans living in cities therefore doubled.

Lesson 9

1. **(4)** *Comprehension/ American History.* The hands marked "Politics" and "Banking" are both grabbing at each other's bases of power. Both are shown as equally greedy, so (5) is wrong. Nothing suggests (3). (1) refers only to the banks and so is incomplete. (2) is not what the main action of the cartoon shows, but is only a possible conclusion suggested by the action.

2. **(5)** *Comprehension/ American History.* The Irishman and the German are shown running away from a polling place, stealing the ballot box. (1) and (3) are not shown by the actions in the cartoon. (2) and (4) are irrelevant to the main action, which is stealing votes.

3. **(1)** *Comprehension/ American History.* The crucial details for this question are that the Irishman is wearing a whiskey barrel and the German a beer barrel, and that they are stealing the votes in a ballot box. No other answer choice mentions drinking and dishonesty.

Lesson 10

1. **(3)** *Comprehension/ American History.* We are told that the U.S. needed new markets because of increasing industrial production. Cuba was a good supply of raw materials and the passage tells us that it was a potential market for finished products.

2. **(5)** *Application /American History.* "Hell On Earth" is sensational language designed to arouse strong hostile emotions. "Dumps" in (2) is slang and "Hit" in (3) is everyday language, but neither is highly emotional. (1) and (4) contain no sensational language, although (4) is about a sensational event.

3. **(1)** *Application /American History.* Imperialism is the act of extending political or economic control over a foreign nation. By capturing Panama's

leader, the U.S. exerted control over the politics of another nation.

Lesson 11

1. **(1)** *Application /American History.* Information from the lesson tells you that high unemployment and drops in the stock market are indicators of economic failure, or "bust."

2. **(4)** *Application /American History.* The writer blames the abuse of prairie soil in the Midwest for the creation of the Dust Bowl. Therefore, he would think that commercial fertilizers *should* be used on soil in semiarid areas. All the other choices the writer would agree with, because they all recommend that damage to natural environment be prevented or repaired.

3. **(3)** *Application /American History.* The tractor driver's remark meant that the forces that took the farmer's land away were too big and impersonal to identify and punish. (3) restates this meaning with reference to the S & L scandal.

Lesson 12

1. **(4)** *Application /American History.* A system with a ceremonial emperor (monarch) and legislative bodies that actually run the government is a constitutional monarchy.

2. **(3)** *Application /American History.* Even though the Italian constitution remained in effect, Mussolini formed a dictatorship by taking absolute control of the government.

3. **(4)** *Application /American History.* (2) is incorrect because this community does not make laws. Since this community does not have a leader, it cannot be a dictatorship, so (1) is wrong. (3) is wrong because nothing is said about elections or lawmakers. Hereditary rulers obviously have no place in this community, so (5) is incorrect.

Lesson 13

1. **(1)** *Application /American History.* These three countries are right next to each other; none of the other groups of countries is.

2. **(3)** *Application /American History.* The cartoon shows Eisenhower the general and Eisenhower the candidate facing opposite directions and acting very differently in each; this suggests he might combine two different political stances in his economic policies. His facing two directions at once also suggests he would not take a distinctly liberal or conservative position, so (1) and (2) are wrong. The comparison implied by the bottle marked "Korea" in the cartoon is to cure-all—that is, fake—medicine, not to natural resources that are being given away: Eisenhower is not giving away Korea, but offering false solu-

tions to the Korean War. Therefore the idea that he would give away natural resources is not being suggested, and (4) is incorrect. Nothing in the cartoon supports (5).

3. **(1)** *Application /American History.* The cartoon shows Eisenhower dealing with the issue of the Korean War by offering quick cure-all solutions as a candidate, and on the other hand, studying a map about it without taking action. (2) is wrong because in the cartoon he is not shown simply turning his back on the issue of the war; only one of the two Eisenhowers in the cartoon is turning his back. (3), (4), and (5) all describe decisive action in one direction, which is not the behavior of Eisenhower shown in the cartoon.

Lesson 14

1. **(3)** *Analysis/American History.* It can be proved that the Peace Corps helped at least some people in underdeveloped countries. (2) and (5) are predictions impossible to prove. (1) can be endlessly debated, in spite of the Supreme Court decision. (4) is a sweeping generalization that can mean many things and therefore is a matter of opinion.

2. **(3)** *Comprehension/ American History.* The lesson states that integration occurred because the courts ordered it. The army did not cause the integration but kept local people from stopping it, so both (1) and (2) are wrong. (4) is an opinion.

(5) makes no sense; no blacks could enter it as the better school without integration's happening first.

3. **(1)** *Evaluation/American History.* The question asks for a probable explanation, or hypothesis. The passage mentions several times the violence confronting the civil rights movement, which would threaten the lives of leaders like King. None of the other choices is a believable explanation for King's statement. He would not speak of the Promised Land if (3) he thought it were only a dream. The information in the lesson gives no support to (4) or (5).

Lesson 15

1. **(4)** *Analysis/American History.* The best hypothesis is that the Army and the Marines were involved in more riskier combat. (1), (2) and (3) are facts, not hypotheses. Nothing in the table supports (5).

2. **(5)** *Analysis/American History.* Only two percentage points divided those who agreed and those who disagreed about American disengagement from the war; 90 percent of Americans were therefore split almost exactly in half on this issue. (1) is true, but the majority (more than half) consists of only two percentage points. This hypothesis therefore does not explain the facts accurately and is misleading. So is (2), which suggests America was decisive about the war when in fact strong opin-

when in fact strong opinions split the country in half. Less than half believed (3), and (4) is not supported at all by the graph's information.

3. **(5)** *Comprehension/ American History.* We are told that after 15 years of war and over 50,000 American lives lost, South Vietnam fell to the Communists.

Lesson 16

1. **(3)** *Analysis/American History.* Reagan's economic policies tripled the federal debt and raised local taxes, but helped to reduce inflation, unemployment, and interest rates. Grenada and START were successes, while Nicaragua was an eight-year stalemate that ended with mixed success. Nothing supports the opinions stated in (4) and (5).

2. **(2)** *Analysis/American History.* We are told that Carter's main strength was his foreign policies—except in Iran. This one policy was much less effective than his other actions in foreign affairs.

3. **(5)** *Analysis/American History.* Even if every person who voted for Anderson and other minor candidates had voted for Carter, he still would have had only 41,629,829 votes, compared to Reagan's 43,201,657. Since none of the minor candidates received any electoral votes, Reagan still would have won by a landslide.

Chapter 3: Political Science

Lesson 1

1. **(5)** *Analysis/Political Science.* In the cartoon the significant details are (a) that the atomic bomb is much bigger than the men and is even bigger than the world, and (b) that the men having a meeting at a conference table are world leaders. The important comparison is that the bomb is pictured as a giant measuring the globe with a tape measure. Measuring the globe with a tape suggests that the bomb is deciding what to do with the world, the way someone decides what to do with a piece of wood or cloth he wants to make something out of. The line under the cartoon— the caption—points up the main idea of the cartoon: that the threat of the atomic bomb makes the discussions of the world leaders unimportant. This main idea is based on the unstated assumption that the atomic bomb is beyond human control. We do not see the bomb in the process of growing, so (2) is wrong. (1) is clearly false. (3) is wrong because only one man at the meeting table even notices the giant bomb. The meeting is at the top of the globe— the North Pole—but this is not a significant detail. If (4) were correct, the cartoon would show people living in the Arctic region, and the effects on the rest of the globe of an atomic explosion.

2. **(5)** *Analysis/Political Science.* America, as Uncle Sam, is shown offering many forms of freedom (in the sign next to Uncle Sam), and freedom from various forms of tyranny (on the sign in the middle of the cartoon). The comparison underlying the whole cartoon is that America is like Noah's ark for immigrants. Uncle Sam and his ark are saving them from the evils of tyranny and the storms of "War" and "Famine" (shown as devils in the sky). (1) is not an unstated assumption but the meaning stated in the caption. Nothing suggests (2) or (3). War and famine are not casting a shadow over smiling Uncle Sam, or attacking him, so (4) is wrong.

3. **(2)** *Analysis/Political Science.* The unstated assumption is that democracy, as the system that offers the most freedom and participation in government, is the most humane form of government. The lesson states that dictatorships differ, so (1) is wrong. (3) is incorrect because a republic has no monarch. These choices are misstatements of details, which (4) is not; but the lesson suggests no assumption that parliamentary democracy is better than the U.S. type of democracy. Since the text states that until recently the Soviet Union had a totalitarian dictator, (5) cannot be true.

Lesson 2

1. **(5)** *Analysis/Political Science.* (5) restates the last sentence. All the details support the conclusion that requirements vary from country to country, so travelers should check them out before leaving. (4) is not true: Mexico and Canada have different policies about car insurance. (2) is an exaggeration because it is stated that in Canada, Americans need a card from their insurer, not just their policy. (3) is a detail, dealing only with Mexico; the paragraph is about Mexico and Canada. No restrictions in Canada or Mexico are called unreasonable, so (1) is wrong. You may have this opinion after reading the paragraph, but it is not the main idea all the details support.

2. **(2)** *Analysis/Political Science.* All the details of the lesson support the idea that the Constitution works by setting limits on different parts of the U.S. government. The second paragraph covers limits in the federal government mentioned in (4); the last paragraph covers limits in the federal system mentioned in (5); (3) restates the limit mentioned in paragraph one. (1) restates what the question stem tells you—that the Constitution has worked for 200 years—not why it has worked, so it cannot be an answer at all.

3. **(4)** *Analysis/Political Science.* The overall purpose of the whole system of separated powers is to keep any one part of government from gaining too much power. That is the underlying belief—the unstated assumption—of the system shown in the chart. (3) sums up the way the system works, and (5) only says it works well: neither gives you the basic belief that made people set it up in the first place. (1) is false, and (2) is an opinion unsupported by the information on the chart.

Lesson 3

1. **(3)** *Analysis/Political Science.* The Equal Rights Amendment had the support of only 35 states in 1982. It needed 38 states (75 percent) for ratification, so it was not passed. (1) and (2) are details that support this conclusion. (4) is false, and (5) is an opinion with no support pro or con in the chart.

2. **(4)** *Analysis/Political Science.* The basic belief, or unstated assumption, underlying the Bill of Rights is that individual citizens (and their individual rights) need to be protected by law against government power. (5) states one assumption about one of the rights, not the basic assumption underlying all the rights in the Bill. (1) and (2) simply list two of the rights in the Bill. (4) is wrong because the Bill of Rights does not seek to use government power to protect citizens; on the contrary, it seeks to protect citizens *against* government power, by means of laws.

3. **(2)** *Analysis/Political Science.* If eight of the 16 amendments on the chart concern voting rights and elections, you can conclude that the category of voting rights must be considered most important in our democratic society. The chart does not tell us what the amendments in the category "Other" are about, so there is no support for (1) and (4). It is not a logical conclusion that the amendment under "Citizenship" is the least important of all of them just because there is only one in that category, since we do not know what it is about; so (3) is wrong. It also is not logical to conclude that the amendments under "Other" are the least important; although the title "Other" may suggest "left over" (and its place on the far right of the chart may emphasize this), you do not know what its amendments contain, so (5) is incorrect.

Lesson 4

1. **(1)** *Analysis/Political Science.* The first paragraph of the lesson states that the division of powers between federal and statement governments resulted from compromises at the Constitutional Convention. (2) and (5) are clearly false. (3) refers to the separation of powers within the federal government not between the federal and state governments. (4) are the powers left to the states by the division; therefore, they cannot be the cause of the division.

2. **(5)** *Analysis/Political Science.* You are told that federal courts try cases that "are interstate in nature (that is, involve two or more states)." (3) is a reason to try the case in a state court, not in a federal court. (1) is wrong because no individuals are mentioned in regard to the case. (4) makes no sense, and (2) is an opinion with no support in the question item or the lesson.

3. **(5)** *Analysis/Political Science.* Since the Pentagon and Congress are rated the least efficient, it appears that Americans (at least those in this poll) think their government is inefficient. The post office and space agency score higher, but all parts of government score fairly low. (2) and (3) are details that do not cover enough information in the chart to be conclusions. Just because supermarkets are considered efficient by 51 percent, you cannot logically conclude that Americans want other businesses to be organized like supermarkets; so (1) is wrong. Commuter rail scores low, but no information about efficiency of private cars is on the chart, so there is no support for the conclusion in (4).

Lesson 5

1. **(1)** *Analysis/Political Science.* This cannot be the cause of the increased number of Republican senators because you can see on the chart that the total number of senators has stayed the same—100. From your reading

thus far, or from prior knowledge, you also would know that changing the number of senators per state would require a Constitutional amendment. (4) explains how Republicans, in fact, got control of the Senate—by winning seats the Democrats had held. (2) and (5) are logical explanations of how the Democrats kept their majority in the House of Representatives while Republicans gained control of the presidency and the Senate. (3) is also a plausible cause. It refers to the so-called coattails effect of a popular president, who carries other candidates in his party into elected office "on his coattails."

2. **(2)** *Analysis/Political Science.* The lesson tells you that the number of representatives, 435, is set by Constitutional law. None of the other choices is a convincing reason for the fact that the number has not changed since 1910. The lesson does not support (5) at all. You probably know from prior knowledge that the U.S. population has grown steadily since 1910, so (4) is false, and that the population of some states has grown more than others, so (1) is false. (3) makes no sense as an explanation because the number of representatives depends on population, not on "shifts in political party popularity."

3. **(5)** *Analysis/Political Science.* You might have to look back at the lesson to check the essential rule of the electoral college system: the candi-

date with the most popular votes in a state receives all the electoral votes of the state. A candidate who won by large margins in small states, and lost by slim margins in big states, might lose the big states and the election although he or she had the most popular votes. (4) describes the opposite situation: a candidate who wins the big states and the election, although he or she may not have the most popular votes. With (1), the candidate would win the big states and the election; with (2), he or she would lose both, and have the fewest popular votes. The candidate described in (3) would not have a majority of the popular vote.

Lesson 6

1. **(5)** *Evaluation/Political Science.* The relevant information is the number of new jobs becoming available between 1985 and 2000, and the total number of jobs in the year 2000 in each city. New York will have four times as many jobs as San Francisco in 2000, and more jobs will open up between 1985 and 2000 in New York than in San Francisco.

2. **(1)** *Analysis/Political Science.* The cities are ranked by the number of jobs that will be opening up. Four of the top five cities are in the western U.S.

3. **(4)** *Evaluation/Political Science.* The graph shows former President Reagan's popularity fell sharply, from 60 percent

to 40 percent approval, around 1990; the timeline shows that 1990 was when he testified about the Iran-contra affair. So the information on the two graphics most adequately supports the hypothesis in (4). Though neither says his testimony was poor, their information suggests a connection between his fall and his testimony. Neither graphic gives us any information to support the other choices.

Lesson 7

1. **(5)** *Evaluation/Political Science.* The last sentences of both the first and second paragraphs support this statement. The second paragraph directly contradicts (3). It indirectly contradicts (2) by saying that students learn more in "high" groups; it is not logical to think they would learn more if they resented having to learn more. The whole passage is about the different ways Japanese and American children learn, so (1) is false. Nothing supports (4).

2. **(4)** *Evaluation/Political Science.* The last two sentences suggest the plan could be gotten around so long as companies could afford to buy pollution points. This does not mean the passage rejects the plan completely; it only means that it provides support for this criticism of the plan, and provides no support for the other statements. (2) is incorrect because the last paragraph of the passage points out a major weakness of the new proposal.

While the rest of the passage describes its possible positive effect, we are told the other solutions also "have some effect." Nothing supports (3) or (5). If "pollution still threatens the environment," (1) is also wrong.

3. **(3)** *Comprehension/Political Science.* None of the countries listed is in Europe. Therefore, (2) is wrong. Only 47 percent have more than two years of college, so (1) is also incorrect. If their "Mean (Average) Age" is 33.5 years, that means some are older than 33.5 years and others are younger. It does not mean that most are exactly that age, and so (4) is wrong. Nothing supports (5).

Lesson 8

1. **(3)** *Evaluation/Political Science.* The passage consists of examples of how Americans "let down our defenses" and withdrew our troops (or most of them) from Europe after both world wars. Even with no clear danger replacing the Cold War, the writer concludes that we should stay prepared militarily. He does not deny that the Cold War is ending, so (2) is wrong. (1) and (4) restate two of the opinions that support or express his viewpoint. The writer stresses the ability to fight wars, not peace, so (5) does not express his viewpoint well.

2. **(1)** *Evaluation/Political Science.* The writer does not even mention (4) peaceful negotiations or (2) trust among nations. The lessons of history (5)

he mentions are all examples of how lack of American military power and intervention abroad led to fascist and communist tyranny. He feels that military security is the only defense *against* military aggression by such tyrannies, so (3) is wrong. His emphasis on military strength and intervention might suggest that he favors military aggression, but he does not favor conquests, only defense.

3. **(5)** *Analysis/Political Science.* The writer of the lesson says "fortunately, most governments prefer to settle their differences peacefully," and gives the examples of the use of diplomacy in the UN and by nations among themselves. Nothing supports (1), (2), or (4). The writer says treaties are good ways to keep peace but does not say economic treaties like the Common Market are "the best way to keep peace," so (3) is wrong.

Chapter 4: Economics

Lesson 1

1. **(1)** *Evaluation/Economics.* Uncle Sam, representing the U.S. government, is forcing the U.S. citizen to give his Social Security number *as his name* before he will give him his Social Security check. Taking away someone's personal identity—his name—in this way is not worth the security given, the cartoon suggests. (2) and (5) are therefore wrong. The small citizen has no

chance to bully the bigger Uncle Sam, so (4) is incorrect. Nothing suggests loss of citizenship, so (3) is wrong.

2. **(2)** *Evaluation/ Economics.* The cartoon's point is that when the President thinks of calling the military to protect him against a threat, the military has become so strong that it *is* the threat. Since the President looks frightened, (3) is wrong, and since the cartoonist does not think the military budget has been made too small, (1) is wrong. Though Bush is shown as frightened, (4) is not shown or suggested. (5) is incorrect because the cartoon makes no reference to the military's increasing the budget deficit.

3. **(4)** *Evaluation/ Economics.* The writer uses emotionally charged language and negative emphasis to describe the demands for free or subsidized health care. Those demanding it are called an "aggressive new lobby." The writer blames the many who cannot afford the high costs of medical care for failing to save enough to pay bills; less emphasis is given to the effects of inflation or bad luck. Emphasis is given to the high cost of national health care programs and their connection to "a welfare state." The writer therefore seems to value a free-enterprise system in which people provide for their own health care with no government help.

Lesson 2

1. **(3)** *Evaluation/ Economics.* (3) is the only logical cause-and-effect statement among the choices given because in *all* the countries shown, the percent of males employed declined slightly from 1980 to 1987. All the other choices state cause-and-effect relationships based on faulty logic. The table does show an increase in female employment and a decrease in male employment, but this does not mean fewer men will have to work, only that more women will be working. Men will still be the large majority of the workforce. So (1) is illogical. (2) is illogical because we do not know if the women are taking jobs that men are leaving or are taking new jobs. As for (5), the table does show that Japanese women are entering the workforce more slowly than women in the other countries; but there is no logical reason to conclude from this that they will "greatly increase" their participation in order "to catch up." (4) is wrong because the percents of employment for both males and females in Canada are actually *less* than these percents in the United States, and there is no logical reason to think this trend will reverse itself.

2. **(4)** *Evaluation/ Economics.* Your friend cannot logically look forward to a year of heavy sales because pools and pool supplies in the northeastern U.S. are a

seasonal item that would sell only in the warm months. You are nowhere told that "people won't want to pay much for a pool," so (3) is not the basis of his faulty logic. You do not know that "supply will exceed demand," so (5) is also not the flawed reasoning involved. Since there is one other pool supplier, there probably will be no surplus, but you cannot tell. Pool supplies would not compete with skiing, so (1) is wrong. (2) is illogical because a new store would not necessarily have to underprice the established competitor if demand were high or if its products were better in some way.

3. **(2)** *Analysis/ Economics.* The cartoonist believes in the classic of law of supply and demand: as determined by other factors (the thrill of using illicit substances), demand will increase. Supply will have to increase to meet the demand, and the producers of alcohol and tobacco will make large profits.

Lesson 3

1. **(5)** *Evaluation/ Economics.* The fact that 17 percent of businesses are corporations does not mean that corporations do 17 percent of all the business. A few very large corporations do a major part of the country's business, so it is possible that even less than 17 percent of the businesses might do much more than 17 percent of the business. (1) contradicts information

in the lesson without providing supporting proof. (2), (3), and (4) give reasons that do not support or contradict the logic of the statement, and are therefore irrelevant. Corporations are not always (or usually) owned by employees, so (3) is also factually false.

2. **(3)** *Evaluation/ Economics.* The number of stocks a company has to sell indicates nothing about their value, pro or con; in fact, a large number of stocks being offered for sale could mean they are undesirable. (1) is not true: stockbrokers are not the only people who understand the stock market. We cannot tell from the item whether (4) is true or not. (2) and (5) are opinions with no support in the item, and do not point up a fault in Sally's logic.

3. **(1)** *Evaluation/ Economics.* The overall population density of a state does not mean that one small town in a state will have the same high density of population. (2), (3), and (4) are not persuasive reasons: probably print shops would be needed outside large cities, where the competition would be greater, and he probably would be able to get supplies as easily. "Central New Jersey has a lot of farms" could mean that few businesses there need printing, but businesses needing printing could co-exist with a lot of farms, so (5) is useless for answering the question.

Lesson 4

1. **(2)** *Comprehension/ Economics.* The passage states that credit unions can offer better rates to their members because they are nonprofit.

2. **(2)** *Application / Economics.* When you use a debit card, money is taken out of your account to pay for an item just as it would be if you wrote a check. Using a debit card does not put money into a savings account (1), or charge expenses which you will pay later as with a credit card (4), or borrow money you will pay back later, like a loan (5), or function as cash directly (3).

3. **(1)** *Evaluation/ Economics.* The passage states that banks invest the money in customer's accounts and charge interest on loans so that they can make money. (4) is not true: only some banks charge a fee to cover the cost of managing your account, and only if your balance is under a certain amount. Nothing in the lesson supports (2) or (5), or indicates that (3) is good advice for everyone.

Lesson 5

1. **(2)** *Analysis/Economics.* The graphs show that fewer banks are members of the Federal Reserve System, but that they hold the greater percentage of deposits. You can conclude that there are advantages to being a member, so (1) is wrong. State banks are also members, so (3) is false. The graph clearly shows that (4) and (5) are false.

2. **(4)** *Evaluation/ Economics.* When the Federal Reserve has a tight money policy, loans are harder to get and interest rates are high. (1), (2), and (3) all contain false statements about this policy. (5) is wrong because raising the reserve ratio would be central to a tight money policy.

3. **(1)** *Analysis/Economics.* When more money is available for loans (by lowering the reserve ratio) and interest rates are low (by lowering the discount rate), economic activity usually increases. (2) therefore would slow down such activity. (3) and (4) contain pairs of actions, one of which would increase economic activity and the second of which would decrease it; so both of these choices would tend to keep activity at the same level. Both, like (5), would tend not to produce an upswing.

Lesson 6

1. **(1)** *Comprehension/ Economics.* You can infer this from the third and fourth sentences: the third states that many AIDS patients would die before FDA testing was finished; the fourth states that the agency agreed to make the drug available before completing testing. (3) simply states the usual FDA rule with no reference to this decision. Nothing suggests the FDA thought the whole country would be infected, so (4) is wrong. Nothing supports (5). The report cited suggests a high success rate

from using the incompletely tested drug, so it is unlikely that the agency "caved in" to the activists' demands; the emphasis of (2) suggests an irresponsibility in the FDA decision that the passage does not support.

2. **(3)** *Application / Economics.* The examples do not concern prices (1), the press (4), or product services (5), and they are not concerned only with children's products or safety (2).

3. **(3)** *Application / Economics.* The Federal Trade Commission controls misleading and false advertising (such as this ad's claim that the food processor will prevent catching colds).

Lesson 7

1. **(4)** *Analysis/Economics.* To find this answer you need to remember that a high inflation rate means that money is worth less and therefore can buy less. A low inflation rate means you get more for your money. The question tells you that the percentages of change in consumer prices on the table are good indications of the rates of inflation. On this basis, you can see that Japan and Germany consistently had the lowest inflation rates, so (1) is supported by the table. The table also clearly supports (2), (3) and (5). Canada had a lower inflation rate than the U.S. in 1979 and 1980, but higher inflation than the U.S. in all the other years, so Canadians did not "consistently" get more

for their money than U.S. consumers; so (4) is not supported by the table.

2. **(5)** *Application / Economics.* Structural unemployment occurs when there is a rapid change in the economy— such as the collapse of the oil industry—that is not part of the usual business cycle.

3. **(3)** *Comprehension/ Economics.* The man on the sled is shown to be terrified by the steep downslide of the recession; he does not seem to even notice the sign that says, "Business upturn just ahead," and if he does see it, does not show any hope, relief, or pleasure at its message. Therefore, (2), which states the message on the sign, cannot be the main point of the cartoon. The downslide is on a sled, not a rollercoaster (which goes up as well as down), and the action of the sled-slide represents a recession, not the economy, so (5) is wrong. Inflation is not mentioned, so (4) is incorrect. Nothing suggests (1).

Chapter 5: Geography

Lesson 1

1. **(4)** *Application /Geography.* It is two hours earlier in Tucson than in Washington, so you would want to place the call at 8:00, when it would be 6:00 in Tucson.

2. **(1)** *Application /Geography.* Pittsburgh and Miami are both close to the line of west longitude between 75° and 85°—

that is, 80°. All the other pairs of cities are clearly too far apart to be at the same longitude.

3. **(1)** *Application /Geography.* These coordinates put you in the middle of Alaska, which is part of the United States.

Lesson 2

1. **(4)** *Application /Geography.* The contour lines are quite widely and evenly spaced, showing a gradual drop. Then there are no lines, indicating that the land levels off.

2. **(2)** *Application /Geography.* Wide, evenly spaced contour lines indicate gentle, gradual changes in elevation. The elevation of 10-100 feet per level of elevation indicates low hills.

3. **(1)** *Application /Geography.* Contour lines that are close together indicate a steep drop. This figure shows a series of 100 foot drops from 900 to 0.

Lesson 3

1. **(5)** *Application /Geography.* These areas are arid, which means they are dry and desert-like. You would expect plant life to be very sparse and limited.

2. **(4)** *Application /Geography.* When it's spring-like weather in the Southern Hemisphere, the opposite is true in the north. The areas marked 5 therefore would be experiencing fall-like weather conditions—cool temperatures, with days becoming shorter as winter approaches.

3. **(1)** *Analysis/Geography.* Because of the tilt of the Earth's axis, the Arctic is tilted toward the sun for 6 months of the year and the Antarctic for the other 6 months.

Lesson 4

1. **(4)** *Comprehension/Geography.* The passage states that the taiga rims the tundra, which is located in the polar region of the Arctic Circle. You can infer that the taiga must lie just below the Arctic Circle. The taiga's "average summer temperature" of "about 38°" would also allow you to eliminate the other choices.

2. **(5)** *Application /Geography.* The oceans have a moderating effect on climate in the temperate zones. Temperatures are still extremely hot in the tropics even in the mountains and by the water, so (1) and (3) are wrong. We are told prevailing winds affect weather inland as well as on the coasts, so (2) is also incorrect. Tundra grows in polar regions where the Arctic climate would not have much of a warming effect on the extreme cold; therefore eliminate (4).

3. **(2)** *Analysis/Geography.* You know from reading in the lesson that winds off the ocean bring moisture to the land, and that winds off the land do not. Therefore, (5) is incorrect. Both coasts border on oceans, so (1) provides no explanation of their differences. (3) could not explain why the northern coast is desert because most other coasts in the northern temperate zone are not desert—for instance, the coasts of the U.S. You also know that it is unlikely that the temperature in a temperate zone—especially part of a zone as near the equator as Africa—would not be warm enough to create much rain; so (4) is wrong.

Lesson 5

1. **(5)** *Comprehension/Geography.* The lesson states that high population growth in developing nations is causing serious problems in terms of famine, disease, and poverty. Knowing what the conditions of a developing nation are, you can tell that choices (1) through (4) are clearly wrong.

2. **(2)** *Analysis/Geography.* It is reasonable to conclude that whites will become a minority in the U.S. if other racial/ethnic groups continue to grow at a radically faster rate. This conclusion takes a logical next step in the growth of population shown on the graph. The other choices go beyond this logical step; they predict other, different developments for which there is no support in the graph—changes in immigration laws (2), in immigration patterns (3), in the main U.S. language (4), and the main U.S. religion (5). They all assume—incorrectly—that the *percentage of increase* in the different groups tells you the percentage of the total U.S. population each group will be in the near future. This is a false inference. For instance, just because the rate of increase for "Asians and other" is 56% does not mean they are, or will be, 56% of the total U.S. population.

3. **(1)** *Analysis/Geography.* The map shows that most of Australia is desert, an environment that is not well-suited to human habitation.

Lesson 6

1. **(3)** *Analysis/Geography.* The passage shows throughout how different parts of the world depend on other parts for resources they must have to survive. The underlying assumption is that this dependence gives some nations power over others: industrial nations over developing nations (and vice-versa), oil-producing nations over industrial nations and tropical developing nations. All the other choices are details that support the generalization in (3), and none covers enough ground to be the underlying assumption of the whole passage. (1) does not include the whole issue of mutual need and exertion of power between nations; (2) leaves out these matters, too. (4) states only half the meaning implicit in the passage because developing nations—for example, oil-producing ones—also take advantage of developed nations. (5) is not true.

2. **(1)** *Comprehension/Geography.* High prices would probably give OPEC nations a positive balance of trade, or trade surplus, because the value of their exports

probably would exceed the value of their imports. (2) is therefore false. (3) and (4) would reduce their income, which would be illogical for them to do. There is no reason to predict (5).

3. **(5)** *Comprehension/Geography.* There is no statement that alternative energy sources are more efficient than conventional ones. However, they are cleaner and cheaper, they don't deplete natural resources, and they make countries less dependent on other countries for oil. So all the other choices *are* reasons for finding alternative sources of energy.

4. **(2)** *Comprehension/Geography.* Northern Canada, because of its high latitude, would not be a good candidate for solar energy. The angle of the sun would not permit strong enough sunlight to make this an effective source of energy.

Chapter 6: Behavioral Sciences

Lesson 1

1. **(1)** *Application/Behavioral Science.* The patient is unable to function normally and has partially withdrawn from reality—symptoms of psychosis.

2. **(4)** *Application/Behavioral Science.* This young man has forced certain memories into his subconscious—the classic sign of repression.

3. **(2)** *Application/Behavioral Science.* The man has modified his urge to kill into a socially acceptable form of anger. This is sublimation.

Lesson 2

1. **(4)** *Application/Behavioral Science.* Tying laces is not naturally in the child's repertoire of behaviors. If he is rewarded first for putting on his shoes, then for making loops in the laces, and so on, successive approximation will eventually lead to his being able to tie his shoes. (1) is wrong because the dancer already knows other ballet routines, while successive approximation teaches actions unknown to the subject. For the same reason, (2) and (3) are wrong: neither the dog nor the kitten learns behavior unknown to it, only to do known behavior differently. A rat would find its way through a maze by trial and error, the way it would find its way through any strange place, not by learning new behavior, so (5) is wrong.

2. **(1)** *Application/Behavioral Science.* Smiling is already in the baby's repertoire. However, smiling specifically in response to being smiled *at* is learned, because it is rewarded while other behaviors are ignored. In all the other choices, the activity learned is not already part of the subject's behavior, as it must be in differential approximation.

3. **(3)** *Application/Behavioral Science.* A girl might want to marry someone who looks like her father because she loves him, but she wouldn't have learned this behavior from her father. All the other

choices show the subjects who exemplify *modelling,* copying the behavior of people they admire and therefore want to imitate.

Lesson 3

1. **(2)** *Comprehension/Behavioral Science.* The boys with "superior" intelligence committed crimes and *none* of them were sentenced to prison (0 percent); 35 percent of the "sub-normal" intelligence group of boys committed crimes while 19 percent of them were sentenced to prison. Since boys of "average" and "dull average" intelligence were convicted of a higher percentage of crimes than boys of "sub-normal" intelligence, (1) is not an accurate conclusion. The first part of (2) is false ("Low IQ does not lead to crime") because "dull average" and "sub-normal" boys committed a slightly higher percentage of crimes than "superior" and "average" boys. (4) is clearly false. (5) is not a valid conclusion because the table is about the relation of intelligence level to crime rate and incarceration, and this conclusion refers to the crime rate "regardless of intelligence."

2. **(3)** *Analysis/Behavioral Science.* Since not one boy from the high IQ group was sentenced, it is possible that judges believed they do not *need* to be punished or reformed. (2) is false: the boys of highest intelligence were in fact convicted. The fact that only 26 percent of this group were *convicted* neither supports or con-

tradicts the hypothesis, which has to do with *sentencing to prison;* so (1) is wrong. The same is true of the facts restated in (4) and (5).

3. **(3)** *Application / Behavioral Science.* While all the other behaviors listed may seem "eccentric," the only one that truly deviates from the norms of society is dressing a baby boy like a girl.

Lesson 4

1. **(3)** *Application / Behavioral Science.* The members of a primary group have close, cultural contact with each other; the primary group is most responsible for the behavioral standards and beliefs of its members. The Mormon church functions in this way for its members. Therefore it is not a secondary group, so (4) is wrong. Polygamy creates a nontraditional family by U.S. standards, but the organization of the Mormon Church itself does not represent a nontraditional family, so (5) is wrong. (1) and (2) clearly do not apply.

2. **(1)** *Analysis/Behavioral Science.* Since we are told the Mormons accommodated the government and the larger society, the unstated assumption is that in general the standards of the larger society are those that are ultimately adhered to. The passage describes attacks on the Mormons for practicing polygamy, but nothing suggests that the author of the passage approves of these attacks or believes the opinions in (2) and (4). Since the whole passage is about Mormonism's existence in the U.S., (5) is obviously false. The opinion in (3) does not relate to the passage, which is about a larger U.S. society that did not believe the Mormons in the 1800s should have this right.

3. **(2)** *Comprehension/Behavioral Science.* The Mormons apparently valued living in peace with the larger society more strongly than practicing polygamy or they would have continued to fight for their right to live as they chose. Likewise, if they believed (5), they would never have given up polygamy; in fact, the violent attacks and persecution the Mormons suffered from other U.S. citizens and from the U.S. government are given as the major reasons for their "adapting" to the norms of the larger society. Nothing suggests (3). As for (4), wealth is not discussed (the Mormons in fact are a very wealthy religious group).

Lesson 5

1. **(2)** *Comprehension/Behavioral Science.* Dr. Mead points out that men and women behave differently in the three societies, suggesting that the roles we normally attribute to one or the other sex are learned, not inborn. Therefore, (1) is wrong. All three societies studied were primitive, not advanced in development, so (4) is wrong. The first society mentioned by Mead shows male and female roles typical of Western society, so (3) is also incorrect. (5) is an illogical statement; the fact that each society was different does not mean no conclusion can be made.

2. **(1)** *Analysis/Behavioral Science.* Humans may well become extinct; it is argued that this is the natural end of evolution. However, we are different from other species because of our brain, and may be able to save ourselves in circumstances in which other species could not. Choices (2), (4), and (5) are very large predictions that have no support in the passage. (3) is a variation on (2).

3. **(3)** *Comprehension/Behavioral Science.* The characteristics listed are those of the Mongoloid race. The lesson states that this race originated in Asia. (1) is an inference with no basis in the passage. It also does not make sense logically: how could cold weather and sparse sunlight cause Eskimos to develop flat faces, high cheekbones, and dark eyes? The passage does not support (2) and says just the opposite of (4). (5) is true, but does nothing to explain the statement.

Lesson 6

1. **(2)** *Application / Behavioral Science.* The Communist movement was opposed to certain basic economic and political beliefs of the dominant capitalist culture, clashing with it in a fundamental way.

2. **(3)** *Analysis/Behavioral Science.* Culture C, because it lies between B and D, would probably

have effects on both of those cultures. B and D might affect C, but not each other. A and E are too far from the others to have much, if any, effect on them.

3. **(4)** *Analysis/Behavioral Science.* Anthropologists should be objective when studying a culture and reporting their findings. Choice (4) includes value judgments (for example, the emotional words, "cruel and painful") that don't belong in an objective study.

Chapter 7: Interrelationships in Social Studies

Lesson 1

1. **(1)** *Analysis/Interrelationships.* The lesson discusses the history of German aggression and the fear that history will repeat itself. It is the unstated assumption of people who fear German reunification that Germans are motivated by a desire to rule the world. The passage asks, "With whom will a reunified Germany ally itself? What will become of NATO?"—which might suggest that (3) is correct. (3) is not the main unstated assumption, however, only part of it; if your main assumption is that Germany wants to conquer the world, you will also assume that NATO will be useless and unable to defend Europe from a reunified Germany. The passage says "Wealthy West Germany, like the rest of Western Europe and the U.S., must give aid to economically depressed Eastern

Europe," which does not suggest that a reunified Germany would be unstable or harmful to the economy of Europe, so (2) is wrong. Since Germany is capitalist and the Soviet Union is changing to capitalism, it is not a logical assumption that Germany will change to Communism and unite with the Soviet Union to re-ignite the Cold War; so (4) is wrong. There is nothing in the passage to suggest an assumption that Germany will ally itself with Japan, so (5) is incorrect.

2. **(4)** *Analysis/Interrelationships.* The passage states that the Soviet economy is already overburdened; this was one reason Gorbachev loosened his grip on the European satellites. The Soviet economy was not, and is not, strong enough to support these countries. The need for Western Europe and the U.S. to give aid to Eastern Europe might allow the former to control the latter, so (2) is possible. We are told that Communist leaders are still in the governments of Romania and Bulgaria, so (1) is also a possible result in some Eastern European countries. Economic instability can produce depressions; therefore (3) is plausible. Through aid from the West and natural ability and effort, a unified Eastern and Western Europe is a potential and likely outcome, too, so (5) is another "logical result of this instability."

3. **(3)** *Application /Interrelationships.* Hungarian Romanians are a subcul-

ture, sharing some of the larger Romanian society's culture but maintaining many aspects of their own Hungarian culture.

Lesson 2

1. **(3)** *Comprehension/Interrelationships.* The lesson mainly discusses the effect of wars in getting women out of the home and into the labor force, and how this had the unanticipated effect of activating the women's liberation movement. There are statements that indicate that well-organized movements were not as important as the unexpected effects of two world wars, so (1) is wrong. The passage states nothing like (2), and contradicts it by mentioning only changes to nontraditional roles in wars. We are told that most women returned to traditional roles after World War II, in which they would have no use for skills learned in the war, so (4) is not the main idea of the passage. (5) overstates the importance of the two books; they helped activate the women's liberation movement, but that does not mean the movement would not exist today if they had not been published.

2. **(2)** *Analysis/Interrelationships.* The table shows that jobs typically held by women (receptionists, secretaries, typists, cosmetologists— even bank tellers and food counter workers) pay less than those typically held by men (all those in industrial and construction occupations,

as well as accountants, bank officers, firefighters, and police officers). (1) is a restatement of information, not a conclusion. The table does not provide any information to support or contradict the opinions in (3) and (4), or the generalization in (5).

3. **(5)** *Analysis/Interrelationships.* The only logical conclusion is that women will have to hold more of the jobs currently held by men if they want to make more money. The other choices are not likely to happen and therefore are illogical. Employers are not likely to pay women salaries equal to men's regardless of the work the women do—(1)—nor are employers likely to achieve equality of pay by reducing men's salaries to the level of traditional female jobs such as receptionist or secretary—(2). Both actions would be illogical and ruin worker morale. As for (3), it is unlikely that male executives, for example, would be forced to take low-paying jobs just because there were more female executives, or that male welders would have to take pay cuts because there were more female welders. If female workers were hired, it is likely that the employer could afford to pay them as well as his male workers. The prices of goods and services go up from many causes; one cause may be higher salaries, but probably not just higher salaries for women.

Lesson 3

1. **(5)** *Analysis/Interrelationships.* It is illogical to produce an even greater need for food by having many more children when there is already a famine. (1) and (2) are extreme predictions for which there is no support in the passage. (1) is not a realistic probability. (2) makes no sense in relation to the question of how many children to have: an such a basis people would never decide to have any children at all. (3) is irrelevant; since the people being discussed are all victims of famine, none of them need food more than others. The government would not be likely to withhold food from the children for the reason given in (4) because these starving people could hardly be suspected of "taking advantage" of such a disastrous situation. The government, according to the passage, would fail them due to lack of supplies, transportation, or because of political conflicts.

2. **(3)** *Analysis/Interrelationships.* Promoting agriculture would enable people to fight insect infestations, provide irrigation systems, and make it possible for people to grow food to feed themselves in the long term. The other answers provide only short-term relief.

3. **(4)** *Analysis/Interrelationships.* The comedian makes his joke by pretending that the country

with the famine has always been a desert, instead of becoming a desert due to the drought; in this way, he can present the people searching for food comically, as foolish and nearly crazy. It is as if he said to victims of a flood, "Why did you put your neighborhood in the water in the first place?" Many people might find his joke in bad taste. Part of his humor is probably directed at the craziness of his own comment, and at the unreasonable, unsympathetic attitude it expresses. The other choices do not have this comic illogic. (1) and (5) are sensible proposals that are not comic. (2) and (3) are unrealistic comments that are not reflected in the idea of the joke.

Answer Key Practice Items

1. **(2)** *Analysis/American History.* The map shows that at the time of the Missouri Compromise, there was an equal number of free states and slave states. Slavery was a controversial issue at this time and threatened to split the country. By maintaining equal representation of both sides of the slavery controversy, the United States was able to delay legislation that a minority representation would fight.

2. **(4)** *Comprehension/ American History.* The first event mentioned in the passage which led to an organized effort to combat racial segregation was Rosa Park's action in 1955. (1), (3), and (5) list events that happened after 1955. The passage does not state when the Supreme Court made its ruling on segregated public schools—Choice (2).

3. **(4)** *Analysis/American History.* The passage implies that the signing of the Civil Rights Bill of 1964 was a result of the march on Washington, D.C. (3) and (5) describe events that helped make possible the march on Washington, D.C. (1) and (2) are conclusions that are not addressed in the passage.

4. **(5)** *Evaluation/American History.* The courts decided against the laws that had been established by the states on the grounds that these laws were unconstitutional. The states had, in effect, passed laws that denied rights that were given to all citizens by federal laws, thereby violating the Fourth Amendment. The Tenth Amendment, which is mentioned in (2), could have been used as support for a court decision that *upheld* the segregationist state laws.

5. **(4)** *Comprehension/ American History.* All the choices use information that is contained in the passage, but the others tell only a part of the story. The main point of the passage is that two national authoritarian leaders, who were corrupt, were forced from office in 1986.

6. **(4)** *Comprehension/ American History.* The illustration shows President Johnson feeding tax money into the Vietnam War, thus either depriving Great Society programs of funds or leaving them only what was left after the war effort was fully funded.

7. **(1)** *Evaluation/ American History.* Because President Johnson is shown in control of Vietnam, the Great Society, and tax dollars, the cartoon implies that he was not coerced into any decisions about how tax money should be spent, but instead freely chose to spend more money on Vietnam than on the Great Society. The representation of President Johnson as the head of all three sectors that are displayed in the cartoon supports (2). The caption provides support for (3). The fact that both vehicles have pulled up to the same gas pump supports (4). (5) is supported because the Vietnam tank is shown to be a much larger vehicle that the Great Society car; it would take much more tax money to fill up the tank than it would the car.

8. **(5)** *Analysis/American History.* The construction of the Panama Canal allowed the U.S. navy to easily shift its fleet from one ocean to another and therefore to meet any threat from either east or west. (2) and (4) are unlikely results because the map shows that the Panama Canal was situated in regions that were already well traveled by U.S. ships. Trade in South American countries (3) could take place without the canal; therefore, the construction of the Panama Canal would be unlikely to increase trade. (1) is also unlikely because in 1914, produce could be shipped across the country most cheaply by train; costs would be unaffected by changes in ocean routes.

9. **(3)** *Comprehension/ American History.* The passage states that the frontier line advanced westward quickly after 1800 and that in 1783, the frontier line "was still largely east of the Appalachian Mountains." Therefore, one can infer that few Americans moved west of the eastern seaboard before 1800 and that in 1800 most Americans could, in fact, be found living on the eastern seaboard.

10. **(4)** *Application/American History.* The passage states that the frontier had crossed the Mississippi by 1820. Kansas is located a little west of the Mississippi, right on the frontier line. (1) and (3) give locations that would be located east of the frontier in their times. In 1783, California was completely unsettled, so (2) does not name a frontier as defined by the passage. (5) is incorrect because there was no longer a definable frontier in 1890.

11. **(5)** *Evaluation/American History.* We are told that the steel plough, an agricultural tool, was one cause of the settlement of the plains, thereby pushing the frontier more quickly to the west. (1) states a confused version of the definition for "frontier," and is therefore unsupported. Likewise, the passage states the center of the continent was occupied 30 years after the settlement of Kentucky's "dark and bloody ground," but does not suggest the settlement caused the occupation, so (3) is not supported. Nothing supports (2) and (4) since other colonial nations and Native Americans are not mentioned.

12. **(3)** *Application/American History.* Only (3) describes an action that would extend the American territory toward the Pacific Ocean. Nothing suggests that the development of the new technology mentioned in (1) was motivated by the idea of manifest destiny. (2) is not an action motivated by manifest destiny but an effect of actions motivated by it which pushed the frontier further and further west. (4) was motivated by desire for wealth, not by manifest destiny. The annexation of Hawaii (5) is an expansion of U.S. territory beyond the Pacific coast and therefore could not properly be considered a part of manifest destiny.

13. **(3)** *Analysis/American History.* All the crimes that are listed in the alternatives, except for treason, are possible crimes with which Watergate participants might have been charged. Treason would involve the selling or the trading of state secrets to an enemy. The crimes that are mentioned in the passage are burglary, the use of secret funds, and wiretapping. (5) is a restatement of "use of secret funds." You can infer that the Watergate conspirators would be charged with (2), "breaking and entering," from the statements that they were arrested in the Democratic Party's headquarters and were trying to steal private papers there.

14. **(5)** *Evaluation/American History.* The Supreme Court decision showed that a president could not abuse the privileges of the office and get away with it. The president must still abide by the law—in this case, by yielding the tapes when ordered to. It did not, as in (1), find him guilty of any crime, nor did it, as in (3), suspend any of his rights as an American citizen. (2) is incorrect because American citizens are not required to prove their innocence; it is up to the state, or to a plaintiff, to prove their guilt. The president does have the right to take the Fifth Amendment, but it does not apply in this instance.

15. **(4)** *Comprehension/ American History.* The only crime of President Nixon that is mentioned in the passage is that of withholding the tapes. These tapes contained evidence that he was involved in covering up the Watergate crimes. His refusal to yield them was a knowing interference with the course of justice. However, nothing in the passage supports the statements that he (1) concealed stolen papers, or (2) was involved in the burglary, or (3) lied to federal investigators, or (5) used his secret tapes to implicate other officials in his administration in the Watergate scandal.

16. **(5)** *Analysis/American History.* To answer this question correctly, you need to distinguish facts from hypotheses. The table gives you no information other than the

number of person-days that workers spent on strike in the years listed. Prior knowledge may lead you to think up several hypotheses about possible causes for the different numbers of strike-days in the table, to explain why some years were so much higher than others. However, the table does not support any hypothesis. This means you can rule out choices (1) through (4). Only (5) is supported by the information on the table: it is a statement of fact.

17. **(4)** *Application/American History.* Being an Eastern European, the Russian is in a group of approximately 750,000 people who emigrated to the United States between 1951 and 1970. This group forms the smallest segment on the graph of any of the groups mentioned in the other choices. The next-largest group is the group of immigrants from the Americas between 1911 and 1930, a group of approximately 2,500,000.

18. **(4)** *Analysis/Geography.* Only the concentration of population in the low-lands is an *explanation* of its distribution. Each of the other statements is only a *description* of information provided.

19. **(2)** *Comprehension/Geography.* The need for caution is the central theme of the passage. (3) flatly contradicts it, while (4) and (5) are opinions that are never implied. (1) is an implication that the passage makes but not an adequate summary of the whole.

20. **(5)** *Comprehension/Geography.* The regions colored for "little or no vegetation" are the same regions that are shown as over 13,000 feet in altitude, the highest altitudes on the map. Regions with desert vegetation are at the lowest altitude shown and also have little vegetation, but the question asks about the "one area" with "the least amount of plant life of all," which is the area of highest altitude.

21. **(4)** *Comprehension/Geography.* You can see the largest network of rivers and the largest rainforest area is between 0 degrees (the equator) and 10 degrees below the equator. Almost all of this area is white on the altitude map, which indicates an altitude of 0 to 1,650. River basins are at low altitudes, and the lush vegetation of rainforests, the richest in all nature, need warm low altitudes.

22. **(2)** *Analysis/Geography.* A high population-growth rate is associated with a situation in which the birthrate is significantly higher than the death rate. This situation is found in Stage 2. Note that in Stage 1 both the birthrate and the death rate are high.

23. **(1)** *Application/Geography.* Strong health services imply a low death rate, while family planning implies a low birth rate. Both of these are characteristics of Stage 4. Every other alternative is characterized by either a high birth rate or high death rate, or by both.

24. **(4)** *Analysis/Geography.* The population will grow if the birth rate exceeds the death rate. You can see on the graph that the death rate never exceeds the birth rate; when the birth rate declines from year X + 200 onwards, the death rate also declines, so the population continues to grow. However, since the death rate on the graph remains at about the same distance below the birth rate, the birth rate does not exceed it at an increasing rate, and so population growth does not *increase*, as stated in (1). The other alternatives are not supported by the data in any way.

25. **(2)** *Comprehension/Geography.* The area that includes New England and the Northeast has 4 states which are in the most urbanized category. The areas mentioned in (1), (2), and (4) each have only one state in this category of 85-100 percent urbanization. The area in (5) has no state with this level of urbanization, though Illinois (83.0%) comes close.

26. **(3)** *Evaluation/Geography.* Only a ranking of states according to percentage of urbanization, or urban population is possible on the basis of the information in the map. The other choices would all require other numerical data as well.

27. **(3)** *Application/History.* This is an example of the government's stepping in to protect the interests of its citizens. (1) and (2) have to do with foreign policy and are not relevant. No monopoly is

discussed, so (4) is wrong. (5) is not correct because regulation refers to efforts by the government to control the activities of individuals or businesses. The FDIC was not an attempt to control depositors' activities but to protect them against financial loss from bank failures.

28. **(2)** *Analysis/Economics.* Of the choices given, the best way to effect an improvement is to import less. Raising tariffs would make foreign goods more expensive, which might reduce the demand for them. (1) would not reduce the trade deficit if the dollar's value kept the price of U.S. goods high and Americans kept buying imports at the same rate. Reducing inflation (5) would increase the value of the dollar (3), which probably would worsen the trade deficit. (4) also might worsen the trade deficit by spending money on military products instead of on commercial products which could be sold abroad to improve the balance of trade.

29. **(4)** *Analysis/Economics.* A strong French franc would enable French importers to buy more American goods, which would become lower priced as compared to French goods. An inflated French economy (3) would lower the value of the franc, while an inflated U.S. economy (3) would raise the costs of production. In both cases, American goods would be more expensive and less attractive to French buyers. United States import-

tariffs (2) would have no effect on French importers of American and other goods. While a depression (1) might affect the value of the dollar, the passage does not discuss its effect on exports.

30. **(5)** *Comprehension/Economics.* The passage states that private ownership and government ownership exist side by side. It does not, as in (4), give details as to the type of ownership allowed to each. Nothing in the passage suggests that government-owned industries are only service-providing and make no profits, or that there are no privately-owned industries that provide services. The postal service serves only as one example of government ownership, not as a model. (1) describes a pure, unmixed capitalist economy, and (2) a pure, unmixed communist economy. (3) uses the example of the U.S. system, which is only one kind of mixed economy.

31. **(2)** *Application/Economics.* According to the graph, the largest portion of the consumer's budget is spent on food. The farming of produce and livestock is administered by the Department of Agriculture.

32. **(2)** *Comprehension/Economics.* The sample family spends $1,200 a year on clothing, while the graph shows that the average family in their income group ($15,000 a year) spends only about $900. The family is therefore not average in terms of annual clothing expenditure. Therefore (5)

is wrong. There is no way of telling from the graph what is the annual household income of "an average family" from all the incomes from zero to 30,000, only what each household spends. So (1) and (3) are incorrect. A family whose income is $30,000 spends about $1,800 a year on clothing, clearly less than double the expenditure of the sample family. Therefore (4) is wrong.

33. **(4)** *Evaluation/Economics.* The line that shows the average relationship between income and clothing expenditure is straight, indicating a proportional rate that is the same (about 6 percent) regardless of income. The graph does not indicate the number of wage earners (2) or people (3) in a household, nor the amount that each can afford to spend (5). A family's annual expenditure cannot be predicted (1), because the graph shows that many—such as the sample family—are outside the average.

34. **(3)** *Application/Economics.* (1) and (2) are examples of tax incentives. (4), although a kind of subsidy, aids the welfare recipients rather than the company. (5) is neither subsidy nor tax incentive.

35. **(3)** *Analysis/Economics.* Federal loan insurance means that the government would not have to provide the loan, but merely guarantee it (paying only in the rare case where the borrower defaults). Therefore, it would be far less expensive than a subsidy, which requires cash, or a

tax incentive, which deprives the government of income. While (4) may be true, it is not an advantage. None of the other choices are implied by the passage.

36. (3) *Comprehension/Economics.* The passage states that owners of proprietorships and partnerships have unlimited liability, while corporate stockholders have limited liability; they all have some sort of liability. Only the owner of a partnership can be a partner, so (4) is wrong, and a partner must share control with the other partner, so (5) is wrong.

37. (1) *Application/Economics.* The six people share both ownership and labor in their business and therefore satisfy the requirements of a partnership. (2) and (3) are examples of proprietorships, while (5) is a corporation that is run by directors. (4) is not an example of business ownership because the farmer is a tenant.

38. (4) *Analysis/Economics.* The passage states that the liability of a corporate stockholder is limited to the amount that a person invested in the corporation. Therefore, no matter how the company fares, a person's personal assets cannot be claimed by creditors, unlike those of owners of proprietorships and partnerships. Nothing supports (1) or (2). (3) is stated as an advantage of partnerships over proprietorships, not of corporations.

39. (2) *Evaluation/Economics.* The need to accommodate the wishes of several owners, as in a partnership or a corporation, often results in management policies that are based on a compromise of ideas. These policies may be weaker than those that are composed by single individuals, which reveals an advantage of a proprietorship. (1) is untrue because unlimited liability can greatly affect a person's life if he or she is called upon to pay all business debts from personal assets such as the car or the house. (3) and (4) imply that there is no money to be made or risks to be taken in partnerships or corporations, which is untrue. (5) is a statement of opinion, not an argument that is based on the passage.

40. (5) *Evaluation/Economics.* As each share gives a stockholder one vote in the corporation's affairs, it follows that many shares give the stockholder a greater influence. (1) and (2) are in no way implied by the passage, while (4) is true of a stockholder in a corporation, not of a partner; a partner has unlimited liability, regardless of the amount of money he or she invests. (3) may or may not be true, but it is not discussed in the passage.

41. (4) *Application/Political Science.* Though the case involves local taxes and local residents, the law contested is a state law. The case is therefore tried in a State Superior Court.

42. (2) *Application/Political Science.* The original case, being a violation of the state drinking laws, would have been tried in a State Superior Court. As the owner wishes to see the ruling overturned, it is appealed in the next highest court—the State Court of Appeals.

43. (3) *Application/Political Science.* Civil rights are administered and protected by the U.S. Constitution at the federal level, and infringements of them are therefore tried in a Federal District Court.

44. (1) *Application/Political Science.* If the reporter believes that her right of free speech has been violated, it is a federal charge and will therefore be tried in a Federal District Court. Appeals will go to the next-highest court, being a Federal Court of Appeals. If the case continues to be contested, the highest court to which is can be brought—and the highest in the country—is the Federal Supreme Court.

45. (3) *Application/Political Science.* Although the accident occurred in Indiana, where the plaintiff lives, the driver of the other car is an Illinois resident. Therefore, the case would be settled in Federal District Court, which handles interstate matters.

46. (1) *Evaluation/Political Science.* Because the United States is now protected by a huge, well-armed military establishment, it is true that armed civilians are no longer necessary for the

country's safety as they may have been during the Revolutionary War.

47. **(3)** *Comprehension/Political Science.* The poll tax, which was not abolished until 1969, required citizens to pay before they could vote. The law therefore discriminated against poorer citizens for whom this tax was more burdensome than for the rich. All the other choices were qualifications for voting that had been abolished prior to 1950.

48. **(4)** *Evaluation/Political Science.* Because there are fewer qualifications for the right to vote than ever before, the proportion of voting to nonvoting citizens is greater than ever. (2) cannot be determined from the time line, while (3) is untrue because a major group of citizens—all those under 18—do not have the right to vote. While (1) may be true, the time line makes no reference to the growing population. (5) cannot be determined from the time line, because it does not indicate which changes in voting rights were by constitutional amendment and which had other causes.

49. **(4)** *Application/Political Science.* OSHA, the Occupational Safety Hazards Administration oversees safety in the workplace. (1) is the Equal Employment Opportunity Commission, which protects workers from discrimination. (2) is the Environmental Protection Agency, which regulates pollution. (3) is the Food and Drug Administration, which tests the safety of products. (5) is the Federal Trade Commission, which regulates business practices.

50. **(2)** *Analysis/Political Science.* The passage describes the various functions of international organizations—judiciary, military, economic, and cultural. Though each of the other alternatives is true, they are statements of fact that support the conclusion. Only (2) summarizes the entire passage.

51. **(2)** *Comprehension/Political Science.* The illustration shows a law-abiding citizen who is willfully and happily breaking the law, as if he had no respect for it. He is compared to someone knocking apart a protective sea-wall. The result of this disrespect would bring a "flood" of lawless anarchy behind it. There is no implication, as in (1) and (4), that the law will be difficult to enforce. (3) is incorrect because the law made the sale of liquor illegal. (5) is incorrect because the illustration shows the citizen breaking the law, not voting against it.

52. **(4)** *Analysis/Political Science.* Big cities, industrial workers, and minorities all benefit from federally funded work programs. If the Democratic Party were to remove these, it might expect to lose a good deal of its support from these groups. (3) and (5) would be beneficial to these groups and would most likely increase their support for the Party. There is no

mention of the defense industry or farmers in the passage and, therefore, no implication that (1) and (2) would be opposed by Democratic supporters.

53. **(3)** *Application/Behavioral Science.* (3) is not an example of reinforcement because the teacher is not seeking to alter the students' behavior, but instead is altering his or her own behavior to adapt to that of the students. The teacher's behavior is not a strategy to change the students' behavior. (1) and (5) are examples of positive reinforcement, while (2) and (4) are examples of negative reinforcement.

54. **(3)** *Application/Behavioral Science.* The colonizing group is forcing the other group to do work; therefore, this is an example of coercion.

55. **(5)** *Application/Behavioral Science.* The teams are competing against each other under a set of mutually acceptable rules.

56. **(2)** *Application/Behavioral Science.* Both individuals want the same piece of land, and they are struggling against each other in order to achieve their ends.

57. **(4)** *Application/Behavioral Science.* In exchange for lending the lawn mower, the owner requires the neighbor to provide some service in return.

58. **(5)** *Application/Behavioral Science.* The new supermarket may or may not be interested in driving the other supermar-

ket out, but, in either event, they are both striving toward the same goal—winning new customers—under the same law of economic competition.

59. **(3)** *Application/Behavioral Science.* Since a defense mechanism is a way to avoid anxiety, it usually entails keeping the truth from yourself, or at least distorting it. In (1), there is no need to get upset because you know the person is not really getting hurt. There is no defense mechanism at work here. Defense mechanisms are not operating in (2) either. It is a healthy response to admit that something is wrong and reach out for help. In (4), while this is certainly not a healthy thing to do, there is no denial or distortion of truth. The person merely smoked too much in response to stress. (5) is the case of someone who is fanatical about looking good. While he or she may work out more than is necessary, the person is consciously choosing to remain in good shape. The person in (3) is using a defense mechanism. Denial of a problem is a classic example of a defense mechanism; the person is avoiding the truth because facing it causes tremendous anxiety.

60. **(4)** *Analysis/Behavioral Science.* To find the correct answer you have to make an inference since the cause of Jenny's changes in behavior is not stated directly. (2) and (5) can be eliminated because no statements support these inferences

at all. (1) is wrong because her smoking and drinking are two changes in her behavior, not *causes* of changes in her behavior: they are effects, not causes. Regular and excessive drinking could change behavior but Jenny only drinks occasionally. (3) incorrectly infers that her stubborn and withdrawn behavior—only two of the changes in her behavior—has been characteristic of Jenny all along and have only gotten worse lately. On the contrary, all the details in the first paragraph suggest she was happy and in harmony with her family until recently. In contrast, all Jenny's new behavior suggests that she is separating from her family and its values and allying herself with the values of "the same group of teenagers."

61. **(4)** *Analysis/Behavioral Science.* To answer this question, you had to first understand the main idea of the chart. It seems that these girls were heavily influenced by peer pressure in Part One of the experiment; they played with the more "female" toys exclusively—the kitchen set, the baby doll, and the vacuum cleaner. These toys conform to the traditional roles of women in our society. The more "masculine" toys—the airplane, the dinosaur, and the baseball equipment—were not used at all by the girls when their peers were present. When they were alone, however, one the of "male" toys—the airplane—was played with

longer than any of the other toys. So which choice in the question supports the conclusion that peer pressure affected play behavior? (4): the girls played with the masculine toys only when they were alone, not when other girls were present. The other choices do not support the conclusion, and are not supported by the graph.

62. **(1)** *Comprehension/Behavioral Science.* The passage states that education is considered to be a sexually neutral field and that such articles, when written anonymously, were taken by most subjects to be written by a man. (2) might be true only after the subjects had decided that the article was written by a man. No statement supports (3), (4), and (5).

63. **(3)** *Analysis/Behavioral Science.* The passage specifically states that the role of men and, therefore, their behavior is thought to have more value in society than that of women. (1) and (2) are examples of the basic prejudice stated in (3). (5) is also a detail, and one that does not explain the findings. (4) also does not explain the findings; it claims that the basic prejudice revealed in the study has been greatly reduced—the opposite conclusion of the study.

64. **(2)** *Evaluation/Behavioral Science.* Only the statement in (2) is directly supported by the study. The study did not test the factors that are mentioned in (1) and (3). There is no discussion of

the writing styles of men and women. (1) seems to be clearly suggested by the passage, but not nearly so definitely as (2): women writers might find it *easier* to get published, for instance, if they wrote on so-called feminine topics and these topics were featured in many publications or became widely popular for all readers (e.g., the topic of male-female relationships). The statement in (4) and (5) are opinions that go far beyond any evidence presented in the study.

Answer Key Practice Test

1. **(4)** *Evaluation/Behavioral Science.* The chart shows that younger children tend to worry more than older children do about such problems as hunger and poverty, violence in the United States, and nuclear destruction, which are all general social problems. The chart also shows that 60% of ninth graders worry about school performance, and that 57% of them worry about their looks, which eliminates (1) and (5). There is no indication that children worry less as they mature (2). (3) is wrong because the chart shows that younger children worry *more* than older children about "My looks" and "How well other kids like me," and "How my friends treat me."

2. **(4)** *Analysis/Behavioral Science.* The two categories on the chart where the levels of concern for younger and older children are most nearly the same are "How well other kids like me" and "How my friends treat me." (1) refers to the two categories about parents who drink and parents who abuse their children, where younger children are more than twice as concerned about their parents divorcing (30%) than 9th graders are (13%); so (2) is wrong. (3) refers to the category "Physical Development," where 5th graders are almost twice as worried (31%) as 9th graders (17%). They are also almost twice as worried about suicide (5).

3. **(2)** *Evaluation/History.* California and Texas entered the Union during the nineteenth century, while Arizona and New Mexico were not admitted until the twentieth. The other choices are hypotheses that cannot be determined by the information provided on the map.

4. **(1)** *Comprehension/ Economics.* The passage states that failure to repay one's loan will result in losing one's insurance. Because the borrower loses the policy in place of the money that has been borrowed against it, the cash amount of the loan will not be forfeited, so (2) and (4) are incorrect. The passage makes no statement about a default being the cause of a change in interest rates. In fact, defaulting on a loan does not have any effect on its interest rate, so (3) and (5) are wrong.

5. **(4)** *Application/Political Science.* Only (4) satisfies all the requirements based on the chart.

6. **(2)** *Analysis/Political Science.* The passage points out many similarities between the situation in South Carolina and that in Lithuania. The key difference, however, is that Lithuania was absorbed into the Soviet Union through an act of aggression. In declaring independence, Lithuanians are basically rebelling against their absorption into the Soviet Union—50 years late. (1) is not correct because war is not a required condition for secession. (3) is incorrect because while secession is a democratic concept, any country— fascist, Communist, or democratic—can attempt to secede. There is no basis for choosing (4); we don't know if Lithuania can survive or not, but this has no bearing on whether its declaration of independence amounts to secession. (5) is incorrect because forming a new federation is not a prerequisite for secession.

7. **(1)** *Evaluation/Political Science.* Growth in population along the Pacific coast will necessarily increase Congressional representation in Pacific coast states such as Oregon and Washington—but not in Eastern Seaboard Southern states such as Florida and Georgia (2). We are not told the whole national population is predicted to grow 10% over the next 50 years, so overall Congressional representation will not increase 10% over the next 50 years (5). Because Senate representation is limited to two senators per state, the Senate will not change (3). No information given supports the prediction in (4).

8. **(1)** *Comprehension/Behavioral Science.* The factors discussed in the first paragraph, plus the discussion of Type A and Type B persons, support this statement (it is really a topic sentence stating the main idea of the passage). Each of the other choices specifically contradicts statements made in the passage.

9. **(4)** *Application/Behavioral Science.* Type A persons enjoy high-pressure situations; they experience the most stress in situations, such as a traffic jam, that are beyond their control.

10. **(4)** *Application/Behavioral Science.* Smoking, lack of exercise, and stress are all factors that contribute to the chances of a heart attack. Only (4) is the type of person who is free of all these factors.

11. **(2)** *Evaluation/Behavioral Science.* The passage makes no reference to the relationship of personality type to smoking. It mentions exercise as only one factor, not the best, in preventing heart attacks. It does claim our ability to identify potential victims. Therefore, only (2) can be correct.

12. **(5)** *Analysis/Behavioral Sciences.* Throughout the passage, the effects of two different life-styles, or general patterns of behavior, on the risk of heart-attack are discussed. All the information given supports (5) as the main conclusion of the passage. All this information contradicts (1). Though the passage mentions smoking as a contributing factor, and says

personality traits "play a part," it does not say smokers are "always" more likely to have heart attacks (2), or that personality traits are "the primary factor" (3). We are told Type B persons seem to suffer less stress from everyday problems, not that they have fewer such problems (4).

13. **(4)** *Application/Geography.* If latitude indicates distances north of the equator, the only way to determine the answer is to compare one latitude to the other.

14. **(2)** *Evaluation/Political Science.* The central theme of the Fourteenth Amendment is the inability of a state to infringe upon the Constitutional rights of its citizens. Of the five choices, that of desegregation refers to a civil-rights inequality that a state is ordered to correct. (1), (3) and (5) all concern legal actions that do not violate the Constitutional rights of individual citizens (they concern, respectively, impeachment of a governor, gambling and sales taxes). (4) is wrong because the 14th amendment applies only to people already citizens.

15. **(3)** *Analysis/Political Science.* The most immediate effect of the Fourteenth Amendment would be to establish federal laws concerning citizens' rights as the most important legal authority in the United States. The amendment does not imply that federal authorization was needed by a state to pass a law (4), merely that no state laws

could contradict federal laws. Note that slavery was abolished by the Thirteenth Amendment in 1865. Therefore (2) is wrong. There is no basis for (1) and (5).

16. **(1)** *Analysis/History.* The passage states that ministers led the colonies, implying a strong connection between church and state. (2), (3), and (4) are untrue; no mention is made of what the ministry was like before Harvard was built, and no discussion is given about college education in general. While (5) is true, it is nowhere suggested or stated in the passage.

17. **(1)** *Application/Behavioral Science.* If she applied for the job, she must have wanted it. Therefore, she is giving a false explanation to hide her embarrassment.

18. **(2)** *Application/Behavioral Science.* The person is denying the existence of his illness.

19. **(4)** *Application/Behavioral Science.* Displaying behavior that is the opposite of repressed unconscious feelings is reaction formation.

20. **(3)** *Application/Behavioral Science.* The person is projecting his hatred of others onto their personalities.

21. **(5)** *Evaluation/American History.* 1970-1980 does in fact show the greatest increase in the debt, but there is no information on the graph to support the explanation of this increase as due to control of the Presidency by the Democratic Party. The

rate of increase in the debt sharply decreased in 1950–1960, but the *debt* itself did not decrease, so (4) is wrong. (5) is an inaccurate statement, anyway, because the Democrats held the Presidency (under Carter) only from 1976-1980. All the other choices are factual restatements of increases in the debt which are shown on the graph in each of the periods mentioned.

22. **(1)** *Analysis/American History.* This is the only restatement of a fact shown on the graph; the graph line does not change from 1870-1900, which means there was no debt increase. All the other choices are opinions or hypotheses which the information on the graph does not support. The choices explain the various increases in the debt by citing spending for wars and welfare for the different periods, when the graph gives no direct information about either wartime or welfare spending. (2) states a cause-and-effect relationship the graph does not support—that Depression relief spending "led to" wartime spending; in fact, the war itself undoubtedly caused wartime spending. (3) and (4) blame the 1960s and 1970s debt increase on welfare spending but do not mention spending on the Vietnam War in these two periods. In the same way, (5) omits mention of Eisenhower's policy of reducing the government's role in business, which was another cause of the slowing down of the debt.

23. **(4)** *Analysis/Political Science.* Sweden, the U.S. and Japan have the three highest per capita incomes of all the countries on the graph and also the three highest life expectancies. In contrast, the poorest countries shown (Zaire, Bolivia, Vietnam, China) have—with the exception of China—the lowest life expectancies. Therefore (5) is wrong. If you compare the infant mortality rates for these three rich countries with the rates for the two poorest countries shown, Zaire and Bolivia, it is clear that (1) and (3) are false. No information is provided about the rate of population growth, so (2) is also incorrect.

24. **(4)** *Evaluation/Political Science.* As a generalization, this hypothesis is supported by the fact that, except for China, the poorest countries (Zaire, Bolivia, and Vietnam) all have the worst health conditions, as indicated by both low life expectancy and high infant mortality rates. In contrast, the wealthiest countries (the U.S., Sweden, Japan and East Germany) probably have the best health conditions, as indicated by both high life expectancy and low infant mortality rates. Taiwan is the exception to this generalization. With a relatively low per capita income, it has as low an infant mortality rate as the very wealthy U.S. and quite wealthy E. Germany. Therefore, despite the exceptions of China and Taiwan, (4) has the strongest support among the hypotheses given. (2) and (3) are wrong because

the table gives no information about birth rates. (1) may be partly correct, but there could be other reasons such as a lack of statistical knowledge on the subject in China and Vietnam. The table therefore provides no information to support this hypothesis, or the hypothesis in (5).

25. **(1)** *Evaluation/Geography.* The passage gives an example of direct pollution of water (factories pouring wastes into rivers and lakes) and another of indirect pollution (fertilizers and pesticides being washed from soils). Therefore, (1) is the correct answer. None of the other choices are supported by the passage.

26. **(5)** *Analysis/History.* The passage states that the Haymarket Massacre had its beginnings in a protest by labor unionists, anarchists and others. (1) and (2) are not suggested by the passage. (3) was the opinion of the judge; it is not a fact. The first sentence of the last paragraph directly contradicts (4).

27. **(4)** *Evaluation/History.* The passage states that the Knights, a reform-unionist organization, gave way to the A.F. of L., a trade-unionist organization. It also says that trade unionists, in contrast to reform unionist, favored strikes and a focus on working conditions. Therefore, (4) is the most likely result.

28. **(1)** *Evaluation/American History.* This answer probably can be found by eliminating the other choices. (2) has no support because, although

we are told that after the bombing public anger turned from the anarchists to the Knights of Labor, we are not told that the public was also angry at other labor groups or workers in general. (3) is wrong because nothing suggests that "most" of the Knights of Labor leaders were "often" associated with anarchists. Also, nothing suggests that the other half of the labor movement, the trade unionists, had anything to do with anarchists. Since they accepted the factory system, they undoubtedly were opposed to the anarchists, as well as to the philosophy of the Knights of Labor. For this reason, the A.F. of L. might have gained later members from the Knights of Labor, after the Haymarket bombing discredited the Knights, but not early members. Therefore (4) cannot be true. It may be true that police violence against union activists was common in the 19th century, but nothing in the passage suggests it. So (5) is wrong. Only (1) is supported by the passage: the first and last paragraphs describe the opposing views of methods and goals in the two main labor groups.

29. **(5)** *Comprehension/ Political Science.* United Press International, the only news source identified as international, is ranked third out of the total of ten news sources, which does not suggest that the newspeople polled thought that international news sources are unreliable. If you know that Associated Press is also an international news service, this will further support (5), because AP is ranked second. The opinions in all the other choices are supported by the information on the table.

30. **(4)** *Comprehension/ Economics.* In every other country, the industrial sector is smaller than either the agricultural or the service sectors, or both.

31. **(4)** *Analysis/Economics.* A smaller number of farmers who produce the same amount of crops suggests that one farmer is doing the work of many. Therefore, farming in the United States must have increased in efficiency. The other choices, although they may be true, in no way explain the ability of few people to grow large amounts of food.

32. **(3)** *Application/History* The Monroe Doctrine specifically stated that the United States would not interfere in European affairs. Entrance in World War I violated this principle. The other choices are all examples either of neutrality or of defense of the Western Hemisphere.

33. **(5)** *Comprehension/ History.* (2), (3), and (4) are all either untrue or not mentioned in the passage. While (1) is a valid statement, it does not adequately define the overall change in the nation.

34. **(2)** *Evaluation/History.* The passage does not imply that food shortages (4) were a problem or that the Revolutionary War was the only cause of

isolationism (5). (1) is untrue because the United States fought naval wars in Cuba, Guam, and so on. United States belligerence (3) was directed at Spain, not Europe.

35. **(1)** *Analysis/History.* In order to maintain needed trade without being able to dock at foreign ports, United States merchants must have relied on the ships of foreign merchants. This question asks you to judge the most probable cause-and-effect relationship between the Embargo Act (cause) and one of the events listed (effects). It is not likely that the U.S. could do without overseas trade altogether (5), or that the embargo would cause foreigners to attack U.S. ships (4). Slave trade most likely would not have ceased (3), because it was too profitable, and too important to the South's economy. Though some sailors may have learned to evade the act, nothing suggests that "most" of them would react this way, so (2) is not the most likely effect, either.

36. **(4)** *Analysis/Political Science.* (1) is wrong because the many steps of the procedure do not suggest that speed and efficiency is the primary goal in passing important legislation. (2) is incorrect because checks and balances were not designed to safeguard against control by one political party, but rather, against control by one branch of the federal government. (3) has no support because the procedure does not

guarantee that any particular candidates will be elected to take part in it, whether as senators, representatives or as the president. The procedure clearly is set up to give opportunities for members of both houses of Congress to consider a bill, debate their differences, revise the bill and vote on it. Nothing is set up in the procedure to allow legislators to reconsider a bill they already have passed. So (5) is wrong.

37. **(2)** *Comprehension/ Political Science.* **The** only information that is contained in the illustration is found in (2). (3), (4), and (5) are contradicted by information in the illustration. Although Congress can override a president's veto, it by no means has to; so (1) is incorrect because the President may successfully veto a bill.

38. **(3)** *Analysis/Political Science.* (3) is the only statement that is accurate and embodies a fundamental principle of democracy (government of, by, and for the people). (1), (2) and (5) are all details of the procedure, not statements of basic democratic principles. (4) is also a detail as well as an inaccurate statement. Since Congresses controls almost all of the process, and can even override the Presidential veto, the procedure does not give the president equal say with Congress. In practice, however, a powerful and popular president might have even *more* than equal say: he could pressure Congress by

appealing to the voters or by refusing to help senators or congressmen get political favors or get reelected.

39. **(3)** *Evaluation/Economics.* (1) is an opinion with no support. (5) is a statement of fact, but it states information beyond the limits of the passage, which does not support it, therefore. (2) and (4), though they might be argued as true, are not conclusions that are supported by this passage. (3) is the only conclusion that is supported by the passage. You can infer this because you are told first that the economy was thriving, and then that the people of the U.S. wanted the government to regulate commerce. Of the two laws mentioned, one restricted and the other destroyed a business activity that had developed under unlimited competition.

40. **(2)** *Application/Behavioral Science.* **Although** (2) describes a situation in which a common language is spoken, no common culture is suggested to exist in a confederation of different nations. (3) describes a situation in which several languages are shared by the nation, which is still defined as a society because of its native language and common culture as a nation. (1), (4) and (5) all describe societies.

41. **(5)** *Evaluation/History.* **The** table shows that, in some cases, more people have immigrated from small countries (such as the Philippines) than from large ones (such as India). (4) is not correct

because the table shows that nearly all Koreans and Indochinese immigrated after 1950. The other choices are incorrect because the table does not give any information about why or when specific immigration took place.

42. **(1)** *Analysis/History.* **The** table states that most Korean and Indochinese immigration occurred after 1950, the period of time coinciding with the Korean and the Vietnam wars.

43. **(3)** *Comprehension/ Political Science.* **As the** cabinet is not an official body, it can make no decisions or decrees by itself that are constitutionally binding. It can only act in an advisory or an unofficial capacity, as is stated in (3). The other choices have no support. The Cabinet does offer the President advice, but nothing supports the idea that he is compelled to follow this advice; so (4) is wrong.

44. **(4)** *Application/Political Science.* **The** secretary of the treasury is not authorized to devalue the dollar; only the president may take such an executive action. All the other choices are actions appropriate to the Cabinet's function of offering the president "advice and opinions on how best to run the government."

45. **(4)** *Application/Geography.* **A** climatic map includes such conditions as rainfall averages, which are important factors in the determination of types of agricultural crops.

46. **(1)** *Application/Geography.* The Continental Divide is a physical feature in the Rocky Mountains. A topographical map would show this feature.

47. **(2)** *Application/Geography.* A contour map gives specific information about elevation. It would detail the slopes and the valley of a given terrain, thus allowing one to determine a flood pattern.

48. **(5)** *Application/Geography.* Potential investors would be interested in the location of natural resources on which to build an industry. A geological map is one source of such information.

49. **(3)** *Application/Geography.* The border between the United States and Canada would be shown on a political map.

50. **(3)** *Application/Behavioral Science.* A self-made, self-educated millionaire would exemplify status inconsistency because the person has a high income status but a low education (and possible family-background) status. The restaurant worker who has a modest income is an example of status consistency (occupation/income), as is the lawyer whose parents are doctors (occupation/family background). Neither a woman truck driver nor a working retiree involve any inconsistency in status, although they may not reflect the traditional notion of roles assigned to them by society.

51. **(3)** *Comprehension/History* The fact that congressional authority was wielded against the tribes indicates that they posed a threat. (1) and (5) are therefore untrue, while (2) and (4) are specifically negated by the passage.

52. **(4)** *Analysis/History.* The acquisition of citizenship entails the acquisition of the right to vote, thus enabling citizens to gain power in their government. The passage contradicts (1) and (3). It is not probable that all Native American lands would be returned, so (2) is wrong. Nothing suggests (5).

53. **(5)** *Application/Behavioral Science.* An unemployed couple who have children is categorized in the table as a no-wage-earner nuclear family, the smallest type of household (1%).

54. **(5)** *Comprehension/Behavioral Science.* The table shows that no type of household is dominant in United States society. (The largest type of household, child-free or post-child-rearing marriages, accounts for only 23%.) (1) is therefore incorrect. The phrase "nonfamily structure" in (2) refers to the category of "other single, separated, divorced, or widowed," which is only 21%; all the family categories far outnumber it. Therefore (3) and (4) are also wrong.

55. **(1)** *Analysis/Behavioral Science.* Single-parent families would probably *increase* in percentage as a result of more divorces. Cohabited households (3)—where couples live together without marrying—would not be affected. Since we do not know whether the people divorcing have children or not, there is no reason to predict an increase in child-free marriages because of increased divorces (2). It is illogical to think that more divorces would increase the number of dual-breadwinner nuclear families (4). More divorces would have no necessary effect on the employment or unemployment of members of the nuclear family, so (5) is wrong.

56. **(1)** *Analysis/Geography.* Only region A has the very high temperatures that would make it a desert. Note that while region C also has very little rainfall, which might suggest a desert, it has extremely cold temperatures throughout the year.

57. **(3)** *Analysis/Geography.* Region C is peculiar because it is colder during the summer months and hotter during the winter months, a phenomenon found only in the southern hemisphere. Since its temperatures go as low as 40 degrees below zero and never go higher than about 20 degrees above zero, region C must be in or near one of the polar regions. Being southern, it must therefore be in, or very near to, Antarctica, the region of the South Pole.

58. **(2)** *Evaluation/History.* The passage states that skilled workers going on strike were believed to have more power than unskilled workers in dealing with employers. The fact that skilled workers were more difficult to

replace would give them this power. There is no logical reason to believe the other choices.

59. **(1)** *Application/Economics.* Tariffs are the main type of indirect influence by the government on the economy that is discussed in the passage. A tax on imported goods such as electronic parts is a tariff. (2), (4) and (5) are all mentioned as examples of direct governmental influence on the economy. Government operation of a nuclear power plant (3) would be an example of the takeover and "direct production and distribution" of certain economic elements, which is cited as direct influence.

60. **(3)** *Analysis/Economics.* The writer argues that tariffs will not benefit special interests who favor them because consumers will buy on the black market rather than pay high prices, and even if there is no black market they will reject the poor quality goods protected by tariffs. (1) and (4) are therefore wrong. The writer tells us that the real value of products is judged by consumers even when there are no black markets selling cheap foreign goods, so (2) and (5) are also incorrect.

61. **(4)** *Evaluation/Economics.* The basis of the writer's argument against tariffs is that they fail completely because they interfere with "the natural laws of the marketplace." By these laws, consumers will reject over-priced and poor-quality goods that are

protected by tariffs. The writer says nothing about getting laws passed to protect consumers (1) or to control special interests (3). He does not recommend consumer activism (2). All these choices recommend actions that would interfere with the operation of the free enterprise market laws which he considers "natural." He believes consumers will turn to black markets if tariffs make quality goods too expensive, but he does not go so far as to say that black market trade "must" be turned to (5). Besides, (5) is included in the larger belief of (4).

62. **(3)** *Evaluation/Economics.* The writer is most concerned with the impending "doom" of American workers (2) and American small businessmen (4). He also expresses concern for foreign labor exploited by American-owned companies (1) and condemns the "dictators and other governments that outlaw labor unions" in these Third World countries (5). Since he sees these companies, owned often by American corporations, as the cause of all these economic consequences he dislikes, he expresses no concern for the profits of American corporations.

63. **(3)** *Comprehension/Economics.* You can infer this meaning because "sweat shop" is used as an adjective for "wages." It is used right after a reference to "cheap foreign labor." The focus therefore is on wages, rather than long work-

hours (2). Nothing is said about the climate (1), the size of the Third World industries (4) or overcrowding in these workplaces (5).

64. **(3)** *Comprehension/History.* The passage implies that the growth of cities and factory work was a new development of the Industrial Revolution. Therefore you can infer that previous to this development most work was done in nonfactory settings, in small workshops or at home. (1), (2), (4) and (5) refer to the period after the Industrial Revolution. (2) and (4) are also contradicted by the passage.

Answer Key Simulated Test

1. **(4)** *Analysis/Political Science.* The people in the cartoon are shown pulling the giant cannon by means of ropes. (4) is the only choice that accurately describes this action in the cartoon. Therefore it is the only one that states the comparison on which the cartoon is based: human beings are like slaves to the weapons of war they have made. None of the other choices accurately describes the action and therefore none suggests a correct comparison. We do not see the people losing (1) or building (3) a weapon. Since the people are tied to the cannon with ropes, they are not escaping, as stated in (2) and (5).

2. **(3)** *Comprehension/ Economics.* The passage states that the main reason that mass-produced goods have almost entirely replaced handmade goods is that they are cheaper to make and less expensive to purchase. It also says that mass-produced goods have the great advantage of making products affordable for consumers who otherwise could not buy them. From this you can infer (3). Though choice (1) may be true, it is nowhere suggested in the passage. (2), (4) and (5) are also alternatives that are not suggested in the passage.

3. **(4)** *Comprehension/ Economics.* The graph of New York City expenses shows that at 22 percent education is the city's second largest expense, after human resources (23%). School maintenance and teachers' salaries would be paid from money allocated to education.

4. **(2)** *Analysis/Economics.* The largest part of the graph showing the groups or agencies that pay for New York City's expenses is "Other taxes and local revenue"—which would include all taxes *except* property taxes, which are shown as 23%. Those in (4) and (5) would pay these property taxes. The choice that lists a group that would pay "other taxes" is (2) New York state residents and consumers. They would pay income taxes and other taxes such as sales taxes. Though New York City real estate taxes (4) would be high because of the high value of the real estate, these taxes could not total as much as all the income taxes and sales taxes paid by consumers in the state. The other choices list (1) federal aid (11%), and (3) state aid (22%).

5. **(3)** *Evaluation/Economics.* The graph shows that New York City must receive aid from the state and federal government in order to pay its expenses. (4) and (5) are incorrect because they are based on opinion rather than on evidence provided in the graph. (2) is incorrect because the graph does not show what other cities contribute to their own budget. (1) is not supported by any evidence in the graph.

6. **(2)** *Analysis/Economics.* The author's statements about the increased upward mobility are positive, not negative, so (4) is wrong. He says that because of this mobility, people's opportunities are not "limited to factory work," and they can get jobs with higher pay, more satisfaction, and better use of their abilities. These benefits we must infer he approves of, since they are obviously positive and he does not criticize them. Since he calls education the "crucial" factor in gaining these benefits, we must therefore infer that he would favor increasing budgets of public colleges (2). Nothing suggests he wants to educate people to go back to factory work (1), or to lower requirements for the newly

available service jobs (3). He mentions but does not discuss race and sex; however, as factors they would largely be barriers to upward mobility, for instance, as biased reasons not to hire women and members of certain ethnic groups. "Using race and sex for advancement" therefore does not make sense in this context.

7. **(3)** *Analysis/Economics.* Because lack of education may be a factor limiting upward job mobility, providing grants to minority scholarship funds would likely help increase mobility. If education is the most important factor helping a person advance, (1) is obviously opposed to this advance. (2) and (4) might help or hinder poor and uneducated people, but neither clearly would affect their upward mobility one way or another. (5) is irrelevant to upward mobility altogether.

8. **(4)** *Application/Behavioral Science.* The passage states that neurotic symptoms are unintentional behaviors that express unconscious troubles. A person who is dieting to lose weight is engaging in deliberate, intended behavior to resolve a problem that he or she is very much aware of. In contrast, the other choices involve behaviors that are not deliberate and that might well express troubles that the individual is not aware of.

9. **(3)** *Analysis/Behavioral Science.* The passage specifically discusses *physical* manifestations of the unconscious mind. Of all the choices, only dreaming is not a physical expression but a mental expression of unconscious stress.

10. **(4)** *Evaluation/Behavioral Science.* The entire passage is devoted to showing how different symptoms are associated with different kinds of neuroses. Therefore, a person's neurosis can, at least in some cases, be diagnosed by examining symptoms. Though (2) and (5) may well be true, they are not discussed in the passage. (3) is incorrect because, although asthma may be a neurotic symptom, it is by no means necessarily neurotic and the passage does not say it is. (1) is contradicted by the passage, which states that early studies of neurosis were made before the beginning of this century.

11. **(1)** *Evaluation/Geography.* The passage states that Third-World nations cannot afford the modern agricultural technology that would help make their soil more fertile and increase the amount of food grown. Thus, low-interest loans earmarked for agricultural technology might contribute to a long-term solution to the problem of hunger in the Third World. (2) and (5) are incorrect because the passage states that shipping food overseas is costly, wasteful, and creates long-term dependencies. (3) and (4) are not logical, because those people who were relocated would still have to be fed.

12. **(3)** *Evaluation/Geography.* The passage specifically states that there is enough food in the world to feed everyone. It is also stated the problem of world hunger is "above all, one of distribution." Therefore if the world's food were distributed evenly no one would starve. (4) is incorrect, since the passage talks in terms of the poor nations as being unable—not unwilling—to spend the money. (2) and (5) are nowhere implied in the passage, while (1) is contradicted by it.

13. **(2)** *Analysis/History.* The passage states that though the debt is rising, it is declining in terms of percentage of annual output. This can only mean that the national output is rising faster than the debt. Though (1) and (3) may or may not be true, they have no support in the passage and have no clear connection to the topic of the question, which is about the decline of the national debt as a percentage of the national output. (4) and (5) are both untrue statements, and have little or no bearing on the issue.

14. **(2)** *Comprehension/ Behavioral Science.* The passage discusses the various social factors that may have contributed to the declining fertility rate in the United States through the greater part of its history. (1) is incorrect because current fertility rates are not discussed. (3) and (4) are incorrect because they do not address the passage's central issue of fertility. (5) only addresses one section of the social issues discussed in the passage.

15. **(5)** *Comprehension/ Behavioral Science.* The passage states that one of the reasons for the decline in the fertility rate was that women were beginning to find opportunities outside the home which were alternatives to child-bearing. From this you can infer that child-bearing and child-raising had been the main socially acceptable activities for women before the decline in fertility. (3) may or may not be true; the U.S. fertility rate before 1800 is not discussed nor are any comparisons made. The passage does not imply, as in (1), that no family planning or contraception was available, or, as in (2), that *only* the rich could afford leisure time. (4) is contradicted by the passage, which implies industrial workers were associated with the period after 1800 and with cramped, not spacious, housing conditions.

16. **(3)** *Evaluation/Behavioral Science.* The decline in the birthrate continued through the Great Depression and increased "after the period described"—that is, in the period beginning with World War II. Therefore (1) and (2) cannot be correct: the birthrate increase began *after* the Great Depression. You can also eliminate (4) and (5) as logical explanations. (4) would be a reason for women *not* to have children, since they would not be able to stay home and care for them if they had to work in wartime. Similarly, it would not be logical for women to "replace" their husbands and brothers killed in the war by having more children; if anything, they would "replace" them by remarrying.

17. **(2)** *Application/Behavioral Science.* Selling illegal drugs could be called a victimless crime because both the buyer and the seller participate willingly in an illegal activity.

18. **(2)** *Comprehension/ Political Science.* The passage states that a copyright is valid even without being registered. Therefore (3) and (5) are wrong. All the other choices mix up information in the passage. (1) is true about a copyright, not a patent, just as (3) is correct about trademarks and patents but not about copyrights. (4) is true about a patent, but not about a trademark.

19. **(4)** *Application/Political Science.* According to the passage, the publisher may publish the book without any permissions, because the copyright expired in 1941, 50 years after Melville's death. The other choices are all contradicted by information in the passage.

20. **(1)** *Comprehension/ Political Science.* Trademarks are used to distinguish a product "from similar products" offered by the manufacturer's competitors. Therefore, (2) and (5) are automatically incorrect. (3) fails to offer an explanation. (4) is nowhere implied in the passage.

21. **(3)** *Analysis/Political Science.* Nowhere in the passage is it implied that intellectual property laws are intended for the benefit of anyone except creators. Though maintaining a government record of ideas and creations may be a useful side effect of these laws, it was not a motivation for their being passed. All the other choices are stated or implied in the passage.

22. **(2)** *Evaluation/Political Science.* Copyrights last 50 years after their owners' death, and trademarks are valid for 20 years. Thus, they all may easily outlive the people who established them. Nowhere does the passage discuss renewal of these registrations, as in (1), or

the intellectual property laws of other countries, as in (5). (3) is incorrect because computer software requires, and receives, protection from exploitation in the same way as other original creations or ideas. Furthermore, the passage say nothing about computer software. (4) is a statement of opinion, not of fact, for which the passage also provides no support.

23. **(4)** *Comprehension/Political Science.* In the 1980 elections, 59 percent of the population—well over half—voted, and a far larger percentage of people aged 65 to 74 voted than did those between 18 and 20. (3) and (5) are incorrect, since over half the population voted. (1) and (2) are incorrect because, in order to determine whether they are true, we would have to know the number of people who voted, and the passage only provides the percent of voters in each group.

24. **(3)** *Analysis/Political Science.* Because nearly two-thirds of the older group voted, while only about one-third of the younger group did, the old can be said to be a more reliable voting group than the young. (1) cannot be determined without knowing both the number of people involved, and whether the older group in fact voted as a group. Unless the old tend to vote along similar

lines, they will not be a particularly powerful voting group. (2) is contradicted by the passage. (4) is a statement of opinion. (5) cannot be supported by the passage.

25. **(2)** *Analysis/Geography.* An inadequate system of transportation from rural to city areas would not be relevant to the problems described: obviously, the transportation is more than adequate for bringing huge numbers of poor people to the cities of developing countries. The passage does not imply anywhere that transportation is one of the causes of the problems. However, you can infer (1) from the mention of "impoverished rural workers." Since the inadequate housing and sewage affects both migrants "and other urban poor," you can infer that the population growth may be partly due to a high birthrate among the poor in general (3) as well as from the big migration from the rural areas. (4) restates the mention of "overburdened city services" which cannot cope with the problems. Since the problems are severe and there is no mention of protest or activism by the poor, you can infer (5).

26. **(5)** *Comprehension/Political Science.* The passage tells us that the Constitution gives the legislature the right to draft all laws, not to veto them or sign them into law. That is a power given

to the President by the Constitution. All the other choices are restatements or examples of legislative rights mentioned in the passage. (1) comes under "regulation of trade." (2) is an example of "impeachment of federal officials." (3) exemplifies "raising of any army, navy and air force." (4) is an example of "printing of currency."

27. **(1)** *Comprehension/Economics.* The chart shows that from 1970 to 1975 the number of unemployed increased by nearly 4 million. This is by far the largest change shown on the chart.

28. **(3)** *Analysis/Economics.* Because the unemployment rate is based on the percentage of people in the labor force who do not have jobs, it is affected by the total number of people in the labor force. Therefore, though more people may have been unemployed in 1983 than in 1982, they still represented a smaller percentage of the labor force because the number of employed increased even more. (1) and (2) may or may not be true, but they cannot be determined by information provided in the chart. (4) is contradicted by the chart. (5) would have no effect on the rates of years prior to 1984.

29. **(5)** *Comprehension/History.* The cotton gin helped to make cotton a very profitable crop,

which it had not been before. (1) is incorrect because the cotton gin was invented at the very end of the eighteenth century. (3) is incorrect because the cotton industry was not a once-vital industry that was now ailing; for all practical purposes, it hadn't existed. (4) is incorrect because the slave-trading industry existed long before the cotton gin. (2) is contradicted by the passage.

30. **(1)** *Analysis/History.* The big plantation owners had the land on which they could grow the large quantities of cotton that could now be processed with the cotton gin. They could afford the slaves to pick this cotton. In this way, the cotton boom had the effect of further concentrating wealth. Thus, (2) is incorrect. (3) is incorrect because tobacco continued to be grown, as it is today, in many Southern states. (4) is incorrect because carpetbaggers did not arrive until after the Civil War. (5) is highly unlikely because Southerners lived among slaves and therefore were well aware of their suffering or denied that it existed for a long time before the cotton boom.

31. **(2)** *Analysis/American History.* (2) is a restatement of the last sentence of the passage. Nothing suggests white resentment over the expense of slaves (1), or rebellious-

ness among the slaves and resulting white fear of them (3). There is no support for (4) or (5).

32. **(2)** *Evaluation/History.* The graph shows great increases in union membership during the Depression and during wars, and very slow increases during times of prosperity such as the twenties or the decade between the Korean and Vietnam Wars. Since union membership increased sharply during all the wars shown on the graph, (3) is completely wrong. (1) is wrong because the graph shows a general increase, not decrease, in union membership from 1900 until the 1930s. The graph shows no information about population, so (4) is incorrect.

33. **(4)** *Evaluation/Economics.* Since the percentage of children living in poverty rose from 1979 to 1984, it is reasonable to assume that public policies and private policies designed to curb poverty among children did not succeed. (1) is wrong because the passage discusses only children living in poverty but in no way suggests that most poor people are children who live in inner cities. There is nothing in the passage to support choices (2) or (5). (3) is incorrect, because the passage is implicitly treating teenage pregnancy as an effect of poverty, not a cause.

34. **(5)** *Application/Political Science.* Impeachment proceedings are an example of the judicial powers of Congress.

35. **(1)** *Application/Political Science.* In proposing the Equal Rights Amendment, Congress was using its constituent powers, which enable it to change the Constitution.

36. **(3)** *Application/Political Science.* In splitting a federal agency into two separate agencies, Congress used its executive powers.

37. **(3)** *Application/Political Science.* The ongoing information-gathering process described here is in an important part of congressional control or supervision over agencies.

38. **(5)** *Application/Political Science.* By deciding that President Nixon was guilty of crimes, and drawing up articles of impeachment, the Watergate Committee was passing a judgment on an individual. This means the legislative branch was exercising a judicial power. It was not exerting an executive power (3) because its judgment concerned an individual, not the administrative sector of the executive branch such as the Postal Department or the Defense Department. Although it was an investigating committee, in deciding that the president committed crimes and drawing up articles

of impeachment, the committee was not exercising an investigative power (4), but a judicial power. The other two choices clearly do not apply.

39. **(4)** *Comprehension/ Economics.* The main idea of the passage is that American productivity has declined and that this decline is, at least according to this passage, explained by a tendency to focus on the present. The other statements listed either support this statement, as in (3) and (5), or are ideas leading up to it.

40. **(4)** *Evaluation/American History.* Only unemployment and inflation are unmentioned as part of the American productivity problem. All the other choices are restatements of statements in the passage.

41. **(4)** *Comprehension/ History.* The map shows Abilene as being near two end-points of the Chisholm Trail. None of the other towns in the other choices are this near to the cattle trails.

42. **(3)** *Analysis/History.* The map shows that all the cattle trails end at a junction with a railroad line. It is thus reasonable to assume that the cows were being brought from the Texas ranges to the railroads, where, as the map shows, they would be shipped to major cities. The map provides no information to support the other choices. It does not show valleys (1), or

deserts (4) or Native-American territories (5). It is not logical to suppose that the cattle were brought from the north to the ranches of Texas (2). Cattle were raised on ranches in Texas and taken north to markets in the cities.

43. **(4)** *Evaluation/American History.* All the cattle trails connect with railroad lines which run east and west through major cities. The best way to find the correct answer to this question may be to eliminate the other choices. (1) is wrong since no cattle trails on the map stop at or run next to any rivers, indicating that rivers never were "the best way" to get cattle to market. (2) is wrong because there is no way of knowing from the map whether San Francisco became a major port only because of the railroads. (In fact, most port cities, such as London, New York and New Orleans were major ports before railroads ever existed.) The map gives no information about regional feelings caused by the Civil War, so there is no support at all for (3). Moreover, Cheyenne is too far north for such feelings to have had this effect. From the map we have no way of knowing if railroads caused cattle trails to multiply, or cattle trails caused railroads to multiply. So (5) has no support.

44. **(5)** *Analysis/History.* The end of the nineteenth century and the early twentieth century were marked by explosive growth of cities as a consequence of industrialization, which had begun after the Civil War. By working in the factories, later immigrants helped meet the need for an expanded labor force occasioned by rapid industrialization. (4) is a reason for the first settlement patterns, not for the change to urban settlement. Nothing suggests that the later immigrants were from urban areas (2) or were laborers rather than farmers before immigrating (3). (1) is true, but is not a reason for change in the settlement patterns.

45. **(4)** *Evaluation/History.* The passage states that the period beginning around 1880 marked the peak of immigration. It also states that immigrants from northern Europe (that is, from the United Kingdom, Germany, and Scandinavia) for the most part came prior to this period. (2) and (3) are wrong because we are not told the ethnic composition of the U.S. population prior to 1850. (2) cannot be true because Americans were never homogeneous (composed of only one kind, or uniform). (1) and (5) are not supported by the passage.

46. **(4)** *Comprehension/ Geography.* The passage as a whole discusses both

natural and human activity as causing soil erosion. The other choices all list specific factors, each of which contributes to erosion but none of which summarizes the main cause of the problem.

47. **(3)** *Application/Geography.* Grazing land on an open plain is vulnerable to soil erosion by *both* natural and human activity. The environments in the other choices would probably be less vulnerable to human activity. Tropical rainforests (4) and a forest in the mountains (1) would suffer only from the human activity of over-cutting trees without replanting. (2) and (5) are examples of human measures to protect nature and prevent soil erosion.

48. **(3)** *Analysis/Geography.* The passage indicates that at the very least conservation measures could cut down on soil erosion that occurs because of human activity. Terracing, and planting trees to replace those removed, are mentioned as measures that can reduce soil erosion. There is no evidence in the passage to support (1), (2), or (5). (4) is contradicted by the passage.

49. **(5)** *Evaluation/Geography.* The passage says that soil erosion is causing a market decline in the productivity of U.S. cropland. Such a large decline would logically affect U.S. farmers. The passage says nothing to

support (4). The other conclusions are opinions not supported adequately by the passage. Agricultural productivity is not determined only by soil-erosion management programs, so (2) is wrong. Nothing suggests that conservation efforts should be paid for by reducing national security spending. In fact, (3) is illogical, because better weather forecasts would not make soil-erosion programs effective if many other long-range measures were not put into practice.

50. **(2)** *Comprehension/History.* The map shows American lumber going both to Great Britain and to Portugal. Every other choice is contradicted by information provided in the map.

51. **(1)** *Analysis/History.* The map shows that the American colonies exported their raw iron to Great Britain and imported their hardware from Great Britain. To preserve this lucrative trade arrangement, Great Britain passed the act forbidding colonial manufacture of steel and hardware. No gold imported from Jamaica to the U.S. (2) or tea from India (or anywhere else)—choice (5)—is shown on the map. Textiles and hardware, the goods shown to be imported by the colonies, are not luxury items, so (3) is wrong. The map gives no information to explain (4) at all.

52. **(2)** *Evaluation/History.* The map shows that colonial exports went to southern Europe and to Spanish colonies in the West Indies, as well as to the British West Indies and Great Britain. In contrast, all imports shown on the map are from Great Britain or the British West Indies. You can infer that this pattern resulted from British restrictions on trade. (3) is therefore contradicted by information in the map. The map provides no information to support (1) or (4), while (5) is an opinion that goes beyond the evidence on the map.

53. **(4)** *Analysis/Behavioral Science.* The focus of the passage is not only on closeness or table manners at meals, but also on people's acceptance of closeness in "similar social situations." Therefore, (1), (3), and (5) are not as accurate descriptions of the subject here as (4) is. (2) is incorrect because the article is about all of Great Britain, not just the Shetland Islands.

54. **(3)** *Analysis/Behavioral Science.* The ratio between single men and single women can be determined because we know the precise number of each and can compare them. For this reason, (1) and (2) are incorrect. (1) requires that we know the size of the total population (not just of New York's) between the ages of 35 and 54, and (2) that

we know the size of this total population. (4) and (5) are incorrect because the graph gives no information to explain that the numbers changed because of marriage or divorce.

55. **(5)** *Comprehension/History.* Each choice in this question describes an immigration trend that goes through two stages; you must read the graph carefully to see if each choice describes *both* stages correctly. (1) is true only in its first part because after the Civil War immigration is shown to have *increased* until 1900. (2) is true only in its second part because immigration *decreased* from 1910 to the Great Depression. (3) is inaccurate in both parts: from 1890 to 1919 immigration first increased and then decreased, and after 1919, after World War I, it did not rise but fell. (4) is true only in its first part: from 1840 to 1859 immigration decreased, but then it increased until 1890. Only choice (5) is accurate in describing both the trends it covers.

56. **(5)** *Comprehension/Geography.* All of the East Coast area of the United States, from Maine to Georgia, remained under British control from 1689 to 1763. The maps show no British control of the other areas named, except of most of the South in 1763.

57. **(2)** *Analysis/History.* The maps for 1689 and 1750 show Florida under Spanish control. Georgia, in 1732, was the British king's only colony bordering Florida. It was, therefore, the outpost against the Spanish. Since the king and colonists were British, (3) and (5) are wrong. (1) is wrong because all of the colonies bordered French territory in 1732. (4) is wrong because Indians are not a subject of the maps.

58. **(4)** *Application/Behavioral Science.* The man's housecleaning is an example of an irrational, repetitive activity that is symbolically related to his problem.

59. **(5)** *Application/Behavioral Science.* The woman has an excessive and irrational fear, which may interfere with daily activities.

60. **(2)** *Application/Behavioral Science.* Instead of confronting his problem, the man allows it to take over, becoming deeply depressed and antisocial.

61. **(1)** *Application/Behavioral Science.* The woman's paralysis is an example of a physical symptom that is expressing an unconscious and unwanted desire. Although consciously the woman is happy about the upcoming marriage and move, unconsciously she doesn't want her life to change.

62. **(2)** *Application/Behavioral Science.* The woman, even if she disguises her feelings from others, is suffering from a depressive neurosis.

63. **(3)** *Application/History.* The passage indicates that colonists resented British measures that restricted their political and economic freedoms. Duties passed by Great Britain raised the prices of consumer goods and infringed on colonial self-government. (4) does not involve the colonies. The other choices would be unlikely to anger the colonists.

64. **(4)** *Evaluation/History.* Because Britain didn't allow the colonists representation in Parliament, and because it was an overseas power, it could make economic and political decisions that didn't serve the colonists' interests. Although economic rights and freedoms undoubtedly would be affected by the British control of colonial political life, they are mentioned only as one of the colonists' main concerns—the right to elect their own leaders, make their laws, and control their own trade. Therefore (1) is not correct. Nothing supports the other choices.